Organizational Culture and Paradoxes in Management

Studies on culture, change and social processes within organizations have been historically organized around orthogonal approaches. While the literature on change has focused in creating pragmatic, generally simple methodologies that bypass the complexity of the data in order to emphasize the possibility of intervention, literature aimed at truly understanding of the firm and its processes has emphasized the ambiguity of organization and the difficulties involved in reaching a unitary view of its processes, let alone creating a single theory of change. Finally, the literature on family businesses has been restricted to limited views of the field, disregarding the rich insights brought by psychology, sociology or anthropology. The result of these trends has been a gap in the creation of knowledge, with a paucity of studies that link theory with practice and ground change on a comprehensive view of the social reality of the firm. This book addresses both the specific need of family businesses and the broader demands of any organization in which the issue of culture is seriously considered.

Drawing on the notions and scholarship on organizations and sociology, the author proposes new concepts and tools for change agents interested in working with culture within organizations, attempting to combine the instrumental rules of the firm with the cohesive tone of the prototypical family. *Organizational Culture and Paradoxes in Management* will be of value to students at an advanced level, academics and reflective practitioners. It addresses the topics with regard to management and organizational studies and will be of interest to organizational scholars, consultants and leaders interested in fostering a meaningful culture within organizations and family businesses.

Saulo C. M. Ribeiro is a psychiatrist, psychotherapist and consultant for organizations in Belo Horizonte, MG, Brazil.

Routledge Studies in Management, Organizations and Society

This series presents innovative work grounded in new realities, addressing issues crucial to an understanding of the contemporary world. This is the world of organised societies, where boundaries between formal and informal, public and private, local and global organizations have been displaced or have vanished, along with other nineteenth century dichotomies and oppositions. Management, apart from becoming a specialized profession for a growing number of people, is an everyday activity for most members of modern societies.

Similarly, at the level of enquiry, culture and technology, and literature and economics, can no longer be conceived as isolated intellectual fields; conventional canons and established mainstreams are contested. **Management, Organizations and Society** addresses these contemporary dynamics of transformation in a manner that transcends disciplinary boundaries, with books that will appeal to researchers, student and practitioners alike.

Recent titles in this series include:

Work Orientations
Theoretical Perspectives and Empirical Findings
Edited by Bengt Furåker and Kristina Håkansson

The Institutional Theory of the Firm
Embedded Autonomy
Alexander Styhre

Organizational Culture and Paradoxes in Management
Firms, Families, and Their Businesses
Saulo C. M. Ribeiro

The Democratic Organisation
Democracy and the Future of Work
Thomas Diefenbach

For more information about this series, please visit: https://www.routledge.com

Organizational Culture and Paradoxes in Management

Firms, Families, and Their Businesses

Saulo C. M. Ribeiro

NEW YORK AND LONDON

First published 2020
by Routledge
52 Vanderbilt Avenue, New York, NY 10017

and by Routledge
2 Park Square, Milton Park, Abingdon, Oxon, OX14 4RN

Routledge is an imprint of the Taylor & Francis Group, an informa business

Library of Congress Cataloging-in-Publication Data
A catalog record for this title has been requested

ISBN: 978-0-367-21154-7 (hbk)
ISBN: 978-0-429-26574-7 (ebk)

Typeset in Sabon
by codeMantra

To John Greden, John Roberts, Woody Powell, Morris Zelditch, Jim March and all teachers who, knowingly or not, helped to shape my spirit. SR

Contents

Preface

This book is dedicated to all scholars interested in organizational culture, to members of any family businesses, and to change agents interested in designing a cultural game that integrates the interests of the actors, of the collectivity, and of the firm into a single, aesthetic, and true organizational form. It thus asks questions such as: "How can one reconcile formal, top-down strategic plans with the emergent, bottom-up processes that give real life to these social systems?". "How can we ground rational claims for cultural unity on the real data, facts and experiences that are available only to the lower levels of the pyramid?". "And how to find the mix of truthfulness and illusion that addresses the practical demands of the firm and family and yet makes for a profound, fair, existentially meaningful and playfully engaging game?". Underlying these themes, as well as many others that emerge in the text, are what we see as two urgent demands of the field: for the leader, the need to develop a solid understanding of the social processes on which motivation and coordination – the two fundamental ingredients of collective action [2] – are based; and for the student of organizations, the need to integrate into a single theory the opposite pulls for an integrative and for a fragmented view of culture, both perspectives competing to explain the social universe and coexisting within the organizational literature [3]. We hope this book provides a useful introduction to these two issues.

Many of the usual conceptions of the firm, focusing on the complexities of the business, deal with these paradoxes by avoidance or simply by reaffirming orthodox perspectives. In the strategic literature, survival and growth are still seen as the meaningful measures of success [4]. Reified organizations are depicted as scanning the environment or reflecting upon themselves to define their moves, mission, or structure [5]. The implicit proposition is that they exist like idealized human beings who would have "significant benefits to gain through an explicit process of formulating strategy" in order to achieve the supposedly logical, discrete, and well-known goals of increasing utility and efficiency while maintaining identity ([6]: xxi). These beliefs become the official or taken-for-granted rules of the game, implicitly guiding the perception of reality and the collective decision-making [7]. Consequently, novel or creative questions, answers, values, or goals are often unable to compete with the demand for efficiency and frequently disappear under the hegemonic rule of the "truth" [8].

Usual conceptions of the family in general reflect the same gravitational power of the abstract nouns. In order to talk about the similarities we forget the differences, the various ways in which the chasms between man and man are more salient than the bridges that unite them. In the same vein, studies of family businesses generally revolve around prototypical distinctions between supposedly well-defined dimensions of ownership, business, and family [9]. Conflict and tensions are deemed to arise because their complex, interlocked social structure leads to the juxtaposition of these three sub-systems. Solutions for the problems derived from the resulting tension should, therefore, be directed toward clarifying the differences between them and designing structures of governance aimed at addressing the specific demands and questions brought by each one [10]. The implicit assumption is that rules really work, suggesting that real organizations and real families are as simple and homogeneous as the words that describe them (see Appendix 2, Figure 1).

Finally, there are few technologies of change in which the "rational" economic interactions, so well described by the dismal science, are treated in parallel with the symbolic games that often cover up the utilitarian demands of practical reality [11]. Strategic plans, focused on the business side of the equation, pay little attention to local actions required for their implementation [12]. Incentive, performance, or promotion systems designed to increase motivation presuppose that players act out of fixed, exogenous (and self-interested) motives, overlooking the relevance of the archetypal need for illusion or the emergent, endogenous preferences that arise as one plays [13]. Governance structures targeting coordination typically evolve as crude refinements of the Weberian bureaucracy, freezing the affective, economic, and pragmatic elements of the system into stylized structures that pay little attention to the predominantly tacit, non-goal-oriented, irrational nature of the game [14]. Change theories thus defy the nature of the reality they attempt to address: the intellectual need to rationalize the firm and the family stays in sharp contrast with the practical reality of social games that always mingle contradictory motives, planning, spontaneity, reason, and illusion into single streams of action that do not accept simplifications.

Directed at this gap, our book is an invitation to discuss how one could increase the chances of reaching common understandings within social systems, given that reality can never be precisely known [15]; how information could be more effectively communicated and transformed, given that news often cannot be reliably transmitted [16]; how tacit or explicit social contracts are put in place, given that decisions about reality never arise from value-neutral rational deliberations [17]; how strategic design may actually be influential, given that problems, decision-making, and organizational action are often loosely coupled as in a politically charged garbage-can process of decision-making [18]; how economic needs and pragmatism can be spontaneously associated with idealism, given this can always be reframed as ideology [19]; and how a leader could influence the culture of an organization, given that local action, bottom-up processes, informal organizations, and diversity of interpretations preclude one from expecting any type of cultural unit [3].

More than a practical predicament, then, the problem of organizational culture unveils a fundamental problem of all social systems - the need to develop a theory that integrates the realism that guarantees individual and collective subsistence with the idealism that allows engrossment in the game. Family businesses, prototypically seen as stretched between the pragmatic demands of the firm and the affective, ethical, or aesthetic goals that characterize the idealized family, are particularly in need of such a theory. For any company in which common values and practices play a role in promoting coordination, however, mixing the organizational need for productivity and the interests of all actors into a single game may help to create contexts that promote both the intangible goals of culture and the practical conditions for the pragmatically interesting organizational learning, creativity, and innovation to occur [1]. The difficulties associated with the management of meaning loom beneath any attempt to develop a culture that responds minimally to top-down influences, emerging rather unpredictably as flimsy displays of unity stemming from the irreducible diversity of the social game.

In the following pages, therefore, family businesses are seen both on their own and as magnifying glasses that help us to better see the paradoxes embedded in all forms of social order. Conflicts derived from misunderstandings about the nature of truth or error, different definitions of the situation, miscommunication and value differences occur independently of the setting in which the social game is played. Moreover, the difficulties involved in integrating the instrumentality, rationality, and impersonality mythically imputed to the firm and the cohesion, spontaneity, and tradition ideologically ascribed to the family can be better framed as a particular example of the difficulties that universally occur when one attempts to accommodate different sets of rules into a single game – in this case, the always-present, contradictory forces of self-interest and coordination, or calculation and spontaneity. We thus propose that change processes in family businesses – or for that matter, in any organization – should be based *not* on a simplistic, reductionist view of these systems, but on broader parameters of analysis that show how players understand, negotiate, communicate, and enact their choices, contracts, and definitions of the situations given the complexity and paradoxical nature of life.

We start by reviewing the broad premises of the argument (Chapter 1). In Chapter 2, we specifically discuss families and their businesses.

Chapters 3–5 focus on general features of the social game – the mechanisms and failures of the processes of information, truth creation, choice, negotiation, and communication that serve as the basis for every form of social order (or disorder). Chapter 6 finishes the book with a more practical reflection about the tasks required from leaders or change agents engaged in the management of culture. In the two appendixes, we shift gears and give a broad overview of how this theory was put into practice. Appendix 1 includes remarks about the methodology and the process of change based on this theory. Appendix 2 contains several illustrations taken from the didactic material used during these interventions. Both serve to illuminate the theory we present in the book.

A special note should be made about a broader goal that guided the writing of this text – the attempt to traverse the bridge between realism and comprehension [20] while acknowledging that "it is impossible for a theory of social behavior to be simultaneously general, accurate and simple" ([21]: 35). To facilitate the understanding, we opted for a single perspective narrative that can work as a heuristic (and hopefully enticing) interpretive lens with which to study the social fact. We have thus avoided the arid format of academic reviews – there are few, if any data about current family businesses or cultural studies (if nothing due to a profound skepticism about the premises underlying the research on these themes); abstract, theoretical vectors are paired with examples and concrete instances of the ideas discussed; references are numbered rather than spelled out; and we seldom mention specific authors in the text in order to facilitate the reading. On the other hand, the extensive bibliography reflects the attempt to be as comprehensive as we could in our approach to the complexity of the problems we addressed. In particular, many citations – some of them with mild modifications within brackets – embed a hidden dialog with the referenced work. They are part of the text, an invitation for the reader to go to the sources and explore additional, potentially richer interpretations of meaning. Whenever time is not a constraint, one should refer to them as a means to grasp the scope, limitations, premises, and blind spots of the intellectual landscape from which our thinking emerged.

As in any book, too many special acknowledgments should be made – every piece of thought is nothing but the final fruit of the confluence of many ideas, which mingled in one's past simply take a new (?) form and strive, once again, to be part of the social reality. In our case, a special note should be made to the various academic institutions that gave us access to these ideas, as well as, a place to discuss them the University of Michigan; University of Oxford; Stanford University; HEC Paris; and Universidade Federal de Minas Gerais, Brazil. This book would not have been written without the support, guidance, and help from Sue Dopson, who with her comments and observations worked practically as a co-writer; to her, my deepest thanks. I am also extremely grateful for the help of the friends who read this manuscript, including my wife, children, and parents. Finally, it is relevant to state that this book is the fruit of two improbabilities. First, the search to combine in a single essay the hands-on experience of a practitioner who looks for patterns and solutions with the inquisitive, open, doubt-prone comprehensive curiosity of a scholar who attempts to address the theoretical problems of the subject [22]. Second, the equally impossible attempt to summarize in a single book the complexity of the social processes in organizations and the trade-offs and difficulties involved in working with them. As any (mythical or idealistic) attempt to organize the beautiful and unpredictable looseness of the practice within the constraints of a logical framework, both are certain to fail.

1 The Premises of the Argument

We can start from the assumption that organizations are inherently complex. Just imagine the evolution of an idealistic entrepreneurial dream – as soon as a project overcomes the liabilities of newness, new objectives arise, failures block some roads, success brings growth, and growth brings layers of complexity that adding on to the initial seed give birth to unpredictable organizational forms that defy the stamp of imprinting [23]. Eventually, almost everything is played out within the confines of an organization. Cooperation, conflicts of interest, agency costs, loyalties, supposedly rational strategies and clearly irrational path dependencies coexist and reflect both the contingencies of history and the preplanned ideals of those who control the system.

Like with organizations, we assume that families are also complex. From an outside perspective, the potent rules of unity, the centripetal forces of kinship, and a succession of generations carrying the same names reinforce the illusion of sameness. But in reality, almost everything is also played out within the confines of a family: ranging from displays of love to clear resentment, encompassing both hidden and explicit games, the powerful forces of group cohesion always counteract the equally strong need to differentiate or the dispute for scarce resources. As complex as the families are, however, they are inherently different from organizations. Distinct rules shape distinct forms; and from the differences in the prescribed appearance, each family emerges as a different reality, another peculiar type of social dream.

Creator of, and at the same time created by the social games he enacts, every individual within the family or in the organization also epitomizes this tension between the complexity of real life and the rational attempt to build coherences. Lived identities, relationships, and values are named and modulated to fit abstract words, which then become currencies in the social market. People believe they are guided by personal goals, forgetting how they follow the unspoken mandate to fulfill the roles to which they are assigned. Words are felt to be true, as if real life were not lost when translated into language. But despite the pressures for conformity, deep down everything is played out within the confines of the individual human mind. Regardless of the social expectations for consistency, incongruent habits always struggle to find their way to action; nouns, verbs, adjectives, and self-descriptions still aspire to be true, oblivious to the antagonisms that surface in thought or interactions; and, as the families and organizations to which they belong, human beings go through their timeline maintaining an improbable appearance of order sculpted out of essential contradictions.

In order to acknowledge this complexity, this book builds on previous studies that cover the social processes of understanding, communication, and value negotiation within organizations [2, 24, 25]. Like them, we take it as a fact that reason is limited in its scope and processing capacity [26]. We assume that all knowledge is interpretive, and therefore relative to the perspectival bases of interpretation that vary at each moment according to context and value [27]. We consider that most of human life occurs beyond the boundaries of the language game, following rules of habit that have little to do with the purported non-contradictions of our logic [28]. And we postulate that all products of reason – the goals, identities, strategies or self-definitions that make up the life of families, firms and people – are both grounded on, and limited by a value-making activity that firmly connects cognition with power [29], capital [30], ideology [19], and aesthetics [31].

These constraints strongly suggest that decisions made in name of the collective body, rules put in place within a system, and what is actually done and lived in the common social space include a host of different propositions that obey logical and non-logical forces, accepting minimal degrees of consistency and, therefore, frequently remaining only loosely coupled. Moreover, the limitations of rationality and the potent social pressures affecting the processes of "self-knowledge" suggest that individuals are equally loosely coupled [32]. If it were not for this slack, which allows players to periodically violate some norms, social games would so deeply constrain the freedom of individuality that life would not be possible. If it were not for rules, which reinforce what must be included, excluded, or transformed to maintain the appearance of each social universe, life would be formless [33]. The values, goals, and culture of each particular family or organization result in a more or less aesthetic game that simultaneously allows, forbids, and disguises the same underlying, multifaceted, deeply controversial human nature.

Definitions of the Situation: Truth, Reality, and Identity

Both the variety of contradictory practices that characterize human life, and the disparate discourses that populate the linguistic universe stay in sharp contrast with the expected objectivity and coherence of the truth-rule normally used to negotiate the conflicts and create the common definitions of the situation deemed necessary for sustainable coordination. In fact, two of the fundamental premises used by individuals or groups to guide their decision-making are one's view of the world, what reality is, and one's definition of one's own self – what actors as being the basic values, goals, traits, or nature. "We tend to assume that we are individuals and that all other humans are individuals as well. We ought to be individuals; we often attempt to behave as individuals; and there is a moral and legal system of rules based on the supposition that we are individuals. (...) To see human beings as individuals involves the assumption that they are actors – entities with clear boundaries, possessing sovereignty and autonomous or self-interested goals and rational means. The individual is assumed to have a strong identity. (...) As individuals, our actions are expected to be controlled by our thoughts, and our identity to be realized in our actions. The assumption that individuals choose and control their own actions and have a free will makes them responsible for their actions" ([34]: 2). Overall, the rules of the identity *game* are subtly transformed into truths and begin to define what reality in fact *is*.

To a naive actor, these premises are not problematic – it is a reminder of our drive to live in illusion, and as a consequence of the need to abide by rules, that the contradictions and paradoxes of reality or of one's self are commonly simply lived as normal for life to be stabilized and go on. Values and intentions are, then, exchanged in the form of the promises by which actors reiterate their preferences, as if these were stable platforms for others to act; imperfect bits of information are put together and used as bases to build "truths", as if the logic of the reasoning made up for the faulty premises; and whenever habitual games come to the fore, individuals, families, and firms ceremonially celebrate their worldviews and identities through private or public discourses, relegating the inconsistencies of practical life to the backstage of unspoken routines [35] (see Appendix 2, Figure 4).

One can allege, however, that illusion is not the only motive behind the persistence of the beliefs in reality or identity. Everything points to the fact that our perceptual apparatus and thinking processes are intrinsically deficient in their ability to grasp the complexity of life. These limitations have made their way into the world of organizations: "It is precisely in the realm where human behavior is *intendedly* rational, but only *limitedly so,* (...) in the boundary between the rational and the non-rational aspects of human behavior" that rests "the central concern of administrative theory". Since habitual truths and self-definitions are products of a language game designed *not* to know the world, but to facilitate the communication of "human beings who satisfice because they have not the wits to maximize" ([36]: xxiv), it is by mapping the steps required for the creation of truths and the sources of ambiguity – and *not* by drawing any fictitious certainties – that one must start the construction of any sustainable organizational change (see Appendix 2, Figure 2).

The first limitation encountered while trying to describe the family, the firm, or even ourselves is that a good part of what is lived is untranslatable into the formal, apparently sharp categories and rules of symbolic thinking. "We can know more than we can tell" ([37]: 4): the collective parameters of analysis, sensations, emotions, intuitions, aesthetic feelings, or automatisms, as well as all "facts" that occur below the threshold of awareness but yet influence decision-making, transcend the simple linearity of the logical thinking or the lexicon and grammar used to explicitly communicate propositions of reality or identity. They form, therefore, a group of experiences that are only tacitly lived and can be transmitted only through the repeated practice of action-oriented social games. The fundamental consequence of this slicing out of part of reality is a mismatch between what is described by words and the real world on which actors live. Since the faulty premises and concepts translatable in language are the ones that eventually compound the deductive chains of inference used to build strategies or goals, many of the explicitly espoused theories, common beliefs, and abstract deductions are often contradicted by one's theories in action and by how facts really occur [38].

Even if one considers only the explicit knowledge, a second limitation of rationality comes from the fact that actors can focus only on one subject at a time. Thus, in the instant a group deals with any object of activity, all are bound to treat themselves, the surrounding community, the technology in place, the rules of the game, and the accorded division of labor as given facts that must be forgotten for the task to be performed [39]; organizations become different realities, depending on the sociological paradigm used as a knowledge-making lens [40]; and depending on the perspective, every family or firm may be seen as having fixed or fluid boundaries, as being homogeneous or fragmented into nested collections of units that follow distinct values and criteria of consistency [41]. Since people alternate moments in which they identify with the firm, with a division, with their family, a coalition, a profession, or even with themselves, each one of these units embodies a particular social actor with different goals and dilemmas. Constantly shifting the perspectives through which they see the world, men are engaged in a permanent ontological oscillation by which they confer reality and meaning to different games and proposals depending on the circumstances, forgetting all other possible realities or interpretations to live the prioritized game of the moment (see Appendix 2, Figures 4 and 5).

Third, this tacit and value-driven choice of a perspective from which the world is seen occurs in parallel with a deeply biased mechanism of information processing of the stimuli that fall into that frame. Both in the individual and in the group, the simple creation of a fact – an apparently objective unit of information that can be passed on to other actors or used as a premise for personal or collective reasoning – depends on how stimuli are selected and organized into a "gestalt" and connected to the imaginary worlds of the future, of the past, of the mind, or of the broader social life that surrounds the actor. This mechanism overlooks the "ignorance of all possible courses of action and other sources of uncertainty, the tendency to search for satisfactory rather than best courses of action, [the existence of] multiple goals and inconsistent values, conflict between participants in decision processes and different sequences of elements in decision processes" ([19]: 166). Furthermore, the ambiguity of most situations contrasts with the certainty required to define one's actions and public proposals for the continuation of life. Of many plausible scenarios of the competitive landscape, only a few can be chosen to guide the strategy of the firm [42]; of many possible unobservable intentions, one has to be taken as true in order for the interaction to go on; of many reasonable versions of the facts, one must be selected to become the postulate over which further reasoning is construed. Because potential errors are embedded in the core of this process, actors are constantly faced with the possibility of having chosen a "wrong" direction. "Objective" facts are thus nothing more than relatively stable interpretive arrangements based on probabilities derived from past experience and on biases that distort objectivity in the direction of a peculiarly human, never neutral way of valuing the world (see Appendix 2, Figure 6).[1]

Fourth, one cannot forget that all the (apparently neutral) information processing occurs in the context of (value-ridden) parallel processes of communication and social negotiation. Rules of consensus or dissensus always add, to the cognitive drive to understand the world, the affective needs to agree, disagree, belong, conform, submit or persuade other players. As information is transmitted from actor to actor, one goes through multiple layers of uncertainty absorption and story creation, a process in which equivocality is gradually smoothened out and validity gives way to reliability until a coherent version of the facts emerges. Responding to social contagion, insecurity, imitation, inattention or conformity, groups and people reiterate truths to each other through self-reinforcing cycles that eventually concretize socialized exchanges of ideas as real exchanges of actions [43]. Shaped by the mechanisms of their creation, the sentences and propositions used in our definitions of the world are in fact compressed stories, which by being socially lived create a reality of their own [15].

Finally, the learning mechanisms by which actors attempt to pursue intelligence and increase their understanding of the environment raise areas of ambiguity related specifically to the methods used to gather and synthesize the acquired knowledge [44]. When one learns from experience, error signals may be inadequately interpreted and cause either hasty change or denial of relevant variables; search processes may lead to small gains that inhibit the pursuit of better goals [45]; risk preferences are internalized as mechanisms of learning that seem adaptive due to self-fulfilling biases [46]; and competency traps arise due to misattribution of successes and failures, biased managerial hubris, or misinterpretation of performance gains that come simply from learning process routines, and not from solving real problems. When learning from scientific models or narratives, one often is prey of errors of induction and deduction that decrease the validity of the symbolic idealization. Intentions, individuality, rationality, or hierarchy are emphasized in interpretative stories and accounts of meaning, creating anthropocentric descriptions of reality [26]; teleology and intention are stripped out of mathematical and formal models, leading to a sterile, invalid structural view of the world; and deficiencies in the codification, storage, and retrieval memory processes lead to poorly accessible, imperfect, value-driven databases that create a pseudo-intelligence of reality characterized by imperfect understanding, faulty communication, and quasi-resolution of the conflicts [47]. Information, communication, and learning are, therefore, mere caricatures of the idealized rationality so keenly pursued by theorists, managers, and people who, in the attempt to use reason as a tool to control themselves and the world, often fall prey of the irrational hope to find an absolute certainty.

It is precisely because putatively objective truths and identities are so deeply intertwined with the (aesthetic or pragmatic?) process of sculpting illusory, relatively fixed worldviews that, under the usual assumptions of truth, our definitions of firms, families, or people are so volatile and subject to dissolution when their inner contradictions are exposed. It is not uncommon to see accidents of life unveiling the discrepancies between espoused values and lived practices; or inconsistencies, pseudo-paradoxes and blind alleys appearing as signs of error; or moments of deliberation in which crossroads bring the need to choose between contrary motives previously bundled together in a single game; or imbalances of power and interest making the disclosure of self-deception interesting to groups or persons and impeding the continuation of the ordinary forgetfulness of daily life. In all these instances, or whenever the tenuous link of understanding that connects the performance to the audience is temporarily lost, one exposes the buffering mechanisms that separate explicit definitions of the situation from the inconsistencies of normal routine. If reality is assumed to be "either 'true' *or* 'apparent', 'illusory', 'unreal' and 'non-existent'" [48], common understandings about the family, the firm or the self must be reframed as cover-ups, illusions, ideology, misunderstandings, or simple consequences of a shared forgetfulness in the game. Truth becomes incredible as a mechanism of credibility or as a guarantee of personal and social consensus, and one is led to search for the answers that explain one's identities and definitions of reality in the field of motives and values for which people behave as they do.

Choices: Value, Power, Status, and Identification

The first, unintended consequence of applying the full power of reason to illuminate the paradoxes looming behind normal people, families, and organizations is, then, a profound doubt about how these entities had been previously understood; and on a deeper level, an equally strong skepticism about the process of understanding (after all, are our definitions faithful descriptions or simply aesthetic falsifications of reality?). Another consequence is the uncovering of the implicit or explicit value choices, silences, hidden strategies, power struggles, coalitions, or compromises that lead to the apparently neutral definitions of identity or "rational" process of decision-making. If the same concrete facts allow for multiple possible interpretations, there are substantial degrees of freedom embedded in the process of the social construction of reality; and if there is freedom, the unconscious or unconscious choices that define the reality eventually enacted are determined by the conscious or unconscious choice of a perspective or viewpoint that necessarily reflects the power or the *values* of the actors.

Each one of the multiple questions usually present in the firm brings to the fore the radical, and ultimately profoundly personal nature of these value differences. Exploration or exploitation, control or foolishness [49]? Realism or comprehension, validity or reliability [20]? Aligned, strong culture or decentralized, emergent counter-cultures [50]? These differences in what is valued by each actor are in the core of the multiple covert or overt conflicts of interest that fill the everyday life of social systems. Only a few of the many possible strategies, routines, tactics, or definitions of the firm gain momentum and become represented in the collective imagination. Even fewer are actually openly discussed as realistic deliberations or possible practical directions for the group; but since "if men define situations as real, they are real in their consequences" [51], the institutionalized truths (or shared fictions) are always more relevant than unofficial truths and usually taken as the final parameter for the resolution of disputes.

Values are thus anything but neutral: every personal decision is ethically and affectively charged as a point of attack, a necessarily incisive action that inserts one's worldview into the core of the public social space. Because actors share a limited stage and have differential access to assets – which include information, communication paths, relationships, influence, or a particular relationship with the patriarch or leader – players are constantly agreeing or fighting not only for space, resources, or prestige, but also for the control of the actions, of the official definitions of reality, and of the prescriptions of normalcy that shape the conformation of the firm or family [52]. To impose the value of a value always implies in taking a position as someone who has a say in how to shape the underlying rules of the game. Grounded in conflicts or negotiations about what should be considered real enough to be true, and ultimately about what should have value to justify an action, all grand, abstract conceptions of the firm and of the family are therefore deeply interwoven with the very mundane and subjective problem of deciding which particular *taste* will drive the choice of the prevailing perspective, or, on a social level, *whose* perspective this is.

As a value choice emerges as the main rule of the game – within the limits given by concrete reality and social structure, *taste* being the single most potent vector that guides the choice of any worldview or perspective in detriment of another – one discloses the deep connection that exists between understanding, communication, and the human value-making or power-enforcing activity. This observation expands the focus of our analysis from the emphasis on cognition and communication to the study of the contrast between selfish and collective interests, and as a corollary to the relative capacity of influence that each one of the actors may have over each other and over the collective stage of the firm [53]. If disparate interests, divergent viewpoints, conflicts, individualism, doubt, memories, pride, control, and ownership disputes always exist overtly or covertly – determining even the definitions of reality – bounded rationality and serial attention allocation are insufficient to explain the contradictions of the social systems.

Competition, prestige, capital, power, cooperation, and negotiable or unspeakable value differences are, therefore, the real vectors driving all interactions, relationships, and forms of organization. It is thus necessary to study the nature of this influence. Essentially, in the core of the game is the strife for expansion, control, and autonomy – exposed to multiple rules, pulled by values that praise both independence and allegiance, impelled by their own (self-interested or group-oriented) motives and forced to respond to contradictory games and irreconcilable ideals, actors always "hold on to a minimum of freedom which they cannot refrain from using to 'beat the system'" (...) and develop a "reciprocal, but unbalanced relation of force from which one party can obtain more than the other, yet in which neither party is totally defenseless". Power, then, emerges as a "reciprocal, but unbalanced, relation of force from which one party can obtain more than the other, yet in which neither party is totally defenseless" [54]. Whatever the wish of the player – a selfish or an altruistic egoism, idealism or efficiency, the good of the firm, of the family, or of any other interest group – it must be imposed or negotiated in the public stage according to the rules of a competition in which all other motives dispute the priority of becoming reality for the community.

Both in the family and in the firm, as well as in any social system, players have different latitude of action and influence in this game. In modern times, control of the relevant resources is mostly what mediates the exchange [55]. Individuals, families, coalitions, or firms who have more access to information, money, supplies, technology, people, symbols, or the rules of the game hold to more freedom and when on open ground are more able to clearly enforce their values. In contrast, those with less economic, cultural, social, symbolic, or political capital are less free and must resort to secret alliances, covert arrangements, or parallel games that occur in the fringes of the public stage. Everywhere, what falls under the scope of the language game becomes subject to the scrutiny of reason and demands a publicly acceptable justification, lest one loses his status as a reasonable social player.

A particularly relevant consequence of this demand for openness and coherence, therefore, is that truth becomes automatically linked with power and capital. For a less privileged player, to accept the moral demand to be truthful implies in bringing the conflict to a ground in which one is bound to lose if the argument is taken to the consequences; conversely, for the strong, the moral (?) imperative to be honest is a useful norm which increases the chances that everything will occur in the domain of the public, relatively controlled stage he commands. The transcendent value of truth and honesty is, then, relativized by the nature of the game in which these are called for. Consequently, all exchanges of ideas are reframed as tactics within a game of conflict or cooperation, and the collective task of designing or implementing a strategy, setting a new organizational structure, making policies, or establishing a governance system becomes deeply enmeshed with the political task of negotiating the ideas and the interests of those involved in the process [56].

The final outcome of the uncovering of this deep linkage between the (supposedly objective) definitions of reality and the (clearly partial) value choices of those who hold a certain belief is, therefore, a deep mistrust about the nature of truth and all public statements. As actors use their discourses to impose or hide their own values, to rightfully preserve themselves from the dangers of being honest, or even to deceive themselves, all purportedly true definitions we commonly use in internal or external dialogs – the inner goals, proposals, identities, and worldviews daily negotiated during social conversations – emerge not only as ambiguous statements, but as imperfect mixes of reality and ideology, inevitably tainted by self-serving biases, social influences, and errors of processing that blur the distinction between science and art, reality and illusion, essence and appearance, or rhetoric and content [57]. Without functionalist fantasies of tradition, adaptation, or duty as putatively objective criteria for consensus, all opinions, suggestions, and theories of change may be seen as social instruments by which actors translate their specific value-perspectives into publicly defensible worldviews. Any calls for cultural unity, cooperation, creative foolishness, or sacrifice can be (often correctly) dismissed as naive or framed as managerial pressures for conformity; disagreements frequently become tacit undiscussables that slowly erode the family or the firm; and the crucial social mandate to be truthful is usually rephrased as a more precise, but substantially more ambiguous, call to be open about what should be said and silent about what should be hidden according to the rules that characterize the game of the moment.

Power, Value, and Justice

Once the combination of not-codifiability, multitasking, cognitive limitations, and conflicts of interest make it impossible to believe in the usual fundaments that justify the existence of the firm, of the family, or of any form of stable cooperation, one is then forced by the "creative destruction" of reason to contrast the two opposing sets of rules commonly used to stabilize the reality, namely, the (scientific) logic of the facts and the (moral) logic of appropriateness [58,59]. For the rational logic of the facts, the inductively observed concrete situations are the parameters used to generate progressively more realistic, complex, concise, and aesthetic views of reality [60]. Conflicts, power, diversity, and loose coupling between identity and reality are, then, seen as a given – and since this mismatch is a condition of existence, fictions of a common structure or coherent identities and meanings are taken as the myth and ceremony that cover up the fragile nature of the connecting bonds and the deep differences among its constituents [35]. Conversely, for the rule-based logic of appropriateness, the parameter of truth is the (moral) fit between idea and action and the differences between discourse and routine, or between espoused theories and theories-in-use, are interpreted as errors that must be corrected enforcing the parameters given by one's professed identity [38]. In this game, sustainable relationships or lasting contracts depend thus on the maintenance of a form that *should* be enforced by rules; conflicts, power, or diversity are violations of an expected norm that ought to be corrected via the constant search for coherence; and error leads not to curiosity, but to definitions of accountability.

As we expose the intimate contradiction existing between two apparently clear and crucial social imperatives – the command to be truthful to the facts, and the equally strong mandate to be fully truthful to one's promises – we reach a dilemma that has been present since the rational disbelief in the traditional or metaphysical fundament for rules [61] has equated justice with power [62] or with social consensus [63]. If norms and laws have no other basis beyond the desire of the strong or the volatile coincidence of the actors' will, it is impossible to find a neutral and stable common ground to justify the collective goals [64]. From this raw pragmatism, eventually, emerges the classic deconstruction of all ideals of justice: "To this war of every man against every man, this also is consequent; that nothing can be unjust. The notions of right and wrong, justice and injustice, have there no place. Where there is no common power, there is no law: where no law, no injustice. Force and fraud are in war the two cardinal virtues" ([65] ch.13). If the full power of Hobbesian dilemma is brought to the family and the firm, one undermines not only the belief in the neutrality of truth, but also the intrinsic value usually given to trust and trustworthiness as the bases of social organization and change [66]. One is then led to a new conception of life, one in which honesty is related not to truth, but to a commitment to the rules of illusion that give particular shapes to the social games players continuously enact with each other.

Games

As soon as one assumes that truth, logic and language are simply peculiar forms of illusion – socially shared and negotiated reductions of reality, which temporarily bring players to the same ground – it is possible to understand how social life can be conceived either as an objective reality or as a set of fluid, abstract, flimsy, or solid shared games based on different combinations of trust, skepticism, truth, illusion, and intermittent omission, struggle, or veracity [67]. Seen from inside, through the eyes of the real persons who are responding to life and making decisions, the other actors, one's interactions and relationships, the family, the firm, or the "self" are palpable realities, directly experienced through the actions, emotions, thoughts, speeches, and acts lived internally or in the concrete world. Seen from above, through the perspective of an observer focused on *why* and *how* men behave as they do, human beings are always responding to, and are made of, games that simultaneously transcend them and direct their actions (reality being simply an illusion that works, a game lived *as if* it were true [68]).

Dismissive as it is of the naive belief in free-will, this game perspective forces actors to momentarily detach from the *illusio* brought by the currently played game situations and concentrate on the multiple, complex, tacit, or explicit structuring conditions that limit, condition, and direct their actions and thoughts by determining, within the constraints of perception, the acceptable definitions of reality and appropriateness. With this movement, all forms of identity are reframed as arbitrary, contingent, socially reinforced mask configurations that simplify the ambiguity and complexity of the real situations and imprison the actors within the confines of specific nouns, names, roles, or rules of a game. When their structure is laid bare by the engagement in another illusory game – the reflective meta-game of awareness – all interactions, relationships, firms, families, and persons that make up our life are reframed as simple enactments, consequences of a social dance that silently transforms the arbitrary, ethereal impermanence of socially shared fictions into the very practical games with which we contend every day.

The two perspectives through which any game can be experienced, from inside or outside, reveal the depth of the antinomies that arise from our ability to be and not to be at the same time: "If the playing out of the game is viewed as simulating the behavior of some aspect of a social system (as it will if the game is well constructed), then there are two naturally separable components: the players and the structure of the game" [69]. When players momentarily halt their drive to live and think about the practice, the illusion of free-will is exchanged by an extra degree of freedom and one becomes more able to explain, criticize, or change the rules of the game. Conversely, *living* a game requires the annulment of the skepticism and the return to the involvement in the drama. It is in the fragile illusion of meaning and identification that emerges during well-played games, and not in the apparent firmness of objective truths, that we find a viable alternative with which to reconcile the ideal world of knowledge and morality – for which families, firms, and people exist as such – with the real, complex contradictions of the practically enacted social life, where everything is immersed in ambiguity.[2]

At any given moment, therefore, all forms of organization and social life can *either* be lived and experienced as true, *or* alternatively be seen from above as a chaotic interplay of simpler games that heuristically simplify the complexity of social reality and reduce it to a series of manageable variables that restrict the possible frames of interpretation by reinforcing roles, connections, balances, and imbalances of power. Since these games force actors to attend to only a situation at a time – the current explicit object of activity and the player or players with whom we are currently interacting and relating [70] – but a number of different, parallel motives are negotiated within each moment, they economically respond to both the cognitive need for simplification *and* to the practical need to integrate instrumental uses, power, and illusion into one single exchange. They thus allow players to attend to just to a few pieces of data while simultaneously living multiple meanings, values, and goals under the guise of the same interaction, relationship, identity, role, or social system.

Games may be serious or ludic; may be based on calculated moves, on passionate forces, or automatically lived as taken-for-granted interactions; and may range from an escape of the daily routine to social constructions deeply embedded in the shared space-time. They are made of rules, but these are loosely consistent or often incoherent with each other, seldom planned or well-thought, and equally likely to be followed, dismissed, or transgressed [71]. They may be played alone, like a solitaire, or involve other actors with whom one plays against or with. Families and firms are both games in themselves, which condition peculiar forms of relation, and social systems that contain an ecosystem of different games, leading to an unpredictable explosion of complexity that defies any attempt of total organization.

Be it in the family, in the firm, or in any relationship or interaction, in the microcosm of personal life social reality demands from all players a certain attitude toward the play. Actors are generally demanded to be honestly immersed in the game and to omit or forget unrelated parallel dramas (as when we play cards); but everyone fluctuates internally between being and not being fully on stage, and therefore knows that the other players may or may not be actually there. Each of the various games played by any single actor reflects a different perspectival view of reality, a loose metaphysical, ethical or esthetic conception of the world that provides the simplifying "absolute" parameters of truth required to act properly in the instant; and precisely because many different interests are played out in every action and the games vary from moment to moment, but the actors are the same, the same conception of truth under one rule may be dismissed as false under another rule of the game. Likewise, the definitions of identity that loosely impose some order to the free flow of perspectives within individuals and firms are seen both as an attempt to give meaning to social action – a playful experiment to capture the chaotic flow of life into the fiction of a rule based on an ideal of permanence – or alternatively interpreted as a falsification of what "really goes on" by the imposition of an appearance of conformance to logical, aesthetic, affective, or pragmatic ideals. Since the stability demanded by the social contracts is always reinforced, but can be only imperfectly and intermittently fulfilled, the question of how firms and families come to exist, given the diversity and instability of the actors on which they depend, is dismissed as an *apparent* paradox that emerges only when different games are compared side by side under the premise that only one of them can be true [40].

For the leader or change agent, the substitution of the relativism of play for the absoluteness of truth also leads to interesting corollaries. If one conceives family and organizational life as a network of interrelated games, conflict is expected as an obvious consequence of the clash between competing interests and frames of interpretation that offer opposing directions for sense-making [72]. However, peace is also expected because attention is serial and players quickly pass from one game to the other, operating within a large zone of indifference in which they automatically accept the rules imposed by the moment without questioning their consistency with other equally relevant existential demands [73]. The contradictory social demands for truth and for omission, and the habitual acceptance of slack, are seen as derived from the tacit understanding that it is impossible to play all games at the same time; but exactly as the relativism of play does not preclude the forceful imposition of a game, acceptance often means fear and temporary obedience rather than the apparent "cultural buy-in". Rules and logics of appropriateness, therefore, are not goals by themselves, but only a step required for man to achieve his arbitrary and intermittent desire to order existence in a particular way that can be quickly dismissed by another equally compelling rule. Truth, consistency, or identities are not states one can achieve, but games one plays with oneself and with existence. Appearance is a value to be praised. And every imposition of a culture, to the extent that it implies some control of the norms, regulations, and structure to reinforce the (ideally) shared goals or assumptions [74], is an act of power that competes not only with the random flow of human nature but also with the other contrary cultures that exist within the individuals, the family, or the firm.

Given that all stakeholders are continuously exercising their power to influence the rules of the game, what is eventually played in the family and in the firm depends both on the various self-reinforcing structuring conditions, which from top to down direct the movements expected from the actors, and on emergent, momentary stances taken by the players as they interact with each other. On the one hand, actors are often taking a step back and analyzing a game from the perspective of another: players consider each other's strategies in order to win the desired prizes [75], search for their "own" motives to judge whether game rules or positions are useful "for them" [76], and see themselves as farsighted economizing actors who attempt to circumvent the unavoidable incompleteness of contracts and the existence of opportunism by designing ex-ante guarantees and governance structures [77]. On the other hand, whenever there is some spontaneity, people become engrossed by the moment, are taken by the game they are playing, and forget themselves in taken-for-granted ways of being that follow the rules of habit more than logical considerations about reality. All aesthetic, affective, or truly cooperative games are therefore fragile constructions, stabilities in which the selfish pursuit of power, prestige, or utilitarian gains sometimes appears clearly in the air and sometimes makes use of the collective meanings, rituals, goals, or shared games to reassert itself under disguised, idealized forms.

Games and Culture

If men had no memory, restricted the exchange of specific motives to specific people, or lived in a single space, the structuration of their social games would be a relatively easy task – a few shifting rules and goals, an increasingly difficult succession of steps, and a right blend of ease and complexity would probably be sufficient to entice the players and immerse them into the illusion. Human beings, however, build their lives as a web of games organized around interlocking networks of people and meanings that extend in multiple times and spaces, feeding decisions and plans that have consequences and are used to stabilize the expectations of all other players. The same action, interaction, or activity simultaneously affects multiple different games, each of them played in a particular section of the collective social space-time. Opposing rules, motives, and actors seem absolute at each moment, but create different path-dependent streams of action and counter-action that shock with other paths in the future or across the stage.

In the real life of the family or the firm, then, slack, inconsistencies, and after-the-fact (romantic or ideological) rationalizations are commonly covered beneath frail dreams of rationality and free-will. This leads to loose, chaotic process of negotiation and decision-making. "Consider a round, sloped, multi-goal soccer field on which individuals play soccer. Many different people (but not everyone) can join the game (or leave it) at different times. Some people can throw balls into the game or remove them. Individuals while they are in the game try to kick whatever ball comes near them in the direction of goals they like and away from goals that they wish to avoid. The slope of the field produces a bias in how the balls fall and what goals are reached, but the course of a specific decision and the actual outcomes are not easily anticipated. After the fact, they may look rather obvious; and usually normatively reassuring" ([78]: 276). Torn between multiple situations that pull them to distinct directions, actors in practice follow the pressures of the moment, while in theory striving to maintain an appearance of unity.

It is when games stop being played only in the relatively private realm of the human soul, or when relationships and ideas people have about themselves clash against each other in the public space, that actors commonly attend to the contradictory forces hidden under the apparently organized games they play. This perspective inaugurates the eternal, all too human contradiction between the world of ideas and the world of practice. From an outside perspective, all stabilities that occult the randomness of practice under the apparent homogeneity of a concept, habit, or ritual are mere artifacts, needed to hide the truths of the facts and fix the illusions needed by social games. From within the game, however, spontaneous life continues being the source of heated passions, conformity, transcendence, or depth – ludic or tense attempts of the spirit to reach a (never reachable) ideal of unity or full realization, sometimes to please or win the audience, sometimes to play the game of meaning. The principle of non-contradiction offers the comforting consistency of the logic, but at the cost of destroying any illusions of stability – under the usual principle of truth, reason is insufficient to deal with the fragmentation of the reality and with the relativism of rules that emerge when one gives up the naively realistic perspective and starts to question the belief that things and people are, in fact, what they seem to be or say they are.

"The nature and quality of leadership, in the sense of statesmanship, is an elusive but persistent theme in the history of ideas. In our time, there no abatement of the need to continue the great discussion, to learn how to reconcile idealism with expediency, freedom with organization" ([79]: 1). As suggested by Selznick, the problem of meaning, and specifically of meaning in the culture, is directly related to the problems of complexity and multitasking. First, actors attempt to extract the maximal benefit and depth from the games they enact by compressing multiple tasks under the same place and people – cooperation and motivation in the firm, companionship, nutrition, and conflict resolution in a joint meal, or coercion, legitimacy, charisma, and rewards in the exercise of leadership. In a second moment, they are engrossed by the game of make-believe or by game-illusions of unity. Later, *in the limit* of the present, or when there is a public demand to justify the contradictions using the logic of the same language game that uncovered them, they go back to the rational principle of coherence as if this could be a fundament on which to rest in order to make an option between one or other pole of the trade-off [80]. Relativism, post-modern deconstructions, and the ambiguities inherent to interpretative flexibility or to trade-offs situations are not characteristic of specific problems, of life, of the epoch of the world in itself. Rather, they reflect the naive use of one set of rules – the logic that characterizes the formal languages, for which opposites exist and cannot be reconciled under the rubric of truth – for situations that do not fit this paradigm because meaningful, sustainable, complex games are crafted not to satisfy our drive for consistency but the more important, adaptive, evolutionary drive for adaptation or the emotional ideal of belonging and consistency [81] (see Appendix 2, Figures 3 and 10).

There is, therefore, an abyss between the abstract perspective of the game and the real life in which actors are always playing or fighting, sometimes according to what is expected, sometimes to preserve their right to violate, change, and define the collective regulations of reality and appropriateness. This instability of meaning means that when situations are simple actors will (*norm*ally) follow norms, processes, rules or engage in expected conflicts; in other situations, we will see rupture of meaning, alertness, and, many times, groundless decisions about what is the true meaning of any truth or action. Since all complex games have exceptions, and exceptions do not allow any rules – multiple objectives are always mixed in any interesting multitasking activity, and it is a *taste* what in the limit defines what is good or right – all meaningful cultures, endeavors, families, or businesses are based on an improbable combination of spontaneity, legitimacy, coherence, inconsistencies, limited truth, and limited justice. As melting pots in which forgetfulness coexists with norms, conflict, arbitrary power, consciousness, and unconsciousness about the game, true cultures, if there are any, probably emerge in the intersection between the top-down structuration of the game and the clash of contrary bottom-up perspectives that express how actors really see and react to them – a set of labile, fragile, semi-organized, and paradoxical fictions that reflect the meanders, obstacles, paths, agreements, and disagreements involved in the institutionalization and questioning of play [82].[3]

The paradox of culture lies precisely in the fact that, despite this complex fragmentation, some *belief* in the uniqueness and naturalness of one's character, identity, values, competencies, stories, accomplishment or culture is frequently essential for any deeper engrossment in the game. "Members do not agree upon clear boundaries, cannot identify shared solutions, and do not reconcile contradictory beliefs and multiple identities. Yet, they contend they belong to a culture. They share a common orientation and overarching purpose, face similar problems, and have comparable experiences. However, these shared orientations and purposes accommodate different beliefs, and these experiences have multiple meanings" ([3]: 58). The irrational belief in the self, the concerns with one's identity, the identification of the individual with the collectivity, and all true cultures are similar illusions – but illusions that stem from the blend of a profoundly interesting, poetic, and recursive language game with the depth, joy, and freedom that are the hallmark of all games of forgetfulness [83]. As says Nietzsche: "Everything that is of my kind, in nature and history, speaks to me, praises me, spurs me on, comforts me – everything else I don't hear or forget right away. We are always only in our own company" ([84]: 166). Meaning is, one could say, the ultimate vindication of the soul against a reality that is never, never objective.

Notes

1 "Whatever we say, as long as it goes beyond mere interjection and minimal communication, is never an immediate and faithful representation of what really occurs in us during that particular time of communication, but it is a transformation of this inner reality, teleologically directed, reduced, and recomposed. (...) Always, we show only a section of [these psychic processes], stylized by selection and arrangement. We simply cannot imagine any interaction or social relation or society which are *not* based on this teleologically determined *non-knowledge* of one another" ([85]: 312).

2 Goffman's concept of engrossment in the game, derived from Huizinga's concept of play [82], is here crucial: "It has been argued that the individual's framing of activity establishes its meaningfulness for him. Frame, however, organizes more than meaning; it also organizes involvement. During any spate of activity, participants will ordinarily not only obtain a sense of what is going on but will also (in some degree) become spontaneously engrossed, caught up, enthralled. (...) [This] involvement is a psychobiological process in which the subject becomes at least partly unaware of the direction of his feelings and his cognitive attention. That is what engrossment means. It follows that if a particular focus of attention is to be maintained, it cannot be maintained intendedly (at least wholly so), since such an intention would introduce a different focus of attention" ([86]: 345–6).

3 The contrast between the institutionalized notions of legitimacy, which require norms, and the real-life serious situations of the family or firm – which often demand quick, absolute, top-down solutions for which arbitrary power is the rule – is well expressed by Schmitt: "The sovereign is he who decides on the exception. Only this definition can do justice to a borderline concept. (...) The decision on the exception is a decision in the true sense of the word. Because a general norm, as represented by an ordinary legal prescription, can never encompass a total exception, the decision that a real exception exists cannot therefore be entirely derived from this norm" ([87]).

2 Families and Their Businesses

As any observer, leader or change agent studies the ties of dependence and counter-dependence that link families and their businesses, the first impression is that of uniqueness. Families' threads of history are drawn from the encounters and accidents of life that mark the memory of their members – a careful, biased, and often tacit mechanism of selection in which unexpected coincidences, special cases, and manifestations of power and status often take precedence over what is routine, common, or normal. Facts are then woven together into a plot, generally privileging the fictions of continuity, purpose, war, and victory. Especially when the business is alive and well, epic sagas that romanticize mundane examples of entrepreneurship and resistance are mixed with family tales, giving the firm a peculiarly personal, heroic touch. The final result is an often fine narrative, not unlike a myth, in which a few apparently distinctive events are commonly repeated over and over in the usual forums of conversation, mingled with the reiterations of identity and value that characterize people's talk about themselves [88].

Monotonous and predictable as it is, this falsification of reality involved in framing actors as being particularly special – a tailor-made story constructed especially for the audience that writes it – has a fundament in the facts. Families *are* made of unique individuals, who through their particular interactions and relationships create an inimitable pattern of alliances, enmities, and connections that explain many of the real, also unique events, meetings, and predispositions that characterize the life cycle of the social system. Likewise, firms *are* the product of an unrepeatable course that begins with their birth in a (historically determined) contingent place of a rugged landscape of multiple capabilities and develops as a sequence of path-dependent, local adaptations to current problems interspersed with occasional leaps of innovation [89]. Moreover, actors commonly *believe* in their uniqueness and make it real through the continuous reenactment of this fiction: enmeshed with what they think they are, and primarily with what they consider they *should* be, identity stories gradually turn into the only possible, or at least more touching, interpretations of reality. As a consequence, these narratives and the parallel reinforcement of the paths of identification relevant for the actors – the

"I- and we stories" that are truly emotional for people – become the main target to be hit if one wants (charismatically?) to implement any process of change or a truly meaningful culture [90].

Understanding and working with the real and purported individuality of families, firms, and actors, however, is a necessary but not sufficient step for any change intervention to be executed. Relevant as they are for the storytellers as they exchange their dialogs and monologs, the explicit narratives that make up one's autobiographies are not only seldom precise, but also frequently crafted to please self-interest rather than practical deliberations or rational negotiations. Consequently, actors often become lost in the meanders of their own beliefs, unaware of the real vectors that need to be touched to disentangle the knots with which they tie themselves as they simultaneously play multiple games with different rules and requirements of identity. How to satisfy the equally important demands brought by the roles of father, founder, owner, son, heir, or successor? How to reconcile the old culture embedded in the matriarchal, patriarchal, clan-, or other kinship systems with the new order brought up by the nuclear family? Should one privilege the alliance to the firm, to the family, or to kin? Which of the many plausible and equally viable definitions of the family and of the firm should be prioritized and made real in the private stage of one's household and business?

For most actors in the family and in the firm, these questions are rarely asked in such way. Rather, they appear in the form of seemingly unsolvable problems associated with doubt, self-doubt, conflicts, polarizations, and radicalizations directed not at the (pseudo) paradoxes of multitasking, but at the concrete situations in which these are manifested [91]. Games, rules, self, and identities are taken as a given or conceived as absolute. Property, affect, sex, labor, cooperation, procreation, and child-rearing are real, concrete, objective pieces of a larger social puzzle that people strive, successfully or not, to integrate under a meta-rule of unity. To a critical observer, on the contrary, families, firms, work, or love are just fragile, labile local orders that arise from the unpredictable emergence and game-interplay of contradictory motives and vectors. Most meanings and practices are necessary components of the social system; other elements are simply fossilized remnants of the past – tacit, automatic, structural but dispensable drivers that were useful at one point but in the present simply shape the actors' lives without their knowing, directing what they are and should do from beneath or above their consciousness [92]. Idealistic or ideological, reflecting the search for a better truth or just self-deception, change depends on new lenses that allow players to reframe the practical situations they face, temporarily solving the cognitive dissonances and recombining in a new way the old, immutable ingredients of life [59]. With new interpretations come new facts; with the new facts, other, frequently unpredictable problems that take the place of the previous ones; and as the (innate?)

tendency to optimism colors the ambiguity of the future with expectations of a better order, one reinforces the illusion that novelty is, indeed, good [93].

This chapter explores some of the ways in which the problem of the family and of the firm can be analyzed today if we consider the constructs, premises, and postulates found beneath some social forms they have taken over time and in different cultures [94]. As we will see, the general theme that emerges from this overview is one of a conflict between uniqueness and generality, or choice and structure. From their perspective, people feel they always are (and indeed are) choosing what to do with their lives and thereby creating unique histories, relationships, and networks. On the other hand, social structure strongly determines what happens and subtly drives actors to homogeneity and isomorphism – even an omnipotent artificer with infinite possibilities of action would soon be bound by the web of consequences and interrelations created by his own choices, by the particular set of options offered by the structuring environment, and eventually by the *belief* in the reality and value of the meanings institutionalized as true [7]. To the extent that man is fully free in thought, but limited in practice to choose between one prison or another, families and businesses are made of this complex blend of moments in which players follow the beaten path of tradition with other times when they "consciously" evaluate the pros and cons of the structuring facts and concepts they face, choosing, to the limit of their ability (and courage), which option to enact.

Some Basics

Whatever the forms taken by family and kinship systems over time, they revolve around the same issues: nourishment, protection, and reproduction are required to preserve the species; man is a social animal; procreation (until now) has required the sexual contact between men and women; the slow maturation of children demands intensive care; and the chronological succession of developmental phases in the individual, of older and younger siblings in the nuclear family, and of overlapping generations in the larger group inevitably brings diversity and discrimination to the core of the (homogeneous?) social structure [95]. To these obvious facts one can then add two psychological motives that push individuals to either immerse themselves in the group, refraining from immediate self-interest to satisfy social egoisms or long-term gains, or, alternatively, to leave the group, exploiting or confronting other players in order to favor individualistic drives at the expense of the benefits (and potentially the sense) of belonging [96]. Both in the family and in the firm, mixed cooperative-conflict games, rather than predictable zero-sum or non-zero-sum contexts, are the norm [97] – the same attachment that allows coordinated action brings restrictions against which men fight, or, alternatively, use to limit to restrict the others' latitude of action (see Appendix 2, Figure 11).

This intimate connection between dependence and conflict is linked to three fundamental features of human life. *First*, there is the inexorability of work, capital, and division of labor, from which come both conflict and the gains of civilization [98]. This mix of cooperation, dissensus, war, and competition, as well as the structures of power, status, and control of resources in which it rests, has always been a central part of the economy of the family. *Second*, there is the inexorability of identification. Men live in a world made of memories, identities, and symbols that persist as stories, names, verbs, and habits located the individual and collective imagination. Families, firms, and the abstract relationships on which they are based are almost solid entities, relatively inflexible equilibria maintained not only by custom and power, but also by how people see, feel, and talk about them as part of their own selves or as obstacles to their realization. *Third*, the application of a single rule of cohesion to different levels of analysis transforms families, firms, and all social systems in (homogeneous) units composed of (heterogeneous) sub-units, all of them created by the same premise that distinguishes an interior from the exterior according to the political heuristic "us" *versus* "them" [99]. The cherished, proclaimed, wished-for common values, practices, and goals that foster illusions of sameness are, due to the constitutive rule that frames social entities as existing facts, a source of divisiveness when one considers the relations among sub-games within a larger unit of analysis [100] (see Appendix 2, Figures 4 and 5).

Conflict, competition, cooperation, capital, identification, and the contrast between levels of organization are, and have always been, the improbable constituents of the fragile equilibrium in which families and their businesses rest. This dynamics infuses *value* into the tangible and intangible elements that form the stage of the change – exactly as other animals fight for the ownership and access to "their" territory, the place where people work, exploit work, or see, live and talk about is simultaneously a domain to be preserved from other groups, a prize to be disputed within the group, and a concrete symbol of stability needed to enact the intangible, affective game of identifying with the past and with tradition. The attachment of the individual to symbols of ownership is the link that connects one's volatile emotions to the equally intangible threads of kin. Thus, the identification of the family with the place has forever been associated with the ownership of the land, goods, business, and house that supported the name, stories, and goods transmitted from generation to generation. Furthermore, rules of diffusion of these constituents follow contradictory, but overlapping logics. Even though the passing of property institutionalizes internal differences of status within the same kin group – ownership being defined by rigid descent and inheritance laws, kindred relationships being grounded on informal networks of affinity – the sense of belonging often spreads like a halo that reaches, albeit softly, even the most destitute of the relatives [101].[1]

Capital and the symbolism of capital are, therefore, intimately connected with the development of the family and of kinship systems. Economic capital, the most obvious, can be directly converted in money or used in concrete exchanges of goods or property; cultural capital, involving the possession of knowledge and educational credentials, supports the (status-based) process of professionalization; and social capital, dependent on the position one occupies in the social network of status and prestige, facilitates the access to special connections, favors, and contacts (all of them eventually convertible in money). When any of these forms of capital become symbolically relevant to the actors, the forms of being, the land, the name, and the particular culture or habitus in which they were socialized become part of their way of seeing the world ([102]: 47). Furthermore, as these various forms of capital bring the dimension of *time* to families, firms, and people, the individuals' struggle for existence becomes deeply embedded in the previous conditions of inequality guaranteed by its possession. Instrumental interests, division of labor, identification, and struggles for power and status are never present as singular, random moments of war or peace emerging in a mythical present time unencumbered by the ordering effects of memory. Rather, they follow directions given by relationships and networks of affinity, power, status, and influence that spread as games in the social space and guarantee that current life is guided by past experience [103]. Like peasants, villagers, or tribesmen transplanted to the modern world – but always imagining themselves special, unique or different – members in the family businesses of our days are, also, always negotiating both the hard facts of economic life and the strong, soft, flimsy, or fragile ties of identification that connect them through (apparently) non-instrumental relationships of kinship, marriage, and alliances.

Ties of Blood and Relatedness

These social structures, which in the long run are constitutive of the free (?) individuals who create them, are not peculiar to human society. On the contrary, fishes, dogs, chimpanzees, baboons, bonobos, gorillas, and many social species also live under the influence of complex social systems that mix multiple rules of association, stratification, and rupture, responding naturally to the constraints given by the social hierarchies in which they are born [104–107]. Primates, in particular, share with humans the existence of fission-fusion societies that mingle larger kin-structures that cross generations with smaller units dedicated to everyday activities, the families and small groups of individuals related through ties of friendship. As a consequence, individuals play different roles in different places at different times, satisfying their biological, affective, and economic needs according to one's place within a larger group of con-specifics [108]. Perhaps the only feature that makes humans unique is that our families and kinship systems make use of the hypnotic power of language to reinforce the habits, relationships, and social structures we copy from our fellow primates [109].

The affective importance given by most individuals to their ties of blood – the main condition for its illusory power as a cover-up for other interests – is deeply embedded in human nature. Most of the affiliative relationships, both in primates and in men, develop around the archetypal connection between mother and children (especially daughters). In chimpanzees, for example, infants and pre-adolescents always stay with their mother; males and females return to greet her affectionately well after adolescence; and solid, long-lasting affinity networks are later established among generations of females or even siblings [108]. A wide range of behaviors, like spatial proximity or dispersion, grooming, formation of alliances, the transmission of culture, mutual tolerance, and help in taking care of the offspring or fighting enemies, are strongly correlated with ties of kinship [110]. In many species, these affinity networks evolve as female-based power and dominance-rank hierarchies – among the Old World monkeys, for example, lineages and genealogies organized around the elderly matriarch define the affective and economic habits of the group, determining who obeys to whom and who has privileged access to the preferred resources and to reproduction [111]. Furthermore, the incorporation of the male in female-based hierarchies or the existence of ties among males, as we see in many businesses of today, is neither a privilege of the human species nor a posterior development of a mythical matriarchal society: one finds coalitions of male chimpanzees in Tanzania, solitary females and promiscuous mating among orangutans, lasting cooperative relationships among males in bonobos, and long-term social bonds between males and females in gorillas [112].

For the human species, however – perhaps as an evolutionary response to the open environment of the savannah, perhaps as a reinforcement of male-based power, perhaps as a contingent, non-functionalistic development [113] – the need to complement the less mobile task of raising children with the exploration of the environment led to the mix of male bands for exploratory and food-finding purposes and the nuclear family, "the smallest hunting and gathering unit possible in terms of efficiency and safety" [108]. Combining into a single game some mobility for exploration, a protected place to raise the children, a stable pair bond to guarantee the needed division of labor, and rules of incest to minimize conflict, the nuclear family has forever coexisted with kin as a form of social order. In fact, what until today characterizes most human societies is their organization as open community social systems that blend three complementary, competing aggregates based on the same distinction between "us" and "them" and separated from each other by the exogamic requirement to mate outside the group. *Ties of marriage*, formal arrangements singled out from occasional sex or illicit unions, guarantee the social control of procreation and the care of offspring and property (particularly relevant needs, given the absence of contraceptive methods, proof of paternity, high infant mortality and short life span that for ages have shaped human life) [114]. *Ties of kinship* regulate the formation of groups of families. *Matrifocal families* of mother and immature offspring, with particularly strong ties between mothers and daughters and the progressive incorporation of the father, complete the regulation of sex, reproduction, division of labor, and hierarchy around rules of descent and affiliation [115]. Everywhere, one sees the association between division of labor and male dominance – even in matriarchal societies, power is generally ascribed to the brother of the mother, and until today men are predominantly involved in the honorific, noble and better rewarded activities (the business), while women take care of the intangible, unpaid, unrecognized, and affective work (the family) [116]. Multiple asymmetries, perpetuated through rigid rules of inheritance and marriage, are hidden under the simile of kin or unity of the family [117].

In the pre-historic era, before time prevailed over the natural flow of life and societies began to respond to past and future, the coexistence of these competing aggregates and rules of game was probably relatively more pacific and one did not fully prevail over the other. In the Nestsilik Iglulik and in the Cooper Eskimos, in the Great Basin Shoshoni, in the Athapaskan Indians or the Hadza in East Africa, as in all nameless peoples who deal intuitively with these three opposing rules of association – kin, family, and marriage – two to 12 independent families aggregated in local bands, forming the center that defined the place of residence, the migrations, and the exploration of resources; larger regional groups of up to a 100 individuals, generally organized around kin, formed the basis of social identification and gave individuals the sense of belonging to a particular group or place; and to accommodate different needs "there was fusion and fission of the communities at different times of the year; nuclear families went off alone on separate trips, and there was great flexibility in residence, [following] a pattern adaptive to constantly changing opportunities and pressures" ([108]: 215). All in all, one could envision a soft equilibrium between attraction and repulsion, a natural response to the need to accommodate the pushes to unity and diversity.

In the Neolithic, when the advent of agriculture led to surplus and consequently to the appearance of capital, this equilibrium was broken [118]. History, permanence, and coherence became, then, the backbones of a line that united past, future, and people around the same path, a game eternized and turned real by the social enactment of the fictions of lineages, clans, and (less importantly) families; and for most of the history of mankind, kin systems, and the productive domestic group competed with families and marriages to occupy the place of the basic unit of social organization [119]. Furthermore, the advent of language introduced the (arbitrary) principle of non-contradiction, by which incoherencies are defined as illogical or irrational. Individuals, families, businesses, and societies are, then, obliged to reconcile the opposing rules of association by creating normative, equally arbitrary rules and regulations that purportedly "explain" why societies are organized the way they are.

In some times and places, kinship systems are the main (legitimate?) form of social organization. In others, families are more relevant. More rarely, marriages and the bond between partners prevail over kin and family. For our purposes, the important observation is that the same archaic, biologically natural but socially institutionalized rules that have forever ruled the organization of society are still present in modern days. Family businesses, as mankind, continuously alternate between equilibria that are always fragile, because when privileging the kin, *or* the family, *or* the couple, *or* specific individuals they inevitably downplay the force of the other, equally strong forces that from the backstage continue influencing the plot. In the impossibility of going back to the clear, strict rules that in the past regulated these contradictions with the weight of tradition, under the spell of the post-modern and sociological relativism, and without new ideologies to justify the status-quo, the same differences of power and status framed as legitimate within formally organized systems work in family business as sources of ambiguity that randomly promote competition and cooperation, bringing people together and putting generation against generation, kin against kin, depending on the moment of the culture and of each family in particular.

Kinship Systems

For a good time in the Western world, and until today in many parts of the earth (or family businesses), the social and economic organization of groups, tribes, and civilizations occurs primarily around the lines given by ties of kinship rather than family, marriage, or the state. In Africa, Australia, Oceania, or Americas, kin systems were generally the single basis of social stratification – individuals were classified according to genealogical relatedness following patrilineal, matrilineal, dual, or bilateral types of descent and required to marry according to strict rules that forbade the incest and favored the exogamy [120]. In ancient Greece, the three basic units of social organization were the set of kindred relatives from both sides, the *phratries* presided by the aristocratic clans, and the household or *oikos* ("the patriarchal center of power, intrigue and wealth", from which we derive *oikonomia* and economy). In Rome, the patrilineal group owning common property was the *gens* (plural = *gentes*, or people) and resources were similarly associated with the household (the word *family* originates from *famulus,* servant) [94]. In medieval Europe, clans linked to a mythical ancestor, lines developed around the domestic group and its property, and lineages that worked as "legal entities owning indivisible property and carrying out military, political and religious functions" always mixed economy, genetic relatedness, and rules of inheritance that defined kinship "from without and by reference to the house" ([121]: 48, 62).

All these forms of organization, as innumerous others uncovered by anthropological research, simply give peculiar shapes and names to social orders that in general prioritize the kin over other equally plausible ways of organization. Arguably, they are so strong precisely because they attend relatively well to three fundamental drives of the living being: the egocentrism of the individual, who as a solitary player needs a social platform to live, reproduce, and have pleasure (and who therefore, for habit or interest, does not question the constraints he faces); the occult egocentrism of the selfish gene, which in order to transmit itself prioritizes the survival of the species and leads individuals to sacrifice their time, energy, and even life to benefit common relatives [122]; and the other-oriented egoisms of the social animal, which have in the common origin, in the common place, and in the common affiliation suitable objects to project a sense of relatedness and belonging [123].

In addition to pragmatically serving the various egoisms of the individual, in human societies kinship systems are legitimated by two layers of meaning that give existence and value to some classes of relatedness, but not to others. Kin categories are framed linguistically, translated into a system of symbols that gives an (apparently neutral) mental existence to relations and social structures that reflect specific value-options of the society – since only some roles and relations are expressed in words, categories of thought not represented in the language game have less power to structure social life [124]. Héritier, for example, suggests that all European kin systems are based on combinations of a few types of (marriage-descent based) relations: the differentiation among generations; the distinction between linear and collateral ties of relationship (a consequence of the marriage alliance); the separation between ties of blood and ties of marriage (a consequence of the incest taboo); the gender of the relative in question; and the differences of age in the same generation [125]. Second, different normative *values* are ascribed to different positions in the symbolic structure of the kin, determining effects of distance, proximity, dominance, submission, exchange, reciprocity, alliance, descent, and access to resources that are seen as taken-for-granted social facts [120]. In this way, the set of connections defined by the systems of kinship is reinforced both by automatic belief and by social pressure, by layers of naturalness that imperceptibly cover arbitrary definitions of rank and by sanctions, norms, and regulations designed to perpetuate the inequalities existing in the game. The same happens in some family businesses, particularly when property, prestige, and tradition, rather than love, are the main commodities that allow the connection to a mythical past (the founder, the genealogy, the reputation in the community).

All kinship systems observed in all human cultures, therefore, structure man's biological, affective, and economic needs according to rules that condition power, status, identity, hierarchies, inheritance, affinity, and identification to one's place within a larger group of kin or related people [109]. In their core is the prominence given to ties of blood and relatedness at the expense of the individual, of the couple, and of the nuclear family. In their periphery, as a condition of the first, are strict regulations of marriage, procreation, and succession. The larger group of kin is then built as a relevant social entity that extends in time and is tied together by the transmission of the common property, by the reinforcement of kin-based hierarchies, and by illusions of identification that hide, under the fiction of the "same blood", several contradictory forms of organization that would be discarded as incompatible if one uncovered the lack of logic of the whole ideology.

Strong as they are due to the power of tradition and biology, kinship systems are, nevertheless, *games* whose stability depends on strict rules that preserve the (arbitrary) form in which they are organized – in this case, the submission of all social games to the higher games of raising children and obeying the kin. *First,* there is the heavily regulated marriage: independently of its form – between men and women, as in "conventional" couples; between same-sex individuals (as in modern gay relationships and in the Nuer, Yoruba, Navaho and Zuni); between a dead person and a living relative (Nuer); polyandric, with several brothers espousing the same woman (Tibet); polygamous or monogamous, as in modern times; and "whether by exchange, purchase, free-choice or imposed by the family, et cetera, – everywhere a distinction exists between marriage, i.e., a legal, group-sanctioned bond between a man and a woman, and the type of permanent or temporary union resulting either from violence or consent alone" ([126]: 268). *Second,* there is the incest taboo, probably developed to decrease competition among siblings, parents, and children within the family or among families in the society [120, 127]. Families, from the perspective of the kin, are just part of a mechanism that guarantees the control of sex, property, power, and access to reproduction and labor within a line, a warranty that by giving up the ownership of "their" women men would have access to females coming from other factions and thus create a brotherhood tie with other male groups [120]. The rules that guide the institutions of the marriage and of families, then, always respect the interval between two poles of refusal that serve the unity of the broader society: the ban on the extremely foreign guarantees the union within the same social class, profession, region, religion or neighborhood; the interdiction of the extremely close led to the taboo of the incest, and consequently to alliances between groups and the institution of relative peace within the household (the bedrock for the ideology of unconditional love between parents and children) [128].[2]

Rules, however, are simply the rational version of irrational values that impose themselves over others through the moral fictions (and the practical enforcement) of bans, prohibitions, and definitions of what *is* (or *is felt* to be) good or bad. The underlying (good) logic of the cohesion-based games of kinship and the purportedly noble identification with the tradition and blood, therefore, introduce by necessity a series of (bad) inequalities within the supposedly unitary system of organization. Regarding women, for example, the widespread use of dowries, the arranged marriages, and the alliances implied by the incest taboo inherently confirm the "intrinsic" value of the male-dominated society and downplay identifications that are meaningful in other contexts. Other relevant asymmetries involve the increased value given to work in comparison to home (which separates affective ties from money, land, or social status); the tensions between the forces of the business (which imply in concentration of the property around ties of blood), and the forces of marriage and nuclear family (which favor the dispersal of the wealth); the contrast between the attachment to children and the attachment to the partner (which puts children over the conjugal bond, or vice versa); or the desire to maintain the differences in capital, power, and division of labor (which puts the individual against all forms of organization that do not serve his or her own needs). Typically, control over the common resources is justified by the adherence and allegiance to mythical ties of identification that placed the group over the individual, and some individuals, who occupied the privileged roles within the group, as superior to other individuals who were inferior according to relations of dominance and submission. Social order, thus, depends on the acknowledgement that older actors are superior to young; that ties of blood are more relevant than ties of marriage; that kin is more important than family; and that men have priority over women [129].

It is unrealistic to think about family businesses of today without taking into account the power of the past, the overt or covert shadow of the genealogy, and the forces of kindred that in the guise of tradition and history are commonly mingled with one's "own" achievements to build the identity fictions felt as necessary by individuals. In the past, kin structures combined economy and affect under the ideology of the blood; within family businesses, the economic side of the kin structure is given prominence by its association with two other mythical institutions of the modern times, the firm and the property. Differentiation of siblings based on age remains common in many families, and often dictates the succession in the firm. Preferences for the maternal or paternal lineage are widespread, often reflecting distinctions of value within networks of affinity (the preferred brother, sister, or relative) and ties of power (those who hold the resources). Ties of marriage are commonly given lower status than ties of blood, with individual and social preferences following the transmission of property rather than the (voluntary!) choice of the partner. Affinity, love, marriage, and family ties, relegated to a secondary role under the ideology of the kin, remain secondary under the powerful, "modern", impersonal, rational ideology of the bureaucratic firm. Particularly relevant, but generally unspeakable and often unspoken, is the tacit rule that legitimizes the superiority of men over women by framing differences as natural or as related to age – an analysis of the linguistic terms used in various cultures, for example, shows that females are classically inferior in rank and seen as younger or daughters rather than older, wise, or parents, making of the apparently neutral kinship terminologies a mechanism that guarantees the reproduction of the social order [95]. This inferiority is compensated only by the central role women play in structuring the affective, intangible, fundamental (but often less valued) pillar of a different form of organization, the family.

Marriages and Families

From the proto-hominid matrifocal dyad of mother and offspring to the recent experiment of the Israeli Kibbutzim, mankind has developed family-liked entities to organize the job of raising children, accumulating wealth, and guaranteeing a privileged place for the exercise of sexuality and reproduction [115]. Families, from this perspective, are a means-to-an-end. *First,* they serve the need to take care of the less mobile, mundane activities related to everyday life and to the management of the household, which are almost universally restricted to women: as recently as in the1950s in Britain, for example, "when a daughter married, and even more when she left work to have children, she returned to the woman's world, and to her mother. Marriage divided the sexes into their distinctive roles, and so strengthened the relationship between the daughter and the mother who has been through it all before" ([130]: 61). *Second*, there is economy [131]. The nuclear family has forever been the fundamental unit of consumption, and for a long time the basic center of production, uniting adults and children in the task of providing for their needs and producing wealth. "Women, men, children and resident nonrelatives such as servants all worked at productive tasks, which were differentiated by age and sex" according to the size of the group and the consequent need for labor ([132]: 54); a single leader, usually a patriarch, ruled over the others and the household; and property, status, and tradition served as the main drivers of attachment and continuity of the bond.

Historically, the two pillars upon which family games have been socially constructed – division of labor and efficiency in dealing with everyday life – prioritize economy over affect, self-interested utility over disinterested identification or engrossment in the game. The fundamental tension between consanguinity and exogamic alliance has been largely dominated by the endogamous pressure to guarantee the production and maintain property within the family [126]. Work and productivity, rather than affinity, have ruled the relations. The size of the domestic group, exactly as it happens today with family businesses, has grown with the size of the holding: the larger the ability to make money, the size of the owned land, and the strength of the political power, the more servants, relatives and nuclear families one single productive group could contain under the common umbrella of the joint property. Given the competition for the (always scarce) resources, players traditionally acquired differential access to the common wealth, succession, or positions of control (typically, actors who stay at home have less privileges than those who go out to work). "Freedom [as in many games of today] could only be exercised within narrow limits fixed by economic, social and in particular demographic factors" ([133]: 1144).

The practical consequences of these value choices are that for most of the history of mankind marriage and family have fit actors into roles that served the needs of the broader group, and not theirs. In Latin, for example, *matrimonium* means the legal condition of *mater,* i.e., mother; there is not a verb that expresses the decision of a woman to marry, rather than to get married or being taken to a home – the verbal root *wedh,* for example, just means "to bring a woman to the house" [114]. The same utilitarianism was reflected in the architecture of the houses: homes, for a long time, did not allow any privacy; promiscuity was common; intrusions were frequent and guaranteed the social control by servants, neighbors, or the whole community; and low affect, patriarchy, authoritarianism, and a view of children as a burden or source of manpower prevailed over the stylized view of the family as a "peaceful retreat" from the outside world [133]. Social organization evolved primarily around the goal of "accumulating capital in the form of land and hence accumulating a symbolic capital with the local community". From the simplest peasant line to the ancient aristocratic hereditary trees or modern industrial dynasties, the basic prerequisites for the sense of commonality included just "a certain genealogical depth, property to be passed, and a family ideology" ([121]: 65–7).

The fundamental paradox that emerges from this superposition of interests – one that is especially important for any work of culture that involves meaning, and therefore engrossment, spontaneity, and valuation of the immaterial ethical, aesthetic, or affective values – is that players *less* interested in the collective game typically have more power over them. Tangible goods and formal contracts associated with labor and capital are easily exchangeable, and therefore have economic value. Affective ties are personal, and therefore useless under standard market rules. As a consequence, players who are more interested in preserving the family – or in giving it any existential significance beyond utility – are routinely deprived of having access to the common goods and do not have the power, means, or courage to enforce any true or idealistic culture for fear of breaking the (usually fragile) ties of self-interest that keep it together [116]. From this tension emerges a pervasive trade-off (or complementarity?) between calculation and spontaneity, power, and love, or individualism and cooperation. In small Japanese family businesses, for example, the *ie* represents the history and perpetuity of the family name and tradition, the maintenance of the common property taking precedence even to ties of kinship; the *uchi,* on the other hand, represents the family as a center of emotional attachment – ties of blood, property, and emotion coexist and compete with each other in the same system [134]. For the typical 20th-century British middle class, on the contrary – unlike the ideal sold in modern concepts about the firm – "the purpose of the business was not the pursuit of profit but the provision of a modest competency for the family" ([135]: 332). The forces of affect and affinity are, as they have always been, in shock with the economic drives and, as a consequence, with the competition to dominate the collectively owned means of production and the place of identification.

The modern emphasis on the ideology of love as a basis of the nuclear family appears as a counterpoint to the older emphasis on tradition, economy, and kin; and, in parallel, as a swing in the pendulum of social valuation away from the ties of blood toward the ties of marriage, privileging the freedom of the individual over the submission to the group. In the West, this trend has been observed since the 1500s. Initially, as in all societies, affect was restricted to the mother-daughter relationship and family mingled with kin-based orders, downplaying the value of the conjugal bond. Gradually, probably under the influence of the Church ideology, the rights of women and children were enforced and the nuclear family gained social more relevance [136] (both St. Augustine and St. Thomas Aquinas, for example, worked for the imposition of stricter incest limits that could weaken the relationships within kin and argued that marriage outside the group "increased ties between communities, breaking down the undesirable solidarity of close-knit groups") ([94]: 61). Eventually, the conjugal bond was prioritized and colored with the tincture of love, rather than interest; the spontaneous, free choice of partners took the place of the goods previously required from the bride's or bridegroom's families; and the formal acceptance of the woman to get married, albeit ceremonial at first, was put in law. The "growing discreteness of the conjugal family as a social group" and the value given to it as separate from kin occurred side by side with the precedency given to the marriage, both working toward breaking the fluidity of the transmission of wealth and power across generations and eroding the archaic rules that shaped the division of labor and the internal economy of the household ([119]: 27).

This double transformation of the marriage and of the domestic group, which led ultimately to the (false, illusory, romantic) separation of love and self-interest, can be seen in the disposition of the physical, affective, and cultural spaces where families actually live. In the houses, the appearance of corridors and segregated rooms for eating, sleeping, and conducting business, the decreasing number of servants, and the increasing worries about promiscuity reinforced the search for privacy, both inside the home and from the house to the environment [119]. The introduction of separate bedrooms for children in the end of the 19th century, the ban on physical punishment, and the focus on the search for happiness reflected a growing emphasis on the individual [137]. Children and adolescents came to be seen as objects of care, rather than just manpower; and despite the continuing relevance of material considerations, "companionship, life-long affection and, slightly later, an 'honorable' sexual dimension (husbands expected to behave like lovers) entered marriage, … sex came to be seen not as a duty ... [and took] its modern role expressing, sustaining and strengthening love" ([119]: 38).

Family law, following the same trends, concentrated on formalizing the (arbitrary, socially constructed) "fair" practices regarding custody, decision-making, legitimacy and adoption of the children; on firming the marriage as a voluntary relationship that involves material transactions between families; and on establishing the rules governing the ownership and control of common holdings or the proceedings upon divorce [138]. A relevant tension related to this issue is still present in how property is regulated in modern-day families – since the game of marriage always involves tangible and intangible goods, but only the first ones allow measurement and partition, there is no perfect contract of association that works fairly for both partners if we consider all possible future contingencies. Societies and family groups have therefore constantly alternated between the extreme regimes of separation of property (which allows the concentration of wealth within the line but empowers the more powerful players) and universal community of property, which guarantees equity at the cost of dispersing wealth, of disempowering the dominant player, and of forcing actors to openly discuss all the economic issues.

In our days, the idealized, romantic, or biased view of the family emphasizes its separation from work, the contrast between home and the capitalistic world, and the "women's special place in the domestic sphere, where they are purported to be the guardians of the key values that had been deemphasized by the shift to market production – intimacy, piety, virtue" ([132]: 10). From this view arises the (normative, value-ridden) view of what *should* be a complete family life cycle: first, the young married couple with no children or children up to school age; second, the domestic group with adolescents; third, one or more young adult children outside of the house; fourth, parents helping their children settle with their own lives; later, the empty nest syndrome and the return to the couple life; and lastly, the ageing domestic group [121]. The implicit assumption is that family games revolve primarily around the individual and affective life of the individuals, following pre-determined paths and rules of progression that hide a potent push toward social harmony.

It is sufficient to scratch beneath the surface of the ideology, however, to find norm violations that unveil the forever-present, covered-up layers of interest and self-interest that defy the prevailing collective ideologies. These are particularly obvious in family businesses. According to the ideology of kin, property and power were integrated around the traditional rule of the patriarch and regulated by strict laws of inheritance; in modern family businesses, the push for the maintenance of property and preservation of the firm within the clan clashes with the overt values of autonomy, education, individuation, and marriage as a free choice. Women, raised to have the same privileges of men and often given equal shares of the family inheritance, still face the reality of a work-world mostly dominated by "male" values and practices that exclude "female" emotions and reserve the specialized knowledge for men, privileging productivity and frowning upon household tasks (but allowing men to have preferential access to leisure, pleasure, and outside activities) [139]. In the milieu of the big dynasties rules of endogamy frequently bring together complementary businesses, putting kin ties against the conjugal bond and introducing pre-arranged nuptial contracts in the core of purportedly spontaneous marriages. Moreover, as in the old times, "whenever and wherever parents have controlled resources vital to their children's future standard of living, they have been able to strongly influence their children's choices of spouses" and life decisions (an observation particularly relevant for members of business families) ([119]: 36).

The obvious conclusion, when we compare kin to family, is that the same contradictions apply to both forms of organization. Within kin, unitary, us-based systems fostered the soft magic of identification with blood and tradition while firmly reinforcing tradition to answer the hard questions related to the differences in power, wealth, and status. In the families, rules of love and autonomy mean that affiliative and economic drives, previously held together in the property-concentrated and individual-diminishing game of the kin systems, are partially divorced. In both, however, the same problems appear: laws of inheritance, strict regulations of marriage, fights for the patrimony and for succession, pushes to fusion counteracting fission effects of diversity, the centrifugal forces of incest opposing the centripetal vectors of tradition and economy. Furthermore, both struggle with the task of reconciling an idealistic ideology – which subordinates the individual to family, kin, and their "common values" of blood or love, deemphasizing the person as an agent – with the potent forces of individuation that separate the diverse players who are members of the "same" unit [137].

It is difficult to say which of these factors, the economic or the affective, the base or the superstructure, is more relevant in shaping the evolution of social systems. If nothing, norms, practices, ideas, and routines systematically differ from each other and circumscribe two different realms for human life. From these different orders and forms in the organization of meaning – both present in the same games and among the same actors, one prioritizing the practice other the language, one focusing on promises and ideals, other on what is really enacted – come different interpretations, and therefore flaws in the desirable (?) homogeneity of the culture: explicit language and overt symbolic displays of identity and intentions, commonly used (and often believed) by the actors, often do not follow or just disguise the real, covert, practical conditions of their lives [140]. Besides, unawareness and unconsciousness are frequently a *good:* in the absence of open conflict or blatant externalities, logical questions do not arise, family laws are not taken into consideration, money becomes a taboo, and it is possible to live and relive the rituals of dinner, the weekend visitations, or the reunions around major holidays *as if* life were pure indeed, separated from the dirtier, mundane transactions of utility. The understanding that loose coupling and soft cultures are the only reasonable answers to the problems of organization is the only way out of this archaic duality.

Family Businesses and Family Property

In many families until today, economic factors related to money, property, work, and capital are tacitly forbidden to reach the collective imaginary and expelled from the explicit checkerboard of the language game. The opposite happens in the realm of the firm. Here, the institutionalization of the bureaucratic ideals has been closely linked with the expectation that one really can (*and should*) create social systems driven solely to the pursuit of profit and production, for which rigid norms of rationality apply [141]. In firms, it is assumed, one should see "equal treatment for all employees; reliance on expertise, skills, and experience relevant to the position; no extra-organizational prerogatives of the position; (...) specific standards of work and output; extensive record keeping dealing with the work and output; establishment and enforcement of rules and regulations that serve the interests of the organization; [and] recognition that rules and regulations bind managers as well as employees" ([142]: 3). Formal, legalistic mechanisms of control and assessment are seen as a means to guarantee justice, and often lead to a strict, fair, logical, but unpractical, search for non-contradictions.

The evolution of the firm, a game that substituted rational exchanges of money and labor for traditional authority, is a well-known history. Until the 1800s, few businesses needed to employ administrators because enterprises were smaller, usually connected to the family. With increasing size, the multi-departmental firm was born. In the beginning of the last century, business education was created and with it the managerial ideology, reserving the "science" of administration to professionally sanctioned specialists. Eventually, larger companies became multidivisional and executives, consultants and (later) board members became indispensable to the firm, pieces framed as absolutely necessary to the "correct" handling of the economic affairs previously dealt with according to the personal, internal rules of the household, family, and kin systems [143]. There are suggestions that the rise of the managerial profession may have happened due to historical (contingent) factors prevalent in the beginning of the last century, such as the pressure of engineers seeking industrial legitimation through the creation of new organizational paradigms, the rhetoric of professionalism, equality, order, and progress, and even the social-political responses to labor unrest [144]. Whatever their source, however, ideologies become true when believed and enacted in social life. The fiction of the firm and the idolatry of work as a rational, value-neutral activity profoundly influence how players of today tend to see their lives, the firm, and its relation to the family.

A good part of the paradoxes and contradictions that mark the histories of family businesses comes from the misunderstandings, false statements, and naive predictions derived from the modern push toward this (never-reachable) idealized detachment from the affect, interests and power that have forever ruled the household economy and the underground of any social system. In particular, the attempt to rationally organize the family, the firm, and their intersection tacitly assumes that rules are an obvious solution for ambiguity; that individuals are rational; that businesses should be freed from affect; that the flow of information between principal and agent is easier than between family members; and that families, unlike firms, are ruled primarily by love, and not economy (!?). Modern systems of corporate and family governance that institutionalize the distinctions between owners, boards, managers, strategy, and execution are, thus, historically created forms of organization that copy the bureaucratic canons and respond to very specific conditions typical of larger, public companies with distributed ownership and dispersion across diverse geographies and areas of business. When engraved as law and enforced as a requirement for the firm, they express the coercive isomorphism that drives people, groups, and social systems to be similar (albeit imagining themselves unique); when taking the form of normative ideals, they bring cohesion at the cost of diversity, precluding the emergence of other, potentially more fruitful, forms of control and organization [7]. They never reflect or can effectively harness, however, the strong, opposite forces and beliefs that must be followed for players to feel they are true members of both the family *and* the firm. Caught in the Procrustean bed of the self-fulfilling rational prophecy, business families are often torn between the loss of their intuitive (but old) paradigms of association around kin or household and the new (but flawed) rhetoric that promises stability *as if* one could assume the existence of transparency, accountability, responsible ownership or fair process in the presence of the ubiquitous, economically driven opportunism with guile that also rules the human relations [145, 146].

Partially convincing to players who are subjected exclusively to the *idealized* loving family or cold environment of the firm – the members of the petit-bourgeois professional or working families, and the employees of multi-national impersonal companies – the ideology that separates instrumental uses from personal affairs is, therefore, unsustainable in the context of business families. In the first two cases, contradictions are easily dismissed as personal failures or as inability of the actors to love, refrain from emotions, negotiate, or act as they "should" do. Family businesses, however, are built upon path-dependent histories and practices evolving around joint property, affect, kin lines, and traditions that both unite their members around material symbols of wealth and separate them as competitors for the scarce resources of money and prestige. The consequence is that these groups commonly follow a double-layered, hypocritical method of organization [147]: the expectation of equality, inherent to the idea of marriage and family as freely chosen games, frequently exists side by side with covert imbalances, unclear systems of domination and submission, and with signed contracts, pre-nuptial arrangements, or dispositions of the property that are in stark contrast with the disinterested love and distributive justice that should (romantically or ideologically) guide the implementation of culture. Since these paradoxes are rarely openly addressed, families and businesses routinely subsist as unstable structures, social dreams in which interest, fear, naiveté and (not uncommonly) joy, pride tradition, or love exist together due not to a true game, but because there is tacitness, acceptance, forced loose coupling [148].

These contradictions, which to students and stakeholders of family businesses seem so unique to merit the creation of a particular field of study, are in fact nothing but repetitions of social forms that from an early history have tried to combine utilitarian and romantic drives into a single game structure. Weber, describing the disintegration of the household, shows how business-oriented medieval houses in Florence gradually created a distinction between private and commercial contracts, personal obligations and commercial debts. One of the products of this severance, by which work became an official vocation to be exercised in the bureaus rather than in the private household, was the firm: a "capitalistic type of association which corresponds to our joint- stock company and [was] completely detached, at least formally, from kinship and personal ties". Another product was the *oikos,* "not simply any large household or one which produces its own various products, agricultural or industrial; but rather, the authoritarian household of a prince, manorial lord of patrician ... [where] the dominant motive [was] not capitalistic acquisition but the lord's organized want satisfaction in kind" ([149]: 380, 381).

To the extent that family businesses can be metaphorically seen as hybrid organizational forms that mix features of the firm with those of the *oikos,* they are just contingent capitalistic entities that contain in themselves remembrances of mankind's past. Initially, they serve the whims of the founder-entrepreneur, whose goals often transcend the mere accumulation of capital and whose (primitive) traditional authority is related to the forces of gerontocracy, patriarchalism, and patrimonialism ([150]: 344–6). Later, when complexity surpasses concentration of power and patriarchs or matriarchs are weakened, they commonly surrender to bureaucracy and substitute control for agility, impersonality for irrationality, or calculation for illusion. This history summarizes the age-old trade-off between centralization and decentralization, tradition and rationality, or between the arbitrary decisionism of the autocratic ruler for whom power and wealth are a means of self-realization and the normativism associated with the legitimate group deliberations of the boards and groups of directors [151]. As fragile social systems that pretend to serve the perpetuity of the common holdings and history (linking the individuals to kin), the valuation of one's home (prioritizing the nuclear family), and the bureaucratic ideology of the firm (privileging the valid, but never completely pure *value* given to profit, capital, competition, or "rational" considerations of utility), family businesses are inherently unstable, diverse, and eminently contradictory.

Deconstructions such as this, however, bring other unexpected deconstructions: the treatment of the paradoxes of families and businesses under the ruling of the principle of non-contradiction breaks up their unity and brings to both the fundamental problem of nihilism, the emergence of a "godless, disenchanted world of hard-headed science" where there is no place for the spirit ([152]: 310). How to believe in families, love, or cooperation when it becomes clear that they are based on the same forces of self-interest, pride, and power that fuel the apparently opposed games of utility? The (transcendent) search for truth, which exposes the ubiquitous economic forces of self-interest and demystifies the false consciousness of a superstructure that idealized kin and family, inevitably reframes spontaneity and identification as errors and erodes the ideals that connect actors to their families and businesses through something more than (immanent) considerations of personal advantage [153]. The same wealth that subsidizes the life of the family also brings with it, in the absence of a game condition that organizes the anomalies exposed by the (pseudo) rational endeavor, the seeds of its own destruction.

Our topic of study may, then, provide a good place for us to reframe the old debate between essence and appearance, or idealism and ideology. If all social constructions exist in the context of rules, goals, exclusions and inclusions that create peculiar conditions of illusion, putting the games of family, marriage, kin, and firm side by side may offer some interesting clues to develop a new form of seeing and approaching the game of organization. Specifically, if the (idealistic or idealized) forces of relatedness attributed to the family are reframed as an expression of the innately human drive to be engrossed in the game, they offer a counterpoint to the blind spots of a rational-bureaucratic perspective that sees all affect and true aspiration as ideological. Simultaneously, the explication of the interests, calculations, and power struggles that underlie all forms of belief may offer the players not a nihilistic disbelief, but a sense of commonality derived from the understanding that personal interest and social order, or immanence and transcendence, are mixed in *all* interesting or meaningful games [11].

The acceptance of this new perspective, of course, is dependent on the acceptance that games substitute illusion for truth as a parameter of value. The unveiling of the contradictions beneath the apparent homogeneity of families or firms, in this case, does *not* lead to their dismissal as untrue. Momentary points of consensus, and not mythical certainties, are seen as the solution for the tension looming behind the trade-off situations [154]. Finally, as explicit practices and concepts integrate into a single meta-view the apparently opposite forces of romance, utility, power, and status, we can bring a new life to the already old, over-rational simplification of the firm as (merely) a profit or production-driven social system or of the family as (simply) an affect-based form of organization. This introduces actors to a second-order dilemma, by which they leave the concrete, immediate fights to define what is "really" true or valuable and become invested in the (rational? emotional?) task of crafting and negotiating the true, genuine, well-intentioned *illusions* that allow fair and pure play (see Appendix 2, Figures 13, 14, and 19).

Organizational Culture in Family Businesses: The Stage of Change

The first picture that emerges from an analysis of history and of the forms of organization that currently give shape to family businesses is one of variety. This diversity, however, is apparent - beneath the multiplicity of arrangements and the various ways in which people have combined ties of blood and marriage we see the same old constituents that have forever formed all social games. "There is a difference of degree, and not in kind, between those societies traditionally studied by anthropologists and contemporary ones. In the former, the basic matter of social categories, the framework of relationships of production, of consumption, of power and so on, is provided by kinship, whereas in the latter, kinship is in competition with other social institutions, and with the state in particular. The way in which the family is currently organized in Western societies is merely one of the possible ways provided by the whole range of cultures" ([121]: 6). Each time and place has its preferred ways of arranging the building blocks of the social game; and in every time and place individuals have a relative freedom to move from one equilibrium to another depending on how social structure is more or less rigidly enforced. Furthermore, as people make their choices, or simply follow automatically a certain path, actions become engraved as memories that shape the interactions, relationships, places, and networks they share with the other players. The history of any particular family and of any particular firm evolves as a line of events that is simultaneously constricted by extraneous forces, created by the actors, and constitutive of itself as past conditions shape present and future in ways often unperceived by the players.

The first task of any leader or changed agent involved with culture and change is to search for these unchangeable building blocks and rules of organization, which beneath all families and firms constrain their diversity and determine the frontiers and mechanisms of change. Missing one of these levers leads to useless efforts to bend what is inflexible, or to introduce novelty on what is bound to remain as it is; creating unnecessary constraints leads to rigidity and myopic learning, inspiring interventions restricted by one's personal, ethnocentric, or culturally limited perspective. As a second step, we must organize the history of the system – the past choices, as well as the habits created by the repetition of choices – in the form of a convincing story that reflects the (apparently) unique character of the place. From the first step come the structuring universals, the unchangeable pieces of the puzzle; from the second come the particulars, the contingent, emergent social and political conditions that give singularity to the universals. Change, if it is to become the seed of a new and lasting culture, requires one to simultaneously respect and softly violate history and social structure.

Some Universal Elements

If one assumes that social actors live upon a platform made partially of hard facts given by perception, and partially of interpretive illusions of truth and meaning made real by their own actions, any player or group of players who engages in an intentional action is singling out one particular game out of the many he simultaneously plays or could alternatively play, were his perspective a different one. All levels of analysis that compose the whole of social life are necessarily interrelated – even if not present in a particular moment, they both define one's perceptions and valuations of reality and are influenced by any change in the system. All should, in consequence, be taken into consideration if one wants to understand the forces that drive inertia and change within the system.

In the case of the firm, these levels of analysis or ontological centers of "being" involve the individuals, the ties that connect them to each other, the coalitions, departments, divisions, boards, the organization itself and its various stakeholders or environmental contexts, such as partner-competitors in the supply chain, the organizational field, the industry, and the "political phenomena, culture, symbols, and myths" that as a sector surrounds the organization ([142]: 262). In the family, the same individuals coexist with other entities, created by different rules of organization: the couple, the children, the nuclear family, the extended family, and the kin. A broader, intangible fiction called culture – the heterogeneous set or toolkit of beliefs, values, practices, and habits, contradictory or coherent, that fill the symbolic cauldron in which actors live [155] – hovers above and constitutes both systems, containing the actions, justifications, explanations, and fundaments known or acceptable as motives for action in the milieu. Each of these entities and forms of organization is made real by habits, laws, institutions, and intuitive forms of order that make people aggregate in that particular way. They are believed to be true. Actors talk about them and lend them their energy as they identify with each one. They are, therefore, common stop-points in the flow of everyday ontological oscillation, fictions to which individuals give life by acting, feeling, and speaking in their name (see Appendix 2, Figures 4 and 5).

Both firm and family, therefore, exist in the context of a multiplicity and instability of games, rules, and identifications. Several structural contradictions emerge from this ensemble. Ties of blood are inherently antithetical to marriage ties – following the logic of kin the partner is the stranger, the foreign, the dangerous element who both introduces a new order and disrupts the closely knit fabric of the same. The bond of marriage is contrary to the individualistic drives or to the collective household tasks, forcing spouses to alternate between the roles of partners, lovers, or enemies. The push for sexual and affective exogamy rubs against the pressure for the endogamy of the land, patrimony, and resources [126]. To these we can add many other examples: considerations of utility are incompatible with the engrossment in a game; promoting the meritocracy expected in a firm contradicts unconditional love expected between relatives; the succession of generations and the branching of the family introduces complexities unmanageable under the private power-rules of the household; the simple inexorability of aging brings different, unpredictable attitudes toward the future, the present, novelty, or tradition (as in the immature idolatry of the blind identification, the adolescent revolt, or the founder's desire to leave or cling to the business with the proximity of death); and eventually, enmities and friendships insert the political dyad of the us-other in the core of the (unitary?) family business. Classically, the same actors that (freely?) make choices later regret the games they choose (the closer the ties and the stronger the pressure for cohesion, the higher the probability and intensity of the conflicts). The various colors of illusion, tacitness, and openness and the many types of compromise taken by the interplay of these forces in each particular era, place, family, and business form the clay from which the change agents can, or cannot, sculpt the structural elements that will favor the development of the culture they see as fit for the place.

Most of these tensions, habitually, are not readily apparent when people are well or the business is flourishing. "Happy families are all alike; every unhappy family is unhappy in its own way" [156]. Rather, it is in the moments of disease, frailty, or difficulty (when cooperation and alignment around common definitions of the situation would be most needed) that fissures commonly emerge and one can distinguish the lines of fracture that subterraneously exist everywhere. As with any group of disparate motives organized economically according to a law of redundancy, the forces that compose family business may both complement and contradict each other, appearing either as well-played games or as conflicts and ruptures of meaning that come from the exposure of the irreconcilable differences between the structuring vectors that give form to the game. This is a universal characteristic of the trade-offs that *appear* when multitasking games are evaluated under the rational rules of the language game: in the fuzzy zone of ambiguity that separates opposite values – the contradictions lived automatically in the practice, but laid bare by the deconstructive power of reason or by the need to make an option in the case of a limit situation – lies the possibility of both the worse conflicts and of the most creative, unexpected, fruitful complementarities of well-crafted meta-games that spread in time, integrating into one direction the apparently opposite or inefficient vectors of meaning (see Appendix 2, Figure 10) [157, 158].[3]

From Structure to Uniqueness: Particulars

Even if one considers that individuals, families, and firms alike are exposed to, and constrained by, relatively similar structural forces, it is also true that each particular system evolves in its own way, shaped by contingencies that are unique to its internal and external landscapes. This single, unrepeatable path gives rise to the various very personal connections and "constellations of sentiment" or definitions of structure observed within any group [159]. It is in them, in the emergent and privately lived contingencies of history, that change agents find the real, concrete opportunities of action. From them come the buttons that need to be pushed and the obstacles that must be avoided for change to be embraced as a meaningful endeavor, and not as merely another piece of rhetoric. Knowledge of the structural factors involved in the organization of the family business is a necessary, but not sufficient step for the management of change.

The theme, tone, rigidity, and flexibility of the particular tales and stories shared by the actors – the good and bad moments that mark one's history, the more or less traumatic conflicts, the experiences of loyalty and unity, the stream of memories engraved as markers of any relationship – must be evaluated taking into account the personality of the actors and the audiences they reach in order to reveal the likely directions where change is more or less possible [160]. These constructs consist of singularities: the nuances, openings, closures, elasticity, transcendence, paranoia, resistances, limitations, and potentialities of each person and personal relationship existing in the place. Consequently, the mapping of the particulars of each place demands a different technique and attitude toward our object of study – only ethnographic and minute attention to details allow change agents to reach a tentative diagnosis of the individuals involved and of the memories, events, "recipes, rules of thumb, social types, maxims and definitions" used by them ([161]: 14). This includes tapping on three different zones of the social terrain: the players' private perspective, shared only in the context of individual conversations; the common content, the facts already in public domain; and the semi-private web of gossips, commentaries, lies, partial secrets and subjects shared only in confidence, which form the interlocked system of alliances and enmities that make of the firm just another expression of the age-old political coalitions that divide mankind in separate groups [162].

In order to distinguish the coalitions and alliances that characterize any specific family and business one must, first, depict the formal lines of relationship, dominance, and submission expressed in the ties of kinship (in the family) and hierarchy (in the firm) – positions that determine both the explicit paths of power and communication and the symbolic value given to them by the actors (a king, CEO or father is intuitively seen as superior, different or special [163]). Second, there are the informal networks – complex, invisible, intricate meshes of pipes and prisms that mediate the exchange of information, affect, reputation, knowledge, and power among the actors [164]. Giving life to the paths, closures and connections allowed or forbidden by these ties are the real people with whom one talks, puppets and sculptors of the particular presentations of the rules of proximity/distance that compose the distinctive fingerprint of the social stage where they live [165] (see Appendix 2, Figure 5).

Depending on how players see themselves, the others, and are positioned in these varied, interconnected formal and informal networks – centrally or peripherally, with more or less connections, acting predominantly as receivers or givers of each specific currency exchanged in the social system – they are more or less influential in each of the various games played within the place [166]. Thus, some actors are sought for advice, others for support; some are central in the distribution of resources, others of information; some are relevant within specific clusters, others precisely because they are gatekeepers of bridges that extend across structural holes (as with different coalitions or divisions in a firm) [167, 168].

Particularly difficult – and of undiscussed importance for our theme, precisely because they are undiscussable – is the existence of actors who resist to change and form hidden networks of silence, hostility, or animosity that hamper any flow of information or goods within the system. In both families and firms, these are associated with the insulated, impenetrable social universes that surround some relationships between parent and children, sibling and sibling, partners, bosses, employees, or other actors that close themselves in loops of self-reinforced groupthink impermeable to change or other rationality beyond their own [169] – preferential ties, tight friendships and alliances, dogmatic groups, and private games that are unique to the actors, and therefore immune to the pressures for organization. For the players, these appear as secrets, taboos, or inconsistencies that should be protected from change or attacked as targets, themes that cannot be touched lest one triggers conflicts that are even worse than the semblance of peace. The private worlds created by these rules explain many misalignments, and also many novelties we see in society – the negative and positive forms of deviance daily seen in families and firms.

Prejudices, information asymmetries, doubt, cognitive biases, dogmas, miscommunication, undue preferences, self-absorbed relationships, stinginess, pride, envy, resentments, dishonesty, self-interest, greed, gluttony, wrath, lust, and sloth – all these ubiquitous in people, families, firms and any social systems – go against the fundamental premises of the social game (rationality, trust, willingness). Seldom spelled out, these are commonly hidden under the guise of the normatively accepted discourses that praise the kin, the family, the group, love, cooperation, or rationality. Often, they make use of the contradictions between the messages and jargon that distinguish families from businesses depending on how they embody the ideologies of love, lust, power, property, or interest. It is thus mostly on what is unsaid or contradictory, on the false or unstable manifestations of peace, on the dissonances between speech and practice, or on the unexpected silences or dark black holes of the apparently absent subjects, and *not* on the explicit manifestations of friendship, love or common values, that change agents ought to focus in order to find the more fruitful pathways of change. In a similar vein, it is upon a few intangible organizing principles around which we build the construction of our perceptions of the players' identities – character, courage, consciousness, and intellectual honesty, the most subjective elements of the social fact – that leaders and change agents, as any players, *ought to* concentrate when trying to map who are the players they will work with in order to negotiate, avoid (or even force) their definitions of the situation and ideals of organization. At this point, culture and change become awfully close to the (apparently neutral) epistemological paradoxes associated with the treatment of information, truth, and learning. It is to these themes that we dedicate our next chapter.

Notes

1 Consider Segalen's description of a medieval family: If one could trace a family tree with a peasant, he would "immediately orient himself in relation to the vertical and horizontal kinship structures within which he functions. (…) This line, amongst all the other lines of descent that are an individual's biological inheritance, is the line that is singled out as of special and unique importance. At the same time, both the individual and the domestic group can identify a collateral line of kin, with whom they share no direct ancestor but only a lateral link. This is the kindred group. (…) As a result of this twofold branching, [each] domestic group is committed to certain prescribed forms of behavior and enjoys particular privileged relationships, rights and duties. Through the line, [it] is tied to the sequence of those preceding and succeeding it in the same place, and through the kindred group it is linked to all those relatives in whose company it is involved in all the vicissitudes of social life: quarrels, friendships and hatreds" ([121]: 63).

2 "Mankind understood very early that, in order to free itself from a wild struggle for existence, it was confronted with the very simple choice of 'either marrying-out or being killed-out'. The alternative was between biological families living in juxtaposition and endeavoring to remain closed, self-perpetuating units, over-ridden by their fears, hatreds, and ignorance, and the systematic establishment, through the incest prohibition, of links of intermarriage between them, thus succeeding to build, out of the artificial [and labile] bonds of affinity, a true human society, despite, and even in contradiction with, the isolating influence of consanguinity" ([126]: 278).

3 In the firm, for example, long-term relational contracts based on trust-bets only appear only when a different logic of interaction – one that considers the advantages of cooperation and the intangibility of the other's soul, and not only the paranoia suggested by the postulates of opportunism and guile – is juxtaposed upon to the economic logic that inspires principal-agent theories [170]. In the family, on the contrary, opportunities arise only when actors transcend the current ideology of naive love or trust and understand that any *true* organization depends on the overt handling of the self-interests for which the ends justify the means. Exactly as affect, kin, and non-instrumental ties are a *desired* violation of the bureaucratic, rational organization of the firm, the stereotyped game-based economic view of the business-game brings a counterpoint to unrealistic attachments or expectations of "benevolent ties" projected on the family.

3 Definitions of the Situation

> Six blind men were asked to determine what an elephant looked like. The blind man who felt the leg said the elephant was like a pillar; the one who felt the tail said the elephant was like a rope; the one who felt the trunk said the elephant was like a tree branch; the one who felt the ear said the elephant was like a hand fan; the one who felt the belly said the elephant was like a wall; and the one who felt the tusk said the elephant was like a solid pipe. A king explained to them: All of you are right; you touched different parts of the elephant. Actually, it has all the features you mentioned (adapted from [171]).

Every conception of a family, firm, relationship, interaction, or problem is based on a certain view, tacit or explicit, of reality. For each individual, the first source of this view is his own experience: as social actors intuitively record their encounters with the everyday facts, they accumulate a loose but comprehensive set of ideas that reflect their private perspectives and are preserved as true, simply because they serve their need to adapt and be happy. The same happens with firms and families: local viewpoints derived from peculiar contexts lead to a series of generalizations and partial truths, put together according to a (dis)order that always opposes or barely resembles the shared, formal logic and (precise?) abstractions of the symbolic languages.

This loosely coupled fabric of ideas, woven together as one's view of the world, can be seen as a partially ordered toolbox of intuitions and truths selected over time as successful answers to the epistemic and evaluative problems faced by each actor [172]. Most of the time, these tools work – grossly wrong ideas are naturally discarded under the intuitive pressures to go on with life and privilege success over failure, while merely satisficing interpretations are accepted as a sufficient sign that search can be interrupted and the response may be recorded as adequate, proper, or "true" [173]. If biases are protected by chance, or collectively shared by groups following the same error, mistakes become immune to disproval, life continues uninterrupted, and one can maintain the usual belief in (or, more often, disregard for) truth. Conversely, whenever situations vary unexpectedly, when actors show different viewpoints, or when there are dissonances between present and past responses, there is pressure to stop the flow of life and integrate the disorganized toolbox. In these moments, one detaches from the local perspectives given by the practice and attempts to find new concepts or recombine old ones, transcending the fleeting, practical world of appearances and creating novel truths that open a different way of seeing the facts or synthesize the different practices under a new viewpoint [174].

Under the current rationalistic premises, the integration of these two similar, but different definitions of the situation – the world of practice exemplified by the various narrow-minded views of the blind men, the world of ideas by the pure, overarching, and absolute perspective of the king – is depicted as a difficult, but feasible task. Like the king, prototypical thinking actors imagine they can really integrate various local, action-oriented perspectives into a few plausible views of reality; choose one from these views, using criteria of rationality; and eventually craft well-aligned strategic and tactical plans to implement the planned change depending on particular contingencies of the problem [175]. Insofar as the tale represents the multitude of theories with which players conceive their common experience, each one of them proposing to grasp the true nature of the organization or of the family, one may say that it aptly describes approach to truth taken by most people in real life.

Unlike the mythical king, however, neither solitary individuals, nor family members or organizational leaders are omniscient or capable of synthesizing the multiple local views into one comprehensive perspective that differs from the minor ones simply by its amplitude. Moreover, to the extent the parable implies the existence of a real elephant, which could eventually be seen as a whole and through a single perspective, the analogy is misleading. *First,* there are always failures in the transcription from the practice to the idea – biases, errors of evaluation, sampling problems, and a potent push to follow fast intuitive views rather than "objectivity" lead to effects of perspective that inevitably taint one's view of the elephant. *Second,* humans always live partial interpretive fictions, and never objectivity – even if one considers only the explicit knowledge suggested by the parable, definitions of the facts are never absolute because the real "reality" with which we interact is always a blend of objective (?) perceptions and interpretative parameters, which are nothing more than a *bet* about how information should be contextualized (i.e., placed in a broader, imaginary, fictional world) in order to have meaning [176]. *Finally,* there is tacitness – all the sensations, intuitions, or tastes elicited by the hypothetical elephant are bound to remain implicit, despite their powerful impact on one's judgments. There are various plausible bird's-eye views of the kings, and they differ on a fundamental way both from each other and from the multiple blind men's hands-on depictions of the elephant.

For most actors, driven predominantly by the instinctive need to quickly solve the differences in order to reach their goals, the disparity between the (often) incongruous interpretations of reality is generally solved by simply forgetting, by conveniently dismissing contradictions as irrelevant, or by creating after-the-fact, coherent stories that romanticize the facts by integrating them into a (hopefully beautiful) unitary plot. This is particularly true for the individual – errors, violations, and negotiations of truths and illusions occur more easily in the private market of one's soul, where inconsistencies are generally solved by a combination of a cognitive loose coupling with a naive belief in free-will (freedom from the limits of the social world, as well as freedom from the tight grip of the instincts, habits, and past learning). Leaders, founders, followers, high- and low-rank people, then, are often content with the blend of truth, omissions, biases, lies, self-deceit, after the fact explanations, self-interested selection of facts, and romance that make up most autobiographies and accounts of reality.

In the collective environment of the group, as opposed to what happens in the privacy of the individual, the sensation of truth (or consensus?) is not only intermittent, but also unevenly distributed among actors who are not necessarily synchronized in the intuitive (or rational) way by which they see and value the reality or themselves. Occasionally, as in the peaceful reunions of the family or discussions about common goals, people *are* in fact united around deeper definitions of the situation. Conflict, of course, always occurs. At other times, actors "come together not because they have the same values [or views of reality] … but because, for a while, their differing ends may be served by the same means" ([177]: 107). As players are deceived by the *feeling* of certainty that usually accompanies their intuitive judgments of truth, by the pride that comes with rational deliberations, or by the illusions of consensus brought by socially shared beliefs, practices, or routines, they easily forget the arbitrariness of the process of truth-creation. They become prey of fallacies, biases, and faulty inferences that reflect more their (innate? normative?) wish to be (or appear to be) in control than the need to precisely assess the complex nuances of the reality [178]. The consequence is an irregular, unstable, and fluctuating set of islands of consensus and dissensus, reflecting effects of the illusions by which players agree, disagree, or *think* they have the same ideas, when in fact they simply share some actions, feelings, or places.

The objective, empirical study of the truths, semi-truths, and errors that make up social life only occurs when the process of knowledge-creation is studied from inside and questioned by the same reason that commonly tries to reason about the world. When this occurs, there is a break in the premise of absolute truth – if one's definition of the situation depends on the momentary perspective through which percepts, thoughts, or feelings are framed and integrated in the form of "facts", the consequence is the acceptance of the empirically true and apparently logical, but still flawed, relativistic axioms (?!) of post-modernism. To the extent that everything is relative, actors should have a total skepticism with reason as a tool to capture the "true" nature of reality or catalyze any rational negotiations of ideas. Leaders', parents', or partners' assertions about reality are, rightly or not, systematically dismissed as self-interested accounts; idealism is automatically interpreted as ideology; every attempt to achieve a true communication is automatically hampered by a fundamental doubt about the premises that give validity to the process of thought (non-contradiction, falsifiability, public reproducibility); and the world of ideas, in which ambiguity should coexist harmonically with (transient) hypotheses, is depicted as a nowhere land where players just compete for the epistemologically illusory, but socially relevant, prize of truth. Eventually, the (flawed) logic behind these false paradoxes and dilemmas is confirmed by the *feelings* of uncertainty that accompany the double bind of negating truth while still longing for it.[1]

Both for the families and for their businesses, the practical implications of these apparently theoretical issues are quite profound. Whenever people are searching for a common ground in the everyday discussions about themselves and the world, developing a single strategy, resolving issues of alignment in the firm, or coming to terms with values, ideas, and goals in the family, the premise of truth is valid. Conversely, when the intuitively obvious, but logically wrong premise of a single absolute truth is taken to the limit and tested in its inconsistencies, what we see are endless discussions, interminable returns to the past, deep resentments, or impervious concepts and prejudices that stall any attempt to reach even temporary common truths. Even in the prototypically rational firm, where conflicts are softened by the need to save face, actors, more often than not, fight for precise definitions of the situation when only ambiguity is acceptable; identify with their own truths, mixing practical matters with managerial or human hubris [179]; and seeing the often unsolvable conflicts of ideas as equally unsolvable personal conflicts, commonly resort to politics or silence as a means to avoid the dissonance [180]. Truth and doubt, reinforced by the potent feelings of certainty or uncertainty, alternate in giving more or less stability to the processes of change and to the culture of the place.

This chapter attempts to contemplate the implications of the cognitive phenomena that inspire the parable of the elephant and the blind men, namely, the need to put side by side the unifying pull *and* the critical power of reason, and thus both construct and deconstruct the truths and definitions of the situation on which we ground the life of the family and of the firm. With this aim, throughout the text we systematically emphasize the violations, biases, errors, and arbitrary interpretations that instill doubt into the supposedly stable truths, justifications, and routines used by players to organize their actions and worldviews – we thus unveil an important source of conflict, the expectation of stability and consensus when ambiguity only allows for transient, unstable, socially negotiated definitions of the situation. At the same time, however, by the simple act of writing about these we are implicitly assuming it is possible to create a rational meta-consensus, a transient kingly view upon which we can agree and proceed with life. By using the logical tools of the language game to illuminate the weaknesses of the same game, we are necessarily enacting the belief that reason, when shielded from delusional self-confidence by the awareness of its limitations, remains an essential component of any technology of change designed to tackle the problems brought by an elusive elephant that cannot be precisely described from any single viewpoint, but that often responds (albeit somewhat unpredictably) to human efforts to direct it.

The World of Practice and the World of Ideas

Doubt, therefore, is as much a product of reason as truth and certainty are. First, one asks *what to do* – even when one's definition of the situation is taken for granted, the variability of the world and of our personal tastes and opinions invites discussions and there are many possible avenues of action. As (social) systems directed to action, individuals, families, and organizations continuously face situations in which players have to deliberate about their options, values, and strategies in order to fulfill the demands posed by their individual or collectively shared definitions of the situation.

Second, if one takes a step back and begins to question the validity of the definitions of the situation for which choices are needed, one questions *what one sees*. Every definition of the situation, whether automatic or planned, expresses a certain perspective, is "theory-laden". In these cases, doubt sits in as a fundamental uncertainty about which interpretation of the facts to choose, and more basically on which perspective and level of analysis – the individual, the family, the firm, the society – to base the definition of the situation that eventually will play the role of the "true" one.

Third, players must ask *what they do not see* – given that common understandings derived from the experience are based on trial, error, and experimentation of strategies already existing to one's mind, simply following the practice may lead to competency traps [181], myopic learning [182] and sub-optimal local peaks of excellence that disregard learning possibilities that exist beyond the everyday practice [45]. Thus, even in the absence of the usual error signals – conflict, dissonances, frustration, mistakes, pain – actors intent on finding alternative, potentially more fruitful definitions of the situation should search for novelty and innovation beyond the restricted world of practice in which they are born, raised, or developed as families, firms, and family businesses.

Finally, players ask *when to doubt* and *when to stop the doubt* and postulate a truth, going on with life. Initially, they exercise their freedom to deconstruct the various points of arbitrariness involved in the creation of the fact – the various inflections of meaning caused by the (often unconscious) selection of relevant stimuli, their organization according to (generally tacit) interpretative frames that form the (always arbitrary) definitions of the situation, and eventually their social negotiation through communication or normative coercion. At some point, however, they curtail their own freedom, postulate a truth, and surrender to the need to assume the existence of some certainties in order to live.

From these four fundamental questions – what to do, how to define a situation, what is not seen, and when to doubt or to affirm – arise the four basic moments in which reason can be inserted in the processes of decision-making and truth-creation: practical deliberations, reflection about the experience, exploration of novel possibilities, and deconstruction of the whole process of reasoning. A fifth moment involves all the instances in which language serves not the need to act or define a situation, but rather the imagination, daydreams, fantasies, myths, and speculations that fill the various times when actors are disconnected from pressures of the world and can go back to their own selves, freed from the constraints of practice and immersed in the self-fulfilling dreams of realization, future, past, or depth. From them come the *ideas* and the metaphysical illusions of meaning and truth that organize the reality and ourselves – the mythical, mystical, true, or untrue models of the world by which we expand the immediate perspective of the practice and create a fictional world that involves multiple potential mental universes made of multiple variations of reality and value (see Appendix 2, Figure 3).

Human beings are, therefore, probably unique in that they are always responding to two worlds: the immediate, concrete facts of the practice *and* the imaginary, symbolic facts that constitute the world of ideas. These are fundamentally different experiences. In the world of practice, archaic mechanisms of perception and immediate loops of feedback increase the chances that we all see the same facts and respond to them according to the preferences of the moment. Chains of stimulus, interpretation, and response trigger automatic responses, emotional and rational, that guarantee the fluidity and speed of action. Reality, value, impulse, and action are blended into a single personal experience that frames all the (objective) components of the present, local context according to our (subjective) interests and tastes. "We do not just see 'a house': We see a handsome house, an ugly house, or a pretentious house. (...) We buy the cars we 'like', choose the jobs and houses we find 'attractive', and then justify these choices by various reasons" that make sense in the social world ([81]: 154–5). Moreover, as people, things and space are tightly connected into the whole of the immediately seen and concrete situation present in the here-and-now of perception and action, one's reactions are generally adapted primarily to the currently perceived context. Survival is maximized and big losses are generally prevented, even if at the cost of restricting the gains to the small benefits of the narrow present.

The world of ideas, on the contrary, is made of symbols and abstract connections that may (or not) represent any concrete reality. These idealized entities and categories can be atomized, fragmented, manipulated, or recombined according to various relations of causality or association – exactly as it is possible to invent many plausible scenarios, futures, or geometries, one can frame social entities, groups, and people in various different ways or imagine as many families, reactions, or people as one wants. At this point, various models of reality – more or less detached from the concrete world of experience, depending on the lucidity or alienation of the thinker – are added to the (monotonous? obvious? hard?) facts revealed by perception. When these are consciously unrealistic, one sees the fantasies, daydreams, and illusions that fill all the inconsequential moments of life. When consequences are at stake, actors check the validity of their models by questioning its internal logic and the laws of correspondence that link it to the concretely perceived facts, constraining the thought in order to minimize the risk of error. This check, however, is often imperfect. The same freedom of thought and imagination that brings the big gains of the brightest ideas also brings the catastrophic losses of unrealism [183].

With a dim intuition of the dangers associated with the recursive nature of their reasoning, which stem from the intersection between freedom of thought and foolishness or alienation, actors feel they are taking advantage of the possibilities of construction opened by the abstract world but seldom realize that the counterpart of the creativity brought by its recombinatory logic is the unreality that often covers their narratives, identity games, or scientific "truths". Rather, since people too easily believe in the truth of their ideas just because they are expressed in language, the definitions of situation on which actors base "rational" deductions and dialogs are generally highly contaminated by tacit premises, biases, and the gravitational power of the present contexts. Alternating between the natural, smooth, bottom-up flow of life and the artificial, top-down exercises of rationality, men commonly profess their belief in reason while surrendering to their own dreams and affect-laden intuitions, the simple absence of error accepted as sufficient proof of truth. Everything happens as if doubt were not an integral component of reason: other validity checks, which could show mistakes and omissions incurred in the process, are seemingly deemed unnecessary, cumbersome, or not even thought of.

In the daily practice of individuals and their groups – families, firms, parliaments, or any social games and institutions – this dualism between practice and rationality has been equated to an opposition between a fast, intuitive, associative, experiential "System 1" and a slow, inefficient, deliberately questioning "System 2" [184]. According to this model, the less costly cognitive mechanisms of truth-creation of the System 1 are seen as hitchhiking on the archaic mechanisms of perception and evaluation of the reality and giving rise to intuitively certain, but normatively flawed, ideas about the world. Generally, "when a stimulus is of a kind that has been experienced repeatedly in the past, the response will be highly routinized. It will evoke, with a minimum of problem-solving or other computational activity, a well-structured definition of the situation that will include a repertory of response programs, and programs for selecting an appropriate response from the repertory. [Conversely], when a stimulus is relatively novel, it will evoke problem-solving activity aimed initially at constructing a definition of the situation and then at developing one or more appropriate performance programs" ([24]: 161). Difficult tasks that require attention, as well as collective action that demands coordination, place actors in the realm of the serious life. There, one needs more precise definitions of what is proposed as being true, valuable, or practical in the moment – it is only when novelty and error bring the need for adaptation, and adaptation engenders conflict, that the flow of experiences that characterize the world of the practice must be halted and one engages in the rational effort of "understanding" the family, the firm, or the facts according to the logic of the "System 2" [185].

The consequence of this multiplicity of definitions of the situation – some brought by intuitive responses to the various contexts of the family or firm, others by equally valid rational interpretations of the facts, some brought by habit or culture, others by experience and reflection – is the creation of an ecosystem of ideas and practices, where many of the conflicts emerge not from different values and interests, but from the contrast between different views of the "same" objective reality ([186]: 198). Although equally plausible, under the premise of absolute truth they are framed as irreconcilable. Thus, in the same moment one actor is immersed in the flow of practice and allows habit to prevail, another may think the issue requires further consideration and engages in serious reasoning (thereby demanding the interruption of action). One person may rely on expert intuitions, another on mathematical models, on metaphorical stories, or on the elaborate, logical syntheses presented in natural languages. A family member may be blinded by deeply seated egocentric biases, while another is prey of other affective heuristics and a third tries (vainly) to use logic to dismantle intuitive beliefs based on feelings of certainty that defy methodological rigor. Furthermore, deliberation, reflection, deconstruction, exploration, and imagination often compete as equally valid, but fundamentally different framings of one's self, of reality, and of how one should approach it: some players ask for action, and concentrate on deliberating about what to do; others are more questioning, asking for strategic definitions and explication of the fundaments and values beneath the potential tactics or logics of action;

many, perhaps the majority, are inattentive to the problem and focused on their private thoughts; a few look for novelty and innovations; and more rarely, one or another asks deeper questions that go to the fundaments of the common definitions of the situation and thus challenge the whole paradigm used in the discussion. All of them, habitually, think they are right. The possibility of a stalemate between the different logics of action and definitions of the situation increases precisely when the freedom that characterizes the world of ideas must give way to the prison of the world of the practice, forcing players to relinquish the lack of consequences and reversibility they experienced when playing with the symbols in their private worlds in order to make the radical, irreversible options required by real life.[2]

The next sessions cover some of the mechanisms, errors, contradictions, and (pseudo) paradoxes associated with the treatment of information, starting from the explicit knowledge and gradually driving deeper into the world of the doubt, of the unconscious biases, and of tacitness. In doing so, we attempt to transcend the typical question of "What is the truth?" and inquire into the various forms in which human "irrationality" is present in social systems. What are the usual errors, byways, and dead-ends observed in the process of truth-creation? What are the difficulties encountered by well-intentioned actors who share common goals and attempt to understand reality, communicate their objectives, or coordinate their actions? And finally, "could we improve the ability to identify and understand errors of judgment and choice, in others and eventually in ourselves, by providing a richer and more precise language to discuss them'"? ([184]: 4). We therefore embrace the utopic, idealistic, or delusional hope that, by making explicit the more common types and pitfalls of reason, we can sketch the draft of a relatively common set of routines, rules, automatisms, and vocabulary that could eventually bring some social unity to processes of cultural change.

The Management of Truth and Untruth

To the extent that the world of ideas includes all explicit statements or practices consciously chosen by the actors or potentially translatable to symbolic languages, conversations in families and firms may be seen as a network of dialogs that cover a spectrum of genres ranging from the most fantastic fables or myths to clearly positivistic attempts to create stories and models that describe people, facts, and the world "as they are". Typically, social actors land midway between objectivity and subjectivity. The lines that separate one genre from another are never sharp or clearly delineated; and even though actors naturally extract meaning from various *valuable* imaginary narratives or whimsical identity stories, as one approaches the more serious questions of property, money, power, status, or deliberations players tend to resort to the common metric of reason and question the *validity* (or truth) of their ideas. Myth and fiction alternate with the serious talk of the identity or sensemaking stories, and with the purportedly objective, scientific accounts of reality to create the foundations for the common views of the world from which emerges the fantasy of a common culture.

The Playful or Emotional Adult: Myth and Fiction

If we were to choose an image to represent the whole fabric of human ideation, the moments of pure rationality could be likened to an unstable archipelago of rocky islands emerging from a vast ocean of fancy and imagination. In the deeper waters of this sea are all the subjective and emotion-based forms of storytelling, relatively unconstrained by objective reality or by consensual accepted norms of truth and meaning. These are first present in the life of children as part of play, of the inspiring fairy tales, primitive art, or any form of unrestrained fantasy; in the life of families, as a common element of dinner or party conversations about movies, novels, poetry, music, dreams, or private wishes, neutral themes that allow players to share their need for an escape from adult life; and in the organization, in all instances in which irony, laughter, joy, emotions, romance, speculations, and imagination are daily brought up (intentionally or not) to embellish the context, to suggest higher goals, to give vent to one's feelings, or to confer an aesthetic, affective, or playful tone to the place.

Especially in the family and in dyadic interactions, but also in the moments of informality within the firm, these fantastic stories, artistic and emotional experiences are the true cement from which springs spontaneity, and with it the volatile, unstable, irrational belief in a shared meaning. This belief is not grounded in objective reality, but rather in subjective feelings that arise during a certain type of experience. Players engaged in a conversation, a party, a ritual, or a performance have different experiences of the same practice, yet *feel* they are reacting to the same thing; loose, abstract, or mythical stories allow actors to believe they are individuals, and still *feel* they partake a common definition of the situation; and all collective aesthetic or affective experiences – the rituals of mourning or celebration, the movies, spectacles, dramas, comedies, presentations, sing-alongs, and all personal scenarios of everyday life – are associated with powerful waves of synchrony in which the ritualized enactment of similar actions rises similar emotions that connect separate actors into one almost identical, jointly experienced social dream. Temporarily forgotten of their individuality, players are engrossed by the illusion of the game and live spontaneously the instant, for a moment distracted from the fact that reason severs them from the original, mythical, wished, or mystical, participation in reality [187].

The common thread explicitly or implicitly present in all these experiences of feeling is the relevance given to one's personal reactions to the objective facts of life, or even to life in itself. Meaning, therefore, is essential: every mythical story or conversation is based on "a symbolic refashioning of the organizational [and family] practices in the interest of pleasure [or pain], allowing a temporary supremacy of emotion over rationality and of uncontrol over control" ([188]: 477). Through this refashioning, truth is put at the service of one's dreams: by manipulating the plot of their stories, players are able to place themselves in the center of the world; one's emotions and ideas become relevant; and eventually, as the interweaving of private narratives results in a collective drama, one sees a range of stories that go from "a terrain that is not and cannot be managed ... in which desires, anxieties and emotions find expressions in the highly irrational constructions stories, myths, jokes, gossip, nicknames, graffiti and cartoons" to (pseudo) philosophical, fictitious propositions of how the world *should* be (for example, fair, safe, open to exploration, allowing freedom as well as safety) ([188]: 9).

In any social system, leaders and change agents interested in fostering the illusion of change or of a meaningful culture must rely on stories that have nothing to do with the immediate negotiations of reality, yet are enticing enough to capture the imagination of the audience and force players to jump out of themselves into a mythical world in which oneself, one's emotions and history are relevant, and thus special, unique, or different. The themes vary with the seriousness one attaches to the illusion. Particularly typical story lines are those in which actors cast themselves as conquering or survivor heroes, specialists, sages, or powerful actors who possess a special type of knowledge or skill and are thus connected to larger sagas, dramas, themes, and plots that enhance the value of the storyteller; as victims of the system, of life, of the firm or of the family, deemphasizing agency and trying to get sympathy through the creation of exclusive, private, fair (and false) interaction-worlds; as love objects, engaged in games of appreciation, gratitude, or empathy that transcend the practical demands of everyday life; or as protagonists of dreams and daydreams that blur the limits of desire and mentally concretize practically unachievable fantasies of wealth, power, or love [188].

In the firm – a social actor institutionally seen as ruled by the bureaucratic impersonality of objective goals, rules, and norms of relationship [189] – these parallel mythical stories seem to be organized around seven major scripts representing three basic dualities relevant to the firm's social game (equality vs. inequality, security vs. insecurity, control vs. lack of control). Generally, stories revolve around some basic questions that bring a personal tone to the impersonal ideals of rationality and hierarchy: "How do high status people relate to rules and rule-breaking?"; "Is the big boss human?"; "Can the little person rise to the top?"; "How will the boss react to mistakes?"; "Will I get fired?"; "Will the organization help me when I have to move?"; and "How will the organization deal with obstacles?" [190]. All these themes involve a selection of events that stereotypically confirm or disconfirm the actors' expectations about reality, blending features of an emotionally desirable world with the practical, harder conditions of the surrounding environment. They (mythically) suggest that life may or should have a meaning beyond the cold calculations of the adult world, allowing players to create private islands of (social) reality in which *they*, the *others*, and the affective element play a relevant role in shaping the outcome of things. They thus pave the way for the more "serious talks" of identity and sensemaking that ground the uniquely human, socially constructed world [15]. They form the ground of illusion on which actors step in order to deliberate, think, and act taking into consideration not only the hard facts, but the social world constituted of the shared and non-shared fictions of culture.

Emotionally relevant stories based on myth and fiction are, therefore, the bedrock of irrationality upon which players build narratives that prioritize what has more importance for them – their own self, emotions, tastes, or choices, which externalized in the world lead to considerations and attitudes about the objects and entities they repel or identify with. When shared as dialogs, they create peculiar social games in which the players' private worlds have a place in the public conversation and put people in the center of the world. They playfully satisfy the need to find a personal meaning in the concrete, impersonal reality. They thus link the action-oriented games constrained by common rules to the feeling-centered whims of one's soul, which suffocated under the cohesion pressures of reality-oriented groups expresses itself in the pauses typical of any loosely coupled form of organization.

Personal feelings, mythical stories, and fantastic constructions of meaning, however, are insufficient to bring any firmness to plans that involve commitments of the future, of common resources, time, or engagement. Rather, people need contracts, pacts, and promises of identity – stories that, although centered on meaning, can still be sold as the expression of rational worldviews that may give a more solid fundament for the collective action. Thus, the explanations with which players make sense of their own reality, self, goals, character, and the world are an integral part of the life of families and firms. It is through the exchange of "excuses, myths, reasons for doing and not doing" that actors reach the more or less transient consensuses required to proceed with work in the firm, or with rituals of companionship in the family [191]; create post hoc sensemaking views of the facts that are used later as a premise of future actions [192]; or show who they are through (authentic?) claims of intentions targeted to audiences as marketing tools in a social game of meaning [193]. These threads of understanding, meaning, or self- and other-affirmation are fundamental tools in the negotiation of reputations and commitments.

They *ought to* fulfill the usual expectations of morality, permanence, transcendence; they must be "true", in the broader sense of the term; they are, therefore, *serious.*

Serious Talk: Sensemaking and Identity Stories

A large part of what we take to be serious talk, then, lies midway between the harsh objectivity of life and the subjective freedom of myth. Narratives about the self and the world are generally serious, because they herald real *actions*; but they are also fictional, because these actions are placed in a (peculiarly human) world in which values exist on a par with facts, and *we* are particularly important. Typically, two types of processes are blended together in this attempt to associate one's (subjective) goals with the hard facts of the (objective) reality: sensemaking explanations and identity exchanges. Directed primarily to the reality, *sensemaking processes* give origin to narratives that attempt to explain and justify past or current events, creating common definitions of the situation upon which actors can work their differences, similarities, and decide what to do; they are generally crafted after the fact, as a response to events that catch the attention or seem (personally) relevant for private or collective decisions; they thus form accounts of reality in which "action shapes cognition", leading to stories "grounded in identity construction, retrospective, enactive of sensible environments, social, ongoing, focused on and by extracted cues; and driven by plausibility rather than accuracy" ([192]: 12, 17). They are, therefore, deeply enmeshed with one's personal view of the self and world. *Identity stories,* on the other hand, are semi-fictional, but purportedly true "I" and "we" narratives with which actors reaffirm to each other their "true" intents, character, stories, and symbols of honor, lineage, or wealth. They are an essential part of a game that permeates all levels of social life. By negotiating identities, actors tacitly pledge to follow the imperative to act as said, creating binding commitments to enact what they display; reaffirm the predominance of socially reiterated, dependable definitions of the situations over the ones given by their changing internal world; and are thus in a safer place to make their plans according to the promises received from the others. It is based on sensemaking processes and identity stories that actors create the imaginary, biased, highly valued and widely believed figures of the self, of the family, or of the firm – apparently homogeneous entities whose existence is tacitly or explicitly confirmed by their ubiquitous presence in the common conversations, by their role as premises of collective deliberations, and by justifications, actions, and interactions grounded in them.[3]

Since the Renaissance, when reason overcame faith as the main justification for collective action – (a battle doubt is now fighting against truth) – passing a narrative through the logical bottleneck of coherence has become a requirement for any topic to be considered a matter worthy of consideration. Thus, the social alchemy that gives legitimacy to identity games depends on the substitution of reliability for validity, or coherence for empirical testing, as the basic criterion that guarantees the value of narratives. Consistency, rather than faithfulness to the facts, is the sieve that defines whether a certain narrative is "true" and the contract embedded in one's identity stories should be socially accepted. Sensemaking and identity narratives are never testable: they "can only achieve 'verisimilitude' (...) – a version of reality whose acceptability is governed by convention and narrative necessity rather than by empirical verification and logical requirements'" ([194]: 4).

After the first test of coherence, the verisimilitude that confers "truth" to players' identity and sensemaking stories is guaranteed by multiple layers of congruence and similarity. *First*, they refer to the common, seemingly stable, and homogeneous things, space, and time that form the world of perception – regardless of the particular interpretation, the more events a story explains, and the more coherently it weaves them into a reasonable plot that follows the chronology experienced by all players, the higher are the chances the narrative will be accepted as true and be used as a basis for collective deliberations. *Second*, in explaining the facts they make use of the shared forms of organization of meaning around which all players revolve – witches, kings, slaves, chivalry, and feudal duties in the Middle Ages, or markets, logic, rationality, democracy, bureaucracy, autonomy, individual rights, love, families, and firms in our times [31]. *Third*, they are reinforced by strong normative pressures for coherence, which expressed as the shared "universal" values of honesty and morality lead players toward a consistency of identities. *Finally*, stories are confirmed by the practice of the same players who share them – meaning, intentions, and goals are then socially established as valid explanations of causality, the stories working as self-fulfilling prophecies made true by actions stemming from the initial prediction [195]. Customarily, if this dance is well danced and is supported by social consensus, actors remain unaware of the arbitrary nature of the personal stories with which they appease their cognitive dissonances. Provided they are reasonably credible, one can continue with them *as if* the socially shared definitions of reality were indeed true, supported as they are by the hypnotizing forces of social consensus. When put together, these claims for rationality and coherence form the basic premises of any serious talk or social contract found in the family or in the businesses (rationality, lucidness, truthfulness, honesty).

It is impossible to expose all the hidden threads of meaning used by mankind to explain itself, the guises and directions in which sensemaking and identity narratives appear. In modern families, for example, they include the (mythical) beliefs that love is unconditional; that feelings linking people to each other are natural, and not game-inspired emotions; that parents and siblings are attached only by ties of affection, and never by sexual interest; that one's identity is innately attached to the ancestors, lineage, or past; or that families, clans, and lines *should* persist, as if they were not fragile, easily dismantled social constructions. In the firm, four major themes have been described: the primacy of calculating rationality, "the idea that human spirit finds definitive expression through taking and justifying action in term of its future consequences for prior values"; the myth of hierarchy, which suppresses other kinds of network structures under "the idea that problems and actions can be decomposed into nested sets of sub-problems and sub-actions such that interactions among them can be organized around a hierarchy"; the myth of the individual leader, "the idea that any story of history must be related to a human project in order to be meaningful and that organizational history is produced by the intentions of specific human leaders"; and the myth of historical efficiency, "the idea that history follows a path leading to a unique equilibrium defined by antecedent conditions and produced by competition", rather than slow processes of adaptation that lead to multiple equilibria. These themes, in turn, inspire counter-narratives that emphasize the role of identity, nonhierarchical networks, complexity, historical inefficiency, chance, or social construction in shaping outcomes ([26]: 55–60).

In family businesses, typical stories revolve around the founder, past relevant obstacles and difficulties, successes, the succession, future plans, and the tradition, honor, reputation, affect, money, or love that join the players around a supposedly unique, but in fact unrealistic, essence. Particularly interesting is the mix between the voices of the families – prototypically based on involuntary filiation, optional marriage alliances, kinship, relationships, love, children, pleasure, affection, tradition, and rivalry – and the opposing voices of the business, which typically emphasize instrumental, contractual, and utilitarian ties (the fantasies of profit, efficiency, capital, markets, sales, merit, competition, success, and failure). This heterogeneous blend includes discourses that "are neither fixed nor unambiguous, [which] are not owned by any one speaker but instead oscillate throughout the system and take residence in different individuals or compete within the same individual", constantly deconstructing each other with their opposing logics of action ([196]: 369). As many other dichotomies looming beneath our stories – such as error and truth, precision and ambiguity, or fact and interpretation – these antinomies express the human need to uncover the deeper roots that drive the constructions of our stories. They provide, so to say, the mythical-philosophical terrain on which social identities, sensemaking narratives, and scientific fictions of truth must be based in order to have credibility and resonance in the broader society.

The same elements that give strength to habitual identity and sensemaking stories, therefore – the search of "coherence by contemporaneity", the emphasis on a "bogus historical-causal entailment", or the teleological attempt to find a meaningful or intentional plot behind the facts [194] – are also the source of their weakness. Well-crafted stories are *enticing*; but for the same reason they are unrealistic, paying a tribute to both truth and illusion. They are crafted to please an audience, including the profoundly social, impure, other-oriented assembly of the soul; and for this they always sacrifice precision for elegance, truthfulness for propaganda. In their search for depth they attempt to blend meaning and reality; they are thus inevitably egocentric, as if men were demiurges "making the world in their image, after their likeness". They suggest that truth, at least in matters concerning ourselves, is never distinct from rhetoric. Furthermore, they are profoundly mixed with value – both in the family and in the firm, for example, prevailing myths of identity, culture, or reality are commonly contradicted by the counter-myths of the flow of generations, innovation, novelty, renewal, or change, which question the veracity of the hegemonic stories and thus offer a rational alibi to the profoundly emotional, self-interested, political, or idealistic, pressures to introduce new orders based on other narratives.

True discourses, stories, biographies, and autobiographies, then, simply reflect one's perfection in the art of persuasion and self-deception. Moreover, as "any particular series of events can be incorporated in many different stories, each of which is susceptible to multiple interpretations" ([197]: 167), within the broader context of the family or firm there are as many accounts of the same reality as there are individuals, groups, and coalitions favoring one or another definition of the situation. Each perspective transforms its private opinion into a truth that is confirmed by the (selected) audience it is directed to please. Without a better metric to solve the differences, one that adds method, logic, and realism to mere explanatory power, it is impossible to transcend the barrier of the opinion and create more public, value-neutral definitions of the situation to effectively guide real life. Such is the role of the idealized (mythical? mystical?) *scientific models and essays.*

The Search for Truth: Scientific Models and Essays

A good part of what is considered serious talk within families and firms reflects, thus, the players' search to explain, illuminate, or predict relevant aspects of the practice in order to create fictions of order, generate useful actions, or persuade themselves and others of what should be done if reality were indeed what they define it is. When social consensus is incapable to sustain the illusions of engagement, however, it becomes clear that private values, private perspectives, and private stories, even when shared, offer only private solutions. It is at this point that reason and truth emerge as parts of a new game, one that supposedly brings the prize of valid, reliable, and realistic definitions of the situation that can direct individual and collective action. This is the domain of science and objectivity – what is considered to be *true* as defined by the scientific method lies beyond the realm of the opinions or of the fictional sensemaking and identity stories, providing a (supposedly) firm basis on which men can rest in order to resolve their personal or public differences and contradictions.

The processes developed by mankind in its search for truth can be summarized as composing two parallel avenues of understanding. On the one hand, players are expected to have some knowledge about the outside concrete reality with which they are dealing, or at least to engage in the pursuit of this objective knowledge in order to minimize error in the execution of their plans – this is typically seen in the firm, whose members are expected to study *and know* the nuances of the market, the behavior of the competition, or the variability and robustness of the processes they use in order to achieve the mythical, truth-based goal of maximal efficiency. On the other hand, in a game that occupies most negotiations that occur in the intimate world of the relationships, families, persons, and their informal networks, actors are called to objectively (?) describe men's subjective motives, values, actions, and perspectives, grounding their actions on a supposedly detached view of human nature rather than on simplistic post-hoc, self-based explanations. Under the rules of rationality that guide this new game, public definitions of reality and meaning are not simply creative endeavors but part of the essence of reasonable players – the often proclaimed, seldom sought, but never reachable expression of idealized unified worldviews that translate the practice in the form of abstract, metaphysical meta-games and logical, well-grounded narratives that give actors a temporary illusion of truth.

In general, the attempts to describe the physical (and social?) reality felt as being "out there" are better served by the methods of the naively realistic, positivistic science: if one postulates the existence of a purely objective world, and if this is assumed to have a stable essence beneath the shifting fluctuation of the appearances, the causal and probabilistic structure of reality can supposedly be apprehended by experimental designs and statistical tools that bring to fore the underlying laws that govern the observed behaviors. Conversely, the understanding of the ways men *interpret* reality depends on descriptions of the cognitive and affective meanings they give to the facts objectively perceived, a process better served by hermeneutic essays and narratives. The fundamental difference between privileging facts *or* meaning, or a positivistic *versus* an interpretive approach, is closely linked to the two major ways by which information is usually registered and transmitted by players. Typically, positivistic, mathematical models focus on the non-teleological texture of the world, extirpating meaning from reality and prioritizing the description of the structural, deterministic, invariable elements that beneath the appearances shape the players' behavior [26]. Natural language narratives, on the contrary, frame the scientific descriptions of reality around time, intentionality and meaning, reflecting more faithfully the many possible individual, personal, interpretative views that characterize the shifting perspective-taking of everyday life.

The mathematical models provided by positivistic science represent the most relevant counterpoint to the idiosyncrasies that characterize intuitive and experiential learning [198]. Their methodology relies on clearly specified initial conditions from which one derives falsifiable predictions that may confirm or disconfirm the proposed law of explanation [60]. In the strife for objectivity, fluctuating values, choices, wishes, interpretations, or people are postulated as stable variables or simply disregarded; concepts are formalized, simplified, falsified in order to observe how they relate to each other; and just because they have (physical or linguistic) borders, objects, persons, families, firms, and groups are treated like enduring entities whose attributes and behavior can then be studied. On top of these (so questionable) premises, one applies standardized measurements from which it is possible to derive reliable, causal and probabilistic relations. Representative samples are assumed to portray the whole population. Since the conditions of analysis are fixed, it is possible to see whether these theories work or not in the shifting world of the decision-makers. Finally, forums such as meetings and journals guarantee that private findings follow the public criteria for what is deemed true in the social world of science.

The main consequence of these methodological choices – by which uncertainty is absorbed a priori in the form of assumptions and certainty is celebrated a posteriori as a feature of objective reality – is an inherent circularity of thought that puts into question the face validity of these abstract models of reality. The weakness lies on the simplifications of disorder required to create order. By treating social or strategic phenomena as single data points and fixed variables, the scientific method may allow one to know *if* a certain correlational or causal interaction exists or not; but it does not show *how* or *when* this relation is manifested in a social world marked by complexity, multiple rules, interpretative flexibility, and self-reinforcing positive and negative feedback loops that create their own truths, independently of the objective nature of the facts. Likewise, *if* measurements are correct and conditions are clearly stipulated, the weakness of the axioms is quickly forgotten and players jump to discuss the conclusions, focusing on what to do with the "facts" they exposed regardless of the source and validity of the initial information used as a premise for the argument. In order to be falsifiable, and therefore simple enough to be testable and communicated in the world of practice, scientific theories lose their explanatory power and (in isolation) become caught in the midst of the validity-reliability tradeoff, offering poor guidance for a decision-maker who needs to respond in real time to a complex, circular, self-contradictory, and profoundly changing human fact.

Interpretative essays, in contrast with the formal scientific models, take full advantage of the imprecise, fuzzy, and recursive nature of the natural languages [83]. Typically, they make explicit the patterns and paradoxes involved in all phases of the fact creation. This involves the discussion of the (arbitrary) assumptions by which one determines whether something is defined as real, permanent, or true in each place; the unveiling of how the perspectives chosen by each actor always imply in a value, an *attitude* toward the facts that determines what is considered real and defined as illusory; and the analysis of the multiple viewpoints and levels of analysis through which the same facts can be seen (it does matter whether facts will be framed as the expression of an interaction, relationship, role, or cultural ideal, or whether they will be described through the perspective of the individual, of the group, of the family, of the firm, or of the broader culture in which they are inserted). From the exegesis of the practical discourses and narratives used by the actors comes an inventory of themes, choices, directions of meaning and interpretation that serve as guidance to understand how people see themselves, the world, and react to it.

For players embedded in the world of practice, and in particular for leaders and change agents who need to respond in real time to the mix of reality and value brought by the actors, these essays are closer to how humans live. Framed according to a language game that shapes how players routinely think about reality and their own thinking, allowing multiple recursive cycles of doubt and assertion about the same theme [199], they allow individuals, families, and organizations to dive into the punctual events of their routine experiences of success and error and learn something from samples of one or fewer [200]. They reflect better how the search to know the objective reality is linked to the subjective search for its value. Since they force one to consider various viewpoints and alternative interpretations of the same facts, they lead actors to think, communicate, and interact more fluidly, shifting the perspectives of meaning in order to understand the contradictions embedded in their identity and sensemaking stories. They are, therefore, not simply the remnants of natural languages whose fate is doomed in view of the rise of mathematical, symbolic formalizations. They express the essential core of life, a social dream whose rules of construction are as relevant to the definition of reality as is the reality itself when it is lived spontaneously. They are, however, limited by the complexity required for the correct study of all perspectives, frameworks, paradigms, and frames through which objective data can be transformed into error, illusion, imagination, or various different, but equally valid, truths.

In the practical life of the families, firms, and people, both types of models are mixed as numbers, words, causality, correlations, and explanations of meaning are blended and used in the creation of (purportedly) true accounts of reality that are as persuasive as they are considered valid. In both cases, the objective and subjective worlds are seen as having a relatively predictable structure – laws, root causes, or forces, in case of the external reality; or meanings, perspectives, values, and interpretative stances in the internal world. Together, both methods create a set of temporary truths and constructs that can be applied to other contexts beyond the here-and-now of the practical world and therefore increase the explanatory power of one's definitions of the situation. These truths, in turn, stabilize the facts and perspectives through which facts are seen, creating the conditions of falsification by which the complexity of reality is simplified in order to be studied. As simplified, predictable versions of the world, they integrate the cognitive and affective connotations of meaning into a single meta-game of truth, a contest for which the prize is the extraction of a thread of order from an existence that is inherently disordered, unpredictable, complex.

As it is always the case, however, the choice of the method determines the reality revealed by it. In the case of positivistic models, the formalization required to treat the phenomena objectively, ideally using mathematical tools – the paradigmatic conditions of simplification that transform the flow of experience into treatable material for modeling – are of as much concern as the truths and untruths disclosed by each model or type of understanding. In the case of interpretative essays, the limitations of single interpretive perspectives have to be complemented by a series of counter-models, counter-theories, and alternative perspectives that reflect the various ways in which one can interpret the same facts – other parallel accounts that can illuminate the blind spots of the first view, in an endless construction that exponentially increases the complexity of the abstraction. Both "stories and models simplify causal relations, reducing the number of variables involved, often ignoring second- and third-order effects, minimizing feedback effects, and glossing over variations in time delays. They often result in over-fitting explanations that provide post hoc interpretations of random variation that offer little subsequent predictive power. They simplify identities and the occasions for their evocation, reducing the nuance of identity fulfillment and the chaos of human obligations. They generally assume that causal stories are decomposable into simple subtexts that do not involve detailed interaction with each other. These simplifications necessarily reflect incomplete representations, but they facilitate comprehension" ([26]: 48). One falls, then, in the midst of a more general trade-off of information, namely, the tension between explanatory power and comprehensibility: as one gets close to the ideal of correctly describing the intricate structure of reality – and especially of human reality, which involves imagination and symbols – the model becomes so complex that it loses its simplicity and heuristic value [20].

The result of this disparity between the complex, unstable reality of practical facts that are always on flow, on one side, and the precise but simplified reality of science, on the other, is a vacuum in the chain of the transmission of meaning. Constrained by its methodology and by the need to offer deep and reliable, but single-perspective accounts of reality, normal science cannot address the complex, shifting world of practice. Absorbed by the immeasurability of the real facts, leaders, change agents, and actors are restricted to their raw intuitions of experts without fully benefitting from the rich (albeit stereotyped) world of scientific systematic thinking; and without a tool for translation, both universes run in parallel as if men, even while thinking about life, had to remain lost forever in their own private universes. Most often, players, families, and firms do not attend to these inconsistencies and respond to difficulties in the pursuit of truth with further pursuits of truth, without thinking that difficulty may be on the limitations of the method that has to be used to create simplified orders and problems. When this occurs and reason puts itself under the scrutiny of reason, we enter the realm of *doubt*.

The Management of Doubt

In the world of practice, the more diverse are the reactions of the audience, the less credible becomes the narrative; and the more stories one hears about the same facts, the more deeply the narrative becomes surrounded with doubt. Usually, this instability of meaning opens the way for conflict or negotiation [157]. "In the moment a hearer is made suspicious of the 'facts' of a story or the ulterior motives of a narrator, he or she immediately becomes hermeneutically alert" and begins to question the canonical interpretation of the narrative, searching for alternative, more compelling stories, plots, or explanations of the facts ([194]: 7). Deprived of the belief in metaphysical, dogmatic, scientific, or interpretative truths, and shaken by the methodical doubt about the automatic authenticity given to information, actors come to see the accounts on which they base their rational deliberations as a huge patchwork of semi-truths, each of them strong enough to justify bouts of local action but never sufficiently absolute to reach the idealized consensus promised by the prior ideal of certainty.

Taken to the extreme, the meltdown of the ideal of truth leads to a total loss of the illusion of objectivity. Consequently, the authority previously given to the voices of tradition in the family, to the institutionalized discourses of each time, to the legitimacy of leaders in the firm, or to the value of change or culture are eroded by the potent forces of subjectivist deconstructions grounded on the (personal, philosophical, or political) dismissal of reason as a reasonable criterion of realism and morality. Information, persuasion, value, and influence are mixed into a single process that transforms everything into a matter of opinion, taste, or power [197]. One hits, once again, the relativistic deadlock – by accepting several alternative explanations of the same phenomenon as equally valid, one implies that truth is relative and violates the rule that propositions cannot be and not be true at the same time; conversely, by shifting "ad lib" from story to story, or from metaphor to metaphor, one is forced to accept the post-modern, democratic, but nihilistic conclusion that "all discourses have the same truth-value, since there are no reliable criteria by which to judge their validity" ([186]: 188). Since there is no definitive way out of this dilemma – the incommensurability of paradigms implying that every worldview may be deconstructed from the viewpoint of an equally compelling account – rationality needs to jump out of itself and study the conditions in which it reveals uncertainty, rather than firmness; and therefore doubt, rather than truth.

In the scientific world, this skepticism has led to two different responses, namely, the dive into relativism and the attempt to transcend it. In the field of management studies and social sciences, where the first response prevailed in many streams, perspectivism and relativism inspired numerous relevant, interesting cross-cultural, historical, and cross-paradigm analyses that illuminate various ways by which the same facts can be interpreted [40, 186, 201]. Practically, doubt has become more and more associated with leadership and with the need to navigate in a world that is naturally complex, many times unpredictable, and frequently in rapid, often turbulent flow: "Reimagining doubt in this way allows leaders to sharpen their ripple intelligence, enhance their ability to make decisions, and mitigate business and decision-making risks in times of complexity and uncertainty ... doubt is a capability to be cultivated rather than a weakness to be cured" ([202]: 14). In the field of decision-making, on the contrary, doubt has led to a reutilization of the same normative precepts of rationality to create a meta-understanding of how humans *really* think and act, divided between objective reasoning and systematic, pattern-following irrationalities that stem from disturbances in several phases of the process of truth-creation [203]. This has exposed how facts always are *created* in the mind. With this study, comes the conclusion that every reality is cognitively and socially constructed through multiple steps of pruning and sculpting that imperceptibly transform the brute clay of life into meaningful facts, which only then amenable to inquiry, choice, or manipulation (see Appendix, Figure 2).

In fact, if one starts from the process of perception and proceed in a stepwise fashion until finding the definitions of situation with which we work every day, it is possible to find three crucial points of transformation. The first involves the (often tacit) selection of the data that will be considered factual – noise, attention, context effects, limitations of perception, and top-down schemata define among all data which are relevant or true, guaranteeing that only some bites of the available information are transformed into building blocks for the posterior process of construction of reality. The majority remains lost and is processed subliminally, as unconscious phenomena that still influence action and choice [204]. The second step involves the organization of particular observations in the form of definitions of the (subjective or objective, mental or concrete) situations – arbitrary arrangements by which certain orders are prioritized at the expense of others, following intuitive biases, heuristics, preferences, and culturally sanctioned patterns of reality description. The third, finally, involves the conscious choice of the interpretations that will be given to the facts depending on the broader context in which they are inserted; and in parallel, the social negotiation of these definitions of the situations in the form of publicly defensible views of the facts.

The certainties created by each of these jumps of organization are the result of substantial amounts of cropping, weeding out, and (conscious or unconscious) choice; they bring, therefore, the possibility of doubt. For players who still believe in the objective existence of facts, doubt lies in the probability of the occurrence of a future behavior, and therefore *uncertainty* – perceptions of risk and stability that involve the predictability but not the ambiguity of the facts, and therefore preserve the structure of reality. For those who question the definitions of the situation, doubt involves the interpretation of the facts, and therefore *ambiguity* – the equivocality that occurs because the same conjunction of perceptions allows multiple potential framings, and therefore gives rise to radically different facts. For those who question the certainty that covers many (if not all) of their automatic beliefs, doubt involves the explication of the unconscious, *automatic biases* and *cognitive mechanisms* through which our apparently simple convictions are created. We will focus on the latter two problems – how to evaluate the various possible interpretations one make about a fact (*ambiguity*) and the hidden errors that exist beneath intuitions that are *felt* as certain (*biases*).

Doubts about Reality: Ontological Oscillation, Interpretive Flexibility, and Ambiguity

All "objective" definitions of the situation inevitably involve an element of interpretation – any action, discourse, movement, situation, emotion, or thought must be framed according to a particular perspective and interpreted in the context of one's hypotheses about the broader reality to which the situation belongs, in order to provide any information that may be useful for the ensuing reasoning or decision-making processes. Messages, perceptions, feelings, or messages only acquire meaning when coupled with assumptions about intentions, character, personality, or goals; fluctuations in sales or consumer behavior, movements of an opponent, or changes in the firm's market value have to be interpreted as real, unreal, bubbles, trends, signal, or noise in order to serve as a basis for action; and the same signal may be framed as an error or an act of war depending on the surrounding circumstances, on (selective) memories of the past and on (arbitrary) hypotheses about the future. It is in the theory with which we surround the facts – the often automatic hypotheses we make about their behavior, relationship with other facts, effects of context, or even the basic assumption that they are *facts* rather than illusions or hallucinations – and not in the perception in isolation, that we ground all thought and action (see Appendix 2, Figure 6).

For a good chunk of the stuff we deal with every day – the established reality, for which redundant interpretations create stable illusions of meaning – this coupling between perception and hypothesis is not problematic: the sun rises every day, the ground is firm, and families, firms, and people follow predictable patterns of actions suggested by their proposals of identity (until they do not do it anymore). However, for more difficult or distant situations, or conditions of silence – the future scenarios stemming from a wicked problem, the behavior of an erratic family member, the simple lack of information, or a crisis in the market, firm, marriage, or family – the interpretation itself becomes a problem. Players face, then, the fundamental and irreducible problem of ambiguity. On one side of the encounter, there is an actor – family, firm, nation, or person – who must radically decide what is the "truth" on which to base the flow of decision-making and reality-creation. On the other side, one sees the fuzzy situations for which many plausible interpretations are possible, each of them carrying an equally ambiguous probability of reality. Between them, a game by which men continuously attempt to infuse meaning – happiness, depth, profit, history – into facts that need first to be (rationally) defined as true in order to receive the (irrational) projection of meaning.

Facts, therefore, only exist as they are to the extent that one maintains the conditions of stability that allow their permanence in a specific form. These conditions of stabilization involve two fundamental assumptions. First, that one sees them according to the eyes of a single entity, which in the moment takes the role of the "self" – objects only exist as objects-for-an-actor, the actor that in the instant occupies the mind of the observer as if it were a real entity. Second, facts are stable only insofar as they are framed following the same rules of organization: the same perception accepts as many meanings as are the reasonable premises of context or bases of interpretation. Both conditions of rigidity are violated by the ontological oscillation and interpretive flexibility that characterize the freedom of human mind. The ambiguities of experience do *not* stem from reality, but from the clash between the inexorable flow of life and our need to tame it, reduce it, fix it in order to satisfy the ordering mechanisms of reason.

The first limitation we face in trying to fit the existence into the framework of language, then, comes from the permanent *ontological oscillation* through which we assume different roles in different times, often successively and according to the whims of the moment. "A man's self is the sum total of all that he *can* call his, not only his body and his psychic powers, but his clothes and his house, his wife and children, his ancestors and friends, his reputation and works, his lands and horses, and yacht and bank accounts. All these things give him the same emotions. If they wax and prosper, he feels triumphant; if they dwindle and die away, he feels cast down, - not necessarily in the same degree for each thing, but in much the same way for all" ([205]: 188). Each of these emotions refers to a specific viewpoint that in the moment is given reality; each viewpoint alternates in catching the actors' attention and motivation, framing the value of the outside reality according to its momentary perspective and the (ordered or disordered) system of value typical of the entity one identifies with. Profit or love, integration or unity, future or present, short or long-term, efficiency or waste, passion or prudence are equally valid options depending on the eyes of the beholder, which change in kaleidoscopic speed depending on the unpredictable factors that direct one's ontological oscillation; this, in turn, gives rise to different conformations of reality by which men give existence to different social entities at different times. Families, firms, people, and all social systems are nothing more than ordered wholes (or meta-games) made of various sub-wholes and sub-games, which gain more or less value and ontological weight depending on the reality conferred to each part by the arbitrary perspective of the actors.

The second limitation to the stabilization of reality stems from the fact that even when observer and things are stabilized the same events can be interpreted in different ways, depending on how one contextualizes the perceived data according to various interpretations of the others' intentions, of future, or of the broader implications of the present situation [42]. Firms are *different facts* depending on how they are framed as homogeneous units – institutions that have legal and social existence within the collectively shared view of reality – or as groups of shifting coalitions, structured formal hierarchies, combinations of competing divisions, or aggregates of individuals who see them as means or obstacles for their personal realization. Families are different facts if they are framed around the dyadic perspective of the couple, as partnerships directed to raising children and controlling property, or as means of perpetuation of a broader line of kin that transcends the nuclear unit of parents and offspring.

From the conjunction of these two sources of instability – ontological oscillation and multiplicity of interpretations – comes the (uniquely human) interpretive flexibility through which the concrete reality of the practice can be transformed into the multiple, shifting, and unstable realities of the world of ideas. "What we firmly believe, if it is neither knowledge nor error, may be called probable opinion. The greater part of what would commonly pass as knowledge is more or less probable opinion" [206]. Many of the difficult situations observed in life or within family business are derived from players' unawareness of how truth is, in fact, a mere result of arbitrary choices of perspective and of interpretation. Legal, medical, and business experts, for example, often become polarized trying to define what is relevant or irrelevant to be included in the situation, how to organize the data, and eventually what is or not real [207]. Couples, partners and work colleagues spend enormous amounts of energy trying to distinguish the "right" version of the facts (even though many are potentially correct). People seldom keep their arguments within the constraints of a fixed perspective, mixing discussions of the future with memories of the past and examples of the present, assuming or denying a relationship, returning always to the same unfinished justification, and eventually becoming lost among the multiplicity of interpretations they can have of the "same" situation.

In all these cases, the solutions for the dilemmas are generally sought outside and not inside – as if one were dealing with the shock caused by the fragmentation of reality and with uncertainty, not ambiguity. The "nature of the problem, [then], is itself a question ... there are multiple, conflicting interpretations [and] different value orientations ... goals are unclear ... contradictions and paradoxes appear ... roles and responsibilities are vague ... success measures are lacking ... [there is] poor understanding of cause-effect relationships ... [and] players use symbols and metaphors rather than precise definitions or logical arguments to express their points of view" ([32]: 45). Families exist or not? Are cultures real or simply an illusion? In fact these paradoxes do not exist, they come from the ability to (recursively) frame the same objective facts through different perspectives, creating different definitions of the situation. To solve them it would be sufficient for men to turn inward and transform the practical question into an existential, metaphysical, ontological problem – to which perspectival dream to give *being* to. Culture, identity, sensemaking, truth, and doubt are then blended in one single proposition, the uniquely human, realistic, but arbitrary dream-game that will direct the preferred avenues for interpretation, action, and interaction in the socially constructed reality of the firm or family. Before we follow this thread, however – which is in the core of any project of culture that acknowledges the limits of its own truth – we will study how the most unambiguous, "certain", and crystalized truths eventually introduce substantial uncertainty in the process by which men reach their definitions of the situation. In this cases, one's ideas about reality are not based on reason, but on deep-seated *biases, intuitions, heuristics,* and *cognitive automatisms* that surreptitiously distort the desired objective view of the facts in the direction of the subjectivity they embody (see Appendix 2, Figures 4, 5, and 6)[4].

Doubts about Certainty: Biases, Intuitions, and Cognitive Automatisms

The dilemma brought by ambiguity, ontological oscillation, and interpretative flexibility is fundamentally different from the problems posed by the biases – selective interpretations derived from the use of heuristics, rather than reason, to construct models of reality on which action and thought can be based. These heuristics (from the Greek *Eureka* and *euriskein,* "to find") are automatic processes of truth-creation by which humans intuitively make use of basic, costless, fast cognitive mechanisms developed to deal with the immediate world of practice – such as perception, pattern recognition, generalization from prototypes, and interpretations based on intention, causality, or teleology – to create (apparently) rational judgments about the structure of reality. This process occurs before any possibility of reasoning about it: "*acceptance* is a passive and inevitable act, whereas *rejection* is an active operation that undoes the initial acceptance. (…) People may change their minds *after* accepting an assertion, but they cannot stop their minds from being changed by an initial contact with it" ([208]: 180). As a consequence, perception, interpretation, emotion, and action are commonly integrated in the form of language propositions that seldom cause doubt, because they come with the *feeling* of certainty. These judgments generally reflect an arbitrary, evolutionarily selected but irrational preference for simplification, which leads to a confusion between prototypical and logical categories; for causal stories and narratives over analyses involving chance and probability; for the present, leading to distortions in the description of the past and of the future; and for abstractions suggesting higher truths, which often lead actors astray in the convolutions of their own thoughts (for good reviews, see [184, 209–216]).

Many times, these heuristics are useful in the context of the small samples offered by experience and give rise to fast and efficient reactions [217]. They prioritize speed, rather than accuracy; action, rather than intelligence; and ecological adaptation, rather than normative validity [218]. However, unaware that neither feeling, nor the language form guarantees the validity or reliability of their reasoning, actors are commonly deceived by the sensation of truth that characterize their intuitions and never reach (or even actively deny) the more stable truths that could be provided by the use of the normative canons of rationality. Doubt is stripped out of the process of reasoning. Players systematically disregard the possibilities of misperception or misinterpretation, assuming "that what appeared to happen did happen", "that what happened was intended to happen", and that "what happened had to happen"

([219]: 19). They are then caught by perseverance and confirmation biases, which lead them to cling to their prior beliefs, to search preferably for information that confirms their viewpoints, to discard data that refute what they already think, and to interpret any new evidence in a way that fits their stereotyped, usually restrictive, perspective about reality [91]. The end result is a loose coupling between reason as theory and reason as practice: to please the first, they search for precision in their inductions and communication; to satisfy the latter, they promise to be swift; and to mediate this trade-off they make use of the language game, which suggests rigor by its grammar but allows ambiguity through its semantics.

Fuzzy sets, Prototypes, Natural and Linguistic Categories

One of the contradictions resulting from this dissociation between idealized thought and pragmatic action is reflected in the dissonance between the precision with which symbolic categories are depicted in the world of ideas and the inexact, vague way in which they are actually used in the practice [28]. Natural categories used for communication and planning on an everyday basis are fuzzy sets, whose blurred boundaries barely separate them from adjacent, superposed classes and whose members are barely distinguished from non-members [220]. The symbols used to describe entities in the language game are exquisitely simple, downplaying the existence of other nested, occult forms of classification; tacitly suggest that there are no differences among members of the same category; and merely by being *nouns* overemphasize the importance of prototypes, which though easy on the mind are seldom representative of the nuances observed in the real members of the category [221, 222]. As a consequence, players often use generalizations when dealing with particulars, make undue extrapolations from single events, or do not understand that classes many times should be seen as mere reminders that a phenomenon has various sides, rather than as precise instruments of categorization.

There are various biases associated with these difficulties. When responding to *the halo effect*, for example, people assume that positive or negative characteristics of a person are predictive of other as yet unknown qualities [223]: a single attribute felt as relevant in a person, event, organization, speech, or internet site – such as the appearance, intelligence, fluency of a CEO or the cleanness of a store – is generalized to the whole entity forming a meaningful and coherent (but often inaccurate) depiction of reality. *Dilution effects* occur when non-diagnostic information weakens (or dilutes) the impact of the diagnostic information on judgment [224] – irrelevant elements such as colors, words, or excessive stimuli distract the observers and make the object differ from the prototypical members of the category, obfuscating the precision of the evaluation. *Focal illusions* come from an undue weight given to specific pieces of information (generally the ones that are by chance more salient in the moment) in the formation judgments and predictions that transcend the present context [225].

Likewise, various errors of judgment and classification involve the *overvaluation of prototypes* inherent to the substitution of logical, well-defined classes for the prototypical, fuzzy categories that in fact characterize the world of practice. Emotions, mood, depression, grief, or sadness, for example, are often treated as distinct, and not overlapping and undistinguishable entities [226]. Prototypes are also overvalued when people classify others as good *or* bad, forgetting the fact that humans have a shifting, complex nature; when projects are radically defined as viable *or* not, as if there were no ambiguities; when people donate the same amount to rescue 2,000, 20,000, or 200,000 birds, basing their decision on the affect they feel [227]; when one decides whether to repeat a colonoscopy based on the feeling experienced in the end of the experiment, and not on the total duration of the event [228]; or when members in a firm believe in (fictional) personality types to make career and employment assessments [222]. *Focal illusions* lead to neglect of important considerations in areas such as affective forecasting or social comparisons: people tend to overestimate the impact of good or bad events in their lives, judging how they will feel in the future based on the narrow prospect of the present [229]; have difficulties in predicting how they will assess other realities, due to the impact of the current perspective on their evaluation[230]; and tend to evaluate poorly their own abilities, giving excessive weight to their characteristics in comparison with targets. In all these cases, the unique, fuzzy, ambiguous experiences that mark the world of practice are (wrongly) translated, using rules of similarity, into the general, abstract and "clean" assessments about the reality used for reasoning and predictions in the world of ideas. The idea one creates of reality – the supposedly objective model of the world, which should reflect its inner structure and not our reactions to it – becomes unduly biased in the direction of the prototypes that subjectively catch our attention, emotion, habit, or customary use of the language game. Moreover, these biases are acted in the collective environment – obeying their intuitions, players tend to focus on their peculiar experiences, stereotypes, and judgments and are often oblivious of how other actors assume opposite, but equally plausible and intuitively correct conclusions about the same reality. The consequence is conflict.

A Preference for the Visible: Narratives, Causality, and Rhetoric

In parallel with the (simplistic) translation of prototypes and fuzzy categories into (apparently clear) symbols and ideas, one of the more relevant biases observed among human beings involves their tendency to privilege descriptions of the reality that integrate the visible or known elements according to rules of causality that provide a good, convincing, or rhetorical story that raises *interest*. These stories are often organized according to a *causal* logic, forming a plot that involves the self, choices, free-will, emotions, the surrounding people, and the more relevant occurrences connecting them – for example, the storyteller in relation to the closer relatives and colleagues or to the more charismatic or older members, the leaders, founders, patriarchs, or matriarchs. Probabilistic reasoning is usually ignored – "the tendency toward determinism is somehow implied in the method of retrospection itself. In retrospect, we seem to perceive the logic of the events which unfold themselves in a regular or linear fashion according to a recognizable patter with an alleged inner necessity. So we get the impression that it really could not have happened otherwise" and other potentially true stories are excluded just because they do not fit the *lived* flow of events ([231]: 369). Moreover, people fluctuate between stories that pursue truth and those that serve efficiency, consensus, or the interests of the storyteller. For the first, coherence, validity, and reliability are paramount and should be complemented by more or less exhaustible evaluations of the alternatives of reality and action. For the latter, "few alternatives should be analyzed, only positive consequences of the chosen actions should be considered, and objectives should not be formulated in advance" ([34]: 37). Stories, thus, maintain the element of coherence but vary in form and content depending on their goal; but because they *fit* the logic of causality and encompass the perceived life into a reasonable storyline, they are intuitively assumed to be true.

The end result of the shock between these disparate tendencies is a number of narratives reasonably good in connecting the observed facts according to a logical plot or in promoting action, but which generally disregard what is not seen (but could have occurred), what happened by chance (but was experienced as a fact), what is merely correlational (but appears to be causal) or the trade-off between understanding and action (which is associated with different lengths of search and moments of suspension of doubt). Realism is usually restricted to dates, periods, and places – the geography and time where the actors' subjectivity is enacted. As narratives vary in other attributes, the imaginary world of a family or firm becomes a complex fabric made of many different threads, in which a few common themes repeated by most players often contrast with the many individual narratives and perspectives privately held or shared in the corridors. Good stories may bring effective coordination, swift action, and the *feeling* of well-being or concordance, but not necessarily truth.

Variations of Memory, Imagination, and Predictions

There are probably no better places for people to exercise their penchant for imagination than past and future. Because they are imaginary, they offer a fertile ground for conjecture; and because they form a good part of the context that gives meaning to present perceptions, they are a suitable place for people to insert their (subjective) values, emotions, and desires into the fabric of the (objective) reality. Furthermore, not only this reality is intuitively assumed to be true, but it also *must* be taken as real for life to go on. Players end up living in a world that necessarily blends, albeit in different proportions and with distinct flavors of realism and illusion, the concreteness of the present with the fiction embedded in the other times with which they construct their lives.

The many possible interpretations one can make of time fill human life with ambiguity and lead to vastly different views of reality. Particularly interesting for the social dynamics of families and firms, because they apply the fictions of choice, free-will, and human action to events in which these were not effective, are the *hindsight bias* and the tendency to *regret*. "Finding out that an outcome has occurred increases its perceived likelihood. Judges are, however, unaware of the effect that outcome knowledge has on their perceptions. They tend to believe that this relative inevitability [of history] was largely apparent in foresight, without [taking into account] the benefit [they have] of knowing what happened" ([232]: 297). The same omnipotence fuels the expressions of regret, counterfactual thinking, and blame that fill many criticisms of the players about themselves or others – even when one's diligence is acknowledged, people usually respond to failures or near-misses with the expectation that they or others could have done differently if they "just had" paid attention or acted in a different way [233, 234]. Moreover, these biases foster many of the (false) premises ideologically used in negotiations of value: guilt, blame, resentments, indignation for past deeds, false belief in traumas are some of the many fictitious explanations that hamper the flow of dialogs in which people discuss their pacts because players become trapped in the illusory belief that they could, or even should, return to the past and redo in a better way what they did poorly at the time.

Self-serving optimism, on the one hand, and negativism, on the other, characterize typical distortions of the future. Anxious or risk-prone individuals, families, and firms relish the anticipation of dangers and spend unrealistic amounts of energy on plans to prevent them, regardless of the actual probability of the occurrence or of their capacity to really do anything [235]. Unduly optimistic distortions lead to *planning fallacies*: actors systematically underestimate the time and cost predicted tasks will take, regardless of how many times they may have erred in the past and of the amount of planning spent before initiating the job [236]. Many times these fallacies are inconsequential – in fact, healthy individuals are anchored in their optimism and typically think they are better than they actually are, privilege the good humor at the expense of realism, tend to interpret their errors as derived from chance and successes as self-driven, are easily prey of illusions of control, modify their autobiographies to increase their competence and minimize dissonances, and systematically overestimate their qualities and achievements while underestimating failures and deficiencies (typically, only depressed people are objective about themselves) [237–245]). However, many trivial or catastrophic errors of prediction that fill the live of individuals, countries, and firms also come from these fallacies – from small promises to colleagues, wrong deadlines, failure in anticipating the time required to study for a test up to mistaken estimations of the "right" budget or time to build a monument, to invade a country or to wage a war, history is full of examples of how these unrealistic biases impact people's estimations of reality and lead players to follow their self-serving, grandiose illusions, and not the hardness of the facts [93, 246, 247].

It is uncommon for actors to notice how the fate of these predictions about the future expresses the ambiguity created by the shock between three equally relevant demands of social life – the parallel, but often incompatible mandates to be happy (coloring the past and future with optimism), rational (having a reasonable account of the facts), and moral (committed to the agreements they make). Especially in the firm, where forecasts normatively must be valid (to be realistic), optimistic (to attend the expectations of growth), and binding (to serve as reliable parameters of value), players are often caught in the midst of the trade-offs generated by this multitasking nature of the social game. The same happens in the more intimate world of the families and relationships: whenever serious past or future events dominate the conversation – in general, when money, honor, or divisions of labor, power, and status are at stake – players commonly become lost in dynamics of blame, guilt, regret, and belief in the over-confidence or under-confidence that marks their peculiar predictions of past and future. Without a clear knowledge of how their interpretation of the present facts is influenced by the arbitrary color they give to events that are distant in time, players cannot devise debiasing mechanisms that decrease the unintended consequences of these cognitive shortcuts.

Statistical Anomalies

Exactly in the same way men live in multiple times – the total, emotional, and focal experience of the present informing the predictions about the future or interpretations of the past – actors constantly use their reactions to the current context as cues to computations of probability that lead to inferences about the broader space. Several heuristics, or cognitive shortcuts, play a role in this process: probabilistic judgments are unduly influenced by the easiness with which a certain fact comes to mind (*availability*), by its similarity of the element with the prototype of the category (*representativeness*), by the emotional weight, valence, and saliency of the experience (*affect*), by the rapidity with which it is remembered (*fluency*), and by the first intuitive assessment, from which they make insufficient adjustments (*anchoring and adjustment*). As a consequence of these preferences, practical, contingent, and deeply personal, emotional experiences – the isolated, but strong criticism of a customer, the initial offer in a negotiation, the egocentric self-perspective from which we start when evaluating others, the surprise, impact, or impression of typicality caused by an event – are translated into numbers and unduly transformed into a feature of the (supposedly larger) overall reality about which actors make their judgments [212].

Several violations of the normatively expected reasoning are described as a result of these heuristics. Intuitive decision-makers are typically immune to the effects of sample size, do not take into account the base rates when judging nested probabilities, overvalue confounding variables such as the affective power of an observation, take correlation for causality, and treat statistical probabilities as truths, discounting the existence of chance [248]. A common error is the *fallacy of the small numbers*, by which players tend to consider that a small sample – or even unique events, such as the ones provided by everyday experience – are representative of the larger population of events [249]. People also consistently disregard prior probabilities or base rates, forgetting that small samples always present more extreme results than larger ones (what leads to false-positive and false-negative findings) [250]. Egocentrically, as if men could never be free from the shackles of subjectivity, objective judgments about the real world are based on the subjective *feelings* that come with the present context or arbitrary movement of their soul.

Various imprecise, real-life judgments, ranging from wrong medical diagnoses based on prototypes up to egocentric biases, are part of the players' routine experience [251]. For example, people consistently fail to abstract from their viewpoint and are unable to challenge their preconceived ideas because they are *anchored* on the self-perspective [252]. Illusions related to the *base rate fallacy* led policy planners to invest billions of dollars in creating small schools just because these were overrepresented among schools with exceptionally high performance (disregarding the fact that these were also overrepresented among schools with exceptionally low performance, a consequence of the fact that small samples exhibit more extreme results) [253]. Both in families and firms, the intuitive transformation of random events into systematic or causal models leads to frequent problems when precise definitions of the situation are needed. Moreover, as players have different propensities to apply one or another heuristic depending on the context, as well as vary individually depending on intelligence, statistical training, and attention, the same objective data can lead to several different definitions of the situation, each suggesting different directions for action. Under the usual ideology of truth, without a shared vocabulary that allow actors to detect and deconstruct each other's errors, conflict is inevitable. This understanding puts into question the very basis of rationality, and leads players to the (freeing or nihilistic) exercise of *doubting their own truths.*

Doubts about Truth

One of the more curious paradoxes related to players' definitions of the situation involves the contrast between the actual imprecision that characterizes many of their opinions and the (innate? normative? socially enforced?) preference, value, and weight they attribute to them as *truths,* just because they are framed linguistically. This paradox is manifested in two ways. *First,* as we have seen, the biases and violations of rationality of intuitive judgments based on heuristics generally go unnoticed and are often believed to be true simply because they are presented in the form of formal propositions. *Second*, players are often so fascinated with reason that they do not realize that the same characteristics that bring freedom to the symbolic thinking can also be used to create parallel, unrealistic universes that give to imagination the appearance of truth [254].

Several errors of judgment derive from logical deductions based on false premises. The more common ones come from the attraction with the beauty and internal coherence of moral, theoretical, or strategic systems – hypnotized by the symbol, players become lost in abstract generalizations and fill their conversations with confabulations about how to define or improve empty abstract concepts that only have meaning when anchored on practical games (common examples are self-esteem, creativity, leadership, courage, wisdom, resilience, or culture). Logical deductions based on false assumptions, unpractical metaphysical and scientific systems, or mythical, mystical beliefs in illusions of transcendence and depth fill firms and families with small talk that simply serves as a respite for the duress of reality. A ubiquitous problem arises from the confusion between the world of things and the world of the values: actors conflate their wishes of how things *should* be with their views of what they *are*, trying to fit the real facts of life into models inspired by their beliefs. All discussions involving indignation, resentment, blame, guilt, righteousness, dismay, or other manifestations of a non-acceptance of the world reflect this type of error, preventing any learning that could emerge from the experience [255].[5]

A second problem emerges because many of people's assertions about reality – true or untrue, arising from biases or careful deliberation, based on intuition or on fundaments – become mingled with the social value attributed to the actors within the collective market of identities. Both in the family and in the firm, people feel more powerful, and are consistently seen as more valuable, when they (even if apparently) discover hidden laws, introduce novel or esoteric ideas, think abstractly, or dominate a vocabulary others do not have access to. Rhetoric, fluency, elegance, and presentation are often more relevant than content, leading the audience, and frequently the speaker, to become lost in convincing, but not necessarily true, mentally created social worlds. Short-term success, especially when confirmed by the institutionalized measures of social value (money, intelligence, power, status) is generally a sufficiently good prize that buffers the drive to question the long-term consequences. Furthermore, criticisms directed at one's *ideas* are commonly mixed and felt as directed to the *person*, leading to extreme (often irreversible) polarizations and ruptures of the social game [256]. Error as the sign of an error is mixed with error as accountability or demerit. At this juncture truth shows its dark side, becoming an obstacle, rather than a tool, to the task of organizing. One of the solutions to break the spell of truth – this common mistake, routinely fueled by both intuitive certainties and human hubris – lies in the understanding that, for all its value, rationality is only the tip of the iceberg of a more vast realm of knowledge that involves different apperceptions of reality and tools to acquire control of it [172]. We, then, open the doors of the *world of the tacit*, in which language plays a limited role and actors are forced to accept their incapacity to grasp the totality of reality [257].

The Management of Tacitness and Unconsciousness

Most of individual and organizational life, and for that matter most of human existence, occurs (or *should* occur?) independently of any awareness. Dancing, driving, running a machine, giving a presentation, or simply interacting are properly executed only without the interference of reason and when embedded in a naive certainty about the naturalness of their rules. Families exist because their members assume they know each other, automatically reenact the expected roles, and cherish the unconscious repetition of practices, behaviors, and beliefs upon which they base their conflicts and experiences (parents *should* behave in a certain way, children and adolescents *are* like this, so and so *is* shy or difficult). Firms only function because their past intelligence is coded in the form of dumb processes, which are thoughtlessly repeated or taken as the traditional benchmark against which one develops new doubts and ideas. To the extent that all games must be first learned and then automatized in order to be well played, unconsciousness is the lifeblood of all forms of practical and social life [258].

Especially in the firm, but also in all attempts to formalize values, goals, careers and other aspects of family and personal life, institutionalized views about this tacitness often equate it with inattention or routine, implying that learning necessarily involves explication. The fundamental assumption is that automatic behavior is the primitive source from which one draws the explicit, presumably more reliable systematic beliefs, methodologies, and best practices; these, supposedly, can be put back in practice and eventually internalized as "logical" habits or processes, generating a virtuous cycle of improvements that leads to a permanent expansion of knowledge. Actors are seen as apprehending the world *either* tacitly *or* explicitly, as if tacit and explicit knowledge were separate and independent modes of relating with reality; these are conceived as being always translatable to each other; and learning is described as a process of knowledge conversion by which individuals exchange and amplify their practical or theoretical understandings through socialization (tacit knowledge to tacit knowledge), externalization (tacit to explicit), combination (explicit to explicit), and internalization (explicit to tacit) [259]. The presumption, then, is that that "tacit knowledge is knowledge-not-yet-articulated: a set of rules incorporated in the activity an actor is involved in, which it is a matter of time for him or her to first learn and then formulate" ([260]: 154). The primacy of the (idealized, false) rational decision-making model is therefore guaranteed.

Nothing is more different from reality. *First,* tacit and explicit knowledge are always present in one's life as two sides of the same coin. The understanding of any fact (for example, an interaction) depends on the implicit understanding of the whole model used for interpretation (who we are talking to, which signs mean what, etc.). In the same way, the study of the model depends on the (tacit) assumption that facts are true enough to be used as parameters to evaluate its validity. "If we switch our focal attention to particulars of which we had only a subsidiary awareness before, their meaning is lost and the corresponding action becomes clumsy. If a pianist shifts her attention from the piece she is playing to how she moves the fingers; if a speaker focuses his attention on the grammar he is using instead of the act of speaking; or if a carpenter shifts his/her attention from hitting the nail to holding the hammer, they will be confused. We must rely (to be precise, we must learn to rely) subsidiarily on particulars to attend to something else, hence our knowledge of them remains tacit" ([260]: 146). *Second,* not only we are always blind to the basis of interpretation, but feelings that depend on (intangible, somatic, tacit) evaluations of valence and salience, as well as on judgments of truth, error, propriety, rightness, wrongness, reality, illusion, or value, are untranslatable to the symbolic languages [261]. The whole task of finding meaning, for example – and particularly relevant for our purposes, of infusing meaning in a socially created, fragmented culture – depends on tacit, unspeakable judgments of what is sufficiently beautiful, deep, touching or right to fit our (also unspeakable) ethical, affective, and aesthetic *feelings* about how life should proceed.

The scope of tacit knowledge, then, involves three types of facts: those that simply remain outside of awareness, due to the limits of our attention; those necessary for the definition of a situation of execution of a practice, which must remain implicit for the task to be developed; and those that necessarily remain tacit because they transcend the grammatical and semantic limitations of the language game. Furthermore, as players vary on which things they pay attention to, on the games they are playing, and on the (tacit) rules by which they evaluate their lives, there are as many barriers between tacitness and awareness as there are communicating or thinking beings in the place. These boundaries shift with the context of communication, with external pressures, with the predominance of top-down or bottom-up mechanisms of attention, and with all movements of consciousness: every time a theme takes the center of the stage the accessory or unrelated knowledge moves to the darkness of the scene, supporting the main line of action or simply waiting to be called again to the awareness. Group dynamics, as it exists in families, business, or any social systems, adds an extra layer of complexity to the interplay between tacit and explicit.

Each of the layers in which we can divide the realm of tacitness involves a different type of management. There are concepts and practices that can be easily brought to attention, because they have already been explicated at some point (the realm of management). There is knowledge that has never been explicated but is potentially translatable into symbolic language (the realm of learning, innovation, and hermeneutics). Finally, there is a lower, inaccessible layer of tacitness that involves all elements than can never actually be made explicit but are daily lived in practice whenever players have repeated experiences with a certain type of game (the realm of the expert). Part of the task of organizing, particularly relevant for cultures intent on breaking the (ideological) spell of truth, involves making individuals and groups aware of these differences so that actors may, at least to the limit of their capacity, understand each other's fluctuations and work toward an alignment that allows some communication.

The more superficial layer of tacitness involves all transient, purely contingent manifestations of tacit knowledge that are implicit just because they have been momentarily excluded from focal awareness [262]. A mechanic testing a car first concentrates on the traffic and pushes his knowledge of the engine to the realm of the tacit, but smoothly and voluntarily forgets the route and pays attention to the noises and feelings when evaluating the machine; proficient social actors are able to swiftly change their demeanor as they move from a collective situation to a private conversation, from home to work, or from work to a pub [263]; and well-informed strategic discussions naturally alternate moments in which they address the competitors, the suppliers, the buyers, the substitutes, and the threat of new entrants as they cover the status of the competitive landscape [264]. In all these examples, as soon as a theme, practice, or way of being comes to the fore, others recede to the background and remain dormant in the expectation of a new instant of attention. Moreover, for the individual the change from tacit to explicit and back to tacit occurs smoothly, automatically, *tacitly*.

Two common problems of organization are related to the management of this layer. First, players who do not understand (or accept) that their conversations are ruled by both top-down and bottom-up mechanisms of attention are easily swept by unnecessary digressions that come from the free flow of the practice *and* by rigid pre-determined directions that prevent the treatment of relevant problems or nested questions. Meetings, for example, are commonly criticized for being too structured or too loose, according to how they prevent emergent meanings or let players follow their intuitions and the flow of the conversation. Both in the family and in the firm, the meanders of conversation, never-ended topics, or abrupt changes are often seen as distractions that ought to be contained for the conversation to continue in an efficient manner; few players see that these are also linked to spontaneity, identification, and exploration. The (unsolvable) trade-off, of course, is between creativity and participation, on one side, *versus* efficiency and power, on the other. Furthermore, in order to shift gracefully from one theme to the other, without feeling they are losing the track, actors must have a sufficiently broad, flexible worldview based on paradoxes, trade-offs, and ambiguities (more than on truths or intuitive pseudo-certainties). Actors, leaders, and change agents need, then, to deal with the limitations of *learning* – the long and difficult task of developing a culture that privileges the mechanisms of reflection and deconstruction and takes into considerations all the problems that characterize the second, less superficial layer of tacitness.

A second layer of tacitness includes all modes of knowledge that are potentially tractable by reason, but have seldom or never been object of explicit attention. All constituents of this layer have in common the "amenability to reification: the possibility of creating products that can be used by acculturated actors (e.g., books and standards), incorporated in technical devices (e.g. gears and software) that can then produce an output accepted within a given collectivity", or that can be used as arguments in the scientific or sensemaking narratives used to explain or predict reality ([262]: 343). The actual extent to which this knowledge is actually codified, however, depends on the technological development of each group, on the awareness that actors have about potentially new forms of organization, and on the resistance offered by social players to the process of explication, self-understanding, and deconstruction.

The attitude that actors have about this layer of tacitness strongly influences the type and depth of learning they experience. In general, the exploitative mode is associated with small, incremental improvements of the tasks, routines, or ways of life that have been successful in the past – families, firms, groups, cultures, and civilizations are then more self-absorbed, and learning is customarily restricted to imitation and restricted to searches in the nearby context or influenced by the fads and fashions that determine the ideal proclaimed by contemporary benchmarks [265, 266]. Slightly more curious actors are open to question their taken-for-granted technologies and ways of life, actively looking for potential novelties or new combinations of concepts and practices reachable through processes of innovation and scientific discovery [59] – disruptive innovations that shake the bases of their technical and organizational routines, or a revamping of the standard interpretations of the family or firm [174, 262]. Finally, in the extreme of this continuum, just beyond what is pleasurably recombined by creative innovations and deconstructions, lies an almost inaccessible mode of knowledge, still translatable to the usual formal languages but seldom brought up to the surface because it falls beyond the precincts of the known practices or accepted paradigms of the person, group, or era [267].

For the individual, this deeper, darker, and often unconscious set of tacit understandings and premises of the game found in the second layer involves everything one is not able to admit even to oneself, the unconscious blind spots whose illumination would shake the foundations of the self- or worldview, the opposites of what is postulated as existent and valuable for the social actor, the anti-truths that destroy the foundations of that particular entity or association, the axioms that guarantee the "firmness" of the prevailing truths about one's identity or reality. For the group, it includes all the hidden agendas, personal secrets, resentments, deviant thoughts, or value choices that openly defy the "being" of the community; and the unspoken or unspeakable truths, the taboos that should not be brought to fore lest they disrupt the engrossment of the moment and lay bare the core of illusion required for actors to feel themselves, spontaneously immersed in the game [71]. Since addressing these practices and themes under the rules of the language game would open up the possibility of doubt, they generally remain deeply hidden, potent distractors that if brought up to consciousness could invalidate the operational purpose of any interaction and invite to a discussion about its bases.

Many of the most important features of family businesses, as of any social system involving personal attachments, are defined by the porosity, overture, or closure of the system to the questioning of the concepts and practices relegated to this second layer of tacitness. Thus, some families accept talking about power and status, others not; in some kinship groups individual differences are respected or even stimulated, in others collective norms are coercively enforced; and in almost all, if not all family businesses one sees some basic points – the myths of foundation or identity, the lines of tradition and belief, the values of honesty, truth and interest, the taboos prohibiting incest, property violation, or fraternal violence – that cannot ever be questioned without breaking the tacit rules of belonging required to be accepted as a member. Similar untouchable assumptions define the existence of the firm: profit, capital, hierarchy, submission to the rules, and institutionalized models of governance usually defy the erosion of doubt and in most cases remain forever true as the solid axioms that form the backbone of the social system. Codifiable in theory, but never codified in practice, these themes are the most difficult to be treated by any work of cultural change based on the proposal of truth. They close the layer of transient tacit knowledge and forecast the beginning of the third and deepest zone of tacitness, one that is completely inaccessible to any treatment by formal languages.

The last, more profound and impervious layer of tacitness involves elements of knowledge that are irreducibly linked to one's physical and social experience of the world and of the self. All this knowledge is self-referential, because it involves an intentional movement of consciousness by which actors apprehend the flow of life in relation to their personal perspective [268]; is physically embodied, because these judgments are ultimately referred to one's feelings, senses, sensations, and emotions [269]; and is socially embedded, because it involves judgments that are made in relation to the total set of (internalized, unconscious, inaccessible) directions, rules, parameters, and prescriptive or descriptive categories that constitute the collective form of life in which the actor is socialized [270].

The physically embodied component of tacitness, or somatic tacit knowledge, refers to "abilities and characteristics acquired in an unconscious way due to the nature of the interaction with the physical world within a form of life" ([261]: 70). In the line, for example, it includes many problems that fall even marginally outside the automated database: any updates, redesigns, or mistake corrections dependent on tacit, action-oriented rules extracted from how workers apprehend the noises, texture, temperature, or color of the raw material and deal in practice with the mechanized product of knowledge [257]. In the family and in the social world, it involves the internalized feelings of disgust, shame, propriety, impropriety, right, wrong, fit or misfit that are physically *felt* as emotional signals of truth or error [271]. Because the actual meaning of these bodily metaphors depends on relating the bodily contact one has with the world to the social meaning of the sensation, it cannot be taught, transmitted, or communicated except by close contact with other experienced actors who have already learned the rules of connection.

The socially embedded component of tacitness – "the ability to fully participate in a form of life" [270] – links our personal experience to the social use we make of it. "This means, for instance, being able to stop the 'regress of rules' with regard to applying instructions and standards as expected, as well as acting smoothly or improvising within a (technical) culture"; it involves displaying a proper behavior in any situation; or just understanding and reacting swiftly to the behavior of others during the nuanced modulations of a social game ([262]: 339).

Exactly as one cannot make a move in game without a grasp of its goals and of all the rules on which it is based, it is impossible to understand a social norm, an entity, a subjective state, or a cognitive category without the (tacit) knowledge of the full set of phenomena from which the particular event is taken; it is also impossible to judge the correctness of an idea or specific practice except in relation to how social players enact, use, live, and judge that same experience. These judgments of value – which define for each task and in different moments what is considered similar or different, relevant or not, good or bad, correct or incorrect – are irreducibly embedded in the social life of actors who are always defining their consensus about what should be done in any particular matter.[6]

Experts, those who master a complex social, strategic, or operational game, are therefore essential to any deep project of organizational culture. "The first ability of a fully acculturated person is that they are able to 'follow a rule' in the Wittgensteinian sense. This stands for the ability to act smoothly and speedily within a form of life, including being able to improvise when facing new and unexpected situations, to evaluate when it is acceptable to break a rule and how to do it. Of special relevance for leaders and change agents interested in fostering a creative environment, "only full-blown members of such groups are able to modify or propose new rules (either explicitly or tacitly)" ([262]: 343–5). Expert thinkers are necessary for families and firms as examples of mastership and creativity in their own type of game, introducing new forms to use a machine, organize a plant, carry a negotiation, or lead people and institutions toward an idealistic goal [272].

Tacitness, then, is an integral part of the life of individuals, families, and firms. It surreptitiously directs how people organize their definitions of the situation, adding another layer of instability to the truths created by cognitive biases, ontological oscillation, ambiguity, and shifting, arbitrary perspective-taking. At the same time, as a reminder of the many paradoxes of organization, it is on these fragile, unstable definitions of the situation that players, leaders, and change agents must ground their strategies and sculpt the change or culture they search for. They are the routine test situations to which actors respond with habit, deliberations, indifference, reactivity, or curiosity. They are the engines of both tradition and change: when prior definitions of situation are confirmed by experience, they are generally accepted as true or categorized as normal problems, which trigger normal mechanisms of search; when there is a dissonance between expectations and how the events unfold, or when novelty appears as a possibility, conflict, doubt, ennui, pain, or inquisitiveness signal an error [273]. Both actors and cultures, if they want to fully embrace their own contradictions, must thus integrate truth, doubt, and error into some form of creative, playful, meaningful learning [274].

Organizational Culture and Paradoxes in Management: Truth, Doubt, and Error

To the extent that players always respond to what they see as reality, and reality is a platform that often proves to be untrue or insufficient, the everyday definitions of the situation that guide one's actions must be framed as part of a process that encompasses past, current, potentially future, and unseen concepts and meanings. Learning, and in particular organizational learning, emerges then as an answer to stabilize the inconstancy of the world of ideas – a second-order solution for unstable theories previously created to stabilize the unstable world of practice, a creative game for the spirit, a tool to promote alignment, illusion, or sensemaking. Whatever its use, this learning always involves some type of translation. To intuitive actors, definitions of the situation appear generally as concrete, specific facts and stories with which they organize their practical life around the typical themes of the place: kinship, relatedness, ties, history, discussions, name, lineage and honor in the family, or the various objects of activity and interconnected problems that surround the purpose and organization of the firm [275]. To learning players, on the other hand, the same definitions of the situation are puzzles to be solved or truths to be deconstructed, riddles that hide more stable patterns, or models that encompass previous theories or practices and may be used to illuminate unseen aspects of the worlds of practice and of the ideas (the two universes that govern human life). One of the fundamental tasks of the organization of knowledge and doubt is to create context conditions that maximize the probability and efficiency of this game.

Regardless as how this back-and-forth translation is conceived – as stemming from practice to theory, and thus grounding learning in experience, or as prioritizing the previous theories about the world, giving prominence to the ideas – learning always involves some type of generalization. The general forms revealed by this translation may appear tacitly as the premises on which the (always theory-laden) expertise, routines, and facts of life are grounded, or may be explicit in the form of theoretical models that explain how the practice works and how people think about it. In either form, abstractions are indispensable tools for the game of learning to be played in its full extension. They need to be explicated and become objects of thought for actors to become proficient in the art of reasoning about their own reason.

Culture as Learning: Abstractions

Any process of learning, thus, involves the development of a tacit or explicit model of reality that purportedly exposes its structure, dynamics, and the causal, probabilistic, or symbolic relations that connect its elements; and a model of how ideas are created and manipulated when actors think about this reality or their own thinking during the process of learning. When explicated and applied back to real life, this framework works as a lens to approach the facts and the ideas about them; from the new perspectives it offers come new contexts of interpretation, language formulations, and tools to manipulate the practice; and from the use of these tools one should ideally reach not only successful responses, but also meaningful generalizations to similar situations. New ideas have to be put back in practice for learning to have any existential meaning – and as in a circle in which ideas and practices revitalize each other, learning, organizational learning, and culture become fused with each other as inextricable parts of the same mechanism of change.

Learning about this process of learning, a third-order game that questions the interplay of truth, doubt, error, and change during the process of creating definitions of situation, involves the study of the processes through which experience, innovation, and scholarship lead to tacit or explicit expertise. Practically, proficiency in this game brings fluidity to the tasks of creating, criticizing, inventing, and deconstructing the definitions of situation that constitute the family, the firm, and their games. Theoretically, it leads to the creation of comprehensive, flexible, abstract frameworks that attempt to explain how learning occurs and the pitfalls on which people commonly fall when trying uncritically to solve the problems of life – a vocabulary, specialized jargon, or organized methodology that works simultaneously as a toolkit of concepts and practices to act on reality, an instrument to effect change, an abstract object of knowledge to be modified with new inputs, and an important instrument of sensemaking that diverts players from the tendency to frame mistakes as conflicts and introduces the possibility of a broader perspective conducive to coordination. The so desired alignment promised by the usual technologies of change becomes, then, anchored *not* on clear strategies, goals, values, or missions, but on a shared understanding of how various, disparate definitions of situation are created and negotiated in social systems - a larger meta-view in which silence, error, truth, doubt, and learning are linked to each other as parts of a process from which (hopefully) arise progressively more ample views of reality.

A first component of this abstract framework involves a typology of the situations commonly addressed by the actors. Weaver, for example, distinguishes between problems of simplicity, in which quantifiable variables can be understood in the form of relations of cause and effect; disorganized complexities, treated by statistical methods that show the patterns followed by a large number of variables that behave randomly, simultaneously, and independently of each other; and problems of organized complexities, such as living beings, people, families, and firms, that "involve dealing simultaneously with a sizable number of factors which are interrelated into an organic whole" ([276]: 538–9). Rittel separated tame problems, commonly treatable by normal science, from wicked problems characteristic of social settings: the latter involve situations inherently "ill-formulated, where the information is confusing, where there are many clients and decision-makers with conflicting values, and where the ramifications in the whole system are thoroughly confusing" ([277]: B-141). Simon showed how these distinctions depend on the granularity of observation and on how they accept mechanization or formalization or defy this form of organization because they are immersed in ambiguity: "In general, the problems presented to problem solvers by the world are best regarded as ill structured problems. They become well-structured problems only in the process of being prepared for problem solvers. It is not exaggerating much to say that there are not well structured problems, only ill structured problems that have been formalized for problem solvers" ([278]:186). Becker and colleagues, echoing Schumpeter and Winter, focus on the problems brought by the pursuit of novelty and innovation – unseen forms of organization and structuration of reality that stem from creativity, genius, lunacy, or alienation, but that nevertheless transcend the limits of the experience because they disregard adaptive success and prioritize novel, unthought-of definitions of the situation [59].

These four fuzzy, intuitive typologies suggest that some situations are better tractable by a technology of truth, others by a technology of doubt, others by counter-intuitive explorations that go beyond the search for immediate adaptation. For the first, it is useful (and many times sufficient) to smoothen the equivocalities and define rigid processes of transformation, sacrificing the potential advantages of finding new solutions or formulations of the problem to maximize the speed, efficiency, and productivity of the already available routines – prototypically, processes that transform relatively well-understood, uniform, and stable raw materials using technologies that use analyzable, rationally developed search procedures to address few, familiar exceptions (several industrial processes, logistics, routines that do not involve the human factor or simple enough to allow the automatism). For the second, doubt, bet, and expertise are the norms – all problems that defy operationalization due to their many exceptions, in which "search processes are always exceptional actions undertaken by the individual" and the raw material is so poorly understood that "continual adjustment to it is necessary" and standardization is not possible [279]. For the third, exploration and acceptance of error, waste, failure, and negligence of the lessons of experience is the rule – since most new ideas are bad, and it is impossible to distinguish which ones will prove true by their initial appearance, actors have to cling their (true? foolish?) ideals of change *despite* error signals that come from their attrition with the practice [1].

The latter two groups comprise the really interesting problems in administration and in life – the complex, multitasking situations in which a single activity aims at satisfying multiple goals and objectives [80]; the consequent trade-offs, which oppose incompatible, equally relevant goals into a single structure of choice [280]; all ambiguous situations, contexts in which equivocality is the norm and many plausible definitions of the situation compete to become the truth [219]; most problems situated in the structural holes that separate different provinces of meaning – issues pertaining to two divisions in a firm, related both to the family and to the firm, to two cousins or employees who do not really know each other, to two people, or to any process of communication that needs to traverse a bridge over a place of scarce information [281]; and everything that lies beyond the realm of the already seen [282]. In particular, we place here all the disputes pertaining to value, justice, good, or evil, as well as the deepest affective issues in a family or meaningful social game and the deeper, paradigmatic changes required for technological, social, organizational, or scientific disruption. In these cases, "there is nothing like the undisputable public good [or right culture]; there is no objective definition of equity; policies cannot be meaningfully correct or false; and it makes no sense to talk about 'optimal solutions' unless severe qualifications are imposed first. Even worse, there are no 'solutions' in the sense of definitive and objective answers" ([283]: 155). The task of organization, then, becomes fundamentally dependent on the understanding of the conditions of the ambiguity, on flexibility in the valuation of error, on the experience of novelty, and on the acceptance that these are expected cases in a continuum of definitions of situations of which the truth hypothesis is just an extreme – contexts of irreducible indefiniteness that require a decision, a transient bet that may serve as a platform for individual and collective action.

The structural, conditioning forms and limits of rationality explored in this chapter suggest that many of the contradictions and complementarities observed when individuals, families, and firms process information occur because the same data are treated (in parallel) in a number of different ways, are organized in various different forms, and serve a number of different functions. The truths reached (or created) by the use of these various channels provide multiple, incompatible directions for one's thinking. They are, therefore, both relevant tools to be used during the task of organization *and* obstacles to any alignment that does not include the meta-conditions that determine the creation of the dissonant ideas and worldviews on which the system's practices and discourses are grounded. At the risk of reviewing briefly of what has already been said extensively, we can organize them by pointing the various ambiguities and loopholes that appear during the long process of truth-creation – in general, four steps of organization that encompass various points of inflexion, choice, and doubt whose unfolding results, as in the plot of a real-life story, in the final the definition of the "objective" facts with which actors contend (see Appendix 2, Figure 2).

The study of the first step of this process of truth-creation shows that most information received by individuals, families, or firms is never processed because it is discarded as noise or simply goes unattended. Even when one discards this deeper layers of unconsciousness, however, two points are relevant for the task of organization: *(a)* a substantial amount of this information is never processed consciously but influences thought, feeling, action, and choice [284–286]; and *(b)* the bases of interpretation to which all data are compared – the rules by which we understand and process the stimuli physically and socially – cannot be made explicit (there is no way a game can explain its own rules) [28]. These points lead to the acceptance that *expertise* – the development of a loose, intuitive framework with which to analyze the common social, operational, or strategic games of every day – is a necessary part of the organization of culture.

Second, once stimuli enter into the individual and collective realm of intelligence where conscious truths are created, the processing of information is made through different lenses and mechanisms. These lead to different definitions of the situation and are then *felt* as paradoxical (we easily forget that truths only exist in relation to the conditions of their creation). Relevant points, here, include: *(a)* there are two systems of thought, one comprising the fast, automatic, intuitive responses to the world of practice (System 1), and another the abstract, costly, deliberate processes of doubt, induction, and deduction that form the world of ideas (System 2) [185]; *(b)* there are top-down and bottom-up mechanisms of attention, each of them prioritizing different stimuli and therefore creating different accounts of the many context [287]; *(c)* explicit and tacit knowledge occur in parallel and support each other [260]; *(d)* the search for knowledge can be prolonged and exhaustive, as suggested by rational maximizing procedures, or obey satisficing heuristics and stop as soon as satisfactory (but not optimal) solutions are found [173]; *(e)* various heuristics developed for several different purposes during the evolution of the species bias the processing of information and lead to different variations in the ensuing definitions of the situation (some of them useful, others detrimental [209, 210, 217, 288]). These points lead us to accept that rationality is not the norm, but a deviation of the expected; and that many times it may be more *useful* to bypass the canonical directions of thought and privilege action, to go on with life.

Third, regardless of their origin, or of how attention, biases, context, tacitness, awareness are combined to create "final" definitions of the situation, these are present to players as explicit propositions organized in the form of language. Conscious thoughts, however, express different truths: *(a)* definitions of the situation may be uncertain, when they involve unknown risks, and may be ambiguous, in the sense of allowing multiple potentially true interpretations [176]; *(b)* definitions of the situation may be created before the fact, as a way to prepare the decision, after the fact, as a form of post hoc sensemaking explanations, or during the fact, as a result of communication. Each goal involves different priorities and leads to different facts [289]; *(c)* language can be used to create myth and fiction, identity stories and collective explanations, or rational accounts aiming for truth; these are often mixed in the same narrative [188]; *(d)* narratives and mathematical formalizations are different forms of treating the same data and transform the object of knowledge by virtue of the methods they use [26]; and *(e)* reason can be inserted in various points of the decision tree (deliberation, reflection, deconstruction, search for novelty, or imagination, each of them with a function). These situations, in turn, are socially shaped by dialogs and counter-dialogs: *(a)* consensus and dissensus are constructed through social mechanisms that, by themselves, create their own truths [15]; *(b)* knowledge is intimately connected with power, identity, emotions, influence, and value [62]; and *(c)* experiential learning is limited by small samples, noise, ambiguity, and effects of context; innovation is risky and, more often than not, fails [26]. Reason, then, is clearly unable to grasp in any reliable way the structure of the world we live in – individuals, firms, and families are bound to live and act based on their bounded rationality, mixing moments in which it works with other instances where the flow stops and it is necessary to halt the action in order to think (and hopefully, learn).

To this realistic, but somewhat gloomy account of human reason, however, we must then oppose the need to live and act. Regardless of how correct, incorrect, consensual, or solitary their definitions of the situation are, people must still daily decide why, when, and how to continue with life or talk about it; to start and end the potentially endless discussions about relationships, future, past, or strategy; to acknowledge the relevance of the always-present nested problems that surround any situation or, instead, focus on a problem and disregard the effects of complexity; to let a meeting follow its emergent course or a pre-planned, rational (or myopic?) path; and to decide when, how, where, and why an error will be treated as a problem to be studied, as something to be discarded because the ideal is too distant, or as a failure to be punished according to the expected (moral) norms of accountability. All these questions, of course, introduce an element of subjectivity in the core of the apparently objective nature of the problem. It is a value, a *taste*, a habit, or a social convention, and never a neutral parameter based simply on the factual reality, what distinguishes the relevant from the unimportant, the good from the bad, the useful from the useless, the right from the wrong (and, therefore, the true from the untrue) [290]. The task of instilling the drive to change and learn inside the culture, therefore, depends in creating suitable contexts for error and conflict to be accepted, and therefore for actors to become experts in the conditions that constrain and give form to the game of information.

Culture in the Practice: Learning from Experience and Novelty

Learning how to learn is an expertise like any other – a mostly tacit understanding acquired only after players repeatedly experience similar situations in relatively repetitive contexts and eventually develop the ability to "intuitively" recognize patterns, discern ambiguities, move quickly from interpretation to interpretation or from an action to another [257, 262, 272]. Change and learning, in these cases, harness several fundamentally human drives – curiosity, dissonance decrease, closure – to counteract the equally innate, path-dependent, or self-interested tendency to inertia. Error, novelty, and the emotional response to them are the main factors that take persons, families and organizations out of the repetitive practices by which they transform their routines, habits, internal processes, rituals, and technologies into needs in search of a discharge and become prey of the (right or wrong) truths they contain [291].

Experiential learning is linked with a mismatch between the actors' theories of action and the problems they are called to solve – facts and events that cause conflict, anxiety, anger, frustration, suffering shock, or surprise. By studying the small, but existentially relevant sample of their personal experiences, people find the motivation to detach momentarily from the practice and see the game from above, trying to distinguish its structuring forces in order to reframe the situation according to a better lens. The more actors are open to spend resources analyzing in depth the context, the thicker are the descriptions from which they can extract the desired meaning [292]. The basic questions are: *What* is happening? Where am *I* wrong? What am *I* not seeing? Typically, when the explanatory template created by these questions is derived exclusively from the experience, it tends to be narrower and limited to concrete situations – after repeated, reflective exposure to the same context actors may learn from the practice and develop some expertise, but commonly fail to take into account solutions that do not originate from the present conditions. This myopic learning, in turn, can be counterbalanced by new perspectives found through innovations and explorations of how other times, cultures and peoples have treated the subjects of interest – families, firms, culture, communication, power, information, or the very process of truth creation (see Appendix 2, Figures 8 and 9).

Attending to one's immediate practice, therefore, is insufficient to illuminate unseen, optimal ways of being. Thus, any culture that prioritizes learning from innovation, novelty, different contexts, or active search, in opposition to only learning from the experience, depends on a willful, methodical or alienated disregard for the error signals derived from the attrition of the invention with the current (supposedly archaic, changeable, or amenable to disruption) conditions of the practice. "Both exploitation and exploration involve searching for improvement. But exploitative search is largely conducted in the course of normal business [or life], looking for improvements in the context of the current agenda and model or for fairly limited extensions of them. Exploration involves search over broader domains, looking for new opportunities outside the current paradigm. It necessarily involves much greater uncertainty, both as to whether anything will be found and then whether it is actually better. It fundamentally depends on slack – that resources be allocated to uses that contribute little or nothing to executing on the current strategy" ([2]: 257).

Given this inherent opposition between exploration and exploitation, skepticism and truth, or constructions and deconstructions of reality, the organization of learning in the culture – the attempt to integrate the ever-appearing dissonances of life into the form of a meaningful cycle of knowledge creation – is never an easy task. In practice, creativity and openness to novelty are associated with positive feelings and hampered by the detail-oriented, while narrow-focus is triggered by pressures and anxiety [293]; a mildly delusional sense of optimism, omnipotence, or courage, often associated with charisma and social power, generally results in real achievements (or at least fame) [246]; and the ability to create good, rather than bad futures, to see oneself as happy, rather than unhappy, or to engage in positive, rather than negative speculations, is a fundamental (although biased) tool to achieve the well-being that fosters curiosity [294]. These (institutionalized) practices and beliefs, in turn, are opposed to the focus, persistence, and perfectionism required to foster incremental, quality-oriented circles of learning. There is a relevant trade-off between accepting error as a material for learning, and not as a matter worthy of punishment – leaders and change agents have to constantly decide, in the presence of strong asymmetries of information, guile, disinterest, incompetence, moral hazard, groupthink, and organizational silence, whether an error should separated for study, punished, pursued, or discarded as irrelevant [8, 1, 146, 183, 295, 296].

Theoretically, the (mythical, idealistic or pragmatic) combination of the world of practice, the world of ideas, and the world of imagination and exploration provides the ideal situation for learning. On one side of the learning field is the abstract lens, which as a common vocabulary or model aimed at more general definitions of the situation structures the practice according to concepts that tend to be general, rather than specific; impersonal, rather than personal; based on the study of the broader contexts, and not on dispositions of character or specific situations; directed to the future and not to the past; and making explicit the variables involved in the irreducible trade-offs and ambiguities that make concrete problems unsuitable to treatment by usual mechanisms of truth. On the other side is the practical situation, which enriches the abstraction by bringing unexpected nested problems or tacit nuances observable only to players who are on the ground, immersed in the practice and attentive to details unpredicted by the theory. Mediating and disrupting this encounter are experts attentive to patterns, tacit knowledge, wicked, or ill-structured problems and also all innovators, deviants, and creative thinkers who explore the imprecisions inherent to the interface between idea and practice and look for new solutions in the culture or in the unknown. In the particular case of family businesses, this three-way avenue of learning is a step toward crossing the chasm created by the traditional rules of the family, by which only the elderly or powerful know what to do, and the managerial myth, by which some actors have power to think while others are supposed to execute (a remnant of the ideals of perfect rationality).

A culture that values both learning and action should, then, blend truth and doubt, emotion and reason, tacit and explicit knowledge into a single set of practices and concepts. Two relevant trade-offs are traversed in this way. The rational search for the fundament (which brings depth) becomes closely associated with the pursuit of action (which leads to efficiency); and doubt makes players more able to ponder, devise hypotheses, or plunge into the infinite regress of the rules, while the ability to halt the skepticism and postulate a truth makes one able to create and use the "knowledge" required to proceed with life. Ultimately, by working as a tool to organize the practice, the ideas about the practice, the ideas about ideas, and how these evolve in time, the process of learning about learning anchors the culture on a basic, archaic and instinctive lever of change – the *taste* to engage in the creative destruction of reason [58]. For the socially constructed fiction of culture, and frequently for the success of the family or firm, it is often irrelevant whether this learning in fact leads to more powerful definitions of the situation, or, alternatively, only colors the ordered succession of paradigms with the *feeling* of evolution. Both bring alignment, and with it the (transient, fragile, unstable) coordination required for concerted action.

When implemented in the practice and shared as a game that marks the culture of the place, compiling the main types of problems, trade-offs, pathways, loopholes, and dead-ends involved in creating reliable and valid definitions of the situation, this abstract framework that describes the process of learning works as a common platform for players to understand how they think and negotiate their differences, an extra tool to facilitate the task of organizing. A vocabulary that embraces ambiguity minimizes the dangers brought by naive realism; substitutes conflict at the abstract level for personal quarrels about what to do; and thus acts as a buffer to unnecessary epistemic disruptions. What it does not do, however, is to solve the irreducible arbitrariness of choice. Eventually, the search for more ample solutions for the dissonances or for an abstract understanding about what is happening is counteracted by the need to go on with life. Meetings and discussions *must* be stopped; doubts and conflicts *have to be* solved; nested problems *ought to* be explored to bring depth or left out to guarantee the focus; and trade-offs *do* demand solutions, lest life stops for lack of a decision. At these moments, in matters of taste and value, there is no criterion of validity to which men can resort to solve their differences.

The ideal of infusing learning into the culture, which in principle solves the trade-off between truth and doubt, does not, therefore, put an end to the ambiguities of life. Ideals have to be socially enacted to become true; and when the world of ideas reaches the world of practice, the irreducible kernel of arbitrariness that looms beneath all routine definitions about preferences inevitably bring actors against each other. Ultimately, there is neither logical nor objective rule that defines *when* to stop or initiate truth or doubt; in particular, there are no common rules that define, for any group in which there are many perspectives about the same fact or decision point, which is the true one. Moreover, actors, leaders and change agents have to sort out themes that *could* be studied and made explicit from those that *should* not, depending on the (always arbitrary) values that guide them. The same values of joy, ethics, aesthetics and affect that for some are worth the pursuit for others are waste, naiveté, or ideological cover-up. There is no ethical neutrality in a project of culture – and this leads us into the world of the choices, the realm of emotions, power, status, values, and taste [297].

Notes

1 Consider Burrell & Morgan's analysis of the interpretive, functionalist, radical structuralist, and radical humanist paradigms uncovered beneath organizational theories: "Each of the paradigms is treated in terms consistent with its own distinctive frame of reference. No attempt is made to criticize and evaluate from a perspective *outside* the paradigm. Such criticism is all too easy but self-defeating, since it is usually directed at the foundations of the paradigm itself (...) Destructive critique would have been a simple task. By assuming a posture in a rival paradigm, it would have been possible to demolish the contribution of any individual text or theoretical perspective" ([40]: xii, 395).

2 "When in the mind of man, appetites and aversions, hopes and fears, concerning one and the same thing, arise alternately; and diverse good and evil consequences of the doing, or omitting the thing propounded, come successively into our thoughts ... the whole sum of desires, aversions, hopes and fears, continued till the thing be either done, or thought impossible, is that we call deliberation. (...) And it is called *de-liberation* because it is a putting an end to the liberty we had of doing, or omitting, according to our own appetite or aversion" ([65]: 64).

3 Weick shows how the seven properties of sensemaking are built around the valuation of a personal perspective of the "I": "*1. Identity*: The recipe is a question about who I am, as indicated by discovery of how and what I think. *2. Retrospect*: To learn what I think, I look back over what I said earlier. *3. Enactment*: I create the object to be seen and inspected when I say or do something. *4. Social component*: What I say and single out and conclude are determined by who socialized me and how I was socialized, as well as by the audience I anticipate will audit the conclusions I reach. *5. Ongoing nature*: My talking is spread across time, competes for attention with other ongoing projects, and is reflected on after it is finished, which means my interests may already have changed. *6. Extracted cues*: The 'what' that I single out and embellish as the content of the thought is only a small portion of the utterance that becomes salient because of context and personal dispositions. *7. Plausibility:* I need to know enough about what I think to get on with my

projects, but no more, which means sufficiency and plausibility take precedence over accuracy" ([192]: 61–2).

4 "Against the positivism which halts at phenomena – 'There are only facts' – I would say: no, facts are just what there aren't, there are only interpretations. We cannot determine any fact 'in itself': perhaps it's non-sensical to want to do such a thing. 'Everything is subjective', you say: but that itself is an *interpretation*, for the 'subject' is not something given but a fiction added on, tucked behind. – Is it even necessary to posit the interpreter behind the interpretation? Even that is fiction, hypothesis. Inasmuch as the word 'knowledge' has any meaning at all, the world is knowable: but it is variously *interpretable;* it has no meaning behind it, but countless meanings. 'Perspectivism'. It is our needs *which interpret the world*: our drives and their for and against. Every drive is a kind of lust for domination, each has its perspective, which it would like to impose as a norm on all the other drives" ([27]: 139, Book 7:60).

5 "In every system of morality, which I have hitherto met with, I have always remarked that the author proceeds for some time in the ordinary way of reasoning, and establishes the being of a God, or makes observations concerning human affairs; when of a sudden I am surprised to find, that instead of the usual copulations proposition, *is,* and *is not,* I meet with no proposition that is not connected with an *ought,* or an *ought not.* This change is imperceptible; but is, however, of the lasting consequences. For as this *ought,* or *ought not,* expresses some new relation of affirmation, it is necessary that it should be observed and explained; and at the same time that a reason should be given, for what seems altogether unconceivable, how this new relation can be a deduction from others, which are entirely different from it" ([298]: 3.1.2).

6 The problem of the regress of the rules – expressed in the proposition that "no rules contain the rules for their own application" – indicates that every proposition of meaning makes sense only in relation to a whole system of meanings that constitute the set composed by all rules of the game (which *must* remain implicit for the conversation to continue). Since games get their fundament from meta-games, which, in turn, need other meta-games to justify their rules, the only solution to stop the epistemological cycle of infinite regress rests in the tacit, sociological realm: concepts, meanings, rules, and practices are embedded in shared forms of life, which by the mere fact of being lived in the world of practice justify the stop of the regress and the (arbitrary) classification of the construct as "knowledge" ([261]: 28) (see Appendix 2, Figure 7).

4 Value, Meaning, and Power

> "Life itself is not a means to something. It is merely a growth-form of power. (...) What decides rank is the quantum of power that you are. The rest is cowardice" ([27]: Notebooks 16 [13] and 11[35]).

The fundamental insight (or metaphor?) of Nietzsche – that regardless of its altruistic or egocentric color, each single value contains in itself an ethereal will to power that is common to all different motives – suggests that every form of organization is, always, the end-result of a composition of different egoisms that compete with each other. Beneath these egoisms are emotions, pointed vectors of meaning that suggest preferred routes of realization. Beneath the emotions are tacit or explicit worldviews, which give them form and direction. Value, meaning, and power are inextricably linked as different facets of the same phenomenon, the joint expression of a drive and a connected worldview that together discharge their quantum of power by forcing a way into reality.

One of the greatest side effects of the emphasis currently placed on describing the world "as it is" is the methodological inattention science has given to the problem of value. According to this view, decision-makers base their choices on more or less realistic definitions of the situation; these choices reflect their attempts to reach what is good for them, the subjective utility that directs action after (supposedly) objective deliberations about what they want; and from the shock between what one wants to have or avoid, on the one hand, and the reality, on the other, emerge the limits of decision. Value is thus seen as distinct from reality, and emotion from reason. The concrete, diverse and antagonistic ways by which people attempt to realize themselves are hidden under the empty catchwords of happiness, goals, or values. Persons, families, and firms are seen as entities who strive to fulfill (irrational), but relatively stable and predictable needs that present in the form of (rational) directions of meaning. Understanding the world and finding effective, sustainable strategies and tactics of action are seen as a means to achieve one's supposedly clear motivations (profit, unity, sustainability, love).

This perspective implies in some blind spots. First, it does not contemplate how preferences, biases, and subjective choices influence the process by which actors frame their observations until they eventually create their truths. Neither does it consider how goals, values, and emotions change and flow depending on the constant, internally and socially determined ontological oscillation by which players give "being" to different aspects of the world at different times. It does not take into account the fact that definitions of the situation are not simple descriptions of reality, but value-ridden worldviews that embed a cherished and only relatively malleable theory of how things *are* and *should* be. A fourth, equally relevant blind spot is the inattention to the intimate relation that exists between choices, emotions, preferences, and the reasoning that supports them: exactly as one cannot understand power without recurring to signs that direct its force, the tastes, impulses, or sensations of pleasure and displeasure that drive our actions cannot be understood without referring to a perspective from which they stem. This perspective is a tacit, fuzzy, ill-defined, often contradictory parameter of reality, which with its power of conviction suggests how the world is organized and what should be pursued or avoided.[1]

What is good or bad at each moment, then, is desirable (or not) *for a perspective* that defines the momentary paradigm of value. To the actors, this point of departure from which emotions derive is seldom consciously examined. On the contrary, the vivid, directly felt emotions are commonly the first and only variable they take into account. "Nature has placed mankind under the governance of two sovereign masters, *pain* and *pleasure*. It is for them alone to point out what we ought to do, as well as to determine what we shall do. On the one hand the standard of right and wrong, on the other the chain of causes and effects, are fastened to their throne. They govern us in all we do, in all we say, in all we think: every effort we can make to throw off our subjection, will serve but to demonstrate and confirm it" ([299]: 1). As in Bentham's classic principle of utility, the inextricable connection that links emotion to reason, the adequacy of the worldview from which good and bad are derived, the errors of judgment and understanding it contains, the partial effects of context, the (generally egocentric) biases, or the unimagined perspectives not present in one's culture remain absent from the chain of decision, from the considerations of utility, and (perhaps more importantly) from the study of the structure of these considerations. However logical, illogical, realistic, unrealistic, shallow or deep a *worldview*, while tacit it reigns absolutely in determining what is *valuable* for the actors at each instant – in the routine flow of life, players are taken by the automatic flow of life and simply respond to the "real" emotions they have when facing the pressures, dilemmas, and choices posed by the "real" people and contexts to which they are exposed.

On a par with the internally felt emotions, these concrete, immediately sensed and observed external situations to which feelings are directed – the command from an authority, an interaction with a relative, the conflict with a partner, a movement from an opponent – are, most of the time, the second major variable taken into account by actors when making their choices. To a naive decision-maker, they are the obvious *facts* present for the self to evaluate, the immediate part of the world on which one's values are intuitively projected to transform the (never existing) world-as-it-is into the existentially relevant world-for-me. Even when alternative values and definitions of the situation spring into one's mind and the deliberation generates a flow of different emotions, the (structural) cognitive constituents of the "objective" reality – the assumptions and premises that create one or another definition of the situation from the same set of data – are generally taken for granted and remain unexamined. Furthermore, reason is satisficing, not optimizing [300] – players are usually content in making their choices based on how they (freely?) react to the immediately present conditions and on the habits that define how to proceed in each context, stopping the processes of search as soon as an acceptable answer appears. Many of the factors that determine the psychology and sociology of value are arbitrarily defined by habit or intent, but often seem fixed, true as if they were indeed real – the architecture of the choice context, the manipulations of truth brought by biased interpretations, the effects of rhetoric and propaganda, the power of the default rule, the effects of social structure, or the socially determined flow, presentation, and functions of the emotions are just a few examples that tacitly define what emotionally moves the actors inside the family and the firm [301–304].

For most (naive) actors in the family and in the firm, therefore, life unfolds as a series of *facts* and *situations* to which they simply respond with some *emotions*. These are the supposedly solid and obvious fundaments used for the (occasional) rational deliberations about value; they are the bases for *action*. The consequence of this myopic definition of the situation is that large portions of the context of choice – specifically, the more abstract, less obvious, but profoundly relevant structuring constituents of what they value – remain out of sight, directing man's actions as invisible threads that from above determined the movements of a puppet. This chapter covers some of the elements that constitute this context, with the goal of furnishing tools for the change agent to understand and deconstruct the system of values, power, and meaning he works with. In doing so, we start with a brief review of the *emotions*, which (rightly or wrongly) are perceived by the actors as the more private, personal, and fundamental signs of value on which they base their choices and interactions. We then proceed with a brief analysis of the *games* on which these are enacted, with an emphasis on the social interactions, relationships, and networks. Following this, these are analyzed as multitasking rule-based patterns of exchange that include four superposed layers (utility, stratification, social contract, and engrossment or cooperation). We see how the consequent rupture of meaning leads to *conflict, norms,* and *contracts*. Finally, we show how *limit situations* brought by the existence of error, deviance, and genius end up with the use of power, expressed by several *mechanisms of social influence* (coercion, rewards, charisma, and legitimacy). Emotions, values, choices, and the real-life games in which these subjective elements are lived become, through this view, the basic link that as a thread of meaning connects the micro-level of the individual with the macro-level of the firm or the family.

Emotions

There are probably few areas of the human behavior that are so inaccessible (and relevant) to the change agent as the field of emotions. For the individual, these represent the key to one's inner world, the most intimate expression of what touches the person and leads to irreducible dispositions of pleasure or pain, approach or repulsion, friendship or enmity. They determine what people identify with as part of *their* world or reject as the *other*, defining the flow of communication and the degree of openness or closeness to the relationship. They are closely linked to one's sense of self as a center of life and power. Emotions are a central component of the inner thermometer that people use to gauge the value that each situation, person, or context has for them. They are, in this way, deeply *private*.

In addition to this private signification, however, since the first years of life humans are also able to voluntarily express, imitate, conceal, or fake their feelings in order to facilitate the flow of the social game. This ability to display, lie, or force the appearance of emotions in order to manipulate the other players means that among adults emotions are never, in fact, experienced as simple or private signs of value [305, 306]. Rather, they are one of the most fundamental tools people (tacitly or consciously) use to respond to, and ultimately shape the reactions of the other players and their view of them as social actors [307]. Moreover, not only the true meaning of emotions is hidden for outside observers, but it is elusive even to the exercise of introspection: momentary feelings felt as true by the players are always enmeshed in a blend of appearance and essence, as a mix of honesty, deception, and self-deception that is not necessarily coherent with how people feel as their perspectives flow or when they have similar experiences in the future.

Finally, to the extent that the family, the firm, and any social institution are always games of expression and impression, emotions are always more than what they appear to the individual and become a means of structuration of the culture. All places develop jargons and norms that define which emotions can or cannot be expressed in each place and time, how long a feeling should last, the acceptable motives to feel in a certain way, and what is considered proper or improper given the status, social class, and role occupied by the players [308]. All cultures, persons, and games, including the family and the business, define how some emotions (and not others) are expected to appear, conditioning pleasure or displeasure as a reaction to the institutionalized (but changeable) rules of the game. The facts and contexts that emotionally touch the actors are the true link between their private, "free" and emergent soul and the structural, fluid but constraining social systems in which they are inserted. This is the realm where, in fact, change occurs.

These three different ways in which emotions can be framed – as private feelings, as (false or true, tacit or intentional) displays of intentions, or as a form of structuring and implementing broader cultural meanings – are associated with three partially overlapping, but potentially contradictory roles played by them in the context of culture and social life. For any individual player who observes himself in the attempt to make better choices, they are indispensable signs of the value acquired by each context depending on the drive that prevails in the moment: both truth and meaning depend on a vibration that intuitively signals what is right, wrong, proper, improper, relevant or not for a certain perspective. For anyone who in the course of social games needs to convey the distance, proximity, dominance, submission, affect, or coldness desired for the treatment of a theme – or, alternatively, to hypothesize the meaning something has for another person – external displays of emotion are a means to go beyond the limitations of the verbal language and traverse the opaqueness brought by the asymmetries of information, giving suggestions about what is taking place on the other side of the mask. For leaders, change agents, or any players who have any say on what the rules of the game are – those with some power to structure the situation – they are potentially useful levers of manipulation. It is possible to affect the context of the place by enforcing norms of behavior that allow, disavow, facilitate, or hamper the expression and flow of some emotions, determining which experiences are naturally *believed* to be true by the players and, consequently, the games that have more or less probability of being played in the environment. This modulation is especially relevant in games that grow on top of the emotional core of childhood, adolescence, and parenthood, like those that occur within family businesses, but it is also important for all social systems in which meaning becomes (for pragmatic, ideological, or idealistic reasons) part of the culture [309].

Emotions as Private Signs of Value

If we could separate emotions from the people and situations to which they are connected, the residue would be a purely affective value signal.

Valence (good or bad), salience (relevant or not), activation (calmness or excitability), and action (approach or withdrawal, fight or flight) are the most important variables. Four fundamental dimensions of value, which connect feeling to movement as orthogonal axes of pleasure-displeasure, activation-deactivation, involvement-apathy, positive-negative affect, and predispositions to action circumscribe the affective space in which choices occur [310–314]. The end result of how this combination spreads in time is the story of a brute quantum of energy searching for realization. First, the situation is intuitively classified according to (egocentric) criteria that reduce the world of facts to the primary, more archaic world of value: good or bad *for me, now,* according to the perspective that in the moment gives the (absolute) parameter for the valuation of reality. If the spark of power created by the valuation finds its way in the outside, there is *action*; when change occurs within the self, there is *deliberation, deconstruction, reflection*; when emotions are projected onto the outside world there is *meaning,* or *conflict.* Regardless of where they are enacted, translated in the form of actual movement or sublimated in the form of understanding or transcendence, emotions are the expression of a need that demands, as an impulse of life, to be fulfilled.

The more or less adequate way with which persons, families, and firms deal with the emotions depends on how much they are able to grasp the worldview that lies beneath the affective pulsation and use it as a basis for efficient action or reflection. For the individual, this amounts to how well or poorly one uses the information conveyed by the feeling to assess the possibilities offered by the practice and by the ideals given derived from his various selves, facets, and inner perspectives – the several ways one can blend realism and value into a single worldview. In the family and in the firm, how actions and games flow depends on the meanings chosen (or imposed) to players as culture. Incentives and force stabilize some definitions of the situation and prioritize one or another type of emotion, catalyzing the transformation of individual self-interest into some form of collective action; openness or closure to conflict lead to more or less clear displays of emotions; and the ability of the players to deal with their values, definitions of situation, and truths leads to more or less easy negotiations and processes of learning about meaning.

The diverse emotional meanings ascribed to the diverse objects with which players deal on an everyday basis can be classified in many ways. Emotions may be seen as being built from a few basic bricks: fear, anger, disgust, happiness, sadness, and surprise are probably present in all species, combining in different ways to produce the variety of sentiments "actually" experienced by the players in everyday life [315] – these are the common final pathways of the feelings observed during everyday life, forming the threads of attachment and aversion that define the connection of players to the family, firm, and other actors. Depending on how fast and clearly these feelings can be attributed to a cause, one may classify them as diffuse (happiness, sadness, anxiety, irritability) or as pointed (attachment, anger, fear, grief) – diffuse emotions forming the basis of the organizational or family culture, pointed feelings giving a tone to particular facts, interactions, and relationships [316]. They may be future- and task-oriented (worry, anxiety, anticipatory emotions) or focused on the present and detached from the flow of action (angst, peace, ecstatic feelings). They can be seen as impersonal and related to physical sensations (happiness, surprise, disgust) or social and related to people (inferiority, superiority, inclusion, exclusion, value, depreciation). Among the social emotions, they can be directed mainly to other players (envy, jealousy, vanity, shame, embarrassment, resentment) or to one's own self and ideal self (honor, pride, guilt, regret, self-esteem). Even languages vary in the way they categorize the emotions, implicitly determining what people in fact feel (or believe they feel): English, for example, contains 2000 categories for emotions, Malay 230, Chewong 7, and Ifaluk 50 (none of them referring to a sensation, but simply meaning "what is inside"); Tahitian has 46 terms to express anger, but none for sadness; both feelings are expressed by a single word in Luganda and among the Ilongot in the Philippines, while other peoples have no words for love, surprise, depression, anxiety, guilt, shame, regret, or disgust [317, 318]).

Fuzzy as they are, these classifications offer relevant hints for the leaders and change agents to assess both how *they* are reacting to the specific contexts and how *others* may potentially react to similar circumstances. They give a direct measure of how each situation is felt according to the prevailing point of view; indirectly, they reveal the internal parameters that define what is good, bad, relevant, irrelevant, meaningful, or meaningless for each particular individual and group in the moment depending on the perspective on which the feeling is based. Furthermore, precisely because they are imprecise they often become a significant point of contention – to the extent that people react to what they feel is right, any culture or project of change only happens insofar as players are induced, directed, manipulated, or convinced to *value* something in detriment of another (potentially valuable) direction. Persuasion directed to the emotions, more than rational arguments conveying any truth, is what defines which definition of the situation is chosen by the players, and therefore what is really played out in their games [319].

Of the several antinomies that express the antagonistic values, emotions, and motives that alternate within the human being, some are particularly important for the change agent: calmness *versus* anxiety, change *versus* tradition, curiosity *versus* recognition, impulsivity *versus* control, and autonomy *versus* belonging. Thus, benefic environments and positive emotions linked to feelings of expansion and being are associated with global, creative, constructive reasoning that lead to more efficacy of exploration, and better cognitive performance, but may increase errors in detail-oriented tasks. Conversely, threatening environments, tight mechanisms of control and emotions linked to non-being narrow the focus of attention and foster local, systematic, deliberative types of thinking that increase the tendency to search for fast responses and decrease the variability of the processes of search [320]. Curiosity, nonconformity, impulsiveness, grandiosity, paranoia, or simply a novelty-seeking temperament may foster movements of change, if nothing out of desperation with the inertia and peace of the status quo [321]. Conversely, risk-aversion, inhibition, shyness, fear, or the pleasure derived from mere exposure and recognition are behind many due oppositions to illogical projects and undue resistances to necessary change (if nothing to preserve the apparent safety derived from the already known) [322–324]. Particularly relevant are the trade-offs between present and future, impulse and temperance, passion and prudence, risk and conservatism, or instant gratification and realism: families, firms, and people alike are always divided between extracting the maximum gain from the present, putting in peril their future, or sacrificing the present in order to guarantee (?) the conditions of tomorrow [325, 326].

In the realm of the social emotions, two opposite drives present since our early infancy remain as potent as ever for the remainder of the adult life: exactly as children initially search for attachment but later react to this dependence with affective movements of revolt and freedom, adults routinely alternate between fear and anger, belonging and autonomy, love and power, or safety and independence when dealing with close relationships [327]. Thus it is that more monotonous games – like a friendship or a work relation, which make use of strict rules of ceremony to foster illusions of unconditional acceptance or rational instrumentality – are easier to play than mixed conflict-cooperation games, such as the ones observed within marriages, families, or partners in a relevant joint endeavor [97]. Family businesses belong to this latter group: their success as a game depends on the existence of some structural slack, on the value the individuals give to the relationship (or prison) they choose, and on the ability to negotiate rules and rules of how to negotiate the rules, preserving the (necessary) space of the players' individualism from the constraints of the common constructions, companionship, and peace involved in any harmonic or coordinated game (see Appendix 2, Figure 11).

Emotions, therefore, flow. *First*, they depend on one's habit to question the impulses of the moment and search for other perspectives of meaning: the more players are used to second-guess their impulses and momentary perspectives of meaning, the more they face the contradictions between different parts of their selves and their emotions vary according to the worldview that prevails at each instant. *Second*, emotions depend on the external context: actors react to the time of the day, to tiredness, to pressures arising from the market, to the end of the trimester, to nuances of the family history, to a particular tone of voice, to the tightness of the bond, and to the multiple interests involved in the relationship. *Third*, they are endogenous to the social situation: rather than stable markers of one's internal state, they both influence and change (unpredictably) in response to the interaction games in which they appear. Encompassing various motives under simpler meta-rules, these interactions and relationships give a single direction to egocentric and social motives, or to the ideal goals and the public image expected from the players in order to translate, in the form of norms, their need for belonging and reputation [328]. *Finally*, they are in the core of every attempt to infuse meaning into culture. "We speak not strictly and philosophically when we talk of the combat of passion and reason. Reason is, and ought only to be the slave of the passions, and can never pretend to any other office than to serve and obey them" ([298]: III: 3). Emotions and displays of emotion form the link that more intimately connects players to each other and to social structure, and as such stand out as a fundamental pieces in the task of organizing.

Emotions as Instruments of Communication and Structuration

In the minute emotions are translated into (public) language and become part of an (also public) social game, they stop being private. Rather, they are always linked to how actors want to *appear*, and therefore to the impression they need to transmit to others or reiterate to themselves, depending on the identity games they espouse. When directed to an external audience, emotions become part of reputation, communication, persuasion. and negotiation games; when directed to the internal audience, they form the private (?) feelings that emerge when people compare what they are with what they should, could, or wanted to be. In both instances, the eyes of another person embody, directly or indirectly, the ultimate standard of value. In this sense, human emotions are never pure. Identification, neutrality, or aversion – all them expressing modes of the fit between internal and external worlds, self and other, real and ideal, feeling and mask – are the fundamental attitudes that show how individual players are connected (or not) to themselves, to the surrounding objects, facts, people, and the family or firm to which they belong.

Social emotions may be prototypically divided as belonging to two larger groups created as actors intuitively feel how they relate to the external audiences (the other) or to the internal third eye of the inner spectators (their ideal self). Embarrassment and shame, related respectively to the breach of minor or serious rules, are sentiments directed mainly to public audiences [329]. Also here are the sensations of obligation, responsibility, loyalty, reciprocity, and justice, which link actors to a logic of appropriateness and connect them to each other by a sense of indebtedness that transcends the narrow scope of the consequences [330]. Both types of feeling associate ethics, morality, and propriety – the supposedly profound values, which deeply determine what each one considers good, evil, right, or wrong – with social appearance (we are ashamed of what we do or feel responsible for what we say, but not for what we think). They are the first step of a magical act of prestidigitation by which emotions directed pragmatically to others are subtly transformed into moral sentiments and transported from being feelings related to a performance in the public stage to affections related to how actors, often unaware of the effects of culture or external environment, experience their purportedly loftiest ideals [331].

In addition to the above social emotions, which are loosely linked to an assembly of "others", actors also respond to internal audiences, and in particular to what they elevate to the stance of an *ideal*. These personal identities, goals, and values are nothing more than internalized instances of external social rules that define what for someone, in a certain era, or to one's culture, is considered good or bad, desirable or not, proper or improper. Once ingrained within one's mind, they become a constant companion of conscious actors. They alternate and compete with their habits, impulses, and momentary drives in directing the flow of attention and action. They often reemerge in the form of reminders of what one should do *if* life were indeed morally or rationally lived; and as part of the public discourses in which players reiterate to each other their "true" intentions, feelings, and ideas, they inevitably become part of the social display of motives by which people are tacitly or consciously transformed into stylized, romantic or ludicrous, characters in the drama they jointly write with all other players in the stage [154] (see Appendix 2, Figures 4 and 15).

For each individual or group in the family or firm, the emotions associated with this internal interaction game – the various dialogues through which actors talk to themselves, discussing how distant or close they are to the self-proclaimed identities – depend on *how* carelessly, rigidly, seriously, or playfully one treats the contradictions that exist between real and ideal. Sloppy, negligent, amoral, or antisocial actors do not commit with long-term goals that transcend the here-and-now gains of mere pragmatism; as a result, they are often unpredictable, internally unstable, prone to sudden changes of route or to small or big lies that conceal the biologically natural, but normatively non-acceptable, variability of the soul. Rigid players, on the contrary, take themselves too seriously and are easy preys of the illusions of merit and demerit. When positively identified with their ideals – as if we could really believe that we indeed *are* what we *want* or *appear* to be – they present as narcissistic entrepreneurs, CEOs, patriarchs, consultants, or employees, who typically imagine they are special and become immune to ideas that go beyond their monologs [332, 333]. When negatively identified with their ideal self, on the contrary, people are usually taken by the (also selfish, omnipotent) feelings of low self-esteem, guilt, remorse, contrition, regret, penitence, and other forms of self-flagellation with which one enacts the paradox of being simultaneously inferior (in reality) while being (ideally) superior.[2]

It is rare that people, families, or firms understand the playful nature of this inner game between self and ideal self and treat it with the blend of seriousness and sportsmanship that characterizes expert social actors. Rather, most people are unable to objectively evaluate what they think, remember what they have done, or anticipate how they will feel (which creates a biased sample of their real self). There are, then, frequent dissonances between what people say they want in theory and the values they enact in practice. Justifications used on a daily basis to explain one's conduct (especially in situations involving money, territory, power, labor, pride, or sex) are clearly different from the abstract ideals professed when there are not any pressures; conscious beliefs and goals are generally restricted to more controllable behaviors, whereas spontaneous and intractable dispositions continue influencing who one actually is without being incorporated into the ideal self; the correlation between the intention to reach a goal and its fulfillment is typically low, the vast part of the variance being explained by factors such as inattention, difficulty to start the task, laziness or indiscipline; and implicit attitudes to minority groups or different ideologies and ideals are more strongly correlated with non-verbal behaviors than with one's explicit self-descriptions [334–336]. In these instances, the ideal self obviously does not represent the archetypal inner center, vocation, core, or deepest side of the individual, the north to which one must go back in order to correct the practice. On the contrary, this ideal self is simply an error, a falsification, a negation, or counterpoint to the real self. The art of organization lies partly in using the transcendent, illusory, or dishonest identity games created out of these truths and semi-truths – what we are, what we think we are, what we think we want to be, and how we want to appear – as the basis of intimacy upon which one designs the public family and organizational games that constitute a meaningful culture.

Emotions, then, are double-sided Janus elements that are central to the context of choice because they obey to several different bosses. The value side of the equation egocentrically reduces the world to what in the moment seems valuable or invaluable for the players (the desire, game, or perspective that in the instant appears to be meaningful); actors then *feel* and name what they feel, giving an initial meaning to the affect and later organizing it according to their self-claimed identity (What am I *really* feeling?). By contrast, the reality side of the emotional lens infuses value into things, contexts, memories, peoples, families, firms, our selves, our thoughts, or identities and is intuitively classified as being part of the *self* – ourselves or everything we identify with – or as an *other*. When relating to the situations linked to *self*, players have the experience of an easy flow, joy, or naturalness – a well-known and repeated game or a well-fit mask, which swiftly translate their inner motives into proper actions that have resonance in the social world. When relating to an object felt as the *other,* sensations of estrangement, introspection, uneasiness, or tension make actors take a refuge in the internal, solitary games they play with themselves or other groups ([71]: 41–2). Finally, as these self- and other-definitions of value are exchanged in games of reputation, image, identity, choices, displays, and propaganda, they close a circle in which ideal, social, and real selves continuously shape each other. In general, the more intense the feeling aroused by the object, the deeper is the connection between the self and the *other* with whom one identifies. The deeper the connection, the stronger the ties of irrationality that bridge the chasm between the microcosm of the individual and the macrocosm of the social structure, fostering the fantasies of identity, value, and free-will. Private social emotions become, then, close to their twin-feelings, the public-directed social emotions that players experience when valued, criticized, praised, honored, or despised [337].

The immense, always imperfect task of connecting individuals to each other and to the group, making of the yoke of the organization a meaningful symbol of personal realization, is probably easier in the family than in the modern, impersonal firm. When people are figuring out how they feel about their families, the gravitational pull of history and redundancy – the same name, the same tradition, the same arms, the same places and rituals – works toward the task of organization. When kin and family systems are seen in their granularity, however, the greatest game of unity appears as it does in any other social system, fragmented and embedded in a paradoxical blend of both attraction and repulsion. "Different men are moved by different incentives or combinations of incentives, and by different incentives or combinations at different times" ([73]: 148). Thus, actors may simply follow their inertia and be players by coincidence, attracted to the system because of convenience, proximity, salary, protection, safety, habit, or other pragmatic factors; may enjoy the tasks they are called to do or become attached to the group, to the rituals of companionship and to the relationships, interactions, and possibilities of affect provided by the system; may be directly affected by the pleasantness, beauty, sacredness, or elegance of the space, light, architecture, or artifacts that characterize the house or place where the game is played [338]; may have in the firm or family a symbol of the structures, rules, roles and institutionalized ideas and forms that are considered good, desirable, or special in the broader society [339]; may even, albeit more rarely, "acquire an attachment or loyalty to the family or to the organization" that surpasses the practical "services and goals, the 'organization objectives'" or the "conservation and growth of the organization itself", to the take the form of personally felt dedication to work or to the rituals of cohesion that mark the place ([36]: 198); and may cling to their self-interest or to other attachments, working against the task of organization. Whatever the value-nature of this connection, however, it always emerges in the context of the *games* through which people interact and establish long-term, interconnected relationships.

Meaningful Games and Their Trade-Offs

If the attention to their emotions forces actors to turn inward, in order to find the vibration of meaning associated with each specific situation, context, or actor, it is in the outside world of the objects, or in the mental, metaphysical world of thought, that one finds the pathways and obstacles for the realization of his wishes. Each time, culture and place has a limited number of games at the disposal of players – from being a chief of the *oikos* in ancient Greece, the matriarch among the Nuer, a businessman in America, or a single, married, or divorced person in the West, people are always evaluating the external reality they have access to, depending on their birth, social status, capital, power, or ability to work with their emotions and with the prevailing standards of value. Each epoch in the history of the ideas also offers a certain number of problems and avenues for the spirit, depending on how deeply the deconstruction of the postulates of reason allows one to engage in the creative task of defining and questioning the ethical, aesthetic, affective, or metaphysical values beneath the conduct. In both cases – whether one searches for social realization or for a deeper, philosophical (?) worldview that opens never-ending cycles of construction and deconstruction of truths – meaning is found in games external to the evaluating self, as a landscape of possibilities that must be explored for the individual to fulfill his needs.

Both in the firm and in the family, the crystallized threads of meaning that constitute these games appear normally as a blend of rituals, routines, beliefs, ways of being, goals, and conflicts that conflate the influences of the broader culture, of the tradition-reinforced path dependencies of each particular place, and of the private pull of the powerful elites. Likewise, collective deliberations and communication occur according to the rules of the established cognitive games: any idea that wants to become a social truth must be expressed in a way that other players understand, relying on the already existing common vocabulary, jargon, beliefs, and axioms of truth to convey a potentially "new" meaning.

This intuitive attitude – by which a self (blind to himself and to other potential values) acts or evaluates the possibilities of acting or thinking – generally occupies most of the actors' time. In particular, positive engrossment in the game is usually enforced by hidden or explicit forms of social pressure – people should look at each other while talking, partners have to repeat promises of solidarity, family members revolve around family issues, players in an agonistic game heed the combat, and employees and executives in a firm repeat themes that reinforce the relevance of productivity, of the market, or of the competition ([71]: 38–40). Meaning and engrossment in the meaning, in the triple sense of intuitive belief, cognitive and emotional significance, form the basis of the identification that counteracts the centrifugal effects of individualism, taking players away from their solitary, calculating attitude and bringing up the fluidity of the flow of life and social life.[3]

The consequence of this intuitive and normatively reinforced belief in the existence (and often in the value) of the socially constructed shared realities is that a good part of the social games – especially their deeper and institutionalized layers, which are *felt* as truths – are commonly taken for granted and used as a basis for communion, negotiation, or conflict. Overall, fluid multitasking hidden under apparently simple concrete activities, rituals, and deliberations is expected in all interesting, complex games – meaningful, sustainable, socially relevant routines and rituals bundle multiple (divergent) motives, emotions, and goals under the guise of the same processes. Since these games are deeply valued, they usually become the common basis that unites players around the same platform of things and beliefs. Even when players question whether something is feasible, or contest the grip that official ideologies or hegemonic categories have over them – as the young or grown-up adolescents of anytime – they generally do not consider any recombination of rules or values that could in fact deconstruct the value of the games they are playing. Resistance, then, occurs *from within* the game they have learned and is limited to concrete situations, without radical changes of the definition of the situation or deeper transformations in the landscape of choice.[4]

The trade-offs – generally defined as "complex decision problems that involve multiple conflicting objectives and where no dominant alternative exists that is better than all other alternatives" [340]: 66) – are dilemmas that appear when multitasking games that otherwise are meaningful cannot be played as usual due to an obstacle or are put under scrutiny through the light of the (coherence-based) language game. The need to choose is then expressed as an irreconcilable opposition between different values or attitudes, both of them desirable but mutually exclusive in the limit of the practical situation. One of the most relevant areas of study, in the firm as in the social life, involves the description and analysis of the trade-offs that appear when individuals and groups have to treat complex multitasking games under the usual rules of rationality. Actors are, then, doubly constrained: first, by the structure of the space-time, which allows only one thing to be done at any instant and therefore forces the option for one or another value; second, by the logical structure of the language game and of the social game of coherence, which define values and situations as real *or* unreal and thus force an opposition that does not exist in the world of practice.

As diverse as they are in their concrete presentation, all trade-offs have the same choice structure: two or more zones of impossibility, representing the radical, unilateral option for one value and the annulment of the other, circumscribe a large area of ambiguity in which various equally valid mixtures of the opposite values can be chosen depending on the context and preferences of the decision-maker. Because players *have to* choose one of these equilibria – all of them equally valid, but involving different definitions of value in face of the trade-off – the exception-situations of choice that characterize this zone of ambiguity cannot be solved by any argument, rule, law, or process, but just by solitary or consensual *bets* that privilege a course of action over another. As leaps into the vacuum of uncertainty, these bets require from players the courage to be radical and the acceptance of the inevitability of error; they defy a basic postulate of rationality, the assumption that decisions ought to be logical or derived deductively from first premises; they thus show that life transcends the limitations of reason, forcing them to respond to the intuitions and feelings brought by each specific context rather than to pre-planned rules, processes, or determinations of appropriateness (see Appendix 2, Figure 10).

It is not within our scope to review all the trade-offs that fill the life of the family or the firm; it suffices to show that they are ubiquitous, looming beneath every single decision that involves a complex issue or when the (arbitrary) demand for consistency shocks against the "ontological oscillation [that] is a constant in everyday sensemaking" ([32]:364). From the archetypal oppositions to the more mundane ones – short- *versus* long-term gains, passion *versus* prudence, risk *versus* safety, idealism *versus* pragmatism, individualism *versus* collectivism, sales *versus* industry, exploration *versus* exploitation, family *versus* business – human life is full of crossroads in which previously harmonic threads of the same game are put against each other by a specific context. These contexts force players to forgo one (certain) value now to privilege the uncertainties of the future, to trust intangible cultural or ideological ideals that (irrationally) guide the choice in the limit situations, and eventually to choose, without any clear rule that conclusively determines what to do, a certain direction of action instead of another equally valid one. It is only when they face the ambiguity and arbitrariness of trade-off choices that men are pushed to define themselves and find the real value they will apply to each context, bringing to the collective world the intimate question of meaning and the groundless, taste-based fundament that forces the common game to one or another direction.

In the practice, players commonly respond badly to the fuzzy texture that characterizes the ambiguity zone of the trade-offs. Often, transformed into a social, and not simply a practical, problem, "the trade-off issue often becomes a personal value question. ... [Since there are] no right or wrong answers to these value questions and, naturally enough, different individuals may have very different value structures", conflict ensues ([340]: 67). Practical problems, for which contradictions, compromises, and uncertain bets are necessary, become enmeshed in the unity-based identity games. The task of organizing – i.e., of inventing complementarities, putting together opposites, creating the unstable equilibria that keeps families and firms together – leads to arbitrariness in the exercise of power, and with it the return to the same conflicts the organization attempts to solve. These antinomies create instabilities in the chain of identification, and often lead players to explicate, think about, question, fight about, or negotiate the three major elements of which social games are made: *instrumental uses, power, rank,* and *meaning.*

Social Games: Instrumental Uses, Power, Rank, and Meaning

Whenever players are normally living what they expect to live, there is no need for any reflection or deconstruction. Life, however, is complex; and during limit situations, when previous truths, identities, or beliefs are dismissed as illusions, or when nuances become more apparent than the previous homogeneity, it is common for individuals, families, and firms to temporarily lose their unity and condition of ontological existence and question the structure of the games on which they are based (if not just to recoup again and be considered as entities in a new moment). Interactions, relationships, communication, or negotiations are, then, deconstructed as exchanges of signs and forces by which people position themselves in relation to each other and the world [76, 341, 342]; contradiction, rather than coherence, becomes the norm; and the power of illusion that gave power to the previous games is demystified as stemming from an (often improbable) combination of utilitarian interests, power, status, and (occasionally) idealism (see Appendix 2, Figure 12).

The more basic and fundamental expression of human nature – the one that gives meaning to all games, as people strive to live, survive and impose themselves in the world – becomes apparent whenever players frame and fragment reality in the form of commodities that can be impersonally exchanged, absorbed, or discarded: money, houses, territory, energy, time, space, labor, slaves, women, men, or sex. Under this perspective, people, groups, things or situations are simply instruments for one's satisfaction, which are then classified as good or evil depending on how they fit the interests of the player. Parents, children, friends, families, or firms do not have then any value in themselves, except as sources or obstacles for one's gratification. There is no engrossment, spontaneity or trust, but only calculating self-interest: fighting for survival and self-realization, men behave and feel as fundamentally economic beings, solitary centers of life and egoism who strive to take the most of the circumstances depending on *their* momentary or future goals and objectives [343].

Regrettably, it is seldom accepted that this satisfaction of self-interested economic needs is, and should be, a goal of every individual, group, family, firm, or game (meaningful or instrumental, utilitarian or "disinterested"). Without proper attention to this natural, egocentric, and inevitable element of the human soul, nothing can effectively prosper because it denies the individualistic life-element of which we are made.

Human players, however, are not moved only by material, instrumental, or impersonal gains. On the contrary: the pursuit of honor, status, power, or dominance underlies every known type of social behavior and makes of stratification a sociological phenomenon that characterizes all forms of organization [344]. Powerful actors, typically, do have a preferential access to the common resources, means of communication, freedom of action, and people they need to use for their goals. Differences are still more clearly observable in the intangible, tacitly lived realm of the social world: players with a high rank in the hierarchy talk more than lower-ranking members; receive more communications and are frequent objects of interlocution; tend to speak to the group as a whole, giving orders, comments, suggestions, and feedback that reinforce their superiority (as opposed to subordinates, who generally attempt to talk to the leader); are implicitly allowed to interrupt, interpret, advise, confirm, or disconfirm the other players, usually framing their utterances in a way that reiterates their experience, expertise, knowledge, capacity, or rationality; and in the group dynamics, determine who speaks what, to whom, and for how long, showing the (often expected) dominance both by the dominion of the social space and by non-verbal signs such as tone of voice, intimacies, or eye contact [263, 284, 345–352]. Men, more than any other animals, are exquisitely tuned to, and permanently asses, the structural conformation of the social games that define how they are positioned vis-à-vis other players in terms of power and status. Time, memory, and social comparison, then, become relevant variables that compete with instrumental interests to determine the outcome of the choice process – it is often more important to pay attention to whom will make the rules of the game than it is to have a momentary gain that would be sufficient from a purely economic perspective.

On top of the individualistic instrumental and power-based drives, of course, there is occasionally the (irrational) feeling of meaning, the ontological and emotional movement by which actors give being and value to the games they identify with. Played with people and institutions who (momentarily) are placed in the friend category, these fragile games of meaning require a disarmed engagement to work – since their power of *illusio* is hampered by any awareness of the activity, they must be lived spontaneously, and are usually seen as games only after the fact, when their rules and structuring conditions of play become object of thought. They form the institutionalized and shared dreams, the conditions of belief that stabilize the multiplicity of interpretations and create the "solid" ground above which actors then live their uncertainties, doubts, conflicts, creeds, and positive or negative evaluations. By them, individuals, families, and firms are believed to exist as they appear in their specific identities, acquiring meaning and value; families, regardless of being categorized as conservative, liberal, open or closed, are felt as "ours"; and firms gain a flavor of transcendence and legitimacy as they become associated with specialization rather than generalization, idealism rather than interest, craft rather than standardization, or complexity rather than simplicity [193, 353, 354]. The paradox of culture, identity and meaning, stemming from this belief in the transcendence of the spirit despite the overwhelming evidence toward fragmentation and individualism, is precisely what gives unity to social games [190, 355, 356]. Romance and stereotyping, more than realism, govern the tranquility of the confidence and feelings of calmness on which we rely to go on with life.

The peculiar, fragile way in which instrumental uses, power, status and romance are reconciled in the form of the idealized tone that characterizes meaningful games lived in the family or firm expresses well the contradictory nature of social life. Complementarities are indispensable. Without the potent engine of self-satisfaction, games would be soulless, fragile like a wind or a random movement of non-animated beings. Without the magic of identification, which links the raw power of egocentric self-interest to the hypnotic dream of the moment, collective action would be loose and easily disrupted by the context-based flow of individualism. Without the idealistic or ideological cover-up that allow players to live their basic needs as if they were transcendent, men would never have the alibi to experience the freedom and spirit of play that characterizes the "true" games of love, joy, depth, or cooperation [82]. Thus, "the more the value to which an action is oriented is elevated to the status of an absolute value, the more 'irrational' in this sense the corresponding action is. The more unconditionally the actor devotes himself to this value for its own sake, to pure sentiment or beauty, to absolute goodness or devotion to duty, the less is he influenced by considerations of the consequences of his action" ([357]: 26). For any (idealistic? romantic? utopian?) perspective, the capitulation to this irrationality of life implies in a desired suspension of doubt, a momentary, even if flimsy, surrender to the naturalness required to live the experiences of joy, affect or cooperation. Families, firms, and people only exist as organized systems insofar as they maintain the tenuous, uncertain, fragile equilibrium between the three different social drives that pull them to different, opposite directions.

The Rupture of Meaning: Social Dilemmas

The opposite way one can frame a complementarity, of course, is by emphasizing the contradictions it synthesizes. Thus, for anyone who sees social games from above, they are falsifications – socially stabilized artifices by which some elements of the total situation are emphasized, others downplayed, and the total flow of motives organized until these are integrated in the form that maintains the (illusory) conditions of the game. Without the awareness of how identification necessarily disguises, covers up, and denies self-interest and social inequalities, idealism would become lost in the gray zone of the alienated illusions, as a manifestation of the players' naiveté. Consequently, if the spontaneity of play is framed as alienation, idealism is ideology – the unacceptable acceptance of a superstructure that simply covers up the inequalities of power, status, and social control required to maintain the present order.

All interesting, *disinterested* games are, therefore, denied by the *interested* exchanges of goods or values that economically support them; all (true) friendships are disavowed by the (equally true) gains derived from them; and as actors are always participating in multiple, nested, overlapping, and shifting games of identification, and yet contend they have a single identity, local experiences lead to a necessary, significant moment-to-moment variability of value and purpose that destroys the coherence and stability of the games they play. For actors and groups who rely on simplistic logics to solve their questions, the result is a rupture of meaning that is as severe as are the contradictions seen between the situations, dialogs, contexts, and discourses that alternate the reinforcement or the disruption of the illusion. Conflict and change always occur in the seas of ambiguities not immediately tractable by the naive use of the language game [157].

The social dilemmas revealed by deconstructions of the unity of meaning are artificial choice situations that emerge when the (equally artificial) rule of non-contradiction is applied to routine games that depend on illusion, forgetfulness, and inattention to flow as they should. They generally appear in limit-situations, when the institutionalized ways to deal with the problem do not work and players need to think about what to do. They express the contrast between the radical pressure for unity, brought by a current limit situation or the need to use the coherence rule, shocks against the normal flow of life, which depends on loose-coupling and illusion. They thus illuminate the deeper contradictions of the system, which materialized as different values within a person, or as conflicting viewpoints among opposing groups, take the form of apparently absolute, abstract dualities that foster the sensation of paradox.

Social dilemmas, then, reflect not only the practical impossibility of choosing two opposing values during limit situations, but also the *logical* impossibility of uniting within a single rule the three different subrules of the instrumental, power-based, and idealistic sub-games that often coexist in a single activity but depend on different attitudes towards existence. As a consequence, they can be solved only in the world of practice, and never in the world of ideas – since the rule of coherence offers no way out of the paradox, players need to muddle through context-based, intuitive choices that often contradict their espoused values in order to craft unique, fragile solutions that only partially solve the question, but avoid (or delay) the interminable conflicts that could emerge by the exclusive use of rationality [358]. They are a fundamental part of the complex problems that need to be tackled by every actor in the system.

Trade-off # 1: The Dilemma of Cooperation

In all its forms – directed to kin or a stranger, as part of single- or repeated-interaction games – cooperative behavior always emerges as a compromise between the egocentric drive to extract everything *we* want from life and the (equally egotistical) wish to derive pragmatic and affective gains from the cooperative endeavor [359]. Players are, then, divided between different structures of space and time that serve different purposes of the social game (short or long-term, private or public, individualistic or collective). One framework involves our own interests, motives, emotions, self, and its relation to others as objects to be used, exploited, or fought in a game of power or status. Another framework encompasses the public games and moments in which we play *with* others. From self-interested action come advantages, calculation, and, for those who feign well, reputation. From cooperation come the benefits of coordinated action, (risky) long-term gains, reputation, and, for those who are truly immersed in the game, belonging.

The dilemmas of cooperation – which involve the so-called tragedy of the commons, as well as the public fence problems – come from the fact that for any self-interested actor who uses a common good, it is better that *others* cooperate while *he* defects, in a way that one can enjoy both the immediate and potential long-term benefits brought by cooperation and satisfy the egocentric drives derived from an individualistic, selfish posture [360]. The obvious consequence of this duality – which depends on the human capacity to lie, conceal, distort, and use the porosity of the mask to manipulate the other's definition of the situation – is an instability of the cooperative dream. Even though groups of cooperators do better than groups of defectors in the long run, "defecting individuals outcompete cooperative individuals in mixed groups" and thus disturb the stability of the organized system on which they depend as individuals [361].

The *right*, intuitive, immediate, economic answer to the dilemma of cooperation is to free ride; and in fact, animals only cooperate consistently when genetically related [361]; people commonly forgo their right to vote; students and employees work less than expected by their share in group tasks; individuals generally do not pay for public radio and television; responsible citizens maintain habits that lead to pollution while demanding public action against it; and participants in a group tend to diffuse the responsibility and avoid conflict when there are others to carry the burden [362]. In all these cases, the marginal gains derived from the contribution to the public good are inferior to the effort required by the cooperation; or the advantages of defection offset the (uncertain) future advantages that could come from cooperation; or there is an (amoral) bet to gain from both individualism and group effort. Furthermore, since there are no logical arguments to define that cooperation, common good, future, or collective goals are intrinsically better than individualism, self-interest, present gain, or egocentrism, any discourse may justify any action.[5]

In the firm, in the family, and in the society as a whole, several mechanisms are generally put in place to limit the scope of the individualistic drives and preserve cooperation. Force and coercion are almost always present – prisons, confessionals, asylums, exiles, families, schools, managerial control, and psychiatric wards systematically (and falsely) link egoism to sin and virtue to altruism or (transcendent?) commitment to the group, instilling the idea that crimes against the collective good *should* lead to internal or external punishment (guilt, shame, fear, repentance). Other control mechanisms include reputation, mutual policing, altruistic punishment, tit-for-tat strategies, indirect reciprocity, aesthetics, and, paradoxically, spite [363–371]. Particularly relevant for our theme is the fact that humans, as many social animals, consistently sacrifice themselves to benefit related individuals and thus assure the transmission of shared genes [96, 372–377] – deeply grounded in our biology, the tendency to protect kin and family may furnish the instinctive basis over which the cultural institutions of the household, lines, lineages, clans, families, and family businesses have evolved [378]. But more relevantly, the deeper elements and tools required for the manipulation of the culture – the ones that affect the actors' personal worldview – lie outside the realm of pure reason, in the irrational drives that foster the illusions of meaning. It is in the identification with the family, culture, or firm, in the adherence to the ideals of altruism, cooperation, or loyalty, and in the intangible values required in games that extend in the future or broader social contexts, that we find the true levers to be touched if one wants to privilege the pursuit of ethics, aesthetics, joy, or friendship in the culture.

Trade-off # 2: Honor, Justice, and Reputation versus Utility

Differently from most social animals, who regardless of their association privilege their own immediate or future gains independently regardless of what others receive, human players are exquisitely tuned to how their share of the concrete world compares to the others' share, and consequently to how they are positioned in relation to other players within the social world they partake [379]. Whenever instrumental and social needs are opposed, we then see a trade-off between two equally important drives, which target two different worlds: the search for utility, for which the value is the exclusive satisfaction of the *self* and of its material or affective interests, regardless of how they are achieved; and the search for fairness, value, or honor, which targets the social world and is satisfied only by a reasonable rank-conformation within the public environment.

The consequences of this trade-off involve a series of economic anomalies – apparently disinterested sacrifices that boost the union of the group by the costly enforcement of fairness, as well as never-ending, irrational fights for empty symbols of identity and status in which players depart from the calculating self-interested pursuit of utility to engage in behaviors that obviously go against their pragmatic interests [380]. Social life is full of these deviations from the pragmatic, purportedly logical courses of action predicted by the dismal science. Humans consistently refuse money offers going up to three months of salary when forced to opt between the economic gain and the sense they are being cheated or unfairly treated [381]; actors often commit to prejudicial courses of conflict, refusing to step back from an initial position because they want to avoid losing face [382]; players regularly punish defectors or unfair offers even when not involved in a situation, putting their resources, integrity, and interests at risk [383]; people are commonly attentive to the effects of social comparison; and families or firms are often torn apart by issues that have nothing to do with the economic pay-off [384].[6]

Several factors extraneous to the immediate situation are also determinant in influencing the outcome of these interactions. *First*, players respond to what is right, wrong, proper, or improper given the hierarchy accepted as normal within a given place and time: "men's indignation, it seems, is more excited by legal wrong than by violent wrong; the first looks like being cheated by an equal, the second like being compelled by a superior" ([385]: 368). *Second*, actors respond to the others' responses to them: negotiations of identity, honor, rank, and reputation, of how one is perceived, and of the fame associated with the name occur on a par with the economic exchanges of money, territory, resources, or other tangible goods. *Third*, men attend to time and consequences: considerations of future and tacit or explicit evaluations of how an action will reverberate in the surrounding social space-time are inextricably linked to the here-and-now weighing of the pros and cons of each exchange happening in every interaction. *Fourth*, people take in consideration the (natural? culturally infused?) ideals that give an ethical, affective, or aesthetic meaning to their social games: legitimate resentments and demands, fairness, justice, and reaction to injustice are, in this case, lofty catch words that cover up the players' reactions to the (mundane, contingent) institutionalized definitions of social value, equality and inequality [386]. Finally, men of course assess what is good for them in the present and in the future, the utilitarian interests that bring economic gain or loss, and therefore more or less utility (the prospect of large material gains commonly offsetting the drive to impose justice) [387].

In the real life of families and firms, especially when there is no pride, reputation, or future involved in the exchange or when the stakes are high, the end-result of the clash between the opposing values in this trade-off is indeed an economic choice that privileges the practical gains. More commonly, however, we also see a tendency to value the social world rather than pragmatism; and consequently, to enforce reasonable degrees of equality or fairness, rather than simply utilitarian gains. This choice leads to different outcomes depending on the context: occasionally, cooperation is helped by the same factors it helps to curb and resentment is put at the service of justice, feeding the (irrational) drive to punish [388]; often, good deals are lost due to social attachments; in both cases, self-interest is passionate and obeys to pride, honor, spite, guilt, empathy, indignation, fairness, or revenge [389–394]. More than on the rational world of the tangible goods, it is on the symbolic universe of social life, a microcosm where time, identity, depth, truth, and meaning are inextricably intertwined, that men build their existence. Both in families and in firms, as well as between nations, churches, factions or gangs, it is common for pride, honor, fairness, and (true or untrue, institutionalized or reflective) attention to "justice" and respect to become relevant sources of dissensus and conflict.[7]

The Social Negotiation of Trade-Offs and Ambiguities

The way trade-offs and social dilemmas are negotiated within families and businesses depends, ultimately, on the two fundamental emotional attitudes they take towards the games they play, namely, engrossment or strategic calculation. Whenever actors are identified with the moment, the family or the firm, they are taken by the game and forget that facts, norms, cognitive categories, and habits of thought, feeling or action are nothing but provisional answers to previous games, which stylized and solidified as final outcomes of past histories momentarily must be taken as reality for the current play to be played. When reality is felt as alien or seen as an obstacle or source of pressure, indifference or antagonisms prevail and actors take a strategic attitude: all players are in the game and know they are in the game, playing with or against each other depending on the circumstances [54]. From these two attitudes stem the simplistic, binary, archaic categorization by which others are intuitively classified as neutral, indifferent, or as good or bad, friends or enemies [99].

Most families, firms, and communities are organized according to a fission-fusion model that buffers the expression of either extreme – total individualism, on the one hand, or immersion in the collective game, on the other – and seldom allows the full expression of the duality friend enemy [395]. Rather, actors are typically linked by double-bind ties of dependence and repulsion that create more or less tense, stable, or unstable equilibria in which social and self-interests both complement and antagonize each other. Thus, at the same time players are unified by their alliances and identifications – giving "being" to any of the various social aggregates to which they belong – they often disagree about values, the route to solve the common problems, the prices to be paid, or the order in which needs should be satisfied or sublimated until the final happiness is achieved. The result is a series of semi-structured, unstable forms of relation that mix cooperation and conflict and always involve asymmetry of information, unstable preferences, imperfect communication, antagonisms between speech and action, and a tacit component that affects the whole tactical structure of the game – mixed-motive games that flow in the unstable zone where only the complementarity between the opposing needs to use the world, to have fairness, *and* to be forgotten in the game neutralizes the contradictions between them [97]. When the gains brought by the complementarity bring a surplus of cohesion that overcomes the forces of entropy and disorganization, there is peace. When dissensions are treated from within the game, one sees innovation, creativity, genius. When tensions and contradictions prevail and the game is at stake, there is disruption, deviance, conflict – and under the commonly accepted premises of naive realism, the radical rupture of meaning that comes from the all-or-none effect caused by the simplistic application of the principle of non-contradiction (see Appendix 2, Figure 11).

Conflict

Whether one considers the under-socialized *Homo economicus,* or alternatively the socialized, but competition-driven actor who strives for power and status, the obvious and more radical consequence of this opposition of drives is conflict. This is the crux of the Hobbesian dilemma: "So, in the nature of man, we find three principal causes of quarrel. First, competition; secondly, diffidence; thirdly, glory. The first makes men invade for gain; the second, for safety; and the third, for reputation. The first use violence to make themselves masters of other men's persons, wives, children, and cattle; the second, to defend them; the third, for trifles, as a word, a smile, a different opinion, and any other sign of undervalue, either directly in their persons or by reflection in their kindred, their friends, their nation, their profession, or their name" ([65]: 86). From the memories and imagination of this conflict comes structural heterogeneity: as players anticipate the possibility of victory or defeat, some people acquire more value than others; some coalitions dominate the means of production, the capital, or the access to communication, while other groups are exiled from the decision-making; and a few players are (implicitly or explicitly) selected to enact plots of submission, while others receive the carte blanche given to positions of dominance. From stratification, finally, comes the inevitable opposition between person and person, group and group, elite and mass – a continuous (overt or covert) strife to break the rules of distance and disrupt the frontiers of separation, the relations of domination and submission, or the possibilities of access to the common resources [396].

The first consequence of this war of every man against every man is the deflagration of the duality between friend and enemy, and with it of the archetypal emotional antagonism between attraction (love, dependence, affection) and repulsion (anger, hate, power, independence). The political enemy "need not be morally evil or aesthetically ugly; he need not appear as an economic competitor, and it may even be advantageous to engage with him in business transactions. But he is, nevertheless, the other, the stranger; and it is sufficient for his nature that he is, in a specially intense way, existentially something different and alien, so that in the extreme case conflicts with him are possible" ([99]: 27). The ultimate, often hidden consequence of this potential war is the assumption that the ends justify the means and, with it, the relativism of justice. In the limit, there are no reasons why any one actor should acquiesce to another or to a social order that eternizes a certain status quo and (always) a proposition of inequality. Both the search for economic gains and the pursuit of power and status inspire zero-sum games where there are only winners or losers, and therefore unstable equilibria that persist while useful, but are easily disrupted when the costs of war are offset by the pressures of a limit-situation or by the loss of the gains associated with the peace [146].

Facing the impossibility of total rupture and the extremes of seeing the other as an enemy, both families and firms walk on a thin line between the dangers of extreme unity, which would suffocate the individualistic drives, and the excess of conflict, which would lead to total disintegration of the social system. When fighting against a common enemy – as in moments of crisis, on the verge of a bankruptcy, or when facing a legal suit – groups tend to coalesce around common values and norms that otherwise are taken for granted. When freed from external pressures, groups often show internal conflicts that expose unseen lines of fissure among the allies or exacerbate the differences between them. In the history of family businesses, these are more easily seen when contradictory rules clash against each other – as in the interfaces between firm and family, individual and group, division and division, different generations, inside a couple or cousin coalitions – and when the weakening of traditional forms of domination requires new equilibria of power (as in the moments of succession or upon the death or illness of the founder). In all social systems and in all times, conflict is the bread and butter of routine experience, the overt or covert expression of the contradictions that exist between the multiple alliances, levels of organization, identifications, and rules that form any loosely coupled organization.

Several conditions modulate the probability, form, and intensity of the conflicts observed within a social system. Some of them are effects of context: the degree in which dissension, diversity, deviance, or dogma color the culture of the family or the firm (excessive orthodoxy leads to splits, ruptures or withdrawals, too much tolerance blurs of the boundaries and dissolution of the common identity) [397]; the presence of, *or search for*, external and internal enemies (battles against a third element increases cohesion and identification with the group); the size and type of the community (small, minority groups usually behave like radical sects, larger and dominant systems lean toward church-like forms of organization); or the extent to which specific conflicts are private and limited to dyads or occur in larger contexts involving triads (which open up the possibility of alliances, coalitions, mediation, despotism, or separatism) [398]. Particularly relevant to our theme are the association between dependence and counter-dependence and the trade-offs between individualism *versus* collectivism, dependence on the bond *versus* autonomy of the parts, or conflict and cooperation. The closer a social relationship, the more intense the emotional involvement of the actors, and the tighter the rules of association of a group are, the higher is the tendency of the participants to avoid conflict through taboos, familial or organizational silence (only to later break the armistice in the form of fierce battles). Furthermore, the intensity of this always-present emotion depends as much on the individuals as it does on the culture: "Greater participation in the group and greater personality involvement of the members provide greater opportunity to engage in intense conflicting behavior, and hence more violent reactions against disloyalty. (...) Intense conflict and group [or interpersonal] loyalty are two facets of the same relation" ([399]: 72). Especially in families and their businesses, where deep ties of affection are always mingled with tradition, submission and domination, conflict is inevitably linked to identification.

Under what conditions, then, is conflict acceptable or even desirable in a culture that strives to be meaningful? Which rules should be in place to minimize the extension of the war, making of the dissension an opportunity for novel forms of organization? How to differentiate fair rules from ideological cover-ups that merely occult illegitimate inequalities and undue stratification under the guise of social contract? This distinction between realistic and non-realistic conflicts - those who belong in a true culture, and those who do not - depends on the philosophical (and most often tacit) beliefs that in any place validate the definitions of legitimacy that give essence to social contracts. In a hypothetical group where all players blindly accepted the legitimacy of all rules, there would be no war (only civilized disputes about priorities); in a mob in which all questioned the validity of any reason for union, radical mutual destruction would prevail; and in all concrete situations of real life, in which players have fluctuating beliefs about the true meaning and utility of the game, conflict lies between both extremes, involving rational and irrational values, local effects, impulsivity, temperament, ambiguity, biases and reason acting together and eventually leading to more or less solvable contentions depending on how realistic it is and on how deeply it involves the foundations of the relationship.

A first (fuzzy, imperfect) difference between potentially functional and unproductive conflict, then, involves the object of the contention. In *realistic conflicts* there is a real point that gives meaning to the feud – a publicly defensible (but often unspoken) motive, which justifies the enmity or war by grounding them on a common worldview. In *unrealistic disputes*, on the contrary, feelings of hostility reflect just an inner need to release the tension, pleasure with the aggression, or, more commonly, displaced, symbolic anger. "A worker engaged in strike activity in order to increase his wages, his status or the power of his union, and one who releases aggression against the boss because he perceives him as an oedipal [i.e., authority] figure, are dissimilar social types. Displaced father hatred may attach itself to any suitable object – boss, policeman or staff sergeant. The economic fight of workers against the boss, on the other hand, is based on their particular positions and roles in the economic and political system. They can choose to give up the conflict and reach accommodation if it seems opportune to do so" ([399]: 50). In the world of families and marriages, probably more than in the firms, symbolic conflicts are commonly due to disillusions that come from the (inevitable) mismatch between the reality of the facts and the usual beliefs that love is unconditional, emotional ties guaranteed, intimacy natural, and couples or children are united only by their affection. In all social systems, they are often associated with the clashes derived from the institutionalized faith in the existence of truth and its symbolic association with morality, value, and identity. In these cases, as in many others that fill the life of social systems, anger is fueled by the (unfair) feelings of fairness, righteousness or logic and becomes "justified", resulting in interminable self-perpetuating cycles where trade-offs, information asymmetry, and ambiguity are interpreted as irreconcilable personal differences, hostility, or disinterest.

It is only when players weed out the passionate, unreasonable or unrealistic reasons for conflict that it is possible to analyze it under the lens of the two fundamental logics of action that govern human behavior: the logic of the consequences, for which the ends justify the means; and the logic of appropriateness, which goes beyond considerations of utility to evaluate the conformity of the conflict to pre-established rules of conduct [330]. Wars, rupture, and disorganization are many times useful, or even morally appropriate. Thus, whenever the disputed issues touch the very basis of the relationship – the core basis of the union, the fundamental and illogical bedrock of trust that guarantees the reliance on the common bond – conflict is justifiable as a means to preserve the idealism that gives a group, a couple, a person, or a family its more profound identity; or may constructively help actors to clarify their differences, to create new norms and rules, and to strengthen the density of the bond by testing its elasticity. For all realistic conflicts – those in which "people raise conflicting claims to scarce status, power and resources, or adhere to conflicting values" ([399]: 54) – the full power of the duality friend-enemy is appropriate and leads to annihilation of the opponent, rupture of the tie or, alternatively, to the treatment of the differences *from within* the game, under its rules.

On the opposite side of the enemy, therefore, is the friend – the group, institution, or person who in the moment is an ally, with whom one forms a coalition against a common enemy, who receives the self-love people naturally reserve for themselves, or with whom we discuss values under the common umbrella of a valued relationship or contract. Empathic or positive identification is, in this case, the rule of this game: any actor, in order to belong to a group, must identify with the features that mark the collective social identity and assume as his own the form of life he is willing to defend. Thus, whenever players rely on any form of mutual interdependence to proceed with a task, goal, strategy, debate, or ritual, they are, at least for a moment, immersed in a game whose features are fundamentally different from the prototypical war. To the relationship with an enemy we apply doubt, reservations, concerns, limited information, and calculation. To cooperative games we apply openness of communication, trust, spontaneity, full sharing of information, disarmament, joint treatment of ambiguities, or respect to the rules – characteristics that necessarily weaken one's defensive or aggressive position in a conflict, and therefore are detrimental for the individualistic, calculating or selfish actor who fights to preserve or realize his self-interest. Especially in the mixed-motive games of marriage, partnership, or participation in the families and clans that surround family businesses, this is a difficult combination – and it is only when players confidently *feel* a relationship is strong, relying on the supposed stability of the social structure they create themselves, that it is possible to engage in the task of working, consciously or not, in reaffirming, polishing, or simply tacitly living the virtual platforms that integrate their individual and collective goals. These are the *norms* and *contracts* that stabilize the players' drives under common (?) rules and regulations needed for any games of engrossment and forgetfulness to flourish.

Norms

Regardless of how precisely one may define the culture, practice or ideals of a family or firm, it is impossible to deny that groups many times convene around certain principles and habits; that this way of life is often taken for granted; and that violations of the expected behavior are often punished with more or less rigor depending on how much they go against the defining characteristics of the group [400]. Thus, certain families accept certain conversations and not others, reinforce some rituals but not others, and repeat stories that emphasize merit, honor or love depending on the prevailing beliefs, creed, values, or habits of the place; likewise, firms revolve not only around the practical tasks and goals that define them as action systems, but also around the values and practices they pursue. The simple existence of families and firms, which share their "being" with a series of (contingent) entities and concepts such as the lineage, the household, the clan, the governance systems, or the separation between work and private life, depends upon a broader (and always fictional) system of social facts that are made real by the actions of the players who believe in them, and who by behaving as expected experience the sensation of fluidity, recognition, normalcy. Since any form of organized behavior depends on the individual, and he is only imperfectly controlled by standard mechanisms of coercion, one needs institutionalized, taken-for-granted definitions of reality and value. Families, firms, groups, people, and nations could hardly exist in the absence of a substantial core of tacit norms.

These tacit, shared understandings of what is real, unreal, right, wrong, desired, accepted, or unacceptable in each context are, then, an integral part of every interaction, game, relationship, or social system. "To be a formal member of a social group, i.e., to be a *part* [or associate] of any partnership [or *society*], one must – before, and beyond obeying the rules that objectively define that association – be imbued with the feeling of *membership,* in other words, accept the rich and flexible vicissitudes with which the players' desires and resistances are articulated in that unit of association" ([401]: 44). These rules unite the essential features of the *pactum unionis* and of the *pactum subjectionis:* at the same time they allow some flexibility due to their undefined structure, attending to the (illusory?) ideals of agency and free-will, they also work to shape automatic behavior or to control members who deviate excessively from the prescribed behaviors [402]. They potently influence players who naively follow the opinion of the "social other" without questioning the various shibboleths that (supposedly) capture the will of the (equally supposed) majority [403]. As double-edged tools that promote both organization and coercion, norms can be accepted, ignored, changed, or subverted; they can be seen as worthy to be pursued or dismissed as ideological cover-ups; they are, nevertheless, potent and always present manifestations of the structuring forces that from the outside define what is right, wrong, real, or unreal in a place and that ought to be taken in consideration by any leader, change agent, or actor in the family or firm.

When considered in isolation and as a series of movements constrained by norms and regulations, therefore, each social game can be seen as "a concrete mechanism that allows the structuration of the collective action, reconciling freedom and restriction" according to half-logical, half-tacit, rule-based flows of actions and reactions ([53]: 391). In the practice of families, firms, and all social systems, however, these games appear to the players as multiple concrete, contradictory situations that only partially organize the flow of normal life. Furthermore, not only there are many games and rules competing for predominance, but these are differently interpreted depending on one's background, perspective, or interest: "the official prescriptive model largely determines the context of the action and hence the resources of the actors ... [But] the system is equally influenced and even corrupted by the pressures and manipulations of the actors" who see themselves as "autonomous agents capable of calculation, ... [and] who can adapt and invent responses depending on the circumstances and the maneuvers of their partners" ([54]: 19). The result of these contradictions is freedom; and as a consequence, despite being presented as a solution by many systems that boost managerial illusions of control, norms do *not* provide a definitive answer for the problem of culture. Leaders and individual players engaged in the game of meaning and organization are, often, forced to search for formal *rules and contracts*, which eternized in words exchange the soft, local, but potent fiber of the unsaid for the logical, public but rigid permanence of the symbol.

Rules, Processes, and Contracts

There are perhaps few places in the modern world where the game of rationality is more vividly defended, lived, and praised than in the firm. Firms exist for supposedly objective reasons; follow supposedly clear rules of governance and ownership; are organized according to supposedly well-demarcated lines of report, power and transmission of information; strive for processes that supposedly capture the flow of practice; and even when dealing with the intangible future, or with the even more inaccessible (and often non-espoused) values and ambiguities of the family business, they still aim for the fiction of the supposedly well-thought missions, goals, strategies, rules, and contracts that emerge from forums dedicated to the specific deliberations. The same search for rationality, albeit more softly, also happens in the family – from an early age children are socialized through the use of (logical?) imperatives, maxims, prohibitions, and definitions of the situation. In order to belong or participate in any form of socialized game, one *ought to* accept that there are rules, that these can be coded in the form of language, and that all players, independently of how they follow or violate the law, are subject to it. Eventually, these laws are engraved in the form of the written contracts and processes that structure the material and economic exchanges of social life.

According to the myth of rationality, formal rules solve several problems that plague the informal deals and commands routinely used by players in the practice – in the moment a direction for action is put in words, players are protected from lapses of memory, honesty, or attention; rules transcend the limits of the present; and actors develop a mechanism to convey the message through complex social systems separated by multiple divisions or spread in different places and countries. As ordered arrangements of clauses, objectives, and contingencies, or of logical steps required to perform an action, rules and processes should, ideally, only be followed as prescribed in order to achieve the desired results. Especially in the modern firm, but also in the mind of many actors who still believe in "rational", bureaucratic solutions for the inconsistencies of real life, the option for the idealized (but false) world of ideas, and particularly for the formalized written idea as a better choice than the imperfect (but real) world of practice, persists as an always elusive, but nevertheless powerful and enforceable, goal to be pursued.

In fact, however, "it is clear that actions are rarely uniquely specified by rules. Rules are generic; situations are specific. Any particular situation has a number of different interpretations and may evoke a number of different identities with different rules" ([404]: 23). This imperfection arises from several sources. *First,* even when rules emerge as some form of learning that attempts to remedy the disorganization of a normatively expected game – as when players are exposed to concepts and habits different from their own, when novel problems require new solutions, when experience needs to be put in words, when negotiations end in hypothetical (consensual) meta-games, or when areas of ambiguity upset firmly held truths – they appear more as quick fixes for the disruption than as well-designed meta-orders truly better than the previous solutions. "Today's rules are often [framed as] the solution to yesterday's problems. Rule changes are often preceded by incidents, crises or controversies … periods in which the continuity and regularity of previous institutional patterns were disrupted" ([404]: 49) – the real spirit of the law, to whom it serves in the power struggle of the system, or how effective it proves to be in the long term, are seldom mentioned factors.

Second, actors participate in multiple games that follow multiple, contradictory rules that reflect different values and privilege different emotions. Since roles and expectations compete with each other, it is logically impossible for any one actor to simultaneously attend to all games he promises to respect – even if we imagined a perfectly rational player, who could consider all rules without overlooking a single one, he would still need a rule to solve the dispute among the rules; but such a rule would be one of many possible solutions, which could be counteracted by another rule; and so ad infinitum, in an endless cycle that ends only when other problems supervene, when players enact an (arbitrary) stop-rule, or when tiredness leads to the creation of institutionalized "truths" that barely remain stable until new paradoxes emerge. It is impossible for any rule or contract to fully cover the reality and the future it addresses – one would need an infinite set of contingencies, rules, and meta-rules that defy the very purpose of making the rule.

Third, rules and contracts are imperfect due to the social contingencies of how they are created – even if we assumed they faithfully reflect true lessons from the past, their proposed clearness and simplicity would always hide the ambiguities and mistakes of the original observation, the political nature of its creation, the fights for its implementation, and the (social) effects of attention, contagion, groupthink, or social conflict at the time of origin and during their path-dependent evolution [24].

The practical consequences derived from these limitations is that some rules are destined to be forever laws, backed up by intimidation and fear; some become conditions of reality, the taken-for-granted and unquestioned features of the world that serve as the realistic bases for the structuration of behavior; some are dismissed as formalistic demands that never find their way into the world of practice; and still others may be reframed as personal goals, the "internalized prescriptions of what is socially defined as normal, true, right, or good, without, or in spite of calculations of expected utility" ([405]: 690). Moreover, to the extent that players are called (and forced) to abide by the laws, a relevant source of power rests then in the control of the rule-making process: rules can be always deconstructed as unfair, illogical, or partisan, giving the subordinates' "legitimate" reasons to disobey or subvert the order. The interpretation and implementation of the rule, more than its validity, becomes the practical problem to be considered in the task of organization.

Written rules, contracts, bylaws, and organizational charters, then, are necessarily imperfect. As fictional pieces of order that work only in specific situations, they are "stable and unproblematic as long as the institutional patterns based on these rules are unproblematic" ([404]: 53). They are limited because players' actions are poorly observable and unreliably measured, opening space for moral hazard, free-riding, failures in accountability and negligence of relevant, but intangible components of the social game (trustworthiness, cooperation, goodwill, effort). They are poorly enforceable, due to asymmetry of information and to the permanent need for a (never neutral) judge to arrange the disputes; and they are always incomplete, as "parties fail to specify fully in their initial agreement what should be done in different circumstances ... [because the actors] do not foresee all the relevant possibilities, or because normal language is not sufficiently precise to distinguish different contingencies unambiguously, or because it is simply judged to be too costly to write such a detailed contract" ([2]:125). The same deficiencies are observed in all systems of rules: tax codes, ordinances, codified statutes, jurisprudences in common and civil law, or routines, processes and standard procedures in a firm are loosely organized according to limited logics that inevitably hide a multitude of contradictions, redundancies, and voids under the apparent formalization. Any formal system of concepts or rules expresses only one of the many possible ways to approach a problem; refers to processes that exist within an ecology of other processes, each of them inspiring contradictory directives for behavior; changes more slowly than the situations and becomes easily obsolete; may or may not be followed; and is inevitably full of ambiguities, which are frequently explored to cast doubt on the value of the rule and introduce non-planned change in the organization. Even long-lasting rules, commonly interpreted as signals of institutional stability, frequently disguise fragile compromises and equilibria that are easily and quickly reframed as unfair as soon as there is a change in the underlying distributions of social, economic, cultural, or political capital. As a consequence, real-life pacts and commitments have to mix formality, informality, trust, and doubt in a way that introduces substantial uncertainty into the process of organization.

In the family, as in all the informal interstices of the formal social systems, these logical impossibilities are dealt with through the tacit acceptance of loose coupling. Partners settle their conflicts with an agreement, just to forget it on the next day; celebrate solid pacts that contradict other accords, following one or another depending on the circumstances; voluntarily or involuntarily forget what they say as a means to go on with life; and make frequent use of silences, taboos, digressions, and pauses, intercalating moments of true, false, or convenient peace with conflicts that recur again and again in slightly different guises to haunt the illusion of order. The same happens in the practical life of the firm. Even in face of formal regimens of rule-making and rule-following, players only intermittently enforce what theoretically should be followed, follow implicit rules about how to react to the rules, have substantial latitude of freedom to act or not according to the prescriptions, and often use rules as a way to divert from problems, and not to solve them. Furthermore, "words are easy, like the wind" – pacts, processes, and promises to respect written processes made in a moment are easily dismissed by the following circumstances and never spread beyond the frontiers of face-to-face interactions, putting a limit on the dissemination of the desired order. One is then forced to a deconstruction of the rules – a metagame in which norms, rules, and contracts are seen from above, and their validity questioned from the perspective of someone who follows other, devious, or supposedly more valid ethical, aesthetic, affective, or metaphysical ideals. *Deviance, error,* and *genius* appear as inextricably linked factors that both foster and hamper any project of organization and development of a true culture.

Deviance, Error, and Genius

From the strict perspective of the law – or for anyone who uses the law as a means to exercise arbitrary power – any deviation from the norms is a (moral) violation that deserves to be punished. Whatever is labeled as abnormal by this audience – typically, those who hold the monopoly on violence – is then framed as more than a conflict between actors who follow different normative systems, or between those who favor the law and others who for any reason refuse to follow a rule. Rather, the dominant group is typically allowed (following laws, customs and regulations that reflect the values of the same group) to sanction, exclude, or discipline the deviant other [406]. Justice is always in the middle of a powerful system of domination, as a tool by which social order is enforced in a self-perpetuating cycle and organization breeds organization, allowing a particular culture to impose the execution of behaviors that reinforce the validity of the same culture.

This viewpoint is central to all mechanisms of control that for ages have kept families, groups, peoples, and firms together. Regardless of how fair, unfair, logical, or illogical a particular cultural ordering appears to an outside observer – privileging certain behaviors and not others, forbidding certain themes to impose "better" values, banishing some truths to reinforce some illusions – an *order* is forced upon the group. Tradition thus serves the interests of those who benefit from it to harness the power of collective action and exploit others, while simultaneously promoting cohesion, guaranteeing conformity, and directing all automatic behavior that does not raise any interest because it goes unattended or falls on the players' zone of indifference. A huge mass of outsiders, unprivileged, incapable, corrupted, devious, eccentric, or just different actors remains at the margins of the system, falling through the cracks of a culture that ranks its members according to arbitrary axes of valuation. Chaos (or a new order?) inevitably looms beneath every apparent organization.

Which comes first in the chain of causality – the adherence to tradition fostering the imposition of an order, or the self-interest of an elite disguising itself as tradition – is irrelevant for our purposes. The important fact here is that both families and businesses are full of lively examples of this antagonism. There is virtually no family in which one does not see a deviant – a child, uncle, cousin, or brother who does not fit the broader or local patterns of socialization and consequently is labeled as difficult, sick, perverted, lewd, stupid, ignorant, or evil in a moral way. Occasionally, the person is a real impediment to the task of organizing, and the group is indeed forced to control or exclude the affected member. At other times, the apparent anomaly is a sign of health and the scapegoat simply illuminates the dysfunctions of the group. More often than not, there is ambiguity – families are then caught between the inability to see their errors and address the unacceptable behavior, moving to and fro between attraction and repulsion in never-ending cycles of aggression, silence, and permissiveness. Commonly, people fear the dissolution of the existing order – an international state of affairs, a family or a group – and normative pressures to maintain (a façade of) love, cohesion, cooperation, or union lead to a subversion of the proclaimed justice and the less sociable, sickest, or more difficult members dominate the game, overtly or tacitly forcing other players to submit lest the ties of connection are lost or made impossible. The consequence, particularly common in intimate relationships, is a (generally secretive) disorganization protected by the same forces of self-interest, fear, pride, and reputation that promote the (proclaimed, and often public) organization and identification to the lineage – as in all games, appearance is more relevant than essence, and families protect themselves by hiding the contradictions that could destroy them.

In the firm, especially when the obedience to the overt rules is more interesting than other covert interests, deviance is usually more harshly punished. This is particularly true if the fundamental mythic themes – the ones that form the backbone of the organization – are called into question. Thus it is that sanctions are typically more severe when one sees violations of the myth of hierarchy, by which the lines of power, domination, and submission are coupled with specialization, delegation, responsibility, and accountability; of the myths of the individual and of identity, by which leaders, change agents, consultants, and employees assume *they* are central to the success (or failure) of a game; of the myth of property, by which the exchange of capital for labor is taken for granted as a fundamental rule of organization (making of dishonesty a lethal mistake); and of the myth of rationality, by which errors are commonly interpreted as signs of incompetence, disinterest, or defiance and thus blamed on the agent, discounting the effects of ambiguity [26]. In family businesses, the clash between the permissiveness and the tradition typical of the family, on one side, and the supposed rationality of the firm, on the other, frequently leads to the imposition of the values, rules, and goals espoused by those who have control of the capital (the owners, matriarchs, and patriarchs of the clan). The same has happened in all places, in all cultures, in all times: apostates and renegades have been systematically fought or destroyed due to the danger they represent to the dominant group and to the values that up to the moment have served as the glue of illusion that maintains players together [397].

The most obvious blind spot of this pseudo-virtuous cycle – by which norms and laws define what is deviance, just to tautologically justify themselves as the right parameters of value – is that errors do happen. Haste, distraction, inattention, information overload, and all the limitations that stem from players being intendedly rational, but only limitedly so, lead to inevitable imperfections in the modeling of reality [173]. Furthermore, ambiguities, interpretive flexibility, cognitive biases, and different backgrounds or viewpoints lead to different perspectives and definitions of the same situation – it is therefore often impossible, except after the fact, for anyone to distinguish what could be a preventable mistake from what is fruit of the inherent fluidity of the reality we try to understand [407]. Thus, both in the family and in the firm, the borders that separate chance, incompetence, disinterest, and mischief are fuzzy enough to cause substantial confusion when one tries to distinguish errors that come from (acceptable) miscommunications or misunderstandings from those that come from (unacceptable) negligence or intent. Is it part of the psychology of deviance and control that vast portions of human behavior – everything that falls outside of the expected – run the risk of being interpreted as a moral issue, and thus crushed by the cogwheels of a mechanism designed to rigidly separate right from wrong, and thus deny all shades of gray.

The second, less obvious blind spot of this mechanism is that many times the error is in the machine that imposes control, not in the deviant. Since the beginning of time innovators have been crucified side by side with malefactors; witches, saints, philosophers, and scientists have been hunted by inquisitions; novel theories, paradigms, and cultures have been suffocated by the existing order; and change has been heralded by moments of turbulence, as if an internal fight between different ways of life were always necessary to introduce a new way of being that taken to extreme could open unseen, often better possibilities. The same happens in the more mundane world of the families and firms: the adolescent mind that brings a new viewpoint, new generations that offer other (but not necessarily good) solutions, the outsider spouse or in-law who from a privileged perspective is able to see the deficiencies of the system are routinely segregated, dismissed, or actively fought as strangers, eventually becoming caught between the alternatives of leaving the group, fighting back, maintaining an obsequious silence toward the dogmatic facts or even, preferably, coming to believe in the traditional, espoused values.

In most cases, this archetypal battle between the old and the new is won by the traditional forces. For one, prudence works against change – since any genius depends on a substantial degree of passion (or irrationality) to succeed, innovation and change tend to occur in the macro-level of the creative eco-systems and at a substantial cost for the actors involved. "Without the advantages of retrospection, what we see are deviants – heretics, fools, and eccentrics. We cannot reliably identify the geniuses among them until that quality of genius emerges in the unfolding of history" ([408]: 226). "Most heretics are burned, not sanctified; most inventions prove worthless, not priceless. Most deviant organizations perish. As a result, persistence in a deviant course of action normally requires, in addition to the more mundane rewards anticipated from patents and copyrights, illusions, conservation of belief in the face of failure, communities of irrational commitment, and adequate social and economic capital to endure through adolescence" [1]. The high mortality of firms and theories that succumb to the liability of the newness, as well as the cataclysmic movements of change observed in the punctuated equilibria of firms, are a tribute to the huge forces of the inertia that subterraneously pull mankind away from novelty and compete with the equally strong, but apparently illogical, drive to change [23].

Genius, however, does exist – positive deviants who cling to their passion despite overwhelming indications that one should follow the tradition [409], secluded groups who stick to their private knowledge despite the official strategy [410], true innovators fueled by curiosity, spirit, hubris, or resentment with a prior underprivileged position [408]. Whatever its source, novelty persists appearing and there is a fundamental trade-off between orthodoxy and identification *versus* heterodoxy and innovation. The more intense is the identification with a traditional ideal, the higher is the commitment with the system, the deeper the blindness to other solutions, and the closer are the ties of union that guarantee the cohesion around the common culture. Conversely, the looser the coupling between mission, values, and action, the more flexibility a family or firm has and the less definite are its identity and boundaries with the surrounding environment, preventing the full commitment that comes from the full identification and the emergence of novelty, change, or (potentially) rupture of the social structure. Centralization and decentralization, tight and loose coupling, orthodoxy and heterodoxy, strict enforcement of the law or norm *versus* soft acceptance of some deviance are features of all organized systems, delimiting a path that is traversed tacitly until *limit situations* require the explicit treatment of the trade-off.

Limit Situations

Leaders and actors alike are, therefore, always facing a limit situation. It is impossible to clearly distinguish whether errors and unexpected events that fill our routine with surprises represent a willful violation of the norm, a mistake due by chance, an alienated dream, or a truly better and innovative definition of the situation. As a consequence, it is also impossible to discern whether the players with whom we establish contracts are indeed worthy of trust, crazy maniacs, or dissimulative rogues that should be punished with sanctions or withdrawal of commitment. How to differentiate a white lie from a forgotten promise? Which spouse should one react to – the joyful, committed, or loving partner of one day or the angry, aggressive, silent, or threatening enemy of the other? When to dismiss the aggressive behavior from a sibling and when to classify it as a true betrayal? What about the differences of perspectives and mutual exploitation implied by the clash between divisions or different firms in a joint venture? How will the other react to persuasion or be willing to share the necessary information for a true communication? In face of a conflict, should we go for open war, bargaining, negotiations, or friendly discussions?

All these questions reveal a fundamental core of ambiguity, which from the center of any human relationship shake the foundations of all pacts on which men ground their social life. For everything that lies outside of the range of legality and formal justice – what cannot be seen or is not punishable, the intangible realm of the future or of the soul, the inaccessible world of the promises, changes, expectations, and beliefs, and everything that involves joy, affect, justice, fairness, or beauty – players are on their own and conflicts must be treated *from within the game*. In fact, *if* it is impossible to really know who anyone in fact is or will behave in the future, *then* all agreements that involve intangibles are based ultimately on trust, and therefore on faulty, inexact bets about the other's identity, intentions, will or personality and on the paradigmatic rules of the game that define how all motives should be treated by the actors who share that type of relationship. Either the social game on which limit situations occur is accepted as the parameter to treat the error – marriage problems being treated *from within* the combined marriage, conflicts in a partnership *from within* the premise of cooperation – or the game must be overturned, leading to the destruction of the particular form of organization in which the contradictions appear (see Appendix 2, Figures 14 and 19).

The full impact of this core of uncertainty that lies in the *bet* that the game is (or not) valid becomes apparent only when we remember that pacts must be backed by a force extraneous to themselves in order to have any enforcement power. If there is no force – as opposed to rules backed up by the state, an army, king, CEO or patriarch – games depend on an act of will: actors *ought to* follow the promises they have made to themselves and others, as well as trust the promises they receive from the players they interact with, for the pact to serve its purpose and work as a platform for the game. It follows from the diversity and fluctuation of the human being – people live many different lives, which occupy many different times – that virtually all actions, words, or discourses lived in the world of practice are ambiguous, intangible, unenforceable, and cannot be treated by formal contracts: their *real* meaning, on which we must rely in order to make any decisions about a game that extends in time, always depends on the fictional hypotheses we make about the other's intentions, character, personality, trustworthiness, or future behavior.

Confronted with the doubt inherent to these limit situations, actors typically take three courses of action. Naive players who firmly believe in the honesty, goodwill, lucidity, or character of anyone are like powerless children, unaware of the dangers of deception and totally at the mercy of chance – *if* they are lucky and the other is indeed trustworthy they succeed by mistake, unaware of the dangers they could have faced or unprepared for any disillusion that could occur. Paranoid actors who do not overcome the paralysis of doubt are prey to suspicion or nihilism – post-modern Othellos seeking for the forever-lost truth, caught in the intricacies of the self-imposed relativism of their own deconstructions. The only solution out of the conundrum is a philosophically illogical, but practically necessary stop in the regress of the rules: by accepting that second-order dilemmas can be solved only by an arbitrary decision to make a *bet*, and not by other deconstructions, players decide then to go for the pact or for the war depending on how the other is classified according the (political) duality that separates friends from enemies, good from bad, or close from stranger [151]. Dismissed as irrelevant by the (naive) belief in trust, fueled by the (paranoid) deconstructions of doubt, or accepted (radically) as part of the bet, the uncertainty inherent to this jump into the unknown world of the interpretations transforms all our social constructions into fragile platforms, whose firmness comes simply from our ability to forget the leap of faith on which they are based (see Appendix 2, Figure 17).

All interesting games that are part of a meaningful culture – the fictions we identify with, whatever makes of play a civilizing factor "of a higher order than is seriousness, for seriousness seeks to exclude play, whereas play can very well include seriousness" ([82]: 45) – depend on the understanding of how dangerous (and illogical) naive trust and doubt are, and consequently on how an uncertain *bet* underlies all decisions to proceed with peace or war. Knowingly or not, automatically following peace or war-games institutionalized by habit, or consciously deliberating about how to proceed, men are always living up to tacit or explicit choices imposed by previous or current limit situations. Moreover, acts of war tend to deepen the war, silence fosters silence, and proposals of peace may (but less certainly) favor the inclination towards amity. Social systems exist as unstable fictions of order always threatened by the self-fulfilling social cycles in which players start moves and countermoves that take their own course, regardless of the initial will of the individuals or of how they change their bets. The task of organization depends on the development of skills to diagnose and deal with these limit situations in which actors are bound to choose between trust or mistrust, without ever being able to fully anticipate the consequences or correctness of their choices.

Family businesses, then, can be seen as prototypical examples of any social system that attempts to integrate pragmatism and idealism – unstable games composed of other unstable games, in which more or less fragile contracts only partially stabilize the centrifugal push of the players' individualistic motives and of the deconstruction caused by clash of conflicting choices. In response to the repetitive, long-term interaction games that comprise the family and the firm, or different rules for action, actors occasionally write down what they want to do and specify the clauses and conditions of their arrangement; but the flow of practice is always more complex than anticipated, and actors only go back to the written pact when extreme conditions require a dispute [411].

Whenever rules are formally made, changes usually take years to be adopted and "the rule-making process itself, not the substance of the rules, is the solution to the problems" ([404]: 75). It is unrealistic to expect that the intricate relationships between board and management, family and business, principal and agent, or family members and family members could be effectively regulated except by broad umbrella agreements that focus on specific manifestations of good faith rather than on the specification of minute rules, which seem comprehensive but never cover the ambiguities of reality. Contracts are inextricably linked to limit situations, and as a consequence with meta-games on which players must agree not only on rules, but essentially on rules about how to negotiate the rules [412].

The profound, paradoxical (?) contradiction that emerges from the (democratic, trust-based) attempt to write down and abide by the rules about how to negotiate the rules – the constitution, bylaws and rules of governance – is that they always include the possibility of a limit-situation in which (authoritarian) power is required to put a stop in the regress of the rules. Second-order dilemmas do not solve trade-offs – they just change the dilemma to a second and more abstract level, in which players are more distant from immediate attachments and may be more prone to exercise the ability to see the game from other perspectives different from their own.

There is a moment, therefore, when a decision *must* be taken because there is not time for checks and balances or because a true exception appears. Power appears, then, in its raw essence: since "the precise details of an emergency [or of any limit situation] cannot be anticipated, nor can one spell out what may take place in such a case, (...) the exception can be more important to it than the rule, not because of a romantic irony for the paradox, but because the seriousness of an insight goes deeper than the clear generalizations inferred from what ordinarily repeats itself. The exception is more interesting than the rule. The rule proves nothing; the exception proves everything: It confirms not only the rule but also its existence, which derives only from the exception. In the exception the power of real life breaks through the crust of a mechanism that has become torpid by repetition" ([87]: 6, 15). Arbitrary choice, in its purity, emerges in these moments as a symbol of the victory of value over truth; and to the extent that "it is the essence of sovereignty *both* to decide what is an exception *and* to make the decisions appropriate to that exception" ([413]: xii), any culture that pursues ethical, aesthetical and ethical values must include in its vocabulary a full treatment of the themes related to *social power.*

Social Power and the Construction of Meaning

Given the need of spontaneity for any illusion to occur, and the inevitable dispersion brought by freedom, the attempt to implement any true culture in a family or firm may be framed as the history of an improbable encounter between meaning and power. On the one hand, meaning is gradually impressed by the players on different parts of the system as actors unwittingly identify with the symbolic forms of everyday life, covering the external reality with value and "freely" lending to it their feelings of selfhood. On the other hand, power is exerted by all players as they enact their drives and emotions or is inflicted top-down by the unilateral action of the elite, spreading laterally, downwards and upwards as actors strive to preserve their autonomy and expand their range of action [54]. Since the restrictions required to maintain the tradition or reason-based hierarchies of the family and of the firm conflict directly with the sensation of freedom demanded for the identification and surrendering, any culture that values transcendent ideals must, therefore, direct and explain the use of power and freedom within the system. Power works simultaneously as a compass, an armor, and a buffering mechanism that allows some slack while straightening the route and covering up the inconsistencies that loom under the broad veil of the shared illusions.

As an integral component of any culture, power must be exercised forcefully and *openly*, to serve as an example whenever basic rules of the game are in danger; *tacitly*, when the geography, decoration, task assignments, institutionalized rules, and other elements that define the conformation of the social networks and structure are put in place and influence the life of the actors, independently of their awareness [166]; and *softly* or *covertly*, almost imperceptibly, when the desired values and categories of thought are introduced as part of the common vocabulary of motives and resonate with the way players think, feel, and act in the world. In order to obey the logic of the facts, the rational rules of intentionality, and the moral constraints of appropriateness, it must respect the complex structure of the game and the limits (legitimately?) assigned to one's authority. It also must be justified by references to accepted forms of domination, to core elements of the order one intends to enact, and to the inevitable areas of confusion and ambiguity in which all actors need to work collectively to preserve the directions they want to give to the system. Leaders and change agents, thus, target both the behavior and the soul of the cultural members, using all forms of influence to ride the waves of an unstable equilibrium constantly threatened by the multiplicity of games and diversity of potential perspectives lived within the social systems they work with [414].

Coercion

Open force, chastisement, and intimidation form the core of the first, fundamental and more *honest* lever of manipulation needed by any change agent implementing an ethical, affective, or aesthetic culture in a place. "Thou shall have no other gods; no graven images or likenesses;

not take the Lord's name in vain; thou shall not kill, thou shall not commit adultery": in all societies, animal as well as human, punishment and threat are used liberally to instill the fear of violating the norms, leading to the formulation of a few negative imperatives that reflect what is undesirable for the controlling groups or for society as a whole [363, 384, 415–417]. These imperatives reflect a relation by which a person or group imposes itself on another one. Beneath this asymmetry is the capacity to define and enforce the law; and beneath this capacity, as an inexorable reminder of our embodied nature, is always the pure strength that allows one to use real or symbolic violence as a means to inflict pain, restrict, or destroy another one. It is only after the outcome of an archetypal battle, or in the fearful anticipation of an impending victory or defeat, that players naturally accept the stratification implied by their positions of domination and submission and there is space for the peace of the contract.

The relevance of this real or imaginary battle in the definition of organization implies that force must be openly used or threatened for "the element of authority to become unequivocal" and its effect on culture to be seen as evident ([36]:129). In the prototypical modern family, normatively and legally constrained by restrictions to domestic violence and obedience to human rights, this authority should not be expressed physically; however, even if one excludes the (frequent) violations of these rules, the simple difference in size or muscles and the common use of menacing words, gestures, postures, verbal and non-verbal signs are a daily reminder that animals are at war, and that with war comes the risk of a direct confrontation. The same archaic mechanisms of intimidation, which speak to how fear and anger were selected as useful for the species, are also present in the firm [235]. Owners of a company and members of the higher management have the right to fire (i.e., kill) their employees, as leaders in a family or clan can impose limits and rules of exclusion; theirs is the monopoly of the violence, the ability to restrict, force a behavior, or give an order that must be obeyed lest the tie of membership is terminated. Whenever strength needs to be proved, when crucial aspects of the definition of the situation are put into question, or when the lust for power leads to unnecessary displays of domination, force reappears as the basic mechanism of social power.

Typically, open manifestations of symbolic or physical violence are restricted to real or perceived limit situations – moments in which it seems necessary to use mechanisms of conditioning directed at the lower levels of the zone of aversion, the deeper emotional core that reacts instinctively to anything threatening one's sense of self, safety, or freedom. Both in the firm and in the family, however, the prospect of violence – in the form of direct confrontation, removal from the job or alienation from the group – is commonly hidden under symbolic forms of imposition or learned by observation, when other actors are fired, punished, or ostracized. "In joining the organization, [the employee] accepts an authority relation. (...). Acceptance of authority by the employee gives the organization a powerful means for influencing him – more powerful than persuasion, and comparable to the evoking processes that call forth a whole program of behavior in response to a stimulus" ([418]:110). The same (partial) process of cover-up and disguise of violence occurs within families and kinship systems: every new entrant – an infant, an in-law, wife, or husband – faces the prospect of symbolic violence and threats of retaliation when clashing against crystalized mechanisms of control and domination that enforce the tradition of the clan.

In most families, firms and social systems, then, the use of force is usually associated with other acceptable forms of illusion that both subtly show and softly hide the exercise of coercion. Initially, rules created as a result of overt or covert power struggles and enforced with violence are framed as legitimate decisions associated with group, rather than arbitrary sanctions that serve the particularly interests of specific actors. Habits are formed by repetition and gradually accepted as normal forms of life. Eventually, with the passage of time, pain and fear become faint memories reenacted abstractly in the symbolic impositions that target the zone of indifference. Ideally, they should completely disappear as submission is internalized in the form of the "personal" tastes, values, goals, and ideals incorporated to the players' zone of identification.

This predictable, gradual construction of an ideological system of deception reflects the contradictory, but complementary way in which mechanisms of power must be used to increase the stability of any contract or culture. On the one hand, it is impossible to sustain any social game without effective mechanisms of control that guarantee (by force) the desired order if one's survival or if the efficiency, cohesion, and core values of the desired culture are at stake. On the other hand, the force implied by these mechanisms of domination often goes against the actors' inner resistances and triggers costly conflicts, withdrawals, or veiled defiance. Humans rarely accept the brutal honesty of force without the addition of other layers of meaning that temper (or hide?) the proposed submission with other, less explicit, false or illusory forms of power. The crude, instinctive or calculated (but honest) manipulation of the psychology of fear and anger is then covered with the softer, enticing, but more dishonest forms of power that target the *reward* system of the players.

Rewards

A second basis of social power appears in those relationships in which actors who possess some form of capital acquire the ability to reward others by the administration of positive valences or by the reduction or removal of negative ones [414]. This form of power is directed at the lower, appetitive strata of the zone of identification that include all reactions to situations agreeable to one's survival, expansion, or pleasure. By it, players are personally and *directly* attached to the salaries, perks, awards, desks, titles, bonuses, or positions of prestige and status through which they can satisfy their personal needs; and since these rewards are contingent to some form of participation in the collective game, they become *indirectly* attached to the job, firm, family, or tasks that are a condition for the satisfaction of their interests (and then serve as means to an end). Contrary to submission, the ensuing attachment and submission are voluntary and perceived as fruits of a choice; target the utilitarian facet of actors, who weigh the pros and cons of the game in order to yield (or not) to the power of social or economic capital; are feeble, based on convenience, shifting with any changes in the conditions of dependence; and are based on the linear association of some specific performance with the promised reinforcement, eroding the possibility of true, disinterested, irrational meanings.

For the modern strategist who attempts to design efficient performance mechanisms in any complex multitasking system, this linear connection between behavior and attachment – inherent to the conditional pairing between the performance and the reward – is a fundamental tool of organization. Through it, subsistence, pleasure, and material gains are exchanged for obedience; and in a social system whose economic efficiency is based on materialistic, self-interested exchanges of goods and services, the (adequate? fair? market-ruled?) remuneration of labor is necessary to guarantee the sustainability of the capital investment. At the same time, however, the use of rewards as a mechanism of control and motivation brings innumerous trade-offs in which the gains received by rewarding one goal are offset by losses in a different realm, intrinsically linked to the first and equally important for the system. In the firm, for example, recompensing individual productivity occurs at the cost of downplaying the intangible gains brought by cooperation; linking individual to group productivity opens the window for free-riders; the second-order problems involved in the tragedy of the commons are solved only with the use of punishment or reputation; coercion decreases identification and de-incentivizes productivity; measurable indexes of performance have greater weight in the design of incentives than fuzzy indicators, although both may be relevant; and so forth [360, 365, 419]. The same paradoxes occur in the family or clan, especially when these are associated with a common business or property – promises implicit in the prospect of the succession, money to be inherited, or donations and financial rewards do promote cohesion, but at the cost of the more fragile, less self-interested ties that keep participants joined by the pleasure derived from (spontaneous, freely lived, disinterested) joy, affect, or pleasure.

There are, then, two dilemmas limiting the use of this mechanism of influence. First, given the difficulties brought by asymmetries of information, the ubiquity of trade-offs and complementarities, and the existence of intangible values that cannot be translated into objective measures of performance, it is impossible to design incentive mechanisms that reliably address all the facets of the complex multitasking games involved in any interesting activity [2]. Second, calculation, self-interest, and utility are frontally opposed to the engrossment, forgetfulness, and disinterest expected in any (true) culture. "Civilization will, in a sense, always be played according to certain rules, and civilization will always demand fair play. (...) But to be a sound culture-creating force this play-element must be pure. True play knows no propaganda; its aim is in itself, and its familiar spirit is happy inspiration" ([82]: 211). The fundamental problem of the use of rewards, thus, lies in the fact that the emphasis on objective inducements has unexpected consequences that go beyond addressing the real value of the transactional exchanges that link actors by economic ties.

Used as a single element of control, therefore, rewards both create situations of injustice *and* downplay the potential identification of the actors with the collective spirit – not only incentive systems are inadequate to address the various tasks and different types of performance expected in normal economic transactions, but the priority given to the realistic, but cold self-interested transactional perspective legitimates the existence of egoism at the cost of weakening the idealism. The habitual consequence is that any new factor breaking the equilibrium of the material gains, of power or of prestige may lead to new calculations of gains and losses and disrupt the agreement that serves as basis for the "shared" cultural game. These drawbacks from reward power can be offset only by mechanisms that address what actors believe to be their deeper and most personal zone of attachment and *charismatic identification*, the "freely" chosen affects or beliefs with which they identify.[8]

Charisma

The third mechanism of social power, one that targets a much deeper affective layer of the zone of identification, occurs when the power of the spirit, the push to transcend the simple conditions of existence, is projected onto a leader – "a prophet, hero or demagogue – who can prove that he possesses charisma by virtue of magical powers, revelations, heroism, or other extraordinary gifts". As in a family where a patriarch or matriarch is revered, or as in a business in which employees are united around a mythical entrepreneur, "the persons who obey such a leader are *disciples* or *followers* who believe in his extraordinary qualities, rather than in stipulated rules or in the dignity of a position sanctified by tradition". Power is personally exercised, and therefore profoundly emotional. "Officials are selected in terms of their own charisma and personal devotion, rather than in terms of their special qualification, status, or personal dependence. (...) Their sphere of activity depends upon revelation, exemplary conduct, and decision from case to case, none of which is bound either by rules or tradition but solely by the judgment of the leader" ([420]: 295). Initially, the ties that make subordinates accept the condition of submission do not include material gains but just the desire to "avoid discomfort or gain satisfaction by conformity based on identification" [414]: 266). Later, the routinization of the illusion happens as the charismatic authority becomes embedded in the total social life of the players and loses its "character specifically foreign to everyday routine structures" to more openly serve the ideal and material interests of all those involved in the game ([421]: 235).

Charismatic power, therefore, is in the core of every form of dependence in which illusion and faith play any part. It is part of the natural fascination with any game, fact, being, or situation that symbolizes depth or transcendence – a person as well as a sacred book, a firm, family, or goal such as the search for truth, identity, power, profit, or the irrational belief in tradition, morality or rationality. It expresses any deep, affective (and generally magical) connection between the actors and the system or those who personify it, the leaders, founders, parents, change agents, or anyone who somehow occupies the mythical role of a bridge between the profane rituals of daily life and the sacred or special state inspired by the idealized game.

Several archaic forces underlie this tendency to alienation and yielding to charismatic power. *First*, the desire to experience the sense of awe, majesty and energy that stems from an unknown source and forces human beings to search for the "mysterium tremendum" – the mystical or mythical union with an ideal, entity, state, or goal that brings them the feeling of closeness to a "mystery inexpressible and above all creatures" [422]. *Second*, the belief that other actors have reached this state and this can be learned by contact, leading leaders to believe they embody the lofty ideals with which they cover their interests, and naive players to engage in a "participation mystique" with anything or anyone that personifies their (unreachable) goals of transcendence [423]. *Third*, the wish to reach a goal without effort or danger, bypassing the work and risks involved in any task of construction.

Regardless of its source, the charismatic fascination with the parents, leaders, consultants, families, or firms is in the core of any form of identification, and therefore of any *belief* that ethical, aesthetic, or affective ideals may indeed signify a real transcendence from the mundane activities of the profane world. Since men make their illusions true by their actions and thoughts, these do influence the system and force it toward loftier, less worldly ideals and forms of game; but paradoxically, the same motives that push human beings toward the supposedly noble, sublime, or beautiful ideals also work to imprison them to the symbols of the illusion, the mediators who by force of persuasion or self-deluded beliefs in their own grandiosity personify the goals they pursue. As importantly, leaders, empires, churches, and political parties commonly become trapped in their lust for power and lose the essence of the dream they wanted (?) to enact – individuals and groups alike are bound by the iron law of the individualism and of the oligarchies, ultimately paying a price for the fantasy that transcendence can be lived in real life without the use of other, less noble mechanisms of domination [424].

It is precisely in the common association there is between affect, illusion, identification, blind faith, fear, and convenience that lie both the power and the dangers of charismatic authority. Without an (irrational) belief on the value of the professed values or in the word of some leader, players are generally unwilling to bear the costs of their idealism, to take the leap of faith into the ambiguity of novelty, or to face the obstacles and risks involved in the implementation of any different, meaningful culture. Simultaneously, without the full consciousness of how this belief is deeply irrational, actors are easily carried by their trust and tend to dismiss the relevance of the underlying structures of domination that control the parallel games of power, status, and access to information, resources, capital, or other actors.

This tension between the asymmetry in status, freedom, autonomy, and control revealed by the brute facts of the practice, on one side, and the idealized similarity of dreams inherent to the processes of charismatic identification that happens in the world of ideas, on the other, generates the inherent instability usually associated with charisma. Generally, this improbable combination can be fully lived only in the first moments of the process, when the profane familiarity brought by economic transactions and the inequalities of the domination system are still covered by the fascination. Commonly, the flame remains in every revered image of the past, of the ancestors, of a business, of a name, or of a lineage – part of the mythical identification with any distant world, which makes people worship the millionaires, scientists, presidents, leaders, and kings of the modern world [163]. But seldom it survives untarnished by the flow of time, which relentlessly shows how the apparently transcendent nature of even the more spiritualized human interaction is, always, surrounded by a web of interests, conflicts, silences, cover-ups, and contradictions that totally undermine the "purely" affective connotation of the tie.

The common reaction to the eruption of the contradictions hidden beneath charismatic domination seals the fate of organizations based on it – even though some players and groups are forever prone to alienation and persist prey of the spell, typically this does not occur. Rather, when power is so deeply blended with soul, or affect is so conditional on behavior, what one usually sees is an alternation between naive surrendering and radical skepticism, a succession of feelings of belonging followed by mistrust, mass movements, futile passions, revolutions, or empty utopianisms that do not reflect any deeper change in the game ([79]: 24). On the part of the leaders, force is often used. Another solution to neutralize this instability is the depersonalization of power. The blind faith of the follower is then supposedly tempered by reason, and one sees the birth of two new forms of domination often associated with the previous ones – *expert* and *legitimate power* [414].[9]

Legitimacy

Expertise, legitimacy, and reference power are grounded on a deeply ingrained habit that underlies every form of human life, namely, the need to ground action and thoughts on models that explain the bases of interpretation used to create information and define how the world "really" is or should be [425]. Once established as the expression of the possible (for the world of things) and of the rightful (for the world of values), these orthogonal axes of reason determine the boundaries of the space within which one finds the meanings at the disposal of the firm, of the family, and of all players within them. *Expert power* is conferred to those who supposedly have a specific, purportedly objective knowledge about parts of this space, and consequently a special ability to determine which meanings and directions for action, among all available possibilities, are realistic. *Legitimate power* is conferred to those who embody "some sort of code or standard, accepted by the individual, by virtue of which the external agent can assert his power" over him and determine which meanings have value within the common space-time ([414]: 264–5). Both forms of domination justify an existing asymmetry in the relative power of influence in the world of practice – and frequently in the access to common resources and positions of power or status – by reference to a moral, legal, scientific, logical, or metaphysical model that is accepted as the source of the rules that should direct the smaller games of everyday life.

Unlike the previous forms of power, both expertise and legitimacy are potentially based on the very practical (and reasonable) needs to know and control the concrete reality, to invent a social world in which meaning plays a role, and to respect the lines of dominance and submission given by the accepted hierarchies of value. Using another's information as a fact in order to bypass the costs of personally assessing the uncertainties and ambiguities of reality – as when one asks for "an attorney's advice in legal matters" or follows the "directions given by a native villager" in an unknown place ([414]: 267) – is often a wise or economic choice by which one forgoes the advantages of immediate contact and relies on someone's view, yielding to the fast pace of life [426]. People need to find doctors when they are ill, rely on teachers as guides to an unknown field of knowledge, and trust experts when dealing with ill-structured problems or complex matters they do not master well. In the same way, it is reasonable to obey a law deemed as fair according to one's view of how the world should be for a desired state to be maintained – it is only the enacted deference in the world of practice what really confirms the validity of the social contracts devised in the world of ideas. Since the rules of the games actors play and the objective reality in which they are inserted form the background that directs their movements, players who (supposedly) have some knowledge of this ground, or who are legitimized by the value structure of the accepted social games and networks, should indeed have primacy of power. In all these cases, legitimate power is indeed legitimate and serves the interest of the individual.

The fundaments that confer legitimacy to social systems, however, also derive from other sources that do not necessarily benefit the players who believe in them. In the clan, for example, commands and directions given by the powerful are backed simply by tradition – those who occupy positions of dominance are followed just because that type of asymmetry has always existed as such, the repetition of the past being accepted and revered as a reason to continue the pattern ([150]: 341). In the firm, institutionalized beliefs in the rightness of the rational (bureaucratic) rules validate managerial power but often work against the good of the firm by hurting the true experts, those who understand the nuances and ambiguities of a necessary game (social, technical, administrative or political) and therefore are beyond the rules. Moreover, the legitimacy of the practices that define the actors' rank and lines of domination and submission is (tautologically) reiterated by broader legitimizing beliefs, which once enacted in practical games confirm the institutionalized prophecies about how actors should behave, interact, think, and feel without being necessarily congruent the legitimate value they express (power creates power, weakness engenders weakness regardless of the legitimacy).

The tendency to unthinkingly conform to legitimate or expert authority happens, first, because of habit – an expected consequence of the speed and automatism of life; second, due to the limits of attention and of a satisficing bounded rationality; third, because processes of socialization reinforce the validity of these models of reality through implicit premises and rules embedded in the explicit concepts transferred during socialization; and finally, because fear, indolence, inattention, and indiscipline often hamper people from questioning the reason behind their choices. "Among all possible sets that might govern a conflict, tradition points to the particular set that everyone else can be conscious of as a conspicuous candidate for adoptions" ([97]: 208). Legitimacy, in all its forms, expresses the power of *habit* over the flow of social life.

In practice, both in the family and in the business, the lack of logic of the (apparently legitimate) forces of habit often appears in the form of untenable catch phrases used to stir feelings of transcendence. People commonly think that firms *should* be able to explore and exploit, combining the incremental learning derived from the practice with the deconstructions needed for innovations that (in fact) decrease the efficiency of the practice [405]; that strategic thinking *ought* to commix ex ante rational deliberations or reflections with after-the-fact, emergent directions brought by unexpected situations or lower levels of the organization [410]; that meetings *have to* both follow pre-planned agendas and adapt to the flow of the interaction, taking into account nested problems exposed by the discussion and preferences or themes endogenous to the context (and thus different from the expected path) [13]; and that patriarchs and matriarchs *must* blend the roles of boss, father, mother, husband, or wife into a performance that counterbalances the (opposite) effects of force, persuasion, charisma, legitimacy, or monetary and affective rewards [427]. Furthermore, identification and (tacit) belief in legitimacy increase with irrelevant factors such as the greater perceived prestige of the group; the pleasure, autonomy, and status associated with the designated tasks; the extent to which goals are perceived as shared; the number of needs satisfied by the common activities; the redundancy and confluence of beliefs and values; the frequency of non-conflicting interactions; and with the (tautological, illusion-creating) alignment between the individuals, their sub-groups, the divisions, and the organization ([418]: 85–94). The impossibility of reaching these disparate goals, all of them usually accepted as legitimate, shows how belief is mixed with consensus or fiction and puts into question the core fundament of this mechanism of power.

The legitimacy of legitimacy and expertise, therefore, falls apart as soon as one puts into question the postulate of rationality on which the idealized conscious deliberation rests. "Individual choices take place in an environment of 'givens' – premises that are accepted by the subject as bases for his choice" ([36]: 88). Blind beliefs come from tacit, habitual, or methodological alienation of the actors to the (always questionable) fundaments of the rules of reality or propriety they accept as legitimate. People surrender to the logic of systems of thought about which they do not think anymore, and consequently submit to the (supposedly) legitimate representatives of these (supposedly) valid ideologies. Without the deconstruction of these premises, the exercise of rationality – be it inductive or rule-based, scientific or moral – is transformed into a deeply unfair mechanism of domination, one that is enacted secretly because the power game is played at another level, the unobserved determination of the cognitive and normative categories from which one derives the lower level games of the social interactions.

Important practical consequences arise out of these reflections. If there is no natural or metaphysical ground for domination or submission, power is not an attribute of any actor, leader, patriarch, or change agent, but is simply the flip side of a dependence expressed in the relationship, the fragility brought by a peculiar attachment by which some deep meaning is conferred to reality. Each one of the different bases of social power is demystified as reflecting a specific stream of meaning, a particular facet of actors who economically strive to realize multiple motives and sides of their selves in the same interaction, relationship, or game. These meanings, in turn, are seen as inevitably contradictory because human beings are ontologically fragmented and cannot be fully covered by the usual linear mechanisms of control, which consider only one perspective at a time. By focusing on one side of the human being at the expense of the other, each of the mechanisms of social power, when used in isolation, contains in its particular strength the bases of its own weakness, and ultimately, self-destruction. It is not in the purity of the ideal, but rather in the dirty, but practical *complementary use* of the various mechanisms of social influence that change agents find the key to fully exercise their power to organize and direct the processes of change and culture in the systems they control.

Complementarities

The contradictions that exist among the various sources of social power simply expose the weakness of each type of manipulation if taken to the limit. Any single mechanism of influence attacks different sides of a complex human being who responds to various motives simultaneously, and who in order to be touched has to be seen as a whole and manipulated according to a framework that integrates the various forms of social power as complementary means, which are effective *only* when used together. This means that the fear, social asymmetries, and decrease in the openness to communication created by force have to be associated with rewards, charisma, or legitimacy to appease the aversive feeling of submission. The self-interest targeted by rewards, which reduce human interactions to byproducts of a zero-sum barter, must be covered up with faith, irrationality, and legitimacy, as well as occasionally be backed by force. The mythical surrender to charismatic influence has to be associated with the belief in truth to become less personal, and simultaneously tempered with rewards and coercion to be less labile. The dogma that lies beneath the belief on legitimate and expert power – forms of social power that anchor the social asymmetry on the access to supra-personal rational systems – must be minimized by the acceptance and practice of doubt; and this doubt should be stabilized by force, by economic rewards, and by the need to be forgotten in the common illusions for families and firms to maintain a relative path of stability. As Weber says, "*purely* material interests and calculations of advantage as the basis of solidarity between the chief and his administrative staff result in a relatively unstable situation. Normally other elements, affective and ideal, supplement such interests. In certain exceptional, temporary cases the former may be alone decisive. (…) But these factors, custom and personal advantage, purely affective or ideal motives of solidarity, do not, even taken together, form a sufficiently reliable basis for a system of imperative coordination. In addition there is normally a further element, the belief in legitimacy" ([150]: 325).

Contradictions and complementarities, therefore, are two sides of the same coin that point to the need of higher-order games that transcend the present choice situation. "When complementarities and non-concavities abound, decentralized local experimentation is not enough. Search and change must be coordinated (...) This means either that realizing the best design must be centrally coordinated – there needs to be a designer – or else the different parties making the choices need to communicate intensely with one another" ([2]: 60). If this is indeed the case, independently of the underlying intent of those who control the system – to create a true culture based on the pursuit of idealism or to guarantee the long-term survival of a purely economic enterprise – the only solution to achieve better results in the task of associating motivation with coordination lies in the creation of a relatively coherent, "rich web of complementary relationships, so the impact of adopting one [strategy] is increased by the impact of doing the others as well [and one] gives rise to systems effects, with the whole being more than the sum of the parts" ([2]: 232). Without the (logical) combination of all mechanisms of social control into a single strategy of power, which includes the (irrational) belief in a unifying culture, any social equilibrium results in a haphazard alternation of pragmatic or idealistic choices that prioritize one or another form of power depending on the circumstances, leading eventually to small peaks of excellence that do not allow leaders a better (?) control of the situation.

Cultures, then, *cannot* be manipulated by successive tweakings in which the system is transformed at the margin, as new solutions bring up new problems that are corrected by even new strategies. Rather, they have to obey a broad, general direction that guides the organization of all its constituents and gives a single tone to the cultural endeavor. They only survive the scrutiny of reason and the attrition of practice if and when one tackles head-on the fundamental antinomies of social life – idealism *versus* pragmatism, cooperation *versus* individualism, identification and romance *versus* calculation, informed bets *versus* naive trust or paranoia – according to unifying ideals and makes use of coercion, rewards, charisma, and legitimacy to reinforce a game that simultaneously serves the individual and the group by focusing on transcendent, future-based, illusory, and not immediate or purely realistic, gains. Because this *bet* on meaning and culture must be radical and global, and not local or incremental, it is, always, dangerous.

Organizational Culture and Paradoxes in Management: Power and Value

From the perspective of power and value, the culture of a family business is simply the final, unstable and only partially organized product of the combination of all vectors of force that from outside or inside its boundaries exert pressure to create the blend of order and conflict of which social systems are made. If one focuses on its homogeneity, it is possible to see a thread of commonality uniting players around common goals and values – the shared rituals, practices, tasks, and encounters on which people exchange values and identities in the form of games of war or peace. If one focuses on the differences, the homogeneity is dissolved and the apparently stable organization is seen as a tense equilibrium always ready to be broken. Different perspectives bring different realities – the more telescopic is the view, the more it tends to emphasize the whole and integrate the parts, reinforcing the illusions of order; conversely, the more detail-oriented is the perspective, the more differences, contradictions, and antinomies are revealed beneath the apparent unity.

It is from the clash between different values and the worldviews they represent that change, conflict, and differences of value and power become clear in social systems. Typically, these occur in moments of transition, when the saturation of a certain form of organization creates fissures in the illusions of sameness or the simple exposure to new environments and players triggers the reevaluation of the prevailing values and creates the possibilities of new forms of organization. "Our mind acts at times and at times suffers; in so far as it has adequate ideas, it necessarily acts; and in so far as it has inadequate ideas, it necessarily suffers. (…) Hence it follows that the mind is subject to passions in proportion to the number of inadequate ideas which it has, and that it acts in proportion to the number of adequate ideas it has" ([428], III: 1). It is in the moments of ambiguity and distress – signalized by unexpected events, failures, conflict, frustration, mistakes, poor performance, false predictions, taboos, organizational silences, or loops of repetitive, circular reasoning – that actors may engage in the creative destruction of the games they used to live spontaneously, opening the door for the recombination of values and meaning that characterize true cultures [157].

The universal elements involved in the diffusion, adoption, creation, and rupture of meaning can be seen as a chain of value-infused worldviews that link the various, nested levels of organization that direct the motivation and coordination of the players. This vector of value and power pervades several levels of structuration: *first*, the culture; *second*, the social units and entities players identify with (including themselves as individuals); *third*, the practical games they play; *fourth*, the exchanges of uses, power, status, and identification embedded in these games; *fifth*, the emotions caused by these exchanges; and *finally*, the mechanisms by which these emotions are triggered are connected to each other and to the system. All these levels are constituted of, and mutually influenced by, the others. It is from the match or mismatch between these links that come either the illusion of sameness – the essence of the fantasy of culture – or the contradictions that trigger the process of change.

Every time a level of structuration is traversed there is a change of boundaries, the delimitation of a different interior world that opposes a different *other* and therefore searches for *its* peculiar meaning. It is there, where individuals, families, firms, partners, or countries freely choose how they will react to an external *other,* that the game of organization is more prone to break or to evolve into unexpected, novel ways. Leaders and change agents, therefore, must have a clear understanding of the elements they face when trying to influence the particular social world of the family businesses they work with.

A Chain of Meaning

The first element to be considered in any project of cultural change is the *broader culture* in which the family business is inserted – the institutionalized practices, forms of life, and taken-for-granted rules and definitions of the situation that are at the disposal of the players at each instant. Since "all real cultures contain diverse, often conflicting symbols, rituals, stories and guides to action", this cultural repertoire is *not* a source of values, but a common well of acceptable (or non-acceptable) meanings from which actors selectively choose "differing pieces that fit the momentary definitions of the situation and thus permit the construction of useful lines of action" ([429], [155]: 277). At the same time, firms, families, and individuals are always exploring the conflicting or ambiguous areas of the system to exercise their freedom. Change starts and ends on the intuition (or manufacture) of ideals that capture the collective imagination while giving the individuals a sense of specialness, uniqueness, purpose.

A second universal element involved in the management of meaning is the organization of activities in the form of *practical games,* coordinated flows of action and identification by which actors are directed to individual or collective goals that have some meaning for them. It is from the shock between the different directions of structuration and multiple goals that exist in the same place and games that come conflict and change. These are often played out *not* in the objective world of the market, firm, or family, but in the circumscribed universe that characterizes the social component of all games.

The third link in the chain of meaning that integrates families, businesses, and social systems – one that is particularly relevant, because it connects the objective activities pursued by the players with the negotiation of the social relationships among them – involves the *themes* and *tone* with which concrete games are played in the local interactions and realities. Concrete practices are embedded in the context of private social games, to whose structuration players respond as potently as they do to the discourses they exchange and the practical tasks they pursue in the real world. Both in families and in firms, therefore, all (higher) pursuits of health, affect, unity, status, or perpetuity have to be translated to the micro-level of the exchanges of uses, power, status, identity, and meaning that in everyday life link actors to each other through mundane activities and contracts.

The fourth universal element that pervades the whole task of managing meaning is the norm, rule, *contract* or agreement that tacitly or explicitly coordinates collective action. To become a meaningful fiction, this pact must encompass in its clauses, goals, and practices the ambiguity and diversity of players and values. As a well-played game of unity, it should take the form of an illusory meta-game that brings together the trade-offs, zones of conflict, and differences between the structuring vectors that give form to the play through the creation of laws, norms, processes, vocabularies, and other prescriptive or proscriptive directions about how to proceed and think.

Given the need for a social contract to give cohesion and direction to the collective action, the fifth element that characterizes the chain of meaning is *the possibility (or desirability?) of rupture*. As a consequence, "the problem of legitimacy continually recurs and cannot be escaped; apparently stable definitions of situations are always threatened, sometimes by heroes, prophets, and saviors, but more frequently by meanings which emerge in the course of everyday interactions" ([177]: 213). The social contract envisioned as a solution for the problems of organization must be simultaneously valued *and* demystified as ideology.

From the double need to have order and to deconstruct this order, finally, comes the last universal element of change – the omnipresent relevance of *power* as a stabilizing factor in the organization. Even when one aims for ethical, aesthetic, or affective ideals, there is need to address limit situations in which actors are asked to bet or define, without any clear rules to serve as guides, how to proceed. Present in every relevant decision in the family or firm, these situations of exception lay bare the thread of power that pervades the whole construction of meaning and reduce it to the unilateral imposition of a value [430]. It is then, when the pursuit of change leaves the abstract plan of the ideas and enters the world of practice, that the cultural project shows its true political nature – an endeavor fraught with all the utopias, truths, vicissitudes, deceits, pressures, or muddling-through negotiations inevitable in any attempt to influence a system [424, 431–433]. This involves touching the players on what is most dear to them, the parts of life and of the world they associate with self or non-self, and therefore with attraction or repulsion.

Touching the Actors

Any of the various social entities or processes nested within complex social systems is a complex mini-game with different rules and forms of structuration that give actors different directions and possibilities of movement [434–436]. Each one of these social universes is insulated, created, and preserved by barriers of separation that delimit an inside and an outside according to rules of inclusion and exclusion that by necessity hamper the effect of top-down forces [71]. The farther these universes are from the controlling leaders, the more players are able to negotiate the rules and outcome of their games depending on the particular contingencies, desires, goals, and propensities that arise in each moment. The closer these are to what directly affects them and the most habitual zone of identification – one's body, soul, relationships, and habitual contexts – the more they are felt as meaningful games. This trade-off, which opposes local order to structuration, is thus a fundamental element to be considered during the process of organizing.

Formal definitions of reality, then, are clearly insufficient to fully determine the local, apparently informal interactions and relationships in which real tasks are performed and information is created and communicated. Rather, players respond mostly to their own *emotions*. These emotions, in turn, are organized according to three layers of meaning-creation that connect the individual to the world and demarcate zones of aversion, indifference, and positive identification. These three modes of attachment are both the soil on which one's actions of structuration fall and the basis from which leaders and actors decide which cultural games are unacceptable, indifferent, or desirable for participants.

The zone of aversion is the one that more frequently and powerfully draws the actors to its gravitational field of meaning. To it we map the deeper motives and more enduring emotions that characterize the human actor: fear, anger, power, pride, vanity, autonomy, sloth, or any other movement that involves an expansion or defense of one's self, and ultimately conflict. It includes all the aversive reactions to situations that negatively affect one's body, territory, property, workforce, freedom, image, reputation, or honor. Blows to this zone are easily felt and seldom forgotten – thus, the closer one is to what really matters to the players, the fiercer the games are, and the less they tend to follow any ground rules; conversely, the more regulated the contend is and the more actors preserve a satisfying level of autonomy, the closer they are to peace and to a zone of indifference in which the cost of conflict is higher than that of inertia, preparing the soil for the development of future attachments. "A prince ought to inspire fear in such a way that, if he does not win love, he avoids hatred; because he can endure very well being feared whilst he is not hated, which will happen as long as he abstains from the property of subjects and from their women. For men forget more easily the death of their father than the loss of their patrimony" ([437]: XVII). Whatever the real motives of hatred are, depending on the times and culture of the place, change only succeeds by forcing a limit of acceptance without hitting the (always ambiguous) limits that demarcate the zone of aversion.

The zone of indifference encompasses all points "within which one's desires can be satisfied without optimization, and therefore without calculus" because basic needs have been satiated and the usually accepted degree of autonomy is not put in check by the game ([438]:106). Here one sees the automatisms and habits, the value-neutral or the minimally disgusting activities, the taken-for-granted social games, and everything that people "naturally" expect from friends, relatives, parents, children, partners, employees, acquaintances, or bosses. These games both accommodate and cover up the themes, conflicts, or wishes contrary to the social organization. Subtle, often tacit regulations of instrumental uses, power, and status define how the domination of one man by another can occur; "methods of handling recurring questions become matters of organizational practice [and] cease to be objects of reconsideration when these questions arise"; choices are "settled by reference to accepted or approved practices rather than by consideration of the alternatives on their merits"; and by identifying with their roles players end up "acquiring an 'organizational personality' rather distinct from their personality as individuals" in other games ([36]:88–9, 198). *If* the actors' basic needs are not endangered, this hypnosis naturally continues and players easily accept any top-down manipulations as part of the expected game. The zone of indifference is, therefore, "the starting point of coordination: it indicates a limit to individual aims, a neutral area in which conflict is in abeyance because no one cares enough", a point where there is some margin of maneuvering to bypass both aversion and awareness, making it possible to create the tacit conditions that facilitate contexts proper to the desired culture ([438]: 106).

Albeit always relevant for organization due to the loose coupling it allows, this indifference has different appearances depending on the social system we study. In the firm, for example, "a highly instrumental attitude and a low level of work involvement can coexist with a high measure of job satisfaction" and shared meanings seem to exist simply because "the vagueness of the general goals pursued by an organization and its sequential attention to goals (which masks their incompatibility) may permit a 'quasi-resolution of conflict' among the many preference orders and the plurality of action systems" that in fact exist within any social system ([177]: 107, 137, 205). The same happens in the family – silences, rituals, meetings, reunions, and tradition often are followed not necessarily because they have an intrinsic meaning, but because they have always occurred in that way and thus *seem* natural. To a naive observer, this repetitive pattern may appear to be love or indicate the existence of a deeper culture. In practice, these manifestations of unity alternate between appearing as unconscious habit, in the intervals of peace, or as relevant facts (as in the dramatic moments, anniversaries, birthdays, or funerals).

The zone of identification is the third, more fragile, illusory, and emotional zone. It involves all instances in which actors positively identify with the system, place, family, firm, and transform them into parts of their own self. In its basic level, meaning is conferred simply to the context – the collective dream is meaningful just because it preserves a sufficient margin of freedom for individuals to participate, leave, value, use, or be indifferent to the public game. When there is more identification, meaning is directly assigned to the tasks, places, buildings, rituals, lunches, dinners, projects, or games that in one way or another constitute the life of the group – self-interest, then, finds its expression in the collective activities and brings life to the work, leisure, aesthetic, or affective games socially played. It is only at a broader, more illusory level that the virtual entities of the family, the firm, or the culture are directly connected with personal interactions and become meaningful by themselves, as the expression of a shared dream that adds an element of belonging to the private dreams that give sense to one's life.

In general, the higher they are in the hierarchy of the firm, the higher are the chances the players may identify with the system as a whole because they *act* in name of the firm or of the family. On the contrary, the lower one is in the ranks, the more distant and abstract the system is and the more the identification occurs only symbolically, through more concrete connections with the surroundings, people, and how work, conflict, power, division, of labor or leisure are lived in daily life. Likewise, smaller families in which participants have frequent, direct (and pleasurable) contact with each other foster identification; conversely, large and fragmented families are connected more by name, myth, or ceremony and provide meager rewards for the identification to happen.

Any cultural project that involves ethical, affective, and aesthetic ideals – or, for that matter, any change that aspires to be implemented in the world of the interactions – must be planned around these private, virtually inaccessible zones of aversion, indifference, and identification. The problem of meaning becomes, at this point, one of translation. A few directions are available. Generally, interventions directed at the zone of repulsion should be used only as a last resort or when the system's interests are actually threatened, lest the fabric of organization becomes fragmented. Manipulations within the zone of indifference should be constrained by the logic of appropriateness, fitting ethical imperatives and being carefully crafted to avoid unwanted repulsion. The enchainment of the rules, goals, and practices by the illusion of identification should allow for some slack in order for actors to satisfy their personal interests and embrace the social contract, yielding to the rules of a game they do not control. Finally, the treatment of the inevitable errors and ambiguities that exist within each zone and in the interfaces should be reconciled, case by case, according to the directives given by a meta-game that integrates the unity, the differences, and the loose coupling that make possible the life of any social system.

Some elements are commonly required for meaning to be part of the interactions of actors among themselves and with the system. First, players must have the sensation they are free to come and go, believe in the feeling that a game is chosen rather than imposed, or forget themselves in the (deceptive) impression of intimacy that comes from a self-imposed constraint. Second, spontaneous identification requires either a placid unconsciousness of the process or a firm belief in the legitimacy of the illusion, a rational leap of faith that the game indeed has a meaning separate from calculations of instrumentality [82]. Third, for the cultural game to fulfill the greatest (utopic or necessary?) goal to reconcile organization and idealism, or freedom with order, players must associate work and family life with joy, playfulness, and affect [79]. Finally, one needs fairness – it is only through the development of reasonable rules, and of rules about how to negotiate the rules, that individuals feel safe to surrender to the collective game *and* maintain their role as free agents who can benefit from, contribute to, influence, forget, or even change the joint endeavor [439]. This leads us to our next chapter, the study of the political world of communication.

Notes

1 "If power resided purely in force, it would be necessary to measure this force by its capacity to overcome a resistance. This capacity would not be regulated, nor oriented, nor determined in space or time, but always subordinated to the organization of the signs. Power only exists, thus, because of the signs and their relations, which are able to establish norms and laws. (...) [Conversely], if power resided only in the signs, it would be reducible to the capacity of the signs to tame the impulses of the force. But only a force can oppose another force: if signs have this capacity, either they are forces, or contain forces, or give rise to forces. Only the force can give birth to power" ([440]: 59).

2 The simple acceptance of the precept that an "unexamined life is not worth living" ([441]: 38a) – the supposedly rational command to "know thyself", as if knowledge were neutral – means that some aspects of the self are more real, valuable, and permanent than others, and consequently deserve to be elevated to the ontologically preferred status of an ideal. All the discussions in which people, families, or firms attempt to determine who they really are, or want to be, imply in the definition of a standard of value.

3 Burawoy describes how researchers, after several months of an experiment in which they or worked as employees in a production line, were "finding values in the piecework system other than economic ones. [They] struggled to attain quota 'for the hell of it', because it was a 'little game' and 'kept [them] from being bored'" ([442]: 64).

4 Thompson, studying the contrast between the notion of time in the unregulated medieval world and in the public, clock-ruled industrial schedule of modern times, shows how the genealogy of belief and value is connected to economic pressures: "The first generation of factory workers were taught by their masters the importance of time; the second generation formed their short-time committees in the ten- hour movement; the third generation went on strike for overtime or time-and-a-half. They had accepted the categories of their employers and learned to fight back within them. They had learned their lesson, that time is money, only too well" ([443]: 86).

5 "If we ask a man who is exploiting a commons to desist 'in the name of conscience', what are we saying to him? What does he hear? —not only at

the moment but also in the wee small hours of the night when, half asleep, he remembers not merely the words we used but also the nonverbal communication cues we gave him unawares? Sooner or later, consciously or subconsciously, he senses that he has received two messages, and that they are contradictory: (i) (intended communication) 'If you don't do as we ask, we will openly condemn you for not acting like a responsible citizen'; (ii) (the unintended communication) 'If you do behave as we ask, we will secretly condemn you for a simpleton who can be shamed into standing aside while the rest of us exploit the commons'" ([360]: 1246).

6 The classical experiment in which economic and fairness motives are dissociated in the laboratory is the one-shot ultimatum game: one of two players receives a certain amount of money with the instruction to give a percentage to the other player; if the other player accepts the offer, both keep the respective share; if not, both lose it and remain with nothing. Humans accept offers somewhat lower than the (idealized) fair split of 50–50, but consistently refuse offers smaller than 30% of the total amount (which should be interesting given the economic, game-theoretic prediction for which any gain is worth more than nothing) [444].

7 Of course, the criteria of justice used to judge the appropriateness of an action conform "justly" to the criterion of fairness that in the moment is, consciously or not, taken for granted as "right". Any successful process of change and organization of culture, then, depends on how players obey, or are able to change, the social concept of justice.

8 "Certain common positive incentives, such as material goods and in some senses money, clearly have an objective existence; and this is true also of negative incentives like working hours, or conditions of work. Given a man of a certain state of mind, of certain attitudes, or governed by certain motives, he can be induced to contribute to an organization by a given combination of these objective incentives, positive or negative. It is often the case, however, that the organization is unable to offer objective incentives that will serve as an inducement to that state of mind, or to those attitudes, or to one governed by those motives. The only alternative then available is to change the state of mind, or attitudes, or motives, so that the available objective incentives can become effective. (...) In some organizations the emphasis is on the offering of objective incentives – this is true of most industrial organizations. In others the preponderance is on the state of mind – this is true of most patriotic and religious organizations", as it is of family business; but it seems improbable that any social system can exist "if it does not employ both methods in combination" ([73]:141).

9 As written by Machiavelli: "It is necessary ... to inquire whether innovators [or any leaders who depend on cooperation] can rely on themselves or have to depend on others: that is to say, whether, to consummate their enterprise, have they to use prayers or can they use force? In the first instance they always succeed badly, and never compass anything; but when they can rely on themselves and use force, then they are rarely endangered. Hence it is that all armed prophets have conquered, and the unarmed ones have been destroyed. Besides the reasons mentioned – [fear, self-interest, doubt] – the nature of the people is variable, and whilst it is easy to persuade them, it is difficult to fix them in the persuasion. And thus it is necessary to take such measures that, when they believe no longer, it may be possible to make them believe by force" ([437]: 9).

5 Communication

If we consider that any information emerges only in the context of (internal or external) dialogs that make use of a public symbolic game, it is only through conversations and exchanges of actions and postures that any negotiations of truth, doubt, meaning, or value manifest the real influence they have on human behavior. By exchanging non-verbal signs and engaging in joint actions in the same space-time, actors are forced to evaluate the appropriateness of their behavior against the metric given by others' reactions. By using language to communicate their ideas and intents, they are forced to explicate their worldview in the form of defensible propositions about reality and themselves; they are exposed to different ways of defining the situation; and are called to exercise their true vocation of rational players, discussing their viewpoints, trying to convince others of their perspectives, or waging war. They are confronted with the fact that every part of human life is influenced by, and directed to, social games of communication that bring freedom from the naturalness of automatic life, but at the cost of the prisons brought by their rules.

This embeddedness of the communication in the concrete system of ties that connect actors to each other suggests that all exchanges of ideas and values "are so constrained by ongoing social relations that to construe them as independent is a grievous misunderstanding" ([303]: 482). Any communication occurs in the context of interpersonal interactions; interactions are shaped by, and simultaneously constitute the relationships in which they occur; these relationships are the bases of formal or informal networks, which, in turn, influence how relationships and interactions occur; and all messages and practices exchanged by the actors are drawn from the same cauldron of the culture that characterizes the particular place and age in which they live. These various parallel stages in which communication occurs – the individual, the dyad, the triads, the small groups, the large audiences of the firm and big families, the interlocked networks through which information and influence spread, and the culture – give particular colors to the process and deeply influence the (always double) negotiation of meaning, rank, affect, proximity, or distance that occurs as messages are communicated.

Every particular communication act is, therefore, simply an instance of the same social game that underlies all negotiations of truth, value, meaning, and social stratification or identification – a deeply ingrained form of framing the reality, by which players circumscribe a particular portion of the universe and give it a special prominence, putting the human world above the concrete things and contexts in which we move. This game is based on just a few pillars. First, there is a relationship between a *self* and an *other*. Second, there is an exchange of signs and messages by which players convey information about who they are, how they see the world, and how they see their position vis-à-vis each other. Third, there is constant accommodation of the individual viewpoint to the view of others. By stabilizing their identities through cycles of communication, actors convince themselves they are agents whose behavior can be relatively well predicted. By assuming there is a common world and shared bases of interpretation, they fix the paradigmatic criteria with which to interpret what happens and build the meaning of reality. By setting the stage and the participants in the game, they define where and how communication occurs and, ultimately, what *exists* for them.

The fundamental assumption that hovers above every act of communication is the premise of truth. Every interpretation is based on concepts that have some meaning within the common lexicon and framework of practices; on the socially accepted principle of non-contradiction and rules of logic; and on the theories sanctioned as sufficiently true to serve as a basis to define what is considered a justifiable argument in the communication game. Even the apparently solitary process of thinking consists of a series of internal dialogs in which discourses are approved, disapproved, refuted, or praised according to tacitly accepted, structured, and socially determined criteria of truth. It is as variations around this premise that one should see the universal phenomena of uncertainty, ambiguity, equivocality, signal, noise, deception, self-deception, meaning, and appearance of meaning – flavors of communication and miscommunication with which actors negotiate their social relationships. Truth and non-truth, construction and deconstruction to build a new truth, this is the hallmark of the thoughts that are superposed upon the more aleatory world of practices ruled by habit, repetition, and local contexts.

In most exchanges observed in the practice, the verbal messages with which actors express their thoughts are *not* encapsulated, fixed sets of contents that link the internal world of senders to that of receivers. Rather, meaning emerges unstably as the result of a fast flow of private interpretations and public actions and counter-actions through which players instantly express their ideas and adapt it to the feedback they receive. Likewise, actors are *not* individuals with clear preferences, tastes, character, and ideas, as one feels when solitarily thinking about his life.

On the contrary, they are constituted through the communicative acts they perform mentally or in real life. The final meaning connected to action and thought is different for all players and appears differently for each player in different moments [445].

This relevance given to the communication, rather than to one's private intentions, character, preferences or pre-planned definitions of the situation, brings a fundamental shift in the paradigmatic bases of interpretation through which one sees people, firms, families, and their identities or cultures. *If* meaning is a questionable fiction that appears as people engage in activities to satisfy themselves in the context of communication groups, *then* the illusions of identity, authenticity, and character are, essentially, artifices that stabilize the game of communication and facilitate the work of building relatively predictable social realities. The real actors who see and describe themselves as agents and free-choosers are, in fact, unstable entities better seen as unstable compromises, created on the spot as people mix what they bring from their soul with the messages exchanged (or not) during the communication and their response to the social game and context where communication occurs. Each relationship, interaction, family, or business is, then, made of a unique thread of communicative exchanges in which the negotiation of messages, interests, and bases of interpretation is blended with the (neutral?) pursuit of truth and identity to define the content, form, and channel of the communication that occur in the moment and prepare what will happen in the future [446].

This chapter reviews some of the elements that are, tacitly or explicitly, present or negotiated in every act of communication. We start by studying the various *stages* in which this game occurs, going from the prototypical face-to-face interaction to the progressively more complex networks and hierarchies that form the family and the organization. We then review several components of the *messages* sent, received, and negotiated by the actors – the *themes* about which they talk, the *tone* of the conversation, the *bases of interpretation* used to create the message, the number and relation of the players involved, the *media* of transmission, and the various games they play with each other. We discuss how interpretations are affected, corrupted, or made more clear according to the number of actors and the relationships they have with each other, to the individual motives that lead each one to communicate, to the media used in the exchange, to the theme and purpose of the conversation, and to the presence of ambiguities and egocentric biases. Finally, we end by discussing how meaning is created (or lost) in self-fulfilling circles of communication and eventually leads to the various processes of conflict, bargaining, rational discussions, and muddling through that create the dynamics of the organized system.

The Place of the Game

The first, fundamental step to understand the process of the communication involves the explication of the structure of the social stage in which it occurs – a relatively distinct partition of the shared social universe, which as a template organizes both face-to-face interactions and all more complex stages where communication occurs. By this structuration, individuals, groups, families, firms, teams, or countries are treated as *actors,* to whom one can apply the concepts of self, identity, privacy, rationality, and free-will. These actors are conceived as participants in interactions with other actors who share the same constitution (intimacy, identity, autonomy). They are simplistically categorized as similar or foreign, good or bad, friend or enemy. Between the *self* and the *other* there are masks, semi-permeable membranes that separate interior from exterior and distinguish three sub-areas within the field of communication: *our* self, which includes one's own thoughts, feelings, and sensations; *the others'* private worlds, which are exclusively theirs and cannot be assessed by anyone; and a *public* field, which is assessable by all the players and observers. Because this field is closed by the obligation of attention, eye contact, or need to respond, signs are interpreted as responses to the other and directions of action, hiding, conveying, or reflecting each other's souls. All messages sent to the public game are liable to interpretation as commitments or indications of how the future interactions, games, and exchanges will occur (see Appendix 2, Figure 13).

The tripartite division of the social space and the embeddedness of every communicative transaction in the total life of the actors introduce several relevant variables that are unique to this game. *First,* there is asymmetry of information – no one but ourselves can tap into our soul, exactly as only the other person has access to his thoughts, feelings, attentions, attitudes, or actions. *Second*, preferences are both reflections of one's attitude toward the world and each other *and* endogenous to the situation – players change what they think and feel depending on each other's reactions, following an unpredictable and emergent course that defies any attempt to fully predict what will happen. *Third*, any information shared on the public space – the data we need to make our choices, as well as any assumptions we make about the choices of the others – is useless without a hypothesis about intentions, character, ideas, or values that belong exclusively to the other person. Since it is impossible to effectively know anyone, actors are bound to make their most important value-choices and communication games based on hypotheses grounded exclusively on past experiences and uncertain bets, introducing an irreducible element of ambiguity in the core of our social life. *Fourth,* each (and apparently unique) exchange of information among any specific players is shaped by the institutionalized, structured and structuring norms, patterns of interaction, categories of thought, bases of interpretation, and already-existing forms of relationship, power division, hierarchy, control, and affinity that link actors to each other. Despite the feeling of autonomy that rises from the options made during the communication – a prerequisite for the (illusory) movement of identification by which players lend their private emotions, energy, and action to the collective endeavor – this is structured from above, from the past, and from the surrounding environment that encircles the players.[1]

The way communication is perceived and felt by the players depends on the effects of game brought by this structure. When the game is well played and rules work according to the expected, actors forget there are rules and are taken by the *feeling* that masks do not exist – the communication is free, the prize is on openness and trust, and the exchange of information is fueled by the temporary, game-dependent absence of antagonisms. Conversely, when break-ups in the flow of communication imperil the identification, actors *feel* estranged and recede to the solitary stance of the self, from where others are experienced as *the other* and information is a good to be kept secret, lest it may be used by the potential (even if transient) enemy in the war. Within most families and firms, notwithstanding the culture (or ideology) of cooperation, love, or tradition, communication is deeply influenced by the effects of these tense mixed games that involve similarity but intermittently explode in open conflict, silences, and taboos carefully preserved from the light to maintain the idealistic or advantageous threads of unity that keep players together [97]. Trust and mistrust, peace and conflict, open exchange and defensive war are mixed together and always potentially relevant in all dyadic communication games.

In the firm, as well as in the family, two relevant social problems are particularly influenced by this tripartite structure. One of them is the principal-agent paradigm. In this model, the principal is the owner, boss, father, mother, or leader who has the power to delegate a task but does not have access to the actions of the other player; the agent is the actor who ought to obey the demand but has some power to act (or not) according to the expected and pass (or not) the information needed by the principal [447]. Under the strong assumption that self-interest governs the openness or closure of the communication field, coloring it with opportunism and guile, players are conceived as constrained by, and benefitting from the asymmetry of information and porosity of the mask that characterize the communicative game.

All difficulties found in the negotiations of the incentives, promises, mutual expectations, definitions of the situation, and the various forms of deceit, conflict, trust or boycott that potentially characterize any hierarchical mixed-motive social game in the firm or family can be seen as stemming from the instability, ambiguity, uncertainty, and loops of socially constructed realities and preferences that characterize the communication between a principal who demands an action and an agent who is framed as accountable for it [80]. The trade-off is irreducible: if the bet is on the possibility of opportunism, principal and agent should develop defensive strategies that hamper the desired cooperation (lies, omissions, hidden cards, secrets) [146]; alternatively, if the bet is on the goodwill, one opens the possibility of being naively deceived by acts of opportunism.

Both in the family and in the firm, the tension between the actual need to cooperate and the (rational?) economic premise of opportunism and guile leads to a common paradox. In theory, games, incentive plans, clauses, and formal contracts between principal and agents should be (and often are) guided by the mistrust and preemptive defense that characterize most distributive negotiations [448]. In practice, for societies, partnerships, or cooperative endeavors to work, players *have to* rely on relational pacts that extend in time and allow for error despite having no guarantee about the disposition of others to refrain for opportunism or guile. These coordinated relationships depend both on bets about the disposition of the other partner (rationality, trust, goodwill) and on continuous checks of the expected behavior [170, 449]. This dichotomy pervades the structure of all regulations that define the dispensation of property and power within families and firms: the written rules created to bring firmness and to guarantee the accountability of the meanings negotiated during communication *never* work in the world of practice, which is organized around the same fragile, flimsy, uncertain meanings that forever have served as a guarantee of the promises of identity and future exchanged in the fast, private world of face-to-face communicative interactions.

Another equally relevant problem raised by the tripartite structure of the communication stage and the asymmetry of information it introduces involves the question of culture. If identification is unstable and asymmetry of information is ubiquitous, it is also impossible to guarantee that any project of culture – the idea of a *self,* the authentic or unique identity personalized by the discourse of the leader, change agent, actor, patriarch or matriarch – is honestly communicated to an *other,* the various individuals, groups, coalitions, and all actors created by different rules of organization that exist within the broader group of the firm or family. Culture emerges, then, as the unpredictable and dynamic result of a series of persuasions, counter-persuasions, distractions, and points of common interest, depending on how meanings, values, or definitions of the situation are taken as the parameters of the proposed "common" reality. In particular, the same culture that is valued as essential for one group can be deconstructed as the cover-up for an established system of domination by another, or, alternatively, seen as a worldview fragmented in so many perspectives as there are actors and moments that interpret the system [3]. The asymmetry of information, an intrinsic component of the communicative game, places all fictions of culture in the realm of the invisible, the *belief* that some common ground exists and is shared by all players.

The so-desired culture that should serve as a glue to the firm or family, therefore, mirrors the relationships and games of communication on which it is based. Shared meanings and cultures exist and do not exist, depending on the eyes of the beholder; may be reified when seen from the perspective of the consensus, decomposed as a clash of conflicting counter-consensuses or deconstructed as a melting pot of "transient, issue specific affinities" that do not reflect any stable form of game ([3]: 120); and may seem relevant for one actor and be irrelevant for another. To the extent that cultures flourish (or are felt to flourish), it is because players at least temporarily are immersed in the same ritual, activities, and (perhaps) internal definitions of the situations. As this synchrony is directly affected by outside influences (and in particular by coercion or rewards), it depends on a continuous dedication of effort, resources, and desire of the leaders to privilege a social dream over the raw, fluctuating reality of the facts. Only when they bear the costs involved in heeding the intangible social side of this trade-off – the mythical reality conferred to one's own self, family, firm, relationship, culture, or way of being – communication is expanded to involve the question of meaning and begins to work as an ample, long-term direction for action that influences the flow of occurrences in the place, despite being erratically confirmed, disproved, or even destroyed by the flow of the experience.[2]

Triads and Small Groups

This same structure – a *self,* an *other,* their masks, and the asymmetry of information these masks bring to the game – is replicated in all other stages where messages and meaning are exchanged. The first of these is the triad – the closed, small group formed when three actors are associated by a common theme or practice and, as a consequence, share a single platform of communication. Any member, then, has the ability to "operate as an intermediary between the other two" and unite, separate, mediate, transmit information, lie, give existence to the triad as a unit, or provoke separatism, triangulations, and scapegoat games ([85]: 135). The consequence is an unpredictable increase in the instability of the process: as one never knows how the third party is dealing with the other two, the communicative stage becomes inherently fragile and always subjected to doubts about how the internal alliances among the members are perceived *and* lived by all. When the connection seems secure, the triad forms a new social unit, a small group that works as the seed of all other groups and coalitions that populate the social systems. When links seem fragile, the triad dismantles as an entity and the ensuing uncertainty strongly potentiates the tendency to return to the more stable (but less strong) dyadic relationships or solitary individualistic stances.

Many of the most important phenomena that characterize the social life of families and businesses can be interpreted under the light of the dichotomy presented by the triad context [450]. On the one hand, any two actors introduced by a third one show a tendency to close a group characterized by rules of affinity. Actors are, then, taken by the atavic drive to connect to people similar to them and privilege the homophilic forces of identification and centripetal pressures for cohesion, creating the bases for all associations based on the (illusory, narcissistic) distinction between a homogeneous interior and a foreign exterior – groups of friends, alliances, coalitions, and all other social aggregates [451]. On the other hand, when the centrifugal forces of doubt and segregation prevail, the same third actor that previously served as a non-partisan mediator sows discord between the other two and benefits from the asymmetry of information to reinforce his role as a preferred or more powerful partner. The power given by the position in the network is, then, used to divide in order to rule and gain attention, power, privileged access to information or control over the channels of communication [168]. Many of the disruptions that commonly block the flow of information and introduce noise or tears within the fabric of the organization – the gossips, rumors, secrets, privately held truths, scapegoating phenomena and (pseudo) preferences, alliances or enmities based on lies, omissions, and silences – come from the combination of these triangular contexts with the widespread inability of actors to deal with the ambiguity of the communication and dismantle their cascade separatist effects.

The differences introduced by the introduction of a fourth, fifth, or sixth actor increase the complexity of the system and the possibilities of understanding it. They introduce variability and unpredictability. However, these become really relevant only when the boundary of the face-to-face context is broken and larger groups bring with them the variables of anonymity, distance, and the complexity derived from the unpredictable interplay of various different self-perpetuating cycles of reality-creation and destruction of meaning. These elements work as counterweights for the predominant role that silence and reputation play in face-to-face interactions. Thus, while the audience is still small, personal pressures are strong and what is communicated within the small groups, double and triple interacts – the local stages where concrete interpretation and exchange are lived – has a disproportionately large effect on meaning and identification [32]. On the opposite, as the number of actors increases the communication is progressively more influenced by anonymity, by the preoccupations with reputation and public opinion, and by the power conferred to the (socially constructed) *other* that embodies how "the group" supposedly perceives and reacts to the individuals when they imagine the full-blown consequences of their actions.

This reciprocal influence and antagonism between the local order and the broader contexts of communication is what eventually determines how this flows and reality or value are created within families and firms. Intuitively, people tend to rely preferably on what they immediately live. Even "rational" organizations are strongly influenced by local networks, board interlocks, and personal ties that reflect immediate, rather than systemic perspectives [452]; "managers strongly favor verbal media – namely, telephone calls and meetings (...) and seem to cherish 'soft' information, especially gossip, hearsay, and speculation" ([453]: 53); and dyadic and triadic communication stages are daily reenacted within the larger groups, giving players the illusion they are playing different dramas, while, in fact, they are repeating the archaic forms of interaction learned in the emotional recesses of private life. At the same time, many of the arguments used in face-to-face conversations involve the use of "the group" as the mythical, homogeneous "social other" that serves as a reference for sensemaking or to justify the legitimacy of an imposed commitment. "Reification of a collectivity justifies commitment. Having become bound to interdependent action, if the person says, 'That's the way we do things in this culture, in this firm, in this family'... the macro is constructed and construed *within* micro interaction. (...) Once macro entities are invoked to justify a commitment, people continue to use them as explanations. And they urge others to use these same explanations" ([32]:15, 19). This jump from the local order of the visible meanings to the macro-system of the invisible culture is paralleled by a departure of communication from the micro-world of the face-to-face interactions to the meso- and macro-world of social structure and culture.

Informal Networks

Even though the communication in small groups appears to be shaped predominantly by the dyadic and triadic fields, every flow of information and influence within larger families or firms depends also on vectors given by the broader, intangible, rarely explicit, but potently structuring social networks. These are characterized by dense clusters of actors separated by structural holes, with fragile ties serving as bridges between the separate aggregates [166]. Generally, actors are first drawn together by the mere effect of propinquity: the simple fact that players are geographically, psychologically, or occupationally close to each other – as when they occupy the same floor, are raised in the same family, share similar tasks, or are randomly assigned to the same floors during the first year of college – is sufficient to serve as the basis for the deepest relationships and friendships, regardless of the initial affinity [454]. In a second moment, choices based on similarity play a role: humans are inevitably attracted to their like, as if they permanently searched in the other for an echo of themselves to facilitate the flow of communication [455]. Finally, from the various threads of similitude that link players to each other emerge various types of ties and networks – the "others" whom "self" preferentially searches to get advice, support, information, friendship, influence, power, or access to specific task expertise [456].

Although dynamic and influenced by the interactions among the actors – in fact, they are created by them – these networks work as an external structure that strongly shapes the flow of communication within the system. They determine which interaction paths are more or less likely, as well as the depth of communication allowed by each channel. They determine the direction and speed with which novelties travel once they are infused inside a cluster [457]. Players *feel* they are freely choosing the cousins, relatives, or co-workers with whom they want to interact, when, in fact, they are following the preferred flows suggested by proximity; think they are fostering their relationships, when in fact they are responding to the pleasure given by recognition; and intuitively believe the *other* family, division, or partner is really different, when, in fact, they simply represent another (frequently stereotyped) cluster ruled by the same propensities to closure, homogeneity, and self-constrained illusions of identity and culture. Social networks privilege habit, continuity, and easiness at the expense of exploration and novelty, and therefore introduce an implicit pressure of the past and of the structure in the form taken by the current flow of communication.

It is not within our scope to review all the forms by which these networks affect how players talk and relate to each other in the firm, extended families and larger social systems. Some points, however, are relevant. *First,* the same forces that work toward a common culture – the effects of homophily, the redundant repetition of the same stories, memories, words, problems, and solutions – work against the integration with neighbor groups located just beyond a small structural hole: members of different divisions in a firm, separate branches in family, or people who must connect despite distinct time zones, countries, districts, or buildings tend to communicate less with each other. *Second,* there is a trade-off between depth and diversity of information: the more connections an actor has, and the more bridges he makes with neighbor clusters, the more likely is the exposition to novelty but the less comprehensive is the understanding of the ambiguities, difficulties, and peculiarities of reality [458]. *Finally,* actors occupying positions particularly central to the flow of communication – such as the ones that receive more connections, or gatekeepers who are in a position to regulate the flow of demands and potentially control decisional outcomes by transmitting, retaining, or distorting information [459] – acquire special status and have a disproportional weight in the flow of communication [164]. The same forces that bring unity and cohesion to families and firms – homophily, redundancy of connections, shared history, values, goals, and vocabulary – introduce surreptitious problems of stagnation and disintegration, creating status differences within the system, separating groups from each other, and introducing a rigidity of meaning that makes change particularly difficult.

Bureaucracies and Hierarchies

A peculiar organization of communication – one that is especially relevant for larger family businesses – involves the (rational?) decision to bureaucratically subordinate the flow of information and influence to the lines of command and to the division of labor that give structure to the modern firm. Formal lines of power, hierarchy, and specialization, rather than just the (desired) freedom and fluidity of communication, become, then, forces that potently influence how actors tend to exchange meaning and value. The consequences to the communication game are widespread. *Downward communication* is generally biased toward privileging job instructions, transmission of procedures and practices, feedback, and indoctrination of goals; *upward communication* toward providing indicators of one's receptivity of the environment, the acceptance of command, questions, and suggestions (but never orders); and *horizontal communication*, albeit unregulated by formal hierarchies, is tilted toward messages that involve task coordination, problem-solving, information sharing, unrelated socialization, and conflict resolution (although myopic specialization, partisanship, and lateralization of conflict also occur as people disregard the relevance of peers and focus preferentially on communication with superiors and subordinates) [460]. Social structure, social game, and one's position within the (rationally predefined) social game, rather than truth, become the main factors that determine the flow of communication within the system.

These distortions in the content and depth of communication introduce relevant effects of position in how players tend to understand and interpret what they say or hear. Leaders in the firm, for example, consistently overestimate the importance their subordinates attach to the official values or economic factors and underestimate the importance of the local, human variables, exactly as parents overvalue their role as models for the children [461]; communication from the superior to the subaltern is generally easier than in the opposite direction [462]; and even relevant messages depend on being transmitted through "official" channels and on being endorsed by someone who occupies a relevant hierarchical position to be heard within the firm (informally putting status, prestige, and power above truth) [456]. The same distortions, of course, happen within families – communication is so inextricably linked with influence and with the position in the hierarchy that the source of the information, more than its content or relevance, becomes the main factor to determine its outcome. "To have a voice is to be able to speak in the context of the organization; organizations, then, exist as a *chorus* of member voices. But not all the members of an organization have an equal voice and not all members of the chorus sing the same tune" ([463]: 389). Moreover, the position in the network strongly limits the information one can receive, as well as the type of communication one may have. Partners, parents, leaders, and members of the family or firm generally cling firmly to their values and positions of power, using the blank slate of silence to project fantasies of communication and feel understood when in fact distance, divergences, miscommunication, or simply a chasm of meaning separates them from the others and impedes the free flow of information they could want to have.

Three problems of communication are particularly important in bureaucracies, hierarchical structures, and larger social systems. *First,* due to pressures of time and attention, messages are smoothened and simplified by a constant process of *uncertainty absorption.* As the information passes through different nodes in the transmission chain, "inferences are drawn from a body of evidence and the inferences, instead of the evidence itself, are communicated". This process substantially hampers the ability of leaders and final receptors to grasp the reality they need to assess: "the more complex the data that are perceived and the less adequate the organization's language, the closer to the source of the information will the uncertainty absorption take place, and the greater will be the amount of summarizing at each step of transmission. (…) [As a consequence], the 'facts' that specific people communicate can be disbelieved, but they can only rarely be checked. (…) The recipient must then, by and large, repose his confidence in the editing processes that have taken place, and, if he accepts the communication at all, accept it pretty much as it stands" ([24]: 187). Both in families and in firms, growth of the organized system is associated with complexity and distance; these, in turn, decrease the access to information and the efficacy of the communication required for the (even minimal) control of the system [464].

The second problem appears when actors attempt to counteract the effects of uncertainty absorption and the uncertainty brought by the lack of contact with reality by increasing the details of the information passed on. One sees, then, the classic trade-off between accuracy and information overload, the advantage of one value being offset by the disadvantages brought by the other. Specifically, if information overload is treated by standardization – in other words, by preprogramming the coordination – one reduces the need for costly feedback but decreases the ability to deal with ambiguity; contrarily, if players and social systems address the excessive simplifications by allowing or reinforcing the passage of details, accuracy is increased but players become unable to absorb and interpret all the data they receive ([24]: 185). Additionally, "the very reward characteristics of an organization tend to develop barriers to adequate communication. When channels prove to be reliable in their regularity, and when there seldom is omission or inaccuracy, these very channels will tend to be used more often. But this greater usage will increase the likelihood of the channel being overloaded, thereby making it less reliable and less accurate. Thus, not only do the very devices invented to alleviate communication difficulties tend to produce new sources of communication trouble, but even success in the surmounting of such difficulties produces new blockages in the already existing structures" ([456]: 561). As actors pursue the (idealized) precision of communication, they move away from ambiguity and thus give up the gains that come from interpretive flexibility (i.e., evaluating many sides of the same problem); communication is then poorer, leading to the endless cycles of error corrections that characterize the intuitive treatment of all trade-off situations.

A third communication problem derives from the trade-off between coordination and productivity, namely, the fact that any organization requires both division of labor and individual motivation *and* efficient or fluid coordination between the parts (what is impossible) [2]. Thus, the more complex is the system, the more the productivity gained by specialization is offset by the indeterminacy and confusion in the treatment of borderline situations, organized complexities, and wicked or ill-structured problems, for which good communication and multidisciplinary approaches are necessary [276–278]. Interfaces between horizontal divisions in a firm, separate families in a multi-family business, or vertical levels in a hierarchy are particularly sensitive to this problem – not only they involve structural holes that separate cluster from cluster in the social networks, but also social voids are typically immune to control systems that could potentially regulate the flow of communication (any third-party element, as a boss, mediator, judge, or other division, would just introduce two other interfaces) [465]. The same mechanisms that facilitate communication in one area, forcing close actors to tackle similar problems through the use of similar techniques and vocabulary, also make it difficult for them to traverse the symbolic and geographic distances that are essential to the development of any complex organization. Centralization allows direct communication, but is inevitably opposite to the decentralization that permits complexity; therefore, both constantly alternate with each other ([2]: 56).

The Game of Communication

In a strict sense, an act of communication could be seen as a simple exchange of signs between two or more actors, who by creating messages about themselves and the world define their directions for collective action or sensemaking. According to this (idealized) framework, semantically neutral symbols or signs – sounds, words, gestures, or any other signifiers that have no intrinsic meaning – are interpreted, combined, and negotiated to create propositions about reality or value. Signifiers are connected to the signified by stable and clear ties; both the set of symbols and the bases of interpretation are known and shared among actors; areas of truth and doubt are well circumscribed, allowing players to reduce uncertainty simply by getting new information; and eventually, definitions of the situation emerge clearly from the communicative process and allow players to engage in fruitful deliberations, fair conflicts, concerted action, or just amusing exchanges of meaning.

Communication, however, is more complex. To start with, the different parameters with which one evaluates the efficacy and validity of a message – and, as a consequence, if there is communication or miscommunication – depend on the goals of the exchange, and thus on how the social game desired by the players and negotiated in real time during their interaction game emphasizes verisimilitude, accountability, persuasion, entertainment, or illusion. *Verisimilitude* – the extent to which a communication appears to be true – is constrained by the need to match the idea to the world it attempts to depict. *Accountability,* a measure of reliability and commitment, depends on *norms,* not on reality – it then taps into an alternative decision logic, "the logic of appropriateness, obligation, identity, duty, and rules" through which players negotiate their promises of permanence and obedience to the social game ([466]: 66). *Influence* – tainted by the need to persuade – minimizes the validity or coherence usually required from truth-seeking exchanges or ethical proposals of identity and accepts whatever is effective to induce a desired belief or action in the recipient. *Distraction and entertainment*, which characterize all pragmatically useless exchanges of stories, affect, jokes, and irrelevancies that characterize the small talk, depend only on themes that reinforce the social bond or fill the vacuum of the moment (stories, myths, jokes, as well as news or truths). *Deception* thrives on ambiguity and noise, privileging the impact, appearance, and form of the message needed to convey unspeakable contents [467]. *Illusion* (or self-deception?) blends truth and value in the form of romantic messages, privileging the engrossment in the game and the deeply irrational nature of men [33]. As all these (contradictory) goals are generally mixed in any (purportedly logical) communication, the final form and flow of the social exchange depend on how they complement or clash against each other to fit (or not) the mix of purposes directing the behavior of the actors in the communicative context they share. Furthermore, they reveal a fundamental trade-off of communication: the stability of the exchange depends on the adherence to the ideal of truth, but all relationships and social games depend on omissions that must be carefully preserved from reason for the game to continue.

The way individuals, families, and firms deal with this trade-off always involves a carefully crafted, and necessarily tacit system of unspoken "oughts" and "cannots", which blended together guarantee the permanence of communication as an improbable coexistence of truth and illusion. Generally, the adherence to truth is widely proclaimed in all speeches that praise the value of candidness, honesty, or openness. However, it is in the requirement to omit or avoid unspeakable themes and to maintain a stable identity – a sustainable illusion, a relatively fixed set of attitudes, ideas, values, and dispositions (ideally) transposed from one stage of communication to another – that one sees the full weight of social pressure. Messages and identities exchanged during any act of communication, therefore, must be consistent with the rules of illusion that give form to the particular type of social game in which this occurs: love in loving relationships, exclusiveness in monogamous marriages, trust in cooperative partnerships, mistrust in conflicting interactions, respect in front of experts and leaders, obedience or submission in legitimate subordination.[3]

Any instance of communication, then, always transcends the solitary world of the information-seeker or the neutral attempt to transmit or receive a message because it adds a distinct type of social exchange to the basic concept of truth. Signs and products of knowledge are as much a means of communicating one's understanding of reality as they are tools to justify the past, to build a future, or to connect actors in an interactive, cooperative, or agonistic (but always illusory) game. Furthermore, for any message to be object of a discussion and for any consensus or dissensus to be reached, people have to temporarily assume the firmness of the cognitive and social premises required for the dialog (or war) to continue. Before one judges the validity of an argument, information, or communication, it is necessary to evaluate the role it plays in the life of the actors involved in the process (validity for what?) [34].

Theme and Tone

It follows from the intrinsic association between communication and social world that any communicative transaction is automatically interpreted in relation to the two universes shared by the actors: the reality they talk about – the things, people, space, future, themselves, or their relationship – and the social world they create in the moment of the exchange, depending on *how* they talk about these issues. The first can be seen as the *theme* of the communication – the denotative component of the conversation, the object of thought or discussion, the message transmitted as actors use symbols, sentences, and (mostly verbal) language to establish, convey and emergently negotiate their definitions of the situation. *The tone* given to the interaction reflects the more primitive, affective, and often implicit proposal of how actors should position themselves vis-à-vis each other. Differently from the theme, this is present in the connotative nuances of the language and in non-verbal cues such as eye contact, facial expression, posture, interpersonal distance, or volume and intonation of the voice. Together, these cues signal the blend of aggression, peace, intimacy, hierarchy, or love players propose to each other as the basis for their common universe; they thus give shape to the social world shared by the players, which is created and changed often independently of the themes they discuss [347, 468–471]. In practice, theme and tone are negotiated in parallel and simultaneously in every act of communication. Messages are embedded in the situation and transformed into parts of a social fact depending on how theme and tone are interpreted based on the (intangible) framework of meanings actors use to contextualize the inputs they receive. This context involves both the objective reality they talk about *and* the subjective social world that will serve as a platform for future interactions [241, 472, 473]. Both need to be studied separately (see Appendix 2, Figure 16).

The theme of the exchange, the component to which players intuitively pay attention and respond to, is in fact the more superficial layer of the communicative process. The stability on which its stability rests – the assumption that communication is ethically neutral and purports to describe and understand reality, rather than to manipulate it or provide a stage for the action and identity games it involves [297] – must remain unquestioned for the practical discussion to continue. Thus, insofar as players are not concerned about their differences of taste, option, or value, and can rely on the firmness of the shared social world, actors in the firm can debate about which strategy to pursue, couples can discuss where to spend the next vacation, or members of a family can define rules of succession, establish limits to be put on the common property, or engage in any form of (productive) conflict. In contrast, whenever there are prejudices, covert opinions, conflict, or value-choices disguised under the objective preoccupations about reality, the proposed definitions of the situation or self are automatically interpreted as potentially false. The communication exchange comes to a crossroad. Players are called to take a stance on the political distinction between friend and enemy, or good and bad, and either continue or break the communication. Intentional or not, momentary or permanent, this step inexorably affects the ensuing flow of transmission and interpretation of information [99].

The tone of this communication – the disposition with which players enter into the game or react to it during the interaction – is, therefore, the soil on which rests the fate of every explicit conversation. Given a positive tone, the communication is likely to unfold as a collaborative construction of meaning and potential difficulties of interpretation tend to resolve within the rules of the game. Given a negative disposition, the exchange is bound to fail or become meaningless as a creative interaction because actors detach from the game and become immersed in *their* interests. It is based on this tone, and on how it is related to a denial of, or engrossment in the game, that all acts of communication and the interactions or relationships on which they are grounded are classified as good or bad, amicable or conflictive, deep or superficial, honest or dishonest, close or distant, cold or warm, smooth or tense, intimate or formal, firm or unstable, or open or secretive. Moreover, the social universe on which any communication occurs extends beyond the present themes to cover all themes that can be treated by the same players in the future or may be communicated to other actors. It includes the definitions of distance, proximity, dominance, submission, and the boundaries between public and private. It determines the disposition for cooperation, expectancy, overt or covert war. It gives the peculiar color with which subjects and choices will tend to be treated in the context of the game.

Although theme and tone are always present (and interconnected) in any communication, the latter is generally more relevant in defining the outcome of the exchange. This preference bears a striking resemblance to the economic anomaly by which players consistently take into account fairness and identification, and not only self-interest, when engaged in their negotiations of value. It shows that the social world on which communication (and life) rest is never simply rational, but also based on feeling, emotion, honor, pride, value, depth, and meaning. More importantly, since the non-verbal cues that convey the tone of the interaction have a rapid, preferential, and involuntary access to the emotional brain, actors often react impulsively to the coarse definitions of the situation suggested by them and disregard the fine, objective nuances of reality that can be transmitted only semantically and by much slower neuronal paths reach the actors' conscious discussions of the theme [471]. The attention to the social field in which the communication flows reflects both our biological inheritance and an existential attitude that gives more weight to the socially constructed reality than to the facts that compose the concrete reality.

Theme and tone, thus, reflect two different, but fundamental facets of the same phenomenon – the stabilization of meaning required to provide an objective view of reality, and the subjective perception and evaluation of how actors position themselves toward the theme and each other. Each of them offers a viewpoint that illuminates different elements of the final definition of the situation; each obeys to a different logic, offering a pragmatically useful direction of action that has clearly stood the test of time; both are processed in parallel and often bring divergent directions for what to do. The decision about how to proceed, therefore, often requires the sacrifice of a perspective that intuitively makes sense in order to privilege another one that is equally relevant but that in the moment (contingently) appears more important. What should one respond to, theme, or tone? Should one prioritize *what* is discussed, focusing on the pragmatic consequences and truth or untruth of the messages? Or, alternatively, should one focus on *how* the themes are treated and shift gears, making of the tone of the interaction and of the relationship per se the real object of the communicative exchange? How to blend both approaches into one single message, manipulating verbal and non-verbal signs to better treat the trade-off between utility and social life? The intuitive, automatic, or planned answers players give to these questions are so inextricably combined that each communication always becomes the weighed sum of their reactions to the issue at stake and to all games they play with their interlocutors, including the present ones. Any act of communication is momentary, present-oriented, and deeply structurally connected to the total social game played among the actors.

The Media

Another relevant, structuring element of the communication, which works in parallel with the number of actors and complexity of the network, involves the media used to transmit the messages. We may start with the prototypical medium, the face-to-face interaction when seen as a conduit of meaning, and not simply as a social game – a multifaceted channel that involves several parallel types of information hitting all the senses and making full use of verbal and non-verbal symbols. In this medium, explicit and implicit messages fluctuate in real time in response to the flow of communication and to the changes of preferences; both are blended in the interplay of narrative and practice; verbal and non-verbal cues address the problem of the tone and words deal with the theme; and the spoken language, allowing multiple digressions, recursivity, and free use of ontological oscillation, creates a suitable means to deal with the complexity, nested problems, and ambiguities of reality [474].

As rich as face-to-face interactions are as a means of communication, however, they do not help in games that extend in time or space. They fail, therefore, in the task of providing a more fixed medium to stabilize message and meaning; they do not address the multiple times and spaces that must be covered by the communication game in larger systems; they are limited by effects of timing, uncertainty absorption, serial diffusion, and the distortions introduced (voluntarily or not) as the message goes from one node to another; they provide depth, but not permanence or scope. Thus, whenever the exchange network goes beyond a few people, extends beyond the present moment, or there is need of documentation, one needs media with more fixedness and higher range of transmission to overcome the unstable dynamism of the social structure [475]. This is particularly relevant in the firm, but also happens in the family. In these cases, emails, memos, written messages, documents, presentations, and other formal means of communication are used to guarantee (?) uniformity of understanding, to serve as a basis for future demands of accountability, and to spread information across multiple groups, levels, or divisions separated by geographic and structural distance. In the same way, phone calls, video-conferences with distant relatives or partners, letters and social media routinely complement, or are used as a (poor?)

substitute for face-to-face interactions. Generally, players use all available means to connect them to others and create a (complementary or contradictory) mosaic of different definitions of the situation, shared through different media and in different times.

The relevant trade-offs, here, involve the tensions between depth, scope and range. Rich or hot media – such as the face-to-face interaction – privilege depth at the expense of range; they are the ones that convey the greatest amount of information, require less attentional involvement from the receptor, capture more shades of meaning, open various possibilities of interpretation, provide a proper setting for immediate feedback, and include various cues, channels, personalization, language variety, and shock of perspectives. Simple or cool media, on the contrary, privilege the range of transmission or size of the audience and offer more stereotyped content, requiring actors to exercise their imagination (or illusions of certainty) to overcome noise, inattention or missing data and eventually contextualize the information received in order to confer cognitive or affective significance to the data (the prototype being a purely numeric document, or a television) [476]. There are the rules and suggested modes of diffusion – this can occur serially, locally, slowly, and costly (for relevant, important information); quickly, in parallel, using mass media in more shallow ways (for simple commands and ceremonial communication); or carefully, by local infusion in the nodal points of centrality of the informal networks (for persuasion and commitment) [457]. Generally, gains in the permanence of the message and range of receptors are offset by losses in depth, in the ability to respond quickly to the context, or in the rhetoric, expression, and co-construction of meanings inherent to the interpersonal communication [456].

Different objectives and situations, therefore, ask for different media and for "communication transactions that can overcome different frames of reference or clarify ambiguous issues" ([465]: 560) – goals and perspectives change depending on how much the focus is on negotiations of meaning and equivocality among players, on the organization of the firm's discourse, on the coordination of the activities, or on the creation of (authentic?) displays of identity [477]. Ideally, the choice of media *should* match the goal of the communication and respond to the structural limitations given by the size, dispersion, and nature of the audience. Players, however, are usually inattentive to the effects of the particular technology or product of knowledge they use, to how the choice of medium affects the interplay of theme and tone, or to the parallel messages they transmit during the same act of communication [478]. The consequence of this inattention is, often, a mismatch between the nature of the situation and the means of communication used to deal with it. Actors are (innately?) pushed by the affective value intuitively given to face-to-face interactions. At the same time, they are trained (and pragmatically or normatively coerced) to rely on the media institutionally seen as adequate in the particular social system where the communication occurs or to use whatever means of communication seems faster or easier in the instant. The medium, and not the content of the communication or the intention of the actors, becomes the source of the problems. Discussions of deep emotional questions done through Tweeter or WhatsApp messages, interpretations imposed on shallow comments transmitted uncritically by email or Facebook pages, private issues inadvertently disclosed in Instagram and other social media, PowerPoint presentations that do not allow the discussion of ambiguities or nested problems are just a few examples of how the choice of the media is often aleatory and responds more to the players' momentary interests, limitations of attention, or institutionalized practices of how to respond [463, 479]. They show how technology and contingent choices of media converge with the stage of the communication, the theme, the tone, and multiple emergent, unpredictable factors to dictate the *flow* of the interaction.

The Flow of Communication

The only way to understand the flow of communication and the traps of miscommunication caused by the naive belief in the naturalness of the game is the permanent recollection that communicative exchanges are indeed *games* – rule-based endeavors by which players pursue arbitrary and contradictory goals, blending them into single messages that evolve in time with the flow of theme and tone. The validity of the game is guaranteed by reaffirming the double postulate of truth and illusion: cheating implies in falsification of a postulate, inappropriateness or naive candidness of the other. To play the game, players *have to* put their egocentric perspective within brackets in order to pay attention to other players and effectively evaluate their viewpoints; *have to* imagine how they are seen by the interlocutors, lest they become lost in their own self-perceptions; *have to* focus on the flow of the exchange at the same time they internally weigh their own preferences, making of the communication both a means of self-expression *and* a form of social negotiation; and *have to* know the common bases of interpretation and the values given to illusion or truth depending on the type of game they play. Closely linked to these premises, as a reminder that tricks, fraud, and truth may have bad consequences, are the expectations that people *should* be rational, commit to the identities they sell, and fulfill the promises made in the public stage.

The stability of this inherently unstable, contradictory game of communication depends on both structural and local factors. The perspective of the structure involves all elements that transcend the players because these are framed as parts of a broader plot that goes beyond the present exchange. Credibility due to status, prestige, power, charisma, legitimacy or by a long-term relationship, for example, contributes to increase the stability of meaning and force the communication process in the directions previously traversed or classified as "normal". Patterns of communication that conform to the institutionalized directions of meaning in the culture tend to be better accepted than those who follow unknown paradigms. The more facts a particular interpretation explains, and the more redundantly this interpretation reiterates the reality of the nested parallel social games played by the actors – like seeing a loving movement in a love relationship, acknowledging the payment of salary at the end of the month, or observing an aggressive move among competitors – the more the communication flows smoothly and the taken-for-granted interpretations are (circularly) confirmed by their own enactment during the communicative exchange. Conversely, dissonances, errors, surprises, or antagonisms between one game and another – like an instrumental demand emerging in the context of a friendship – tend to destabilize the meaning and increase the chances that the communication exchange will fall apart due to inattention, tiredness, resistance, or animosity of the tone.

In parallel with the forces that from top-down constrain the communicative process, the emergent and unpredictable components of the message-exchange game result from the peculiar way in which meaning, doubt, ambiguity, peace, conflict, theme, and tone are combined with each other and from bottom-up determine the flow of the interaction [445]. Commonly, communication follows erratic paths that reflect the limitations of attention, speed, and information overload of routine life. Communication then occurs by chance, and players find islands of true exchange (or feeling of exchange) and accepted satisficing, but not optimal solutions for their definitions of meaning and reality. At other times, as in all the desired (but rare) effective communicative transactions, problems are more focused, the relationship is clear, or players more used to the game they play with each other succeed in negotiating the common definitions of the situation maintaining an amicable tone that reinforces the stabilized shared meaning. Although fragile and dependent on effort, and not on naturalness, these perfect dialogs should probably be kept as an ideal to which players can return as in a (mythical?) search for the consensus or for the consensual ways with which to treat their dissensus. They are the standard of organization, the transient goal of common cultures insofar as they accept differences among their members.

Games, however, are simply games – desired or institutionalized social creations whose rules are made to guarantee that players depart in a predictable way from how they *would* behave if left to their natural inclinations. All the violations of communication observed in the family or firm, thus, should be seen as willful or involuntary errors in a game, instances in which uninformed, boundedly rational or strategic actors are lost in the ambiguities, biases and self-fulfilling cycles of communication or take advantage of these contradictions to foster conflict, reach a social goal, or provoke change [157]. In these cases, the communication is marked by the fear, inability, unwillingness, pride, dishonesty, or inflexibility of players that do not question their bases of interpretation or fail to move smoothly between various hypotheses about each other's identities. Exchanges that fall into this trap then turn into endless voyages into the regress of the rules, in which players search for impossible guarantees that trust, good faith, or lucidity do exist; or end by fatigue, if and when players satiate their nihilistic thirst and forget their skepticism in order to (again and again) move on; or turn into make-believe games that substitute the premise of doubt for the premise of trust – all players tacitly agree to maintain the appearances despite being untrue, betting the messages they receive are untrue and betting that all players are fully aware of the true nature of the untruth-game (an outcome not rare in organizations and even in the family). All forms of organization always go back, as in an endless circle, to the need to discuss the possibilities of doubt without violating the premise of truth.

The epistemic essence of any communication involves, then, "two interrelated discursive practices: collaboration to negotiate meaning and cartography to adjudicate interests" ([478]: 343). Both bring the possibility of miscommunication. Under the premise of truth, even well-intentioned rational actors are deceived by semantically contradictory, but similarly rigid interpretations or definitions of the situation. Likewise, the (always partial) selection of the themes brought to the table, the choice of the media, and the depth and form in which themes are treated depend on the value-based match or mismatch between the players' expectations or emotions. It is not in the institutionalized ideals of objectivity, but in the value-laden social world and in the drives for adaptation, power, control, or identification that we find the key to understand the flow of communication and the origin of the divergent meanings openly shared in the public space or privately held in the soul of the participants of any communication game. This involves the study of the *ambiguities*, *biases,* and *self-fulfilling cycles of communication* that, by themselves, hamper the flow of the game.

Ambiguity

"Any theory of organizations is necessarily also a theory of hypocrisy, a theory of the role of lies in sustaining human institutions and commitments to ideals, and a theory of the emotional response to involvement in a system of lies" [480]. With these words, March rhetorically exposes the pseudo-paradox raised by the fact that families, firms, and people continuously search for solid truths to go on with life even while knowing that truths are, always, unstable social creations negotiated within equally unstable communication games. This dichotomy introduces a fissure in the ground that supposedly stabilizes the communication.

Specifically, for actors who search for certainty, illusions are either error or willful deceit, but never legitimate objectives of a game; and as all players are involved in multiple, contradictory games, any unveiling of the conditions of multitasking is commonly framed as a limit situation potentially linked to conflict, and rarely as a ludic crossroad in a game of communication designed to stabilize the (unmanageable) fluidity of life. Ambiguity, then, emerges as a problem that apparently resides in reality, and not in the (vain) search for perfect coherence.

The more superficial zone of ambiguity in the communication involves the lack of precision due to noise, contradictory signs, foggy perceptions, or complexities that preclude easy contextualization. This includes, first, the intrinsic difficulties brought by the object of the message. "People are raw materials in people-changing or people-processing organizations; symbols are materials in banks, advertising agencies and some research organizations; the interactions of people are raw materials to be manipulated by administrators in organizations; boards of directors, committees, and councils are usually involved with the changing or processing of symbols and human interactions, and so on" ([279]: 195). Every communication involves, always, the transformation of the raw material of experience – a volatile, fast, and mostly tacit flow of events and sensations – into a fixed definition of the situation or well-structured problem, which can be treated verbally precisely because it was simplified, symbolized, falsified.

The consequence of this (necessary, desired, willed) falsification is that safer and more predictable materials, for which there is a well-established system of meanings, provide easy themes that generally allow for smooth communicative exchanges. These include the day-to-day subjects, observations, questions, answers, commands, or comments that reiterate habitual practices of relationship or work. In contrast, materials that present many exceptions, that are less understood, more variable, and unstable, or that involve many facets are inherently ambiguous and lead to imprecise or inefficient communication. For this reason, any attempts to define the firm's identity, the character of the players, the "true" values of a family or culture, or how these values should be applied in each case are bound to unleash interminable discussions in which players typically become lost in the (pseudo) paradoxes brought by the contrast between the complexity of reality and the simple, stable meanings required for the social game to proceed under the usual assumptions of truth. Complexity, as well as ambiguity due to complexity, are always present.

A second zone of ambiguity in communication emerges from doubts about the transmission, reception, or interpretation of the message. In this case, the bottleneck in the communication shifts from the interface between man and reality to the interface between man and man. Does the message convey all ideas of the emitter? How did the audience understand what was said? How many variations of meaning can be imputed to the same content? The ambiguity brought by these questions is increased by the fact that any message simultaneously serves many (contradictory) purposes – inquiry, explanation, persuasion, manipulation, filling up, or illusion in the meaning. Actors, leaders, and change agents in the firm or family are *not* necessarily attempting to increase the clarity, redundancy, and simplicity of their messages. Rather, they are *always* negotiating the trade-offs that exist between the excessively simple and the hard-to-understand communication, as well as between attending to the practical demands of reality *and* the purposes, social impact and tone of the communication game they are playing, depending on how the fluidity or ambiguity of meaning attends (or not) their contradictory goals [467].

A third zone of ambiguity comes from the fact that actors always fluctuate across different levels of analysis, giving "being" to distinct social entities in different times and thus bringing up various instabilities associated with ontological oscillation. Moreover, even when the epistemic bases of interpretation are firm, noise and signal are hardly distinguishable; multiple nested games lead to changes of focus; the same content passes through similar channels and the same channel accepts various different contents simultaneously; and players are often unsure about the match between what they wanted to convey, what they did express, and what was, in fact, understood by the other player. When seen from close enough, virtually all exchanges defy the postulate of truth and have in its core a large gray zone in which doubt, if taken to an extreme, makes it impossible to continue with the communication.

A fourth area of ambiguity in communication, finally, stems from the complexity of the underlying social games that give support to the exchange. The primary assumptions of identity commonly used to stabilize the communication game are in sharp contrast with the fact that people often change their preferences in view of the circumstances and often during the same act of communication [481]; belong to multiple social systems and follow various rules of appropriateness (hedonism, affect, religion, work); identify in different levels and times with themselves, with their relationships, families, firm, or cultural ideals [482]; include past, present, and future in the same conversation; use the same communication for understanding, persuasion, and self-expression [474]; may use the communication game for various goals, honest and dishonest, covertly or openly; and as a consequence are variable, confused, and in flow, rather than stable and predictable. Ambiguity is a natural, inexorable consequence of the fact that during communication reason engages in the game of *distorting* the real structure of reality by fitting it into the logical, stable meanings and propositions usually seen as necessary for life to go on.

Either in the firm or in the family, the habitual response of players to these ambiguities is the tacit acceptance of the loose coupling between emission, signal, and reception. In fact, unlike suggested by managerial, patriarchal, or matriarchal fantasies of cultural alignment, players are (and probably should be) more occupied with acting and living than with obeying the (ceremonial) rule of consistency that normatively directs the communication game [483]. "The subjective meaning need not necessarily be the same for all the parties. (...) A social relationship in which the attitudes are completely and fully corresponding is in reality a limiting case" ([150]: 119). No relationship, family, firm, marriage, or friendship would probably persist if players were fully aware of what players really think, of how others receive the messages they send, or of how many plausible interpretations are routinely given to their purportedly consistent definitions of situations and identity.

These observations, we can conclude, strongly suggest that ambiguity in communication is *not* as an error to be solved, but rather the only possible *solution* to maintain a reasonable level of organization in face of the inevitable contradictions and complexity of real life. "A loosely coupled system is not a flawed system. It is a social and cognitive solution to constant environmental change, to the impossibility of knowing another mind, and to limited information-processing capabilities" ([32]: 44). It is only by accepting the (desirably) ambiguous and loosely coupled nature of communication that players can overcome the epistemic prisons of the ideals of truth and pave the way for softer communication games based on bets, trust, presumptions, fewer social comparisons, freedom from the pressures of coherence, less hubris, and the ability to improvise that are required in any true cultures.

Egocentric Biases

Beyond the doubt (or playful acceptance) introduced by ambiguity, communication is also potently influenced by biases that introduce relevant points of irrationality, blindness, and (undue) belief into the process of the exchange. These biases lead to predictable omissions and distortions in the messages passed across the system – players consistently disregard important details, condense information, accentuate specific parts of the plot according to their attitudes or vocabulary, and tend to fit what they hear and speak to prior knowledge and own attitudes, values, or social pressure [456]. Simultaneously, recipients accustomed to the facts of communicative life "ordinarily use counter-biases to adjust for such biases as they anticipate in the data they receive" ([25]: 71). In the world of practice, communication games are always half-conscious, half-unconscious adaptive attempts to find consensus and reach (or create?) a reasonable understanding of reality despite the forces that work against a common definition of the situation.

Particularly relevant obstacles for the flow of the communication are the egocentric biases – eruptions of the (natural) self-centered perspective in the context of a game that requires fluid perspective-taking for its continuation. These are a function, first, of the archaic, potent affective heuristic that from inside pushes living beings to a constant, egocentric search for power and value [484] – even when attempting to be objective in their communication games, players are stuck with the limitations of a mechanism of fact-creation that inherently privileges of what has value, and in particular value *for them, now* [485]. Second, there is the cognitive pull that comes from the fact that actors are inevitably bound (and used) to *their* perspectives. "People see the world through their own eyes, experience it through their own senses, and have more access to theirs than to the others' cognitive emotional states. This means that one's own perspective on the world is directly experienced, whereas others' perspectives must be inferred. Because experience is more efficient than inference, people automatically interpret objects and events egocentrically and only subsequently correct or adjust that interpretation when necessary. The automatic default occurs rapidly but correction requires time and attentional resources, meaning anything that hinders one's ability or motivation to expend attentional resources will systematically hinder correction" ([216]: 173). As a result of this push for egocentrism, individuals, families, and firms are inexorably self-absorbed and biased toward themselves. The more ambiguous is the stimulus – what includes the silence, and in our case family and organizational silence – the more the vacuum of meaning is filled with private interpretations and hypotheses that when spelled out become public facts, endorsed by the unimpeded flow of the communication. Players are obviously less rational than expected by the rules of the game, and this alone would be sufficient to explain many instances of miscommunication.

Although egocentric biases are inevitable, problems generally occur when this cognitive and affective egocentrism is coupled with the postulate of truth. This postulate can be decomposed in three premises: "(1) *I* see entities and events as they are in objective reality, and my social attitudes, beliefs, preferences, priorities, and the like follow from a relatively dispassionate, unbiased, and essentially 'unmediated' apprehension of the information or evidence at hand. (2) Other rational social perceivers generally will share my reactions, behaviors and opinions – provided that they have had access to the same information that gave rise to my views, and provided that they too have processed that information in a reasonably thoughtful and open-minded fashion. (3) The failure of a given individual or group to share my views arises from one of three possible sources: (a) the individual or group in question may have been exposed to a different sample of information than I was (in which case, provided that the other party is reasonable and open minded, the sharing or pooling of information should lead us to reach agreement); (b) the individual or group in question may be lazy, irrational, or otherwise unable or unwilling to proceed in a normative fashion from objective evidence to reasonable conclusions; or (c) the individual or group in question may be biased (either in interpreting evidence, or in proceeding from evidence to conclusions) by ideology, self-interest, or other distorting personal experience" ([486]: 110–11). Because these (naively realistic) misrepresentations violate a basic premise of the communication game – players must be on equal standing for their messages to be worthy of consideration – they become important sources of conflict, silence, or polarization.

There are innumerous examples of how self and other are erroneously (and self-servingly) construed by social actors who persist in naively believing that they are what they think they are, that they are perceived in the way they see themselves, that their mask conveys what they want to show, and that what happens in the public communication game indeed reflects who other players are. People consistently consider themselves better than average [487]; have a tendency to overestimate their contributions to group tasks [488]; believe their reactions, feelings, preferences, knowledge, or perspectives are more common than they really are [489]; are overconfident about their ability to persuade [490]; tend to overestimate how much others talk about and pay attention to them [491]; imagine their internal states are more transparent to others than they really are [492]; explain their behaviors taking into account all the circumstances, but easily stereotype others [493]; frequently fall prey of self-serving optimistic biases [494]; and think they are more clear, more precise, and less ambiguous and biased than they really are [495].

To these preferences about oneself one can add systematic distortions about the *other* players. People consistently believe that others are more influenced by public opinion, propaganda, or irrelevant information than they are [496]; are particularly aware of how others are influenced by extrinsic rewards, false consensus, or biased perceptions of reality (which they do not recognize in themselves) [490]; are often cynical in predicting how others accept or deny responsibility for their actions [487]; underestimate the impact of situational factors on the actions of others, commonly attributing their errors to character, disposition, or attitude and (wrongly) inferring they know their personality [497]; pessimistically explain others' attitudes by self-interest, minimizing the role of alternative motives [498]; and generally classify "others" as more homogeneous and less complex or diverse than they actually are or than themselves, making broad (and firm) inferences about the other actors' behavior despite the small samples offered by their outside perspective [499].

These inequalities between the perception of self and other, of course, lead to equally biased inequalities in how players rank themselves in comparison to the interlocutors. "People perceive their own self-knowledge and insight to be more accurate and complete than that of other people, and perceive their knowledge of other people to be more accurate and complete than other people's knowledge of them" [500]. All premises of the communication *game* are daily violated because its rules are insufficient to curb the natural, more potent affective and cognitive tendencies to egocentrism.

Most commonly, these biases are not relevant for the flow of the communicative exchange – players go on with life, oblivious of the fact that their views are not shared and assuming there was communication when in fact there was just soliloquy, self-referential thought in the guise of publicly shared silences and narratives. There are two instances, however, in which they potently affect the outcome of the communication game. *First,* they are in the basis of many (apparently dispassionate) moral judgments: players' evaluations of right and wrong, and consequently the bet they place on the trustworthiness of others, most times "are not based on stable attitudes or preferences, but are constructed based on an egocentric assessment of what is good and bad from their own [momentary] perspective" ([216]: 178). Although built after the fact to justify the emotional reaction, these judgments are believed to be, and brought to the communication as if they were, absolute truths that potently influence (and often determine) the flow of the game. *Second,* egocentric biases also potentiate the tendency to polarizations – when holding divergent views about a fact, "both sides in the conflict believe that although their own views reflect the complexity, ambiguity and contradictions of objective reality, the views of the other side have been dictated and distorted by ideology, self-interest, and other biases. These attributions in turn lead the conflicting partisans to see the other side as extreme, unreasonable, and unreachable" ([490]: 651). The end-result is an undue, self-reinforcing loop of mistrust that exacerbates the distinction between "us" and "them" and underestimates the potential common ground where consensus and communication could occur.

Attempts to avoid the detrimental effects of these biases have generally been restricted to stabilizations of the flow of information-action. Firms, for example, try to minimize distortions by transmitting the same content through various channels, by repeatedly reinforcing the desired message (a technique often used by parents), and, often, by standardization – the processes, manuals, best practices, and formalized directions for action that normalize the sequence of communication in such a way that the organization "only needs to know what kind of stimulus it is confronted with in order to execute an elaborate program" ([24]: 185). By doing this, of course, managers are simply reifying the ideas and biases of those who write the rules. They are also making an option for speed while treating the trade-off accuracy-efficiency – the preprogrammed absence of feedback minimizes the waste of time, but at the cost of precision in the treatment of ambiguities. Consequently, as a defense against undue simplifications, "specialists engaged in organizational problem solving [often] evade official prescriptions in order to get the job done" ([501]: 111). This attempt creates islands of isolation, often perceived as silos, power strongholds, and barriers to "new" knowledge (purportedly) aimed as a substitute for expertise. It is uncommon for players to understand that deep games require the tacit knowledge of the experts, and that this can be acquired only through the continued experience of a game in the context of rich communication with other experts [257]. Attempts to clean the communication game of its imperfections in the micro-level of the interactions create second-order difficulties at the level of the social system.

Similar difficulties are observed in the attempt to individually treat the egocentric, evaluative, and moral biases by which actors consistently misconstrue the interactions and identity games upon which their communication is based. Usually, techniques directed to the cognitive side of the equation, such as suggestions that players should see the others' perspectives, disclose conflicts of interest, or read about their self-serving biases are easily dismissed as empty ideology and prove useless as debiasing mechanisms [216]. Slightly more effective is to act "before people have even developed a perspective to bias their judgments, or to make disputants actively generate and focus on the weaknesses in their own case" ([216]: 182). The transcendence of our innate egocentrism is not something to be reached by rational or moral evolution, but an obstacle to be daily faced in all everyday, mundane communicative exchanges. The desired, utopic, fluid, and fair ideal speech situation, which theoretically should be the ground for any true culture, is not achievable in the macro-level of the large family or business but only intermittently lived in the practice, as actors learn (by experience) how to better communicate.

Self-Fulfilling Cycles of Communication

One of the big obstacles for players to learn from their experiences of communication comes from the inherently circular nature of the communicative process. This circularity may be seen as a transposition, to the field of communication, of the strong *confirmation biases* that distort players' perceptions of the reality in the direction of previously held viewpoints. In face of small ambiguities, actors generally deny or quickly restore the potential rupture of meaning in order to reduce cognitive dissonance [273]; tend to interpret confirmatory evidence as a proof that they are correct, forgetting that different hypotheses could be compatible with the same data [502]; prefer known ideas and stimuli simply because they have been exposed to them [324]; and are overconfident about their beliefs, partly due to an ingrained tendency to neglect contradictory evidence [503]. Likewise, in face of doubt or when facing new problems, players generally start by looking for confirmation rather than error, stopping the search process prematurely without examining potential mismatches [504]; tend to disregard the possibilities of misperception or misinterpretation [219]; insert spurious logic into the fabric of reality, creating and firmly believing in messages and explanations that defy or over-explain the facts [47]; and, consequently, "often prove to be rationalizing rather than rational animals, and as such are influenced less by logical rigor or objective evidence than by the interests and preconceptions they bring to their task" ([490]: 636). Communication exchanges may amplify these biases: *if* attitudes and fictions of truth have an echo in the other person or are validated by the game, *then* ideas are ratified by the facts and shared truth becomes absolute truth, as if there were no other possible, better or worse, perspectives about the facts.

These confirmatory biases, which in isolation lock individuals into their narrow worldviews, are, thus, often reinforced by the tendency of players to respond to others according to the rules of the game. If the expectation of peace encounters peace, the conjecture is assumed to be right; if war meets war, there is no need to review one's premises; if a meaning matches a similar meaning, the obvious deduction is that the idea is right. Silence is commonly interpreted as agreement, when in fact it may mean boredom, inattention, or defiance. "Action, perception, and sense-making exist in a circular, tightly coupled relationship that resembles a self-fulfilling prophecy" and redundancy, lack of error, and the *feeling* of recognition are automatically mistaken for truth ([21]:159). Furthermore, since players *have to* rely on the underlying social game in order to concentrate on the theme of the moment, it is common for the premises of the communication game to be taken for granted. As a consequence, they often become blind to errors that originate *within* the process of communication – *if* the unquestioned assumption is that all players are collaborating to find the truth, or, on the contrary, that all are competing against each other, *then* socially created cycles of consensus or war tend to be naturally misconstrued as true [26]. Often, "a *false* definition of the situation [evokes] a new behavior which makes the originally false conception come *true*. (...) The prophet will then cite the actual course of events as proof that he was right from the beginning" ([505]: 477). Players socially construct, forget they have built, believe in, and enact the fictions they share, reinforcing each other's beliefs through narratives and silences that introduce an essential element of illusion into the communication process.

Most instances of communication in the family or firm are not deep enough to fall into the trap of the more potent self-fulfilling cycles of communication. Consider, for example, Barbara Czarniawska-Joerges' observations about a meeting in a firm (the same, of course, can be said about a family reunion): "It is often assumed that collective action requires shared meaning. This is true to a certain extent (to carry a table together we must agree about what is up and what is down, what is forward and what is back). The plural form in the definition, however, suggests that a collective action is possible in the face of many meanings that are only partly shared. It is the experience of a collective action that is shared, more than its meaning. My two colleagues went to hear a speech given by a well-known businessman. One "participated in a most exciting encounter between the wisdom of practice and curiosity of theory", whereas the other "took part in an extremely boring meeting with an elderly gentleman who told old jokes". They were each, nevertheless, members of the same organization, and what was common for them was that they went to the same room at the same hour, sharing only the idea that their bosses expected it" ([506]: 33). What the description does not show is that by the simple act of communicating their ideas players are already bringing or imposing *their* meaning to other players. Not in a touching or deep way, but exactly as in the more powerful and lasting idealistic or ideological movements in history – the wars and illusions in which belief, action, commitment, collective belief, and collective action were synchronized for some time – this routine imposition of meaning, the so-called agonistic side of communication, covers the whole range of identifications that go from "us" to "them", suggesting attitudes of peace or conflict. It is in these extreme forms of the self-fulfilling prophecy, in which the depth of belief meets the duality friend *versus* enemy and both create excesses of trust or mistrust, that that we see the *illusions of consensus* and the *paranoid cycles of mistrust*.

Illusions of Consensus

Every communication among friends, from the joint endeavor to solve a problem to a debate about values or ideas, aims at some form of consensus; and the prototypical presentation of how powerfully this illusion shapes communication games lies, probably, in how these tend to hypnotize players through the creation of redundant, self-reinforcing, dogmatic, pacifying cycles of truth creation. In these extreme moments (and to some extent in every conversation of everyday life) the process of communication is characterized by a closure of belief reinforced by the match between expectation, reality, and collective repetition of meaning. With repetition, comes redundancy; with recognition, pleasure; and validated by the *feeling* of success and the congruity brought by repeated instances of a match, the triad is tacitly (and many times explicitly) accepted as a marker or synonym of truth [324].

The identification that emerges in these moments is among the most potent motives driving the life of individuals, families, and firms. In its maximum degree, the hypnosis may result in excessive reliance on the shared concepts, morality and values, leading to self-imposed censorship, punishment of deviance, groupthink, and collectively reinforced blind communication [169, 507, 508]. On a more daily basis, the same process is present in the practice of friends who repeatedly remember the same experiences; in the ritualized displays of affection and commitment that make the life of happily married people or good partners;

in the pleasure brought by endless conversations about abstractions and explanations that do not offer tools for action; or in all the useless demands for (virtual, unreal, social) emotional support hidden under the everyday confidences, secrets, and emotional outbursts. These islands of consensus do not have any validity, but are valuable.

Every family, firm, history, or legacy, in fact, depends on a constant, almost monotonous mantra of reiterated stories, myths, memories, interjections, collective tasks, and common rituals that ratify the (illusory) existence of the group and give it unity, often at the expense of other equally valid perspectives. Regardless of how true they are, shared truths are profoundly economic (and therefore rational): by the simple fact that a message is fed back by a similar message, actors suspend doubt, surrender to automaticity, pay a tribute to conformity, satisfy the need to belong, and have social confirmation of their private biases [403, 485, 509–511]. The social corollary of this (tacit?) disregard for validity is that the repetition, recognition, and identification allowed by the closed game of communication mingle to form the core of any form of organization as a closed system. They are an integral part of what people identify as culture, and therefore work as a glue of commonness that unites players around similar themes. They may, or may not, be congruent with the practice or even with the shared practices (and often are not); they form, however, a place where players temporarily rest in order to discuss common issues and solve the problems brought by the collective tasks. They are the rational, delusional, or realistic platform on which "rational" actions, plans, ideals, and ideologies based on the illusion of commonality are grounded.[4]

From the perspective of the actors who live the game from inside and share these illusions – all of us, most of the time – the obvious conclusion is that communication is, to a substantial degree, an important part of a socially institutionalized game of falsification. By committing to the communicative game, players become (morally) obliged to talk about the valued themes that bring them together and to be silent about the untouchable themes. They are expected to ceremonially respect the rules of exclusion that create the social entity of the relationship, family, or firm, while accepting to be truthful about all other games and thereby apparently respecting the rules of the primary game. They thus reenact the ideal of the perfect dialog as an idealized prototype of the process of creation and negotiation of meaning, reinforcing the players' illusions of identity while (mis) construing silence for consensus, practice for common values [71]. When seen from outside, of course, all cherished illusions of any era or place are easily deconstructed as error or ideology – Tayloristic manuals that ignore the complexities of tacit knowledge, managerial practices that preach standardization as an easy response to social complexity, or all-too-beautiful family expectations that deny conflict, individual, and group differences [141, 144, 512]. The unveiling of the illusion is a potential source of new ambiguities, which become a fertile ground for miscommunication and conflict [157].

At least officially or in relation to some main themes, families, and "organizations, then, tend to move toward reliable – that is shared – interpretations of history. Not necessarily valid interpretations, but shared ones. In the face of historical ambiguity, actors gain confidence from the fact that several share the same interpretation, and tend to treat agreement as equivalent to validity. These pressures toward consistency and diversity are constrained by the formation of subcultures of belief, subcultures which are sustained by conflict and competition within the organization [or family]" ([513]: 85). The clash between these cultures and subcultures may indeed lead to learning and to the creation of more ample (reliable or valid) views of reality; but may also force the pendulum in the other direction and trigger the polarization of the game toward the exacerbation of the duality friend-enemy, contaminating the communication with the expectation (or certainty) of conflict.

Paranoid Cycles of Mistrust

Exactly as players are drawn together by social pressures for consensus and cohesion while dealing with those they classify as friends, they may also identify with the centrifugal forces that trigger doubt and put them *against* any communication partner framed as an enemy. This duality, of course, does not exclude (and generally involves) all cooperative games implied by social organization. Cooperation means dependency, institutionalized dependency means contracting; and with the bond of the contract come imprisonment, conflict, and all the dangers that arise from have opened the door of communication to a now potentially untrustworthy player. "Almost every intimate emotional relation between two people which lasts for some time – marriage, friendship, the relations between parents and children – leaves a sediment of feelings of aversion and hostility (…) In the same way, every time two families become connected by marriage, each of them thinks itself superior to or of better birth than the other" ([514]. This hostility comes from the observation that the previous friend has momentarily or permanently turned into an enemy who may not be reliable for future communication. Doubt and paranoia are substituted for trust as premises of the social game, introducing a deep source of instability that leads to a completely different communicative exchange (see Appendix 2, Figure 17).

The paranoid disposition is a common ingredient in the history of grandiose, proud, or rigid geniuses, leaders, entrepreneurs, CEOs, patriarchs and matriarchs who identify with power or status and therefore see every communication as part of a dominance-submission game [332, 333, 515–519]. It also comes as a common attack-reaction to previous experiences of fear, shyness, or defrauded naiveté. It is a well known personality trait that involves two sorts of people: "furtive, constricted, apprehensively suspicious individuals and rigidly arrogant, more aggressively suspicious, megalomaniac ones" ([520]: 54). Regardless of the type, suspicious or grandiose, driven by fear or pride, the presentation of the paranoia is the same: "interpretations, illusions, delusional perceptions, hallucinations, fables, intuitions, all of them reducible to a pathology of belief ... polarize all affective forces towards the meanings given by the delusional construction that subordinates every activity to its goals. (...) Moreover, the so-called paranoid character (distrust, pride, aggressiveness, false judgment, rigidity) is an essential component of their personality" ([521]: 451). As a reflection of this (innate), deeply ingrained evolutionary tendency to categorize others as friends or enemies, and to react to the latter with suspiciousness or aggression, paranoia is present in some way in all players, in all times, in all families and firms [522].

As part of the communication game, however, the paranoid bias can be better seen as a consequence of the combination of dissonances, naive realism, and the complex, multitasking games that underlie any deep communication. Mixed-motive games do not allow any repose because they always involve dependence and counter-dependence, and consequently disputes for power that occur in the core of deep, profound affective, material, or political ties [97]. Rightly skeptical about the naive premise of trust, players taken by the paranoid bias readily exchange that postulate for the assumption of doubt about the others. However, despite being systematically incredulous about any of the bets that could preserve the flow of communication – the presupposition that the *other* is honest, rational or has goodwill – they maintain the naive belief in truth and continue to search for certainty, confirmations, permanent dispositions of character, and proofs of good or evil intentions to confirm the desired (even if negative) stability of meaning.

Successful communication games, however, depend on overcoming the distances of meaning; and as a consequence, the social enactment of this bias usually brings significant disruptions to the stability of organization. Limited to what is observed in the public field, incapable of definitely interpreting or dismantling the rigid belief of the paranoid actor, and generally prey of the same bias (enmity produces enmity), others usually react to what they see. Habitually, the initial aggressive attitude associated with the paranoid disposition provokes paranoid counter-reactions expressed in the same tone; these counter-reactions confirm the prior suspicious or aggressive attitude and beliefs; the distance associated with the conflict prevents the appearance of new information, confirming the correctness of the doubt-assumption by simple lack of evidence; and interpretive hypotheses of war frame every communication as deceit or falsehood. Commonly, regardless of how true the original suspicion is, the ambiguity and asymmetry of information inherent to the communication game fuel the self-fulfilling, autonomous paranoid cycle of mistrust.

The eruption of this bias is a common occurrence and frequent source of miscommunication in families, businesses, marriages, and every relationship in which material interests, power, prestige, and hierarchy are relevant for the future of the players. Many times, the enmity is real. Paranoia, however, introduces a potent element of irrationality and repetitive, biased considerations about power, dominance, submission, and suspiciousness that close many potential avenues for peaceful, productive communication. Frequently, the duality friend-enemy is triggered not by reality, but by misinterpretations, ambiguity, and self-fulfilling prophecies that create unnecessary conflict. Once instituted, these cycles tend to remain forever as players are unable to leave the dependence or accept the possibility of giving up the illusions of doubt and make a new bet on trust. More rarely, their intensity is untenable and leads to the pursuit of other forms of communication that deal, in different ways, with the dispute.

Communication, Conflict, and Appeasement of Conflict

Insofar as they are enacted in the context of mixed-motive social games that intuitively trigger the dichotomy friend-enemy, rational communication games are, therefore, always played in the narrow space demarcated by the extremes of excessive unity, which leads to groupthink; the unmanageable paranoia, which leads to silence, rupture, or deception; and the biases, unpredictability, and effects of complexity derived from the superposition of different rationalities, values, and games within the same place. Fuzzy as it is, this intermediary space is the only possible ground for the idealized productive conflict that characterizes true forms of organization [439]. In real practice, however, communication often suffers or breaks up when voids of information, asymmetries of information, or internal conflicts of interest expose relevant lines of fissure in the shared illusions and in the underlying social game – in family businesses, for example, in the vacuum of meaning that separates firm and family, different generations, or cousin coalitions, as well as when the weakening of traditional forms of domination requires new forms of stratification, disrupting the stability of the power game. In all these instances, fluctuations in the normal way of communicating reflect the saturation of an illusion or condition of equilibrium, forcing players to renegotiate the adjudication of meanings and interests that form the epistemic bases of communication [478].

Communication, then, is a virtual game that leads to irreconcilable attitudes in different moments. War leads to silence, withdrawal of information, and intentional ambiguity as tools of manipulation; self-interest minimizes the common game to the limit required by the useful instrumental uses players make of each other; peace and cooperation privilege openness to discover richer meanings; and as all of them tend to persist in the future once they are started, players naturally have fluctuating beliefs about the true purpose, advantages, dangers, meaning, safety, and utility of the communication games they play. In particular, if we start from the (obvious) fact that the world is neither moral, nor can be described as a single game, relationships, families, firms, and the communications from which they are made are inherently unstable and unpredictable. The form with which meanings and practices are negotiated in each case then lead us to an (arbitrary, prototypical) distinction between communication during *conflict,* in which the tie is thin; *bargaining*, in which self-interest predominates; and *rational negotiations,* in which theme or tone are logically treated by formal rules and clear directions for the communication or by practice-based attempts to deal with the points of consensus and dissensus created as actors *muddle through* the complexity of their problems.

Communication during Conflict

It is not within our scope to analyze all different forms taken by communication in conditions of open war. In this case, the ends clearly justify the means and players have to become masters in the art of using force, silence, deceit, threats, or intimidation to manipulate how the enemy defines the situation and may be fooled into actions that provoke his own defeat, annihilation, or surrender. The common ground on which players agree is simply that there is a war – and even in the case of limited war, when previous arrangements, common interests, or codes of honor restrict the use of the violence, the frailty of the link prevents the belief in any safe platform to rely on (if there ever is one). "Limited war requires limits; so do strategic maneuvers if they are to be stabilized short of war. But limits require agreement or at least some kind of mutual recognition and acquiescence. And agreement on limits is difficult to reach, not only because of the uncertainties and the acute divergence of interests but because negotiation is severely inhibited both during war and before it begins and because communication becomes difficult between adversaries in time of war. Furthermore, it may seem to the advantage of one side to avoid agreement on limits, in order to enhance the other's fear of war; or one side or both may fear that even a show of willingness to negotiate will be interpreted as excessive eagerness" ([523]: 19). Willful manipulation of silence and truth, as well as strategic interpretation of situations of ambiguity in which all know that ambiguity is the norm, are the hallmark of the exchange of meanings.

In (ideally unitary) family businesses, the existence of overt conflicts is generally denied or minimized – the simple existence of a pre-defined valued form of social order transforms any clear manifestations of hostility into a threat for the desired cohesion, and therefore into something to be hidden or left to the secretive dialogs of opposing actors or coalitions speaking of each other. Some type of war, however, is always present when players make a negative bet about the disposition of *another* and classify him or her as an enemy, changing the tone of the communication in a way that provokes (rightly or not) counter-reactions that shape the posterior flow of communication. In these cases – all types of serious discord between parents and children, siblings, mistrusting competitors for a promotion, or partners linked by self-interest but opposed in the soul – communication moves alongside a continuum that ranges from an almost clear war to the more acrimonious forms of bargaining. In the fiercer contentions, players generally respect the (ceremonial?) adherence to the good of the family or firm while openly talking about the personal disputes they have with the others (the more personally a conflict is framed, the less threatening it appears to the organization); as in criminal gangs, actors then "use limited war, disarmament, attack by surprise, reprisal, retaliation, and threat of retaliation; worry about appeasement, reputation and loss of prestige; and establish pacts and alliances that suffer from the same deficiency of those signed by nations: the impossibility of appeal to an authority to enforce it" ([524]: 25). In the other extreme of the spectrum we see all forms of bargaining, in which players are simultaneously contenders in a zero-sum game and equal below the rules of contract that regulate the form of the competition. Multiple, unpredictable equilibria can be found within this range. In fact, "the problem of limiting warfare involves not a continuous range of possibilities from most favorable to least favorable for either side; it is a lumpy, discrete world that is better able to recognize qualitative than quantitative differences, that is embarrassed by the multiplicity of choices, and that forces both sides to accept some dictation from the elements themselves" ([523]: 34). Leaders and change agents dealing with conflict are, as in any other facet of the problem of organization, dealing with complex and unpredictable games, and never with clear rules.

Privileging Self-interest: Communication during Bargaining

Bargaining, then, may be seen as a peculiar communication game that allows conflicts of interest and unilateral pursuit of personal gains within the context of minimal identification and relative agreement about the rules of the game. Although players pledge to adhere to the rules of negotiation, in a typical bargaining game many strategies of war are valid to reach one's goals: threats, falsifications, bluffs, lies, true or false promises, intimidation, revenge, alliances, trust, and betrayal of trust are appropriate (or not) depending on the context and on how they serve to reach one's goals [525]. The emphasis on a theme may hide a more relevant hidden agenda given by the tone of the relationship; the escalation or submission in tone may distract the attention from a relevant theme; or actors may alternate between discussing theme and tone, following disparate directions of action that are never reconciled by the persistence on a single subject or by consensus. Uncertainty, ambiguity, and interpretation, rather than perception and truth, shape the formation of the messages. Gamesmanship, façade, and disguise of the façade are the rules of the game [418].

In a typical bargain, although players acknowledge the self-interested nature of the exchange, force and coercion are forbidden. Also commonly, actors commit to openly behave according to the professed ideology while covertly acting (and knowing that all act) according to their interests – spouses should talk about mutual love, employees about the commitment to the business, salesmen pledge their duty to the customer, businessmen say how they are honest, gangsters repeat the official code of honor. Paid the tribute to the common thread of commonality, however, bargaining serves exclusively the utility drives of the players. Ethical, aesthetic, or affective goals are means to an end, alibis for the games of instrumentality and domination to occur without slipping into open conflict. Communication is contained, calculated, making use of the asymmetry of information to prioritize the (covert) games that are really relevant for the players.

Bargaining inspires the most observed patterns of communication in many families or in the contested terrain of unstable and informal relationships – many of the dissensions between parents and children, husband and wife, or members of a clan or family are blends of self-deception and cover-up by which people try to keep open, but limited channels of communication while subterraneously satisfying the deeper interests that fuel the discord (and often maintain the relationship alive). The same, of course, can be said from the firm. "Political processes evolve at the group level, from the division of work in the organization, and at the individual level from associated career, reward and status systems. Sub-units develop interests based on specialized functions and responsibilities; individual careers are bound up with the maintenance and dissolution of certain types of organizational activity and with the distribution of organizational resources" [433]. From the perspective of these actors – people or groups who look for their interests, despite accepting the need to maintain the relationship – there is limited commitment to the basic tenets of the communication game. Life is more fluid, and occurs beyond the limits of any restraining rule.

Despite the personal advantages (potentially) brought by this fluidity, politics, bargaining and covert war put substantial strain on any illusion of organization or open communication. Consequently, culture and meaning are preserved only insofar as players minimally respect the myth and ceremony needed to maintain the appearance of integrity of the official illusions [35]. In the business, for example, actors generally end up framing "all conflict as though it were in fact individual, rather than intergroup [or ideological] conflict. Disputes in the organization are defined as problems in analysis; the initial reaction to it is problem-solving and persuasion; such reactions persist even when they appear to be inappropriate; there is a greater explicit emphasis on common goals where they do *not* exist than where they do; and bargaining (when it occurs) is frequently concealed within an analytic framework" ([418]: 151). Also in the families, the true motives of money, power, status that drive the exchange are seldom openly acknowledged. Rather, they are commonly reduced to concrete, practical and limited problems that do not lead to questions about the mode of organization, relationship, character, or intentions of the players. The end-result is a general superficiality of meaning, and, many times, slow rupture or radical effacement of the bond. This contrasts starkly with the depth searched in rational discussions.

Privileging Common Meanings or Actions: Rational Discussions and Muddling Through

As much as players agree that they disagree during the (ubiquitous) process of bargaining, they many times really need to play the communication game in order to integrate and coordinate the values, definitions of situation, or behavior that in a group determine the collective action. Institutionally, this is the task of the leaders; privately, this is the scope of any actor who pursues a sense of belonging, who thrives in the experience of engrossment, or who needs to engage other players to benefit from their effort, expertise, or capital. In these cases, players have to (at least temporarily) agree on *what they think* or on *what to do;* and consequently, on whether to adopt a logic of meaning or a logic of action as the primary parameter of coordination. In the first case, the communicative exchange serves to reason and to the world of ideas, under the assumption that common definitions of situation will eventually lead to organized action. Conversely, under the logic of action the exchange serves to the practice and stops as soon as a pragmatic decision is reached and a movement occurs, resulting in the desired joint effort or *feeling* of consensus regardless of the existence of common meanings.

The prototypical differences between the two types of logic – the rational negotiations of truth or meaning exemplified by scientific discussions and sensemaking narratives, the rational pursuit of efficiency appearing as muddling through – reveal a fundamental trade-off of communication. Besides serving self-interest *or* common goals, communication is always split between privileging common meanings *or* common actions. The opposition is obvious: privileging the logic of action through *muddling through* leads to short-term commitments, but at the cost of depth and consistency. Alternatively, privileging the logic of meaning favors the coherence and epistemic stability of *rational communication*, but at the cost of digressions around nested problems and interrelated levels of analysis or interminable dives into the (infinite) regress of the rules. Both, in fact, alternate with each other and compete with habit or simple disorganization as (tacit or explicit) models of how families and firms use the communication game (see Appendix 2, Figure 16).

Rational Communication

Prototypically, for any form of rational communication to occur, actors must agree on certain definitions of a situation and on a "belief that at some level objectives are shared and that disagreement over sub-goals can be mediated by reference to common goals" ([24]: 150). These agreements are organized in levels – *first*, players must at least temporarily rest on the (irrational) bet that the other is a friend; *second*, they must share a relatively common cognitive and moral ground – some rules of how to negotiate the rules, even if to break or deconstruct them; *third*, they must accept that rational communication is a proper tool to define the shifting themes of every day, the processes, truths, values, and definitions of situation on which normal life depends. All these phases allow the possibility of *doubt;* and consequently, every form of human communication is grounded (?) on certainties and premises that depend on arbitrary stop-points on a potentially endless circle of constructions, deconstructions, and digressions about related problems. Any negotiation of rules about how to communicate depends on prior negotiations of what *should* be accepted as a rule, in an infinite, unjustified spiral of search for the fundament that exposes the core of irrationality that exists in the center of every, rational or irrational, communication. Every definition of a problem circumscribes an arbitrary area of analysis, which necessarily excludes other relevant points to be studied.

For players engaged in developing a meaningful culture, understanding how this mix of irrationality and rationality stabilizes the communication is a crucial step in the task of organization. From it comes the postulate that any reasonable conversation must obey certain constraints in order to run smoothly – conflict and ambiguity, for example, ought to be accepted as normal; truth should be doubted; all abstractions should be grounded in the practice; unless the relationship itself is a theme of the conversation, actors should be forbidden to question each other's honesty, good intentions, and rationality (to prevent the fall of the communication); and so on. It is only by assuming that all players are truly participating in a legitimate game, and by fixing the perspective, paradigm, time and viewpoint from which reality is framed, that one stabilizes the field and can proceed to the practical task of finding the truth, negotiating the meaning, or defining the common values on which action will be based.

In the life of families and firms, these rules are generally tacitly accepted as a necessary basis for all the serious talk involved in the definitions of truth, sensemaking explanations of the facts, or identity definitions. They are also formally studied as part of the conditions that allow the growth of knowledge within the field of science: "Normally, members of a mature scientific community work from a single paradigm or from a closely related set. Very rarely do different scientific communities investigate the same problems. In those exceptional cases, the groups hold several major paradigms in common. (...) What scientists share, however, is not sufficient to command uniform assent about such matters as the choice between competing theories or the distinction between an ordinary anomaly and a crisis-provoking one. (...) If all members of the community responded to each anomaly as a source of crisis or embraced each new theory advanced by a colleague, science would cease. If, on the other hand, no one reacted to anomalies or to brand-new theories in high-risk ways, there would be few or no revolutions or change. In matters like these, the resort to shared values, rather than to shared rules governing individual choice, may be the community's way of distributing risk and assuring the long-term success of its enterprise" ([526]: 162, 186). In science, like in the firm and in the family, the norms that govern the flow of rationality are looser than reason would expect and limited to broad, unenforceable commitments to some ideals (see Appendix 2, Figure 18).

It is not within our scope to review the many nuances that negotiations and communication may take in the family or firm, depending on the various effects of context that exist within a family, a firm, or any society – communication flows differently if it occurs between siblings, partners, lovers, spouses, parent and children, cousins, acquaintances, friends, or bosses and employees. Most of it, obviously, flows at the margin of these rational rules and does not need any ground or fundament to continue. On the contrary, players rely on fluid, changing rules to negotiate these dissensions – not on the formal agreements of the rational perfect dialog, but on non-contractual, non-enforceable, intangible, and unsafe bases of a unity that echoing the spirit of the game suggests reasonable ways to keep them connected. Furthermore, rational negotiations, when they occur, lead to a mixed outcome. Occasionally, themes are restricted to the initial scope, the question is addressed with proper (but limited) consideration of nested problems or related levels of analysis, and discussions are both productive and profound. Often, however, reason fails in addressing problems of complexity due to the same rules created to guarantee its method – coherence to avoid mistakes, and comprehensiveness to disclose blind spots. Rational communication, in these cases, loses its power to create meaning and players fall into the trap of the endless discussions, digressions, subjectivity and lack of clarity often seen in the day-by-day of social systems (just think of the flow of communication during most meetings in a firm, disagreements between partners, or debates in the parliament).

The failure of reason to tackle the real problems faced by players in a communication stems, in a substantial proportion, not from their inability but from the very nature of the game. *First*, all interesting problems defy any easy solutions – the theme of communication is unstable. *Second*, the archetypal duality between friend and enemy forces every actor to revisit the initial bet whenever a conflict arises – the tone of any relevant communication is equally unstable. *Third*, in order to address this complexity players cannot stick to rigid rules of rationality that depend on a single perspective to avoid ontological oscillation and generate stable truths. *Fourth*, the rules that govern the symbolic or abstract meanings created in the world of ideas do not address the deeper questions of communication because reason fails on two extremes – rationality is either satisficing and stops as soon as a first choice is found (what introduces confusion and ambiguity in the process), or, alternatively, is optimizing and never stops the interminable search for the fundament and gets lost in interminable digressions, regresses of the rules, or evaluations of interlocked nested problems. Actors must, then, opt between sticking to the (rational? irrational?) ideals of reason – which independently of being logical or not, of leading to a perfect dialog or fostering illusions of certainty, are always unattainable – or follow the pragmatical need to minimally organize the practical, political, and logistical features of the tasks they address. This need, which is directed to common actions and not to common meanings, forces players to use communication as a tool to *muddle through* the problems they face in order to proceed with life.

Muddling Through

One of the rules of communication proposed as a solution for the deadlock of rationality comes, in fact, from the explication of what people already do. When discussing serious questions, actors routinely "avoid grand questions", evade the fundamental difficulties of evaluation caused by "the multiplicity, fluidity, and conflict of values", and muddle through their problems, searching for small or incremental steps in which local, rather than long-term negotiations privilege the practice and not the values. By muddling through, players violate all premises of the idealized, rational process of decision-making – they show more preoccupation with potential ills than with the positive goals; the analysis of options is divided among various (partisan) stakeholders, preventing single-side views of the problem; and aim not for alignment, but for incremental, disjointed improvements in the situation [358]. Their communication is, by design or intuition, limited to few alternatives – in public life, policy goals, values and practical aspects are loosely considered; in the families, trivial everyday questions, rather than deep conversations about the future, fill the conversations; and in the firm, operational immediate demands are commonly chosen in detriment of long-term strategic questions. It seems that the social or complex problems can (or should?) only "be attacked (not well, but with some reduction in incompetence) by 'resultants' of interaction rather than 'decisions' arising out of anyone's understanding of the problem of hand" ([431]: 524).

In fact, the science of muddling through just substitutes concerted action for common meanings as the basis of organization. Its main advantage lies in the (pragmatic) denial of the need for interminable discussions, empty searches for the fundament, or impossible considerations of the "one best option" or of all competing alternatives – all rhetorical exercises of meaning by which actors in the family or firm cover up their real motives for action under the guise of rational worldviews. The blind spot lies in the shallowness of the immediate decision – if the bases of interpretation are not questioned, but just utility is considered according to frames that are (by definition) biased and self-interested, the expectation is of formalized pacts that do not necessarily follow any axiological meaning (as the world of practice really is).

Despite its utility, once the pragmatic option for muddling through is rationally formalized and accepted as a canon for the negotiation of values and ideas, one turns upside down the whole normative edifice of communication. It is true, the disbelief in idealized forms of consensus acknowledges the ambiguous, multifaceted nature of most situations and brings the theory of communication closer to the ambiguity of the practice – ontological oscillation, changes of perspectives, emotionality, and values are accepted as necessary elements of the exchange, which can be tamed but never denied by the rigid simplifications of standard rationality. However, the acceptance that solutions are always influenced by effects of context and perspective, "settled *ad hoc* and therefore differently on different occasions", introduces an irreducible element of arbitrariness and capriciousness into the core of the decision-making process ([527]: 244). If contradictions among values are not only allowed, but actually expected in view of the various (equally valid) utilitarian considerations of partisan groups, and if "grand questions" *should* be evaded, then idealism and ideology, exception and cover-up, lie and truth are undistinguishable, and human life is reduced to politics, struggle, or to unmanageable effects of complexity. In the extreme, this breaks the top-down effects of hierarchy by which power, control, and tradition tilt the communication in favor of the elite. Taken to the limit, the conclusion may be that families and clans will have to deal with the dispersion of power, and "managerial practice [in the firm] will have to learn how social structures can act as a form of distributed intelligence, blurring the boundaries between management and employees and between companies, suppliers, and customers" ([464]: 336).

The radical consequences of this trade-off decision – to stop the search for the idealized good communication by accepting compromises on its depth – are, therefore, not without consequences. Deprived from the common metric given by the idealized shared values, tactics, and fundament – the basic rules and the rules about how to negotiate the rules, which as codified bases of any social game give stability to the communicative exchange – actors, leaders, and change agents are easily caught in the obscure ambiguities that separate "really" feasible solutions from self-interested compromises that just reflect the momentary power of some actors or coalitions to control the information or process of decision. Simple inattention, habit, automatism or decisionism, arbitrariness, and power – of those who control the force, of the group, or of the majority – and *not* norms, rules, or fundaments, appear as the bases of the flow of communication; and ambiguity and imperfection, and *not* consistency, become the standards for the decisions that come from the exchange. One is, then, led again to the utopic, idealistic, or functionalistic search for an ideal (?) contract, one that can serve (at least temporarily) as a basis for efficient communication. This contract, as in every romantic, mythical, or omnipotent attempt to influence a component of a culture, involves the interplay of top-down effects and the acceptance – and many times the surrender – to the bottom-up, emergent effects of complexity.

Organizational Culture and Paradoxes in Management: Communication

As the expression of a game based on transmission and negotiation of meanings, every act of communication seemingly celebrates the mythical, prototypical contract that unifies sign and interpretation of the sign in the form of shared definitions of the situation. For the players, it represents the shock between their solipsism and the *other*, an encounter that puts their private views to the test and defines whether they are publicly defensible. For leaders and change agents, it is the place where the macro-world of the structure meets (or not) the micro-world of the actors' minds. Whatever their shape and content, truths, values, organization, disorganization, or culture only seem to become real when enacted within a communication game.

Ubiquitous as it is, this encounter of perspectives is anything but natural. First, because various limitations intrinsic to the communicative and social games profoundly direct, constrain, and bias the process. As a consequence of these features, actors – "sometimes in harmony, sometimes in bitter conflict, sometimes in webs of ambiguity, paradox, and contradiction" ([3]: 3) – are, always, imperfectly touched by the messages they receive. They have limited possibilities to check if their interpretations match the reality they talk about. Moreover, this reality is fugitive, shaped, and socially constructed in real time by the flow of the same communication that "objectively" attempts to grasp it. Consequently, the real meanings eventually enacted in the private space of each soul are certainly different from the others' internal ideas and feelings and from what transpires in the public space; and meanings placed in the public space are only partially shared, invariably distorted by the effects of mask, and affected by the autonomous life they acquire due to self-fulfilling cycles of truth-creation. The final factor that triggers individual and collective action – a coincidence, a fortuitous action, a common meaning, or simply fatigue with the discussion – depends not only on how messages are crafted and transmitted, but on the contingencies of the social space and of how the actors' interests, dispositions, and tacit or explicit bases of interpretation appear in the local contexts where communication occurs (see Appendix 2, Figures 13 and 16).

Communication, then, is a game, a tool, the expression of a sometimes efficient, but always imperfect attempt to twist the complex, fluctuating reality of solitary actors by tying them to other players through exchanges of meaning. Any power (or freedom) to influence its flow is exercised only within the (narrow) constraints of this intersection. Moreover, the message of change is only one of multiple messages within an ecosystem of (always contradictory) ideas, practices, and explosions of life and stimuli that come from both inside and outside the organization. There is a competition for the prize of truth and for the attention of the audience: narratives are "the ground on which the struggle for power is waged, the object of strategies of domination, and the means by which the struggle is actually engaged and achieved". From the perspective of communication, families, firms and organizations are "socially constructed verbal [and non-verbal symbolic] systems … where some voices are louder, more articulate and more powerful than others" ([197]: 174–8). To communicate something to somebody – insofar as this communication implies in any emotional impact, and therefore in any understanding, adoption, or negotiation of a meaning – is always an act of force and a tribute to chance, the belief that a flash of common understanding will succeed in creating a bridge between the players.

The drive to persuade, convince, influence, or win an argument, then, is the fundamental element that transforms communication into an agonistic game. Tastes, opinions, dreams, jokes, or acts or faith can be part of the public space but remain forever private, ebbing and flowing at the sole discretion of the actors who espouse them. They fill the life of the family and firm with spontaneity and grace; they are not, however, strong enough to direct collective action. Moreover, there is more in life than stories and narratives – the simple need to act, habits that flow independently of the communication, emotions or impulses that need a discharge, and everything that provokes movement and feeling independently of any communication. The art of using communication to provoke change or tweak culture within a firm or family business is, then, equated to the (always limited, but real) capacity of actors or leaders to act or make a presence within the limited space of the total life that responds to words and symbols; and, from inside this place, influence the "ensemble of rules according to which the true and the false are separated, and specific effects of power attached to the true" ([62]: 133). Truths, or at least reasonable *bets* about what could be these truths are needed to build the social platforms of the common meanings.

Every communicative transaction, therefore, is a game within a game, which, in turn, is only one of the many games played inside each family or firm: any exchange of messages between two or more actors occurs within the context of a large mesh of communicative exchanges, which constitutes only a small fraction of all the other games and stimuli that fill the place with life. Small as it is, this subset of interactions privileges the human, and foremost the *social* element within the human – the negotiations of truth, doubt, power, legitimacy, and identification, which by the simple fact of being put in the public space connect actors to each other and create a reality that transcends their private worlds, binding them to the social universe. For a message to be heard it must be significant; appearance, rhetoric, and content are required for the emotional impact; and for this impact to be favorably interpreted, players have to be engrossed by the game of communication, feeling they are agents who are *freely* choosing to participate in the organized system.

Ultimately, this sense of freedom, spontaneity, or engrossment depends on a fragile, unstable but potently motivating projection of the self into an activity, family, or firm that is always also an *other,* and in other moments appears as a source of pressure or as an obstacle for the realization of the individual. This antinomy – by which the (always) forceful imposition of a meaning must be framed and felt as coming from voluntary acceptance in order to work as a personal truth – means that leaders and change agents must be able to transmit the messages they want in a way that carefully preserves the players' sense of freedom. This involves the study of how to (honestly? ideologically?) manipulate the elements of the communicative game to eventually create sufficiently competitive narratives and discourses – practices and contents that, at least intermittently, may acquire some prominence in the jungle of meanings that shock against each other in the local universes where they are interpreted.

Some General Elements

The first elements that limit (and shape) the communication are the trade-offs related to the contact between information and audience: accuracy *versus* information overload, realism *versus* comprehension, detail *versus* simplicity, and, in the limit, essence and truth *versus* rhetoric and form. "It is impossible for a theory of social behavior [or for any account of a serious problem] to be simultaneously general, simple (or parsimonious), and accurate. The more general a simple theory, the less accurate it will be in predicting specifics. The more accurate a simple theory, the less general it will become – the less able it will be to account for anything more than the most specific or contrived situations" ([528]: 406). Any choice for one side brings to the foreground the advantages of the counter-choice, in an interminable zig-zag of local, context-dependent, momentary, and transient equilibria.

Second, there are the always present, improbably combined, and equally valuable goals of communication – inquisitive behavior, persuasion, commitment, sensemaking, illusion, meaning, deception, or self-interest. These are linked to how communication always addresses theme and tone, the object of the discussion and the (often tacit, always subjective) proposal of how to shape the common social game. Of relevance, theme and tone travel differently in space and time depending on how the distance between the interlocutors increases or decreases the percentage of fiction used in the interpretation: the farther one is from the players who receive the message, the more this may be framed as true, false, or interpreted according to arbitrary criteria depending on how it is felt by the receivers or generalized based on the (supposed) attributes ascribed to the actor who spoke. Immediate context, implicit biases, and present situations define the direction of interpretation, but people *feel* meaning is outside, in the leader, family, firm, or culture that appears as the owner of the message [529].

Third, there is the paradox of language. The same reason that legitimizes any practice or discourse, linking it to a (supposedly) common conceptual or metaphysical ground, inevitably opens the possibility of doubt, and therefore of deconstructions and erosion of belief. This tradeoff explains why many sustainable changes occur only when effected tacitly, through manipulations of the context of choice or nudges aimed at changing habit, and not awareness [301, 302, 530]; it also explains why the same repetition that reinforces the message may cause mistrust, disbelief, and disengagement. The *feeling* of meaning and identification, like the engrossment on which it depends, only flourishes when left implicit, unconstrained, and untainted by the logical categories of the language game.

Fourth, we see interpretation and negotiation of the interpretation. All in all, *if* and when players are attending to the game, outward behavior is taken to be a valid sign of internal understanding and the validity of the communication is measured by its ability to provoke action or put an end to the interaction. Information as truth, then, becomes barely distinguishable from information as illusion and from the self-fulfilling cycles of trust or mistrust created by the exchange. A similar point involves silence and the manipulation of silence – everything left out of the explicit verbal exchange, but that nevertheless works for the players to project their inner self, is construed as part of the imagined meaning. Particularly relevant, in this case, is the use of ambiguity for the creation of the feeling of *true* meaning, and, consequently the trade-offs between rational and emotional depth, language and tacitness, or logic and poetry. "The unremitting glare of the ideological spotlight degrades the experience which, perhaps, can flourish only uncontested, in the dark" ([483]: 216). Be it in families, firms or nations, true cultures require an (irrational) absence of doubt that appears only during the execution of habit and the more emotional immersion in the idealistic, charismatic, legitimate, or ideological, meaning.

Fifth, one has the channels and how they are connected with truth and power – reminders that communication does not exist separately from the way it is done, because the choice of the medium affects which information can be transmitted, the form it takes, how potently it reaches the other part, and the possibility (or prohibition) of negotiation. The first trade-off is between efficiency in the transmission of the same message for a broader audience (at the cost of interpretation and depth) and accuracy and impact through the creation of small forums in which meaning can be co-created, rather than imposed (at the cost of time and resources). The second trade-off is between exchange and persuasion, the first privileging the joint attainment of common meanings (at the cost of power), the second the forceful imposition of a message or command (at the cost of identification).

Communication, then, is inevitably linked with power and influence. The competition is, openly, for the local spaces where meaning is created and enacted; and, intimately, for the (impossible) sustained attention and goodwill of the players. Those who hold positions of dominance defend their control of the places, media, and meetings where messages are more frequently and loudly voiced; less powerful actors defend their freedom to hear or not, exercising the right to do what they want to do within the confines of their private territories. A special, subtle form of control involves the ideology of social cohesion. In this regard, the often proclaimed circles of feedback, suggestions that players should be open with each other, or calls for cooperation do *not* offer any solutions for the intrinsic problems of crossing the bridge between self and other, or friend and enemy. Rather, they only take out of the weak a relevant and legitimate weapon, the possibility of lying and concealing; and bring culture to the proximity of the extremely close, raising the loops of doubt and suspiciousness that preclude the emergence of any true, spontaneous, legitimate surrender.

Finally, there is complexity. Everywhere, local order emerges as a weak point – private, secluded, immediate, personal, emotional universes that are distant from the mediate, global, willfully communicated plan of change or proposal of culture. When taken to the core of each private world, communication is directed to actors dispersed in the middle of a web of different games, rules, meanings, messages, discourses, and narratives that take them to different directions, the one emotionally closer to them winning the temporary place in the podium of truth. Distance and overcoming of distance through feedback and (social) exchange are, always, fundamental aspects of communication and of how it is translated into action and talk, creating the socially constructed reality of the culture.

Local Aspects

Given the constraints inherent to the simplest act of communication, and how deeply this is linked with definitions of power, influence, and truth, any attempt to fully structure the communication within a family or firm appears, if taken to the limit, as a futile exercise of omnipotence. It is impossible to reach a significant amount of actors without simplifying the message one wants to convey; but when critically interpreted, this simplification becomes ideology. Any idealistic project of culture depends on meta-concepts that synthesize the contradictions of practice; but these truths hide counter-truths that could be used to build other, equally valid systems of thought. Social dreams are necessary to bring players to common goals; but they always imply in positions of power, status, and control that can be interpreted as the real fundament of action, demystifying the playful or transcendent essence of the game. Solutions, then, vary on a case-by-case basis depending on nuances of context and local, intuitive judgments of value that have nothing to do with the absolute truth imagined as a solution for the more common everyday questions. This manipulation involves interventions directed at four levers that define the *context* of the game: the concrete *stage* where communication happens; the formal *social structure*; the *vocabulary* and bases of interpretation used in the place; and the official, as well as some of the non-official *messages* transmitted within the system. Beyond this, it is impossible for anyone to define with any certainty how the exchange of meanings will flow depending on the elements that become (emergently) relevant in each place or moment.

The first lever to structure the communication within a family or firm, then, involves the definition of *where* the exchanges occur, the stage of the communication. No architectural choice is ever neutral – whether players have privacy or not, the floors, corridors, noise, decor, light, windows, openings, colors, artifacts, symbols of decoration, and the predominance of the vertical or horizontal dimension influence how people attach or not to the environment and how they relate and communicate to each other [531]. Particularly relevant is how space is enclosed to create an interior with centrality, rhythm and aesthetic, transforming the locus of communication into a meaningful *place* [532]. In family businesses, for example, many of the more important messages are expressed in how the house, the farm, the castle, the garden, the dinner table, the factory, or the dining room come to symbolize a sacred space with which players identify, making of the family or the business a place of communication separated from the profane world by walls of identification and history. The manipulation of space creates the structure; and from the structure come permanent effects of propinquity and fluidity of communication, which in often unobserved ways affect the whole subsequent flow of the game.

A second definition of local context involves the *time* and timing when communication occurs – the moment, interval, and duration of meetings in a firm, the periodicity of family reunions, how much time will be allotted to private or group activities. Of relevance here are the classic trade-offs between centralization and decentralization, collectivity and individualism, or power *versus* autonomy. Families that do not share meals, partners who do not talk regularly, colleagues in a firm who do not exchange information, or parents who do not see their children become attached only by forces that coincidentally bring them to communicate or not to each other. Conversely, tightly coupled demands for conformity, social cohesion, obedience, or obedience to rituals or dogmas, as we see in the more traditional families and firms, stifle individual actors and make the social game uninteresting. It is part of the role of the leader to structure (and often impose) when communication should occur in a way that players feel constrained but not coerced, and eventually find meaning in the collective construction.

Formal social structure defines which are the easier, more efficient, preferred paths for the flow of communication and link it to the lines of power, status, proximity, or distance that characterize the stage. In the firm, this depends on how the organizational design integrates people, hierarchy, incentives, information flow, routines, and common or banned values, practices or concepts in a more or less aesthetic, pleasing or efficient whole [338, 367, 533]. In the family, formal structure includes the legal arrangements of property, marriage pacts, inheritance, or access and control of the shared resources. Of relevance is the issue of governance, and particularly of family governance – the whole logic of the system depends on open communication, which never occurs; disregards the effects of power and opportunism, which always cloud the transmission of information; minimizes the role of informal networks and tacit knowledge, which are essential to organization; and does not take into account a fundamental trade-off of communication, namely, the need to simplify (and therefore falsify) the message as a means to address the risk of information overload. Formal structure gives a shape, blocks some paths, and privileges some directions for the communication, but in no way guarantees what happens in the private space of local action or in the subtle spaces created by the multiple interlocked social networks of the place [166].

A fourth lever of manipulation involves the relevance given to some *bases of interpretation* (and, as a consequence, some meanings) in detriment of others. "Conversation is immediate in its claim on attention, instantaneous in its moment to moment occurrence, and fleeting or ephemeral in its form, yet it relies on patterns that become culturally sanctioned, frames that presuppose prior knowledge, and macro processes in which individuals speak as representatives for others" ([463]: 391). It is possible, therefore, to indirectly affect how communication occurs by spreading novel forms of seeing the factors – for example, by enforcing a common vocabulary that involves the main trade-offs associated with truth, power, and communication, as well as a broader, inclusive view of the particular themes, themes, problems, and zones of ambiguity and conflict that characterize the history of the family or the type of business with which it engages. Here, two points are relevant. First, communication becomes linked with learning and memory within systems that by definition are complex, loose, impermanent, marked by fluid participation and with no precise center for the processing and disposal of the information [176, 181, 534]. Second, it is impossible for any interpretive framework to encompass all potential perspectives by which facts are see or adopted as true by all actors – any new framework always competes (and *should* compete, lest culture turns into dogma) with other systems of meaning that emphasize other, often contrary, aspects of the problem. When seen from close enough, communication, as the culture that directs it and the people who live it, is loose, fragmented, and never unitary.

Finally, leaders can select some of the messages that will be transmitted and the media to be used in this transmission. Higher values, in general, just give a north. They bring a layer of commonality that allows players to *feel* they communicate, but *not* a prediction or direction about how to act in the future, and rarely a description of how real life occurs. As creatures of the world of ideas, however, these values are "essentially nonoperational and do not provide a rod for comparing alternative policies". Thus, in order to be implemented in the world of practice, they must be translated (?) in the form of processes, routines, habits, and sub-goals that encompass all the themes touched by the communicative game and "whose connection with the broader 'general welfare' [that characterizes them] is postulated but not testable" ([24]: 177). Without this translation – a loose, minimal but supposedly well-intentioned connection between the communicated ideals and the practices that direct the flow of action in the place – culture becomes ideological and loses its power of illusion.

Particularly in the firm, or in the families where feeling intersects with tradition, property, or status, this is a sensitive area. Specifically, it is only when money, incentives, control, status, ideology, or coercion become acceptable themes of the communication *and* match the spoken discourses – i.e., when one puts to the test the deepest, individualistic attachments of the human being and openly treats the hidden themes, taboos, and undiscussables commonly preserved from the discussion – that culture begins to be believable. It is in the nebulous interface that connects the public symbolic language game to the secret language of the private actions, practices, and routines – and *not* simply in the coherence, transcendence, and power of illusion of the ideals communicated to the players – that lie both the solutions and the problems involved in the structuration of the communication.

Even within individuals, and let alone in families and firms, it is rare to see a reasonable level of coherence between the concepts and values espoused during the communication game and what is really lived in the world of practice. Coherence implies acceptance of imprisoning – prison to what is said, concordance between how one deals with the private egocentrisms related to the baser aspects of human nature and the social egoisms praised as noble in any attempt to craft reasonable messages for a common culture [535]. The usual solution for this dilemma is a (conscious or unconscious) loose coupling between the verbally communicated ideals of culture and how they are interpreted or lived in real life. "Problems are often solved, but rarely by the choice to which they are first attached. A choice that might, under some circumstances, be made with little effort becomes an arena for many problems. The choice becomes almost impossible to make, until the problems drift off to another arena. The matching of problems, choices, and decision-makers is partly controlled by the attributes of content, relevance, and competence; but it is also quite sensitive to attributes of timing, the particular combinations of current garbage cans [in which decisions occur], and the overall load on the system" [18: 2]. Eventually, the attrition between this ceremonial enactment of some noble goals and the (incongruent) relinquishment to inattention, indiscipline, laziness, pride, or self-interest leads to a corrosion of the belief in the social game, and as a consequence in the communication.[5]

For actors, leaders, or change agents engaged in overcoming the effects of inattention, indiscipline, lack of knowledge, or unbridled self-interest, communication must, then, be part of a meta-game of culture in which the (desired) surrender to the illusion coexists with the openness to talk freely about doubt, errors, and disputes of power, status, or interest that happen during conflict. When these are appeased – due to consciousness, contracts, habit, custom, belief, idealism, or simply acceptance of a certain social order that fits the zone of indifference – players stop questioning the bases of their communication and begin to pay attention to themes of everyday life. Fairness in the conflict, on the one hand, and joy, affect, and productive or creative work during peace, on the other, are two different types of soil that require different approaches to communication.

It is in these moments of peace or enthusiasm, when reason does not need to be used, that messages or signs of the communication game are more likely to reach the zone of attachment, creating the basis of a meaningful culture. The more the family, the firm, and the collective good are present in the memory of the players, the more they will be relevant in the architecture of individual choice and will impact the joint deliberations that occur in the secluded world of the players' interactions and relationships. This influence depends on subtle, but efficient measures that affect one's identification with the place. In particular, meaning only emerges in the space created by the intersection of a series of strict negative constraints with softly implemented, but clearly defined directions of action that delimit the point of equilibrium to which actors tend to return after the (expected) ruptures of the link between speaker and audience. Communication is then left to be lived spontaneously, on the spur of the moment, depending on the private and contingent experiences of the encounter. For an instant, or for the duration of the dream, power and necessity give way to freedom and allow the constraining structure and the unrestricted spirit, by chance or design, to flow in the same direction.

Notes

1 "There are some people – and I am one of them – who think that the most practical and important thing about a man is still his view of the universe. We think that for a landlady considering a lodger it is important to know his income, but still more important to know his philosophy. We think that for a general about to fight an enemy it is important to know the enemy's numbers, but still more important to know the enemy's philosophy. We think the question is not whether the theory of the cosmos affects matters, but whether in the long run anything else affects them" [536].

2 From a functionalistic perspective, culture is a "pattern of shared basic assumptions that the group has learned as it solved its problems of external adaptation and internal integration, that has worked well enough to be considered and, therefore, to be taught to new members as the correct way to perceive, think and feel in relation to these problems" ([537]: 12). Due to "the human need for order and consistency, these assumptions become patterned into what may be termed cultural 'paradigms' that tie together the basic assumptions about humankind, nature, and activities" ([74]: 3–5). According to a fragmentation perspective, on the contrary, this homogeneity is an illusion and "the boundaries of subcultures are permeable and fluctuate in response to environmental changes in feeder cultures. The salience of particular subcultural memberships wax and wane, as issues surface, get resolved, or become forgotten in the flux of events. In this context, the manifestations of a culture must be multifaceted – their meanings hard to decipher and open to multiple interpretations" ([538]: 132).

3 "There two types of actors in modern society: individuals and organizations. In Western culture, actors are assumed to be bounded, coherent, coordinated, and sovereign entities with intentions, who are able to talk, decide, act, and who control their own actions. Hypocrisy is a kind of inconsistency within an actor. Inconsistencies *among* actors in society are generally seen as routine and are not necessarily perceived to be problematic. Inconsistencies *within* actors, however, seem less ordinary and more problematic. The general norm is that actors should be consistent in what they say, decide, and do" ([34]: 112–3).

4 "Important as it may be to know the motives from which humanity has acted so far, it might be even more essential to know the belief people had in this or that motive, i.e., what humanity has imagined and told itself to be the real lever of its conduct so far. For people's inner happiness and misery has come to them depending on their belief in this or that motive – not through the actual motives. The latter are of second-order interest" ([84]: Aphorism 44).

5 A rare, apparently harmonic relationship between culture, practice, strategy, and the evolution of communication in the firm is well expressed by the case of Lincoln Electric Company, which dominated the American market for arc-welding equipment for over a century and associated decades of productivity gains with uninterrupted quarterly profits and no lay-offs. The complementary, emergent development of the productive technologies and of culture started with the adoption of strong individual incentives given by a piece-rate reward system. These incentives led to increased productivity, but decreased quality and cooperation, caused difficulties in synchronizing pace of work in the assembly line, and led to mistrust in managers (who could increase the rate with higher performances). Multiple counter-measures, all of them individually inefficient but effective because they were complementary, were put in place: significant amounts of work-in-process inventory was kept in order to allow each employee to work at his maximum; bonuses were based on quality of output and perceived cooperativeness; the company kept the promise to adjust the base rates only in case of breakthrough technology; ownership without voting rights was extended to employees; there was a promise of no lay-offs; and culture was backed by the fact that "Lincoln was run by the founder and his brother until 1965 and then, for the next three decades, by career Lincoln employees. They were personally committed to the system, and they well understood its logic and the need to honor the worker's trust" ([2]: 37–46 and [158]).

6 The Organization of Culture

> "Imagine that individuals in a culture are each assigned a light bulb. When an issue becomes salient (perhaps because a new policy has been introduced or the environment of the collectivity has changed), some light bulbs will turn on, signaling who is actively involved (both approving and disapproving) the issue. At the same time, other light bulbs will remain off, signaling that these individuals are indifferent to or unaware of this particular issue. Another issue would turn on a different set of light bulbs. From a distance, patterns of light would appear and disappear in a constant flux, with no pattern repeated twice" ([3]: 94).

Exactly as human beings are ontologically fragmented and in flow, so are the cultures of the families and firms in which they play their games. Resembling fuzzy zones of commonality to which players tend to return, rather than normatively rigid games in the strict sense of the term, these cultures get their peculiar form from the joint action of duty, habit, and pleasure. They are, then, "loosely structured and incompletely shared systems that emerge dynamically as cultural members experience each other, events, and the organization's contextual features", personal interpretive dreams lived as communal illusions only when the game unfolds spontaneously and actors become truly engrossed in the collective tasks or rituals ([3]: 58). Actions are taken half-spontaneously, half-consciously, following the interests that prevail in the instant. Even when ethics, affect, joy or aesthetics seem to be present, bringing feelings of obligation, attachment, or identification with the joint endeavor, these always appear in the context of a complex blend of egotisms that for a moment unifies the conflicting forces of self-interest and the various contradictory local commitments brought by the players' personal objectives, interactions, relationships and alliances into a single, common vector of action.

Arguably, no culture or social system could survive without allowing this chaos and the expression of all the antagonistic, yet complementary drives that coalesce to give impetus and direction to social games. Players have to satisfy their needs of subsistence, pleasure, control, power, prestige, and dominance – they are, thus, inevitably put against each other by the oppositions of war and pushed to search for higher means of realization, through which they express their ability to transcend or (proudly) prove the superiority over others, the destiny and themselves. Paradoxically, the same egocentric motives that push actors to create and maintain ties of utility, self-interest and convenience also create the conditions for the emergence of games that bring affection and identification, driving players to "naturally" lend their own individualistic *pathos* to collective tasks and groups they belong to. In the firm, in the family, as in any civilization, the same deep, individualistic core of our divided human nature – a blend of animal self-interest and lust for power, of the soft need to belong, and of illusions of transcendence – is needed for games to be sustainable, economic, grounded on the real life of the players.

Yet, despite the aleatory nature of the flow of self-interest – what serves *me, now,* is good – every relevant people or group in the history of mankind has given a particular meaning, a color to the mundane games played in their stages. Materialism, spirituality, joy, pleasure, affect, rationality, peace, and depth are some of the more common directions of meaning – a layer of illusion composed of loosely organized concepts, ideas, and ways of being that shape the surface, but never the depth, of the games they give a color to [31, 539, 540]. For our purposes, it does not matter whether the real drivers of change lie in the Marxist substructural base or in the Hegelian superstructure, if idealism stems from self-interest or pragmatism from beauty, or whether man, in its core, is transcendent or immanent, sacred or profane – these are all remnants of the old search for a single truth, for the fundament to which the complexity of existence could be reduced as if one's (momentary) lens were the only, single way to explain the reality. It suffices to say that the fiction of a culture that could unify family and firm lies precisely in the goal of developing a game that gives a particular *tone* to these contradictions – a relatively harmonic symphony, which with its recurring theme and leitmotivs creates preferential avenues for individual realization and brings a certain form to the collective endeavor.

Every project of change and culture, then, involves the creation of a cover-up of transcendence, a façade of meaning that simultaneously allows the actors to satisfy their self-interest and gives a general direction to the collective manifestations and choices of action. "If man is an animal suspended in webs of significance he himself has spun, and culture [is taken] to be those webs" ([541]: 5), the particular cultural form that characterizes any family or firm expresses the specific threads of meaning that are more commonly lived by the players or that have been institutionalized as habitual games in the place. These threads are both imposed from outside, as an implicit or explicit manifestation of social structure, and lived emergently by human beings who see themselves as free thinkers – it is only when the desired dream is inserted into the practice that one infuses the world with signification, transforming the supposedly objective reality of the facts into a blend of objectivity and subjectivity. Actors are, therefore, always enforcing, enacting, communicating, and writing their stories, the plot of a play in which facts are perceived at the same time they are interpreted by a subjectivity that permanently assesses the significance of the situations for one's life. Leaders are simply the (contingent) embodiment of a collective, historically determined will to power that demands some direction of permanence of change. They do, however, exist; and it is in their hands that falls the institutional task of defining the rules and tone of the game.

Leading Change

One can think that all individuals are similar in their capacity to exercise local action, to think about this action from above, and to (partially) structure the games over which they have power. Only those who occupy authority roles, however, have access to both their share of local action and a position that confers the right to craft the rules of the whole game or to broadly influence its execution [163]. Social status confers power; and because status stems from a position of centrality in the system, the game-perspective, focused on the top-down, structuring or structured facet of human behavior, is peculiarly relevant to leaders or change agents. The task of designing and implementing a cultural game is always an act of influence, which serves the needs and interests of particular actors or groups and prioritizes some values, goals, and *tastes* in detriment of others that could be equally valid if one used a different definition of the situation.

Change, then, depends on power, status, and capital – without the leverage given by forces that back the ideals of the culture, any personal intent to change fails because players do not have the tools with which to insert their private ideas in the public arena [62]. Sure, the exercise of this power is constrained. First, by the nested, overlapping structure of the social world – multiple levels of integration that allow fragmented identifications and local worlds that need to be reached for any project of change to become part of the economic exchanges and identity games that occur in the micro-level of the interactions and relationships. Second, change is constrained by the institutionalized definitions of meaning – without the resonance with the playful spirit and ideals of transcendence of the era, men are seldom hypnotized by the illusion of the game and do not put their self-interested egocentrisms at the service of socially directed egoisms ([82]: 110). Finally, change is constrained by the range of control available for each actor – one's soul and body for the individual, the family for the parents, the clan for the patriarch or matriarch, the firm for the controlling groups, the whole system for the majority if the fantasy is of democracy. "A leader will just as surely fail if he too readily yields to the limitations of his organization as if he ignores those limits. The problem is always to explore and test apparent restrictions, to see which must be accepted as inevitable, as areas of true recalcitrance, and which may be altered as to create the institutional conditions for achieving the goals retained" ([79]: 91). The larger and the more complex the system is, the more power is shared and dependent on communication, negotiation, and identification in order to reach the distant, private worlds where life really happens.

In family and firms alike, leaders and change agents are both empowered and limited by their positions. Formally, the power of any controlling group or organized coalition to influence the game starts with its ability to define "the conditions of membership, the goals towards which the participants are supposed to orient their behavior, and the means that may legitimately be used to attain them" ([177]: 203). A relevant point is the monopoly of violence and rewards – only leaders can fire, hire, promote, or punish undesired actions. They control the larger forces that affect the behavior of the group, shaping the flow of all automatic, taken-for-granted forms of being and defining the rules and interdicts that set the tone for the official illusions of the place – the explicit or implicit meanings that, expressed in the form of the structure and norms that direct the behavior of the cultural members, become eventually embedded in the world of practice. The more power they have, however, the more distant they are from the local places where change is implemented and life occurs, generating the information they need for any realistic planning. Norms, laws, and commands must be followed to become truth.

As structuring as they may be in theory, therefore, in the practice rules are followed only as a function of habit, fear, or belief. Whenever there is any contrary wish or margin of freedom, or when the crisscross of different games does not offer any clear direction, violation is the norm. "The acceptance of rules in social life may imply something quite different to the acceptance of rules in a [circumscribed] game. In the former case, there need not be an implicit agreement that rules should be equally fair to all actors and, as a consequence, they may have different types of commitment to any existing set of rules. The participants may be involved in the interaction for varying reasons and differ, therefore, in how they conceive 'winning' or 'losing'. Finally, their strategies may be designed to overturn the rules of the game rather than to obtain a larger slice of the cake (as presently defined) by means of legitimate actions" ([177]: 12–13). Culture and change depend, then, on the interplay of chance, unpredictability, complexity, and the contradictory complementarity between open force and illusion of meaning; and meaning, in contrast with forced behavior, depends on self-imposed tasks, spontaneous games, legitimate doubt or conflict and fair demands – normatively institutionalized practices that are accepted by players as good, natural, indifferent, habitual, or so intrinsic to how things should be that they imperceptibly define how things are.

For ages mankind has tried to find proper justifications for the belief in truth, justice, beauty, or love as sources of meaning. First, there was only God – the sacred commandments, maxims, and givens that from the height of metaphysics directed men to follow certain directions. Then, there was reason – the search for laws that could ground the need for the social contract despite the overwhelming evidence that men strive for freedom, and that this freedom is often contrary to the accorded collective goals. Almost imperceptibly, then, morality and rationality have been equated to each other: "The *fool* has said in his heart, there is no such thing as justice, and sometimes also with his tongue, seriously alleging that every man's conservation and contentment being committed to his own care, there could be no reason why every man might not do what he thought conduced thereunto" ([65]: 91, my underlining). Until today, in some hidden corners of the family or firm, players still feel compelled to profess their belief in justice or in the collective good while acting, in practice, according to what pleases them in the moment.

It has not been until the deconstruction of rationality as disguised metaphysics – an event that had its climax in the last century – that it has become clear that there is *no* reason why one should believe it is indeed *foolish* to break the law and act according to one's own interests. After all, when the darker side of reason ventures in how things really happen in the private and public worlds where people show who they are, it is only based on one's power and on the individual taste for a certain direction of meaning, on the more irrational and groundless desire of the players, that a goal, tone, or game prevails and actors find the fundaments that give meaning to their actions [542]. Morality, transcendence, justice, aesthetics, ethics, and affection are, exactly as self-interest, utility, pragmatism, power, and status, equally irrational (and legitimate) motives for one's action and thought [271, 331, 543, 544].

From a purely pragmatic perspective, therefore, "a compelling vision is neither necessary nor sufficient for a successful business strategy. A firm that is well positioned with clear competitive advantage can succeed by tweaking its current strategy at the margin", as are family leaders who want to maintain the group together but do not think or want to pay the prices of implementing the culture they profess ([545]: 802). Genuine, idealistic proposals of change, on the contrary, must be grounded on practices that are convincing both to the public *and* to those who espouse them, to the external spectators *and* to the private audience of the actors, leaders, or change agents who (truly) search for meaning. The problem of the management of culture then becomes one of poetry and translation, the manufacture of a (hopefully beautiful, necessarily touching) narrative that integrates into a single plot the belief and the disbelief in meaning. Only when games of transcendence acknowledge, include, and embrace the contradictions of the practice where they are lived, forcing action in the direction of the dream, they are able to pass the test of doubt [546]. Then, taken honestly and with the right blend of seriousness and playfulness, like a lighthouse that from the horizon guides the ship but does not determine its immediate course, the family and firm's identities and propositions of value may exercise their real task, to create and maintain a sustainable illusion that gives form to the organized activity.[1]

Setting the Tone

Any ethical, affective, or aesthetic ideals that abstractly represent the directions wished for meaning are, ultimately, only words. It is only when enacted in the daily life of the social system, that they anchor the transcendent idealism with the ballast of practice and serve as reminders of the commitment to collective goals. They tag as negative the games that are frontally antagonistic to the culture; modulate acceptable egoisms to fit the *form* of the desired illusion; offer a range of plots and possibilities of identification through which actors can simultaneously enact their personal drives and feel part of the community; and independently of the motives by which they are followed, still color the outward manifestations of culture [31]. As hybrid creatures made of a blend of reality and dreams, individuals, families, and firms then transcend the limitations of the material and power games by enacting the dreams they believe in, the memories they remember, and the objectives they put in place as if goals had, indeed, any meaning beyond the ludic pleasure of beating a self-imposed limit.

The ethical tone given to a cultural game reflects the decision to restrain power according to justice, and thus constrain the individualistic games by the enforcement of (tacit or explicit) rules that define what is considered fair at the time. This goal expresses the overt commitment players pledge to each other, to the collective good, and to the social contract they celebrate among themselves. This commitment, in turn, involves a few hard and clearly spelled out imperatives that define for all actors what can or cannot be accepted in the game – the basic rules that guide the practice and the meta-rules that define how to negotiate the rules. In addition, it involves a personal, unobservable, and unenforceable determination to do to others what one would like to see done to himself, a guide to action that binds players to the promise they will take into account the others in moments of conflict. For the leaders, this includes restricting the use of power to actions that serve the system and the culture, avoiding both the excesses and the omission commonly associated with authority; for all players, it involves promising to avoid any actions detrimental to the social or productive purposes of the family or of the firm.

Intangible as intentions always are, it is in this internal determination to stick to the shared illusion that lies any realistic possibility of a bet on trust – an informed and always conditional leap of faith by which actors temporarily give up war, or the preparation thereof, to engage in the construction of peace. The burden of reinforcing the rules of this game falls on the leadership – it is only when leaders uphold the proposed social contract and redundantly reaffirm their adherence to its spirit, consistently placing coherent actions in the public stage, that other actors become (potentially) more likely to be taken by the shared illusions and consequently more open to engage in the process of negotiating the relational contracts that must be enacted in practice for the system to evolve. In addition to the usual clauses, these contracts have to predict the possibility of trade-offs, paradoxes, contradictions, distractions, and errors; set clear rules to negotiate the rules and allow multiple rounds of negotiation, provided these occur within the implied spirit of the game; predict the irreducible, final right of the sovereign to define what is an exception and what to do about it; and overcome the limitations of formal contracts by emphasizing the need to use uncertain trust commitments grounded in the bet on the future and on the spirit of cooperation, rather than just on short-term considerations of utility [547].

Differently from ethical behavior, which can to some extent be reinforced in the form of law, *the affective component* of the cultural game depends completely on the spontaneous reaction of the players. Attachment, companionship, love, friendship, gratitude, and loyalty come from the tacit, *free* choice of the players to privilege the bonds and ties by which they are connected and focus on each other, their joint constructions, and the common well-being. Joy, pleasure, and peace, on the other hand, privilege states of action or tranquility that come from being *above* the game, laughing at its paradoxes and contradictions or reposing in the serenity of understanding. Both types of emotions depend on the players, not the leaders. Affective ideals, therefore, can never be imposed – at most, leaders, and change agents can use their power to create the context from which the desired feeling may (or may not) emerge depending on the (uncontrollable) disposition of the actors and on the (unpredictable) loops of communication and negotiation that develop at each moment.

Uncertain as they are in guaranteeing any form of culture, these contexts depend, first, on the definition of the places and time where players have to encounter. Second, on ground rules that establish the accepted forms and tone of conflict, thereby diminishing the chance of games that fall into the players' zones of aversion; third, on the use of charisma and legitimacy to reinforce peace; and fourth, on the disposition to add a personal, disinterested tone to the instrumental gains brought by the simple contracts that regulate common exchanges of interest. In the main forms that inspire productive cultures – joy, peace, attachment, curiosity, and engagement – the resulting affect brings intimacy and irreverence to the culture, coloring the tense equilibria of the zero-sum games of power, status, and self-interest with the engrossment and forgetfulness that come with the feelings of affectivity.

Perhaps more than justice, widely seen as required for the organizing, the institutionalization of affectivity works against many directions of culture because it erodes its bases of power. Even in the modern family, tradition and emotion are generally in tension with each other – during routine life, friendship, love, joy, and mutual support are tacitly dependent on the respect for the rules that from above determine how the common resources, space, periods, and rituals will be dealt with. The same happens in the firm: the bureaucratic ideals of rationality, professionalism, specialization, division of labor, accountability, respect for hierarchy, and impersonality tend to discourage, minimize, or even prevent the emergence of real affect among stakeholders – joy and attachment are, therefore, lived on the fringes of the system, in the context of private relationships that have little to do with the network and thus develop independently of the system and often at odds with it. As peculiar social creations that draw from both sources, family businesses require the ability to deal with the two different logics of action in order to prevent the rupture of the illusions that constitute the family and the pragmatic game played by the organization. Insofar as they concentrate in the same stage the usual pragmatic demands for merit or efficiency *and* the spontaneity of the family nuclei, these firms typify the tensions that exist in any intimate, complex relationship or social system. It is only by developing common understandings and clear rules about the basic facts of conflict, power, peace, contracting, and self-interest – and not by trying to artificially separate their contexts – that one develops the ability to create more sustainable illusions and then engage disarmed in the affective or aesthetic games that give the place its transcendent, non-utilitarian flavor.

The aesthetic component of culture, finally, belongs to the intangible world of the "nuances and impalpable elements that cannot be apprehended cognitively but only through the sensations they provoke in the players. These sensations cannot be separated from the pathos [they acquire] for organizational actors" [338]; and jointly with the affective reactions, they are radically severed from any direct managerial action. "Different strokes for different folks" – within the rules of the broader social game, whether one considers something beautiful, sublime, ugly, comic, humorous, gracious, picturesque, tragic, or sacred falls in a fundamentally norm-free zone and is determined solely by matters of taste, related to the individuals' immediate and private sensing of the organizational environment. Virtually untranslatable to the usual categories of the language game, aesthetic feelings are therefore among the most directly felt experiences, the strand of meaning that more intimately and freely connects the actors to the place or to the games they play.

For the leader or change agent, the aesthetic game works like the rhetoric of the artist – a form designed to please the audience and the actor, to show as well as to disguise, to recreate the world painting it with the colors of another and more touching dimension. In this sense, it is closely related to the identity games with which people, families, and firms simultaneously make up and enact their ideals selves rather than the crude facts. "In producing an aesthetic, what an organization does, intentionally and/or unintentionally, is to structure both form and content in such a way as to elicit a positive response from all those with whom it has any transaction. The way in which this is done generally involves a profound denial of the reality of the organization" ([548]: 189). When such a denial occurs on top of a (sometimes open, sometimes tacit) fair treatment of conflict and ambiguity, it presents not as an ideological twist of reality, but as a full embracement of the true role of illusion in human life, an attempt to cover, and potentially adorn the raw reality of the facts with the softer varnish of beauty or grace.

If it is the way in which ethical, affective, and aesthetic ideals are practiced what truly distinguishes idealism from ideology, the attrition between the world of ideas and the world of practice is never an easy matter. In the firm, an action generator whose function is to perform well the task it proposes for itself, work has a double meaning. As a solution in search of a problem, it creates demands, searches for markets, increases the complexity, and expands the scope of the activities covered by the always-evolving technologies and forms of organization of labor [549]. Its members are, naturally, simple means to an end; and depending on how this utilitarian core of life is treated within the system, work becomes estrangement, alienation – alienation from the product, "when human beings become estranged from the things they produce"; alienation from productive activity, when they "lose control over the capacity of their labor to affirm and define their self-existence"; and alienation from the species and from fellow humans and the community, "when the sole aim of life is competition and social relations are transformed into [purely] economic relationships" ([550]: 88–96). One way to counteract this perspective is by reframing work as a socially embedded, personally relevant process of transformation by which disorder, or entropy, is shaped, pruned, and organized to create a certain type of order [343]. The innumerous practical negotiations and commitments that need to be made for this to happen – the compromises between profit and culture, an internal design that may serve the culture and the competition, the use of complementarities, the pursuit of fit between strategy, operations, technology, and people – inaugurate a never-ending cycle of successive manipulations of the frontier where the maximum motivation required for engagement meets the maximum coordination required for collective work and for the experience of meaning (see note 4, Chapter 5).

The same happens in the intangible games that give life to most families, especially when these are directly linked to the very tangible games associated with family property, family business, and traditional rules of power. Faced with maneuvers directed at their soul, and generally aware of their ability to accept or reject the manipulations, members often react to the pressures they receive with different exercises of freedom. For them, culture is *not* a direction for action but a disjointed group of concepts and practices from which they choose, according to the values and contexts of the moment, what to do. The pursuit of identity, common values, aesthetics, playfulness, or affect becomes, then, a fugitive ideal that may threaten both the firm and the family, whose reason of existence and conditions of illusion are constantly impacted by private interests, facts, rules, processes, and truths that menace the illusion of meaning and free-will. Grounded on two radically different pillars – one reflecting the aesthetic need for illusion or forgetfulness in the common game, and the other the equally true requirement to enforce the demands of work – this integration of several disparate forces into a single mode of life transforms the change process into a game, a profoundly difficult game for which the goal is to make of the place a mix of the technical demands of work, the political interests, and the affective, ethical, and aesthetic utopia to create a type of order that maximizes human realization and cooperation [551].

Drafting Some Rules

If the individual's feelings of meaning depend on spontaneity, and therefore on unstable and constantly negotiated combinations of identification, slack, and constraining, cultures – to the extent they are assumed to be homogeneous – are necessarily based on a mix of rule-following, rule foisting, rule violation, war, forgetting, and jazz-bounded improvisation that occurs in the ground of formal contexts, rules, and structural designs that foster the desired goals [552]. This fluctuation poses a series of pungent problems for the leaders: how to craft a superstructure of meanings that reflects the value-perspectives of those who control the stage, the player's social and economic needs, the interests of the firm, and the best parts of the collective spirit of the age; how to reconcile coordinated action or feeling with the forces of individuality; which limits to impose and how much slack to tolerate, in order to prevent the stifling and anonymizing effect of the group forces; and ultimately, how to translate, into a relatively ordered and repeatable system of rules, what can, cannot, or should be part of the game [552].

All these questions, naturally, go back to the universal duality between individualistic and collective identifications and the need to deal with the mixed-motive games that constitute social life [553]. This duality leads to a crossroad. From the fact that actors and rules are many, but the stage of the play is a single one, comes the inevitability of conflict – war, with all its implications for the transfer of information, communication, and dis-organization, is in the core of any intent to change that involves influencing a culture in the direction of any specific form of social order [554]. In the opposite pole, one sees the "passions that incline men to peace: the fear of death; the desire of such things as are necessary to commodious living; and a hope by their industry to obtain them", which ultimately lead to the social contract ([65]: 86). These rules of the game, to be idealistic, must both touch a chord of transcendence already present in the collective imagination *and* solve the political dilemmas brought by the intersection of the various different motives and levels of identification.

Even when this broad contract *is* accepted as a solution the political friend-enemy duality, emerging as an *apparent* solution for the war, any ideals of justice, in fact, simply substitute a second-order dilemma for a practical predicament. Discord about practical matters – whether one should prioritize the present or the future, choose one or another strategy, or give a certain (and not another) direction to the common endeavor – still inevitably occurs despite any commitment to the collective dream. Furthermore, the very nature of justice is a matter of debate. Players may agree that fairness and social order are worth pursuing; but they may still define the "good" by taking into account the utility of an action *or* its conformity to a moral rule; may consider moral rules as absolute *or* accept that each rule has a specific validity depending on the context; may ground ethics on rational deductions of right and wrong *or* on emotional intuitions that define what one *feels* should be done in each moment; and may shift haphazardly among different ethical criteria, depending on what they believe in the moment and often without noticing they are incongruent [555]. Conflict, again, is inevitable – the dissension is just played out in different stages, on more and more abstract levels in which ideals *always* cover up, romanticize, and serve the private interests of the players.

Any attempt to delve into these questions would lead us into a swirl of meta-ethical constructions and deconstructions, reflecting the second-, third-, fourth-, and n-order dilemmas that arise whenever players attempt to find a fundament for the fundament of their actions. It suffices to note, then, that this desired, mythical, utopic, idealistic, or ideological social contract that serves as a basis for rational communication games depends, necessarily, on an arbitrary stop in this interminable regress of rules. As remarked by Rousseau, our problem has always been "how to find a form of association that will defend the person and goods of each member with the collective force of all, and under which each individual, while uniting himself with the others, obeys no one but himself, and remains free as before". In this ideal contract, "the articles of association are reducible to a single one, namely the total alienation by each associate of himself and all his rights to the whole community; (...) each man, in giving himself to all, gives himself to nobody; and as there is no associate over whom he does not acquire the same right as he yields others over himself, he gains an equivalent for everything he loses" [63]. It does not matter whether this idealized equality under a common contract is, or is not, true (and it never is). It suffices for players to believe in the fairness of the proposed solution for idealism to work, making players sufficiently happy with the underlying social soil to stabilize the tone of the communication, believe in the culture, and go back to the themes of life.

All simplistic premises of game commonly used to deal with the problems of honesty, dishonesty, alignment, coordination, identification, and legitimacy that may help or hamper this desired contract – strict observance of the identity game, rigid adherence to the law of coherence, reaffirmation of one's character, intentions, values, or binding commitment to follow up with one's promises – are clearly insufficient to cover the complexities of real life. They reflect the immediate and intuitive needs of players who still believe in truth, and who from inside the game face the possibility of cooperation or defection, the instability or firmness of the promises on which they need to rely in order to go on with life. They satisfy the mythical need for a solid platform on which to ground the proposals for the future – an expectation as uncertain as is time, inasmuch as it depends on the others' soul. They do not, however, address the complex decisions required in situations of ambiguity or the "more serious problem that occurs when moral rules or rights appear to conflict", offering distinct, but equally valid directions for one's choice based on identity, appropriateness, or truth ([555]: 71). For these, we need *relational contracts*.

Relational Contracts

If it is not simply on written rules, on formal systems of governance, or on rigid norms of conduct that the stability of family businesses lies, the management of the family and of the business becomes closely associated with the irrational, contingent, partially ordered, partially aleatory management of meaning as it appears in each particular situation. This leads us to the fragile, ordered but relatively unpredictable relational contracts – commitments focused not only on the exchange of interests, but on continuous negotiations based on time, trust, doubt, limited error, ambiguity, and uncertainty [449]. These contracts place the long-term relationships, like the marriage, the firm, the family, the joint venture with a partner, or the collaboration with a supplier, above the present situations in which players contend with each other. This means that the paradoxes of information, communication, power, status, and identity are acknowledged; and that conflict, individuality, and cooperation are reconciled. But more importantly, for the cultural game to be played out of calculations of instrumentality and give meaning to the contract, the exchange of self-interests must follow the ethical, aesthetic, and affective spirit that determines, as in an underground meta-game, the legitimate way to negotiate the remnant rules.

All practical, daily enacted relational contracts that make part of everybody's life – the arrangements based on trust, the acts of loyalty, gratitude, or retribution that form the basis of good marriages, friendships, partnerships, or relations of employment – depend, for their stability, on the juxtaposition of the awareness of error, ambiguity, doubt, conflict and of the same intangible bets that gives solidity to any social game (honesty, truth, and will). Practically speaking, by the mere act of engaging in any communication actors are tacitly or explicitly validating the idea that some problems are worthy of negotiation and that this negotiation can occur under common rules of interpretation. By assuming they share a common basis of interpretation, they are validating each other as competent social players. They are, therefore, reinforcing the social game in which they are inserted and the socially negotiated premises with which they define what is good, valuable, or real for them in the moment. It is only when these premises of the game are explicitly assumed as forming the primary basis of negotiation, however, that one can stop the regress of the rules and create the (artificial, choice-based) space for the (rational) negotiations that occur under a single premise or perspective.

For relational contracts to work despite the arbitrariness of the definitions of legitimacy on which they are grounded, they must include a vocabulary of change that covers a discussion of the limits, deficiencies, and areas of confusion and ambiguity that inevitably exist beneath any system of truth, morality, aesthetics, and idealism. This loose lexicon of concepts and practices involves, in first place, the translation of nonnegotiable goals and values – those deemed indispensable for the game to continue according to the perspective of the players who have the power to maintain or dissolve it – into the form of strict, publicly defensible limits and directions of action that set the required points of coordination. Every culture rests primarily on a group of "nos" and "shoulds", which in the form of prohibitions or imperatives determine what is unacceptable and absolutely required in the game. Generally, these involve regulations concerning the common property, work, body, obedience, decision rules, and the codes of honor and honesty legitimately accepted (and imposed) as due reason for the use of force. Even when fair, these limits are the reminder that every game, family, or firm, insofar as it requires (always arbitrary) decisions on divisions of capital, labor, energy, and what to do with ambiguity, are the game *of someone,* the person or persons who have the power to decide on the exception [99] (see Appendix 2, Figure 14).

Established the limits that define what is not allowed in the place, leaders and change agents who want to optimize the chances of steering the social system to a certain direction of meaning must rise "above and beyond the specification of formal structure to provide members of the organization with a sense that they are organized, even amidst an everyday feeling that at a detailed level everything runs the danger of falling apart" ([556]: 260). For change and culture to penetrate the private social universes of where individuals reign, they have to find an echo within the potential, personal, volatile, unmanageable core of idealism that may exist in each actor. Furthermore, since the spontaneity of play is intrinsic to culture – and in the absence of naiveté consciousness is often required to justify this spontaneity as legitimate – one must study the conditions in which actors tend to feel some illusions as true or false, and as a consequence become more prone to create, accept, resist, modify, or pay more or less attention to the rules that give form to the social system.

There are a few clear rules about how to negotiate the rules. Actors should not dwell on the past, except to exemplify rules about the future. Assumptions about each other's honesty, character, identity, or intentions are not allowed unless explicitly discussed from within a basis of agreement, lest one breaks the (always uncertain) pact of trust. Generalizations about the past, the future, the relationship, the family, the firm, the other, and the self must be limited and restricted to (solvable) practical problems, to avoid the risk of useless abstractions. Future, not past or present, should direct the focus. Discussions should be maintained within a scope to avoid chaotic ontological oscillation, while simultaneously opening the space for the discussion of nested, relevant problems and emergent reflections or strategies. All these rules, of course, can be disputed and introduce new areas of ambiguity. The consequence is that the less important is a situation, the more it can be dealt by rules; the more relevant and difficult, the less important becomes the formal law or process and the more relevant are the tacit, intangible rules of how to negotiate the rules.

These rules about how to negotiate the rules have to strike an (always contingent) balance between normativism and decisionism, opening a space for a final decision to be made based on the legitimate power to define what is an exception, and how this should be dealt with [557]. This is, perhaps, the fundamental trade-off of choice. On the one hand, the more elasticity and openness there is for the process of joint decision – between board and management, parents and children, across the various levels of the system or among suppliers and customers and managers of different divisions – the more one can create context conditions that foster learning, collaborative work, sharing of experiences, and identification. On the other hand, the speed, ambiguity, emergencies, and exceptions that make life interesting often cannot wait for the endless circles of the deliberative decisions; leaders must, then, exercise the solitary power of deciding, without any ground beyond their tastes and feelings of the moment and based on intangible values that accept multiple interpretations, when to act and what to do [87].

Relational contracts, therefore, do *not* solve the antithesis between power and consensus, fix the dilemma of cooperation, or give any solid foundation to the games of organization and culture. They simply assume that truth is inextricably linked with ambiguity, perspectivism, and error, and that all interactions, relationships, families, and firms are mixes of self-interest, pride, power, status, and (occasionally) the romance on which the contract is based, giving the tone for all the interactions. They frame deviance as a fruit of chance or creativity, as well as opportunism or guile. They shift the dialog from the practical problems to the abstract considerations of whether a bet is or is not reasonable. They interpret the problems brought by concrete trade-offs and divergences of value as particular instances of a more general second-order dilemma, namely, whether one should respond with a *bet* of continuity or rupture of the game. Actors in the family and business are, then, called to keep in mind their relationship and first deal with dissonances from within the game, under the assumption that others will, in the limit, surrender to the cooperative endeavor (see Appendix 2, Figures 17–19).

If all players are conversant with the dark side of meaning, if all know that all know everything, and if concrete problems are reframed as trade-offs and ambiguities, the abstract conditions of choice force men to make radical decisions in face of the peculiar moment they are facing, projecting the resolution of the (inevitable) down-side of the choice to the nebulous world of the future and of the (always uncertain) irrational bases of the social contract. By introducing players to a new game, to which belongs a second-order dilemma, they allow them to momentarily forget the embodied, emotional nature of life-in-context and consider other potentially true, future, imaginable, or unimaginable conditions of life which allow, because they obey to different rules of the game, different solutions for the disputes of organization. While acknowledging the fragmented nature of culture, the inevitability of conflict, and the role it plays in the generation of novelty and freedom, they put an (arbitrary) end to the regress of the rules by assuming that (irreverent) order is preferable to disorder, (ludic) organization to dis-organization, (loosely coupled) family and firm to non-family or non-firm.

It is at this moment, when one takes the radical decision to stop the regress of the rules and accept a practice, contract, culture, or order as truly *legitimate*, that the task of organization benefits from the same limitations of rationality that are so disruptive to coordination at other times. As players follow cognitive biases that privilege consistency over inconsistency, closure over fragmentation, and truth over error – which in normal times lead to many half-truths, pseudo-explanations, and (false) intuitive judgments that seem valid just because they are logical –

the sensation of coherence brought by the comprehensive, logic relational contracts based on a meta-ethical acknowledgment of doubt and truth overcomes the dissonance that comes from their (inevitable) lack of fundament. Likewise, tired of the endless constructions and deconstructions aimed at finding a valid (but unattainable) fundament for social order, players stop the search as soon as they find a *satisficing* answer and automatically accept the validity of most reasonably crafted rules – reenacting a heuristic that in daily practice is a source of many problems, such as myopic learning, competency traps, or fixation in small peaks of excellence [45, 182, 558]. By the same token, as the game moves out of the battlefield of practice to the more abstract, idealized, beautiful (and difficult) world of ideas, the task of organization benefits from the mythical value given to reason and from the detachment brought by perspectives that privilege the impersonal, impartial, neutral second-order dilemmas over the concrete, emotional, personalized, and socially embedded ambiguities and trade-offs of real life. In general, if rules address the obvious contradictions related to error, truth, ambiguity, power, conflict, autonomy, and power to decide, and if practice is loosely coupled with theory, actors tend to accept that the contract is reasonable and probably take it as a symbol of the higher goals that (always ambiguously) guide the lower level processes of decision-making. This leads us to our last topic, the implementation of culture.

Putting in Practice

The first conditions that influence the outcome of any process of change include the contingent, historical ways in which the particular social system targeted for change evolved. Family businesses, for example, are different depending on the degree of diversification, on the percentage of family involved in management, ownership, and governance, on the number of generations, firms, family owners, and members, and on the corporate configuration of the firm (whether it is managed by the owner and entrepreneur, by a sibling partnership or a cousin consortium, for example). Soft, cultural indicators – such as identification, social ties to community stakeholders, succession intentions, or the family philosophy and practice – are equally important in the diagnosis and planning of the directions of change imagined for the place ([559]: 9). Family businesses also diverge depending on the institutionalized definitions of family, kin, market, or society, on the nature of the task performed by the particular firm (industry, retail, technology), or on the shared stories, practices, rituals, and property passed from generation to generation. The same happens with firms. Imprinted from their birth by the particular conditions of the market, technology, governance, and culture, they evolve as social creations only partially amenable to change because the present conditions embed all compromises, past and current, that find a reasonable equilibrium in the existing games of the place [23]. The gravitational pull of this tradition – the path-dependent forces of the particular past of each person, organized group, or social system – creates an inertia that strongly influences the ways in which change can or cannot occur at any time.

Resistance to change also comes from divergences of interest. It is true, leaders involved in the pursuit of meaning have in their hands the institutional task of defining the rules and tone of the game. Their rules, however, simply express the official illusions about the place – every structuration of a game is a subtle or clear imposition of an order that serves the needs and interests of particular actors or groups and prioritizes peculiar values, goals, and tastes in detriment of others that could be equally valid, if one used a different definition of the situation. Furthermore, since instrumental gains, power, pride and illusion (or self-deception) are always, implicitly or explicitly, satisfied by the pursuit of any ideal, all propositions of cultural identity, authenticity, and legitimacy are fraught with the same inconsistencies they pretend to overcome. If actors are in flux and continuously influenced by ideals and habits that come from their personal lives, "the wider society, *and* the finite provinces of meaning specific to the organization" ([177]: 184), true cultures cannot be imposed as a project of change and emerge relatively unpredictably, in the narrow spaces created by the intersection of the negative constraints of social structure, the economic pressures, the indifference of habit, and the (playful?) exercise of the actors' free-will.

It is precisely the moment of this brief flash of freedom, in which actors feel momentarily unconstrained because they respond to what they immediately see and jump smoothly from one perspective, value, or meaning to another, what marks the end of the effect of structure and the beginning of local action. Family and firm, as entities, are just two of the various circles of influence to which players respond when defining what to do or how to feel, think, and act in their practice. Virtually inaccessible to anybody beyond those present in the instant, these personal reactions are a powerful counterpoint to the deterministic constraints of the concrete world of the facts and to the normative, rigid interpretive solutions which prevail in the structural cultural meta-game. One of the tasks of organization, one may argue, is to deal with the game of emotions in a way that one can avoid or minimize hitting the zone of aversion, push the limits of the indifference, and create contexts that bring to fore identification and the old, abstract pursuit of meaning. One could, then, temporarily or apparently, solve – but only in practice, never in fact – the divergences of interest that hamper any pursuit of change or management of meaning.

The devil, however, is always on the details – and it is precisely in the interface between the world of ideas and the world of practice, when the abstractions that give meaning to the culture shock against the real choices that must be made on the spot (and in haste), that one sees the third and more subtle source of resistance, one that is inherent to any form of organization because it arises from the exposition of the multiple contradictions that have to be ordered as a game for life to flow. These contradictions simultaneously go against, and are necessary for, the experience of true meaning. Families and firms only subsist *because* they put together irrationality, bounded rationality, calculating self-interest, union in the war, calculation, spontaneity, meaning, identification, and differentiation from the outside at the service of the group. Strategies only confer sustaining competitive advantage when based on "clear patterns, with all the complementary choice variables tending to be done together or at comparable levels" – system effects that lead the whole to be more than the sum of the parts and therefore involve losses on particular options when analyzed individually ([2]: 36–7). People only seem rational *when* they integrate their various (logically opposite) egocentric and other-directed motives into the single, romanticized identities framed as values, ideals, or (authentic?) displays of image and reputation. Furthermore, it is only *because* players intuitively lend their "I-motives" to social entities, forgetting themselves in the roles they play, that collective games of self-preservation, identity, morality, love, joy, or patriotism acquire personal meaning [71, 184, 324]. The sense and sensation of organization, culture, and unity only emerge strongly, and the game of culture only succeeds in having some say in the competitive social ecosystem of practices and beliefs, when various vectors of power are united temporarily in a single direction – love, friendship, family, firm, personality, profit, or any convincing "truth" – that *seems* real in the moment it is lived.

In all these cases, of course, what we are seeing are just the inherent contradictions that arise from seeing the game as spontaneity or as rationality, or respectively according to a truth- or to a game-perspective. When institutionalized in the local world of practice, when there is identification, and when the ideas in the family or firm echo what is generally considered good, beautiful, or true for the individuals, groups, era or society as a whole, meaning emerges. When there is a shock of reality and the local good of the players prevails, or when they have a different conception of the good for the whole, meaning is ruptured. The result is a fragile, transient, always questionable thread of commonality that integrates micro and macro, immanence and transcendence, practice and idealism, percolating (in an always imperfect way) all levels of social life. Diversity is necessary to create and strengthen this thread, but only works *for* meaning when contradictions are forgotten and players are immersed in the illusion of commonality; otherwise, incongruities become salient and force actors to their own stance, from where they work *against* the surrender to meaning because this seems contrary to the perspective that has more force in the moment.

Institutionalizing this back-and-forth conversation between the various shifting micro-and macro-levels of organization, of course, is never an easy task. In the firm, for example, the complementary fit between the various operations required to perform a task, the desired strategy for the company, and the cultural and strategic environment causes a series of conflicts, misunderstandings, partial views, and antagonisms that, in the present moment of the limit situation, lead to choices that are always apparently arbitrary and intuitively lead to conflict – short-*versus* long-term, centralization and decentralization, rational or intuitive thinking, risk *versus* prudence, or, more locally, finance *versus* production *and* sales. The same happens in the family: the good of the clan, of the individual, or of the group, the values given to the common property or financial liquidity, what seems right and proper for each player at each moment combine as an always unstable mosaic of preferences and prompt players to respond preferentially to their immediate needs than to any direction of culture given by the leaders. It is only when the broader ethical, affective and aesthetic ideals that inspire the culture are translated into the practical values, habits, and tastes that direct the (free?) choices of the participants that this culture becomes part of the collective tasks and personal goals that blend one's own emotions and values with duties, obligations, and allegiances to other players and to the social system in general.

Instability, contradiction, and contingent confluence of top-down choices and emergent courses of action, rather than homogeneity and alignment, are then the hallmark of true cultures. When players are engrossed by the game or just following the automatisms that characterize the zone of indifference, they are expected to live as usual, as if life were normal or meaningful. When awaken from the dream of practice by the clash of its (inevitable) dissonances, they can (hopefully) be distracted from conflict and be briefly directed to a meta-game, a common vocabulary of motives that allows them to review the concrete emotional flow of action usingthe more abstract game-perspective, in which (individualistic) vectors of power are less tense because embedded in the (common) ground of human rationality.

The alternate use of reason and forgetfulness – the first to deal with calculating games, the latter to engage in games of peace – is a crucial point of any technology of change directed at the creation of meaning. By this taking-turns, the diversity and conflict usually associated with capital, power, ambiguities, and trade-offs of the practice are openly acknowledged to prevent misrecognition and false consciousness; at the same time, engrossment, joy, spirit, affect and spontaneity are fostered as manifestations of the culture-creating play-element that infuses all creative forms of civilization [82]. It follows that true cultures should *never* be based on strong, shared (positive) values; rather, the management of meaning ought to depend on the artful combination of strict (negative) constraints with softly implemented, tacit definitions of context that determine the points of equilibrium to which actors tend to return. Be it in the family, in the firm, or in any social dream, it is in the middle of this complex trade-off between rationality and feeling, freedom and constraint, or consciousness and forgetfulness, that one seeks the hypnotic feature of the culture, its power of illusion or cooptation.

Note

1 Unlike the zero-sum games linked to instrumental uses, power, or status, the pursuit of justice, of engrossment in the game, or of a genuine culture requires the *belief* in the ideal. Observe Hobbes' distinction between external behavior and internal commitment: "The laws of nature oblige *in foro interno*; that is to say, they bind to a desire they should take place: but *in foro externo*, that is, to the putting them in act, not always. For he that should be modest and tractable, and perform all he promises in such a time and place where no man else should do so, should but make himself a prey to others, and procure his own certain ruin, contrary to the ground of all laws of nature which tend to nature's preservation. And again, he that having sufficient security that others shall observe the same laws towards him, observes not himself, seeks not peace, but war, and consequently the destruction of his nature by violence. And whatsoever laws bind *in foro interno* may be broken not only by a fact contrary to the law, but also by a fact according to it, in case a man thinks it is contrary [to the spirit of the contract]. For though one's action in this case is according to the law, yet the purpose of the action was against the law; which, where the obligation is *in foro interno*, is a breach. (...) The same laws, because they oblige only to a desire and endeavor, are easy to be observed. For in that they require nothing but endeavor, he that endeavors their performance fulfills them; and he that fulfills the law is just" ([65]: chapter 15).

Appendix 1
Some Remarks about the Practice of Change

The concepts presented in the previous pages are closely linked both with the empirical observation of the facts and with the theoretical understanding we currently have about families, firms, and social life. The practical problem of developing a technique to work with organizational culture, on the contrary, involves mixing these realistic (?) interpretations of reality with the idealistic goal of provoking change in social systems that are, by their very nature, complex, contradictory, and fragmented. Developing *a* culture necessarily implies in some type of unity; this unity is in stark contrast with the diversity introduced by the various difficulties, dead-ends, and irreducible ambiguities, trade-offs and paradoxes observed in the processes of communication and negotiation of truth and value. Applying these concepts in practice, therefore, requires both the creation of a coherent set of techniques to deal with the social fact and a (blind?) faith that these techniques and frameworks will really work when used by real actors, who in the real world follow several other systems of organization and interpretation of reality.

As we worked with several families and firms, our approach to organizational culture has evolved as a loosely organized methodology that attempts to encompass, within a single process, the tools to deal with the realities of misinformation, miscommunication, power, and conflict while maintaining the ethical, affective, and aesthetic ideals required in a meaningful culture. Fundamentally, this framework attempts to address a fundamental question of our times, namely, "the problem of relations between the symbolic and material aspects of social life and between structure and agency" ([560]: 40). Practically, it intends to overcome the nihilism introduced by modern and post-modern deconstructions through the creation and diffusion of a new vocabulary and set of practices in which culture and meaning are not grounded on truth, but on the willful playing of a game that alternates awareness with forgetfulness, calculating strategy with engrossment in the illusion. The organizational commitment to treat all common themes under the rules of rationality becomes, then, the element that paradoxically legitimizes the call for actors to (temporarily) suspend their rationality and fully engage in the collective game.[1]

Following these lines, the first premise of our technique was that any project of change must be based on a thorough analysis of the contradictions, ambiguities, complementarities, trade-offs, and complex feedback systems that characterize any social system: simple answers value comprehensibility at the expense of comprehensiveness, and therefore do not give agents sufficient knowledge of the variables to allow them maximum autonomy. Paradox and skepticism are continuously used to foster understanding of the rules of the game. We thus hope to demystify charisma and blind faith in legitimacy as instruments of social power, increasing the agents' power to both question the institutionalized structures of meaning and to choose and shape their own movements of change.

Reason, however, is constraining as it is freeing: within current rules of rationality, any argument must refer to facts observed in the (public) world of the facts and follow the logical syntax of the (public) language game in order to be acceptable as a ground for change. Thus, by making facts explicit one is implicitly constrained to think about them according to common standards that define what is a proper way to reason; by accepting that thoughts should have a fundament, one is automatically restricted to publicly defensible worldviews; and by stating an argument before thinking audiences, one is tacitly committing to follow that line of thought and action. The degree of freedom gained by the explication of a game occurs at the cost of imprisonment in another (also social) game, the game of language, which seems freeing just because it follows other rules of structuration. The methodology of change derived from this study involves the use of open communication and rules of explication to analyze, treat, and talk about all problems practically lived and spontaneously brought by the actors as part of their reflection about their own practice, implicitly forcing them to be coherent (i.e., moral).

A second premise of our change methodology, therefore, is that when openly and honestly used in social systems reason works (and from the perspective of the organization, should work) as a powerful moralizing tool, the more so because its association with the modern institutions of agency, free-will and individuality makes it less prone to accusations of partisanship and disguises its constraining effects. As a consequence, a crucial element of the technique involves the open treatment of self-interest, egocentric biases, ambiguity, error, miscommunication, irrationality, and conflict as facts that ought to be clearly understood and dealt with, rather than avoided or proscribed. By creating a common vocabulary that includes these themes, actors are tacitly forced to treat them according to the public rules of the language game; common contradictions between espoused theories and theories-in-use are exposed [38]; and, either by fear of disclosure or to smoothen cognitive dissonances [273], players become more prone to take into account the logical (i.e., moral) rule of coherence during their decision-making. Consciousness and (forced) cognitive congruence are then added to reputation, spite, coercion, kinship, punishment, and reciprocity as tools that help to stabilize organization, a powerful new mechanism to reinforce cooperation [363, 365, 366, 368, 380, 419, 561, 562].

The third premise of the methodology is that social organization is unsustainable without substantial measures of slack that preserve lower orders of organizing from the isomorphic constraints of the collective games. Thus, we assume that a fundamental task of the change agent consists precisely in mediating the negotiation between actors with different levels of power in the system, buffering (undue?) manipulations of truth by the dominant coalitions and taking into account all the stakeholder's (legitimate) interests when defining the direction of change. As a corollary, we imagine change as a process that separately and simultaneously addresses several levels of organization, namely, individuals, small and larger groups, divisions, families, coalitions. By using these four parallel settings and approaches to change, private issues can be dealt exclusively with the change agent and remain preserved from conformity pressures related to public exposition; one can help players to understand the advantages, disadvantages, dangers, and trade-offs involved in maintaining secrecy or engaging in open dialog, weighing the pros and cons of omission, truth and lying; areas of attrition are potentially worked on; and change agents may have a more open channel to continuously tap on the perspectives, information, and structure of the informal organization that often determines what happens in social systems, thus going beyond the usual homogeneity of managerial discourses [563].

The fourth premise, the proposal to give a particular attention to individual and micro-sociological levels of organization, is also related to our assumptions that efficient learning is personal, that it must be theoretical as well as practical [257], that experiential learning in social matters ought to involve emotional as well as rational inputs [564], and that knowledge is codified both as formal rules, processes, and concepts and embodied or socialized as tacit capabilities that are irreducible to symbolic language [181]. Following these assumptions, a formal (rational) exposition of the basic constructs involved in social organization – done through plenary lectures, didactic material, or through other readings (see an example in the figures on the Appendix 2) – is systematically associated with the practical, tacit, emotion-laden, experiential learning that occurs in parallel private and smaller meetings, whose aim is to blend theory with the real life of the players [261]. Privately or in group, these discussion-meetings bring memories, conflicts, and dissonances to the surface; show, in action, the contradictions and difficulties inside and between actors; pressure all to solve the dissonances and make difficult choices; allow the enactment, in the relatively protected environment of the mediated encounters, of the concepts presented theoretically; and provide a setting for the experiential learning required to achieve the desired (necessarily tacit) expertise regarding the social matters related to the task of organizing. By bringing reason, emotion, action, and social action into an immersive context, we thus hope to increase the fixation of learning and provide individual actors with the repeated exposure required for them to become expert change agents, freed from the need to contract external mediation or consultancies [565].

The fifth premise of our methodology is that organizational change cannot occur without support from the leadership. Be it in the family, in the firm or in any social organization, the right and the power to define and "protect the institution's distinctive values, competence or roles" belong to an internal elite that has been able to preserve a "condition of independence sufficient to permit a group to work out and maintain its identity" ([79]: 119, 121). Thus, in designing this method we have assumed a relatively centralized system in which some stakeholders are strongly committed to the process. In particular, given the a priori ethical, affective, and aesthetic ideals that guide our practice, we assume that projects such as these will work only when directed by leaders who are willing to use these goals as the parameters with which to question their own roles, mistakes, or doubts in the game that exists both within the leadership group and between the organization and its internal stakeholders [17]. Without this intent – a desire to embrace change as a personal and internal, in addition to institutional and external project – any change project is just another version of the (too frequent) discourses that hitchhike on "culture" to disguise caricatures of meaning with which to manipulate the collective endeavor.

The last premise of this methodology refers to the peculiar type of engagement required from the change agent. In particular, we assume that when leaders, consultants, and decision-makers face the pressure to go to action, the real drive that determines the direction to be taken is always the subjective, value-ridden choice about what is really taken to be true or relevant at the moment. Commitment to the success of the enterprise must then be based not on an (impossible) ethical neutrality, but on an equally ethical determination to be explicit about the value premises that ground any practical intervention [297].

The Methodology

Several elements that characterize this theory of change and the methodology designed to work with organizational culture have their origin in the career directions taken by the author as a psychiatrist, psychotherapist, professor, and more recently as a consultant. Learning, of course, occurs differently in these different contexts. In the protected environment of a medical office, for example, the social power involved in directing change is conferred not only by legitimate knowledge, but often by the mythical forces of idealization and charisma – an obvious invitation for change to be lived from inside and as if it were "normal", a self-realization that invites explorations and deconstructions without any dramatic stories standing out. In the public, more complex settings of the firm and of the family, on the contrary, learning is brought from outside in. Change, then, occurs side by side with negotiations of values and choices in contexts that demand coherence but at the same time require decisions in face of trade-offs, ambiguities, doubt, conflict, and fuzzy definitions of power, status, and identity.

Given that firms, families, and families businesses exist both as social entities *and* as a group of individuals that follow their own values and ideas, the technique of change associated with the theory we discussed in this book mixes the deep self-learning sought in any psychotherapeutic office – a setting that privileges explorations about one's personal perspectives and issues, which many times cannot or should not be exposed publicly – with the learning that occurs in everyday practice, as players agree, compete with, or rub against each other while exchanging concepts and decisions. In the office, in order to promote the emergence of limit situations and foster the development of autonomous learning, actors are exposed to different approaches and stimuli – individual and group sessions, family or couple meetings, and mediations between partners in a business. Clients are invited to bring the real problems they face in the outside world and reflect about them in the private, insulated context of individual or group sessions, while being exposed to an extensive didactic material covering the topics of emotion, cognition, social interactions, and relationships to have a broader cultural perspective. This particular mix of information-giving, study of the experience, and tacit understanding within the interpersonal context of change provides a meaningful live-as-you-learn type of experience and makes powerful use of the social interaction to change habits and infuse concepts drawn from theoretical, as well as practical sources. The trade-off is between depth and (cognitive) egocentrism. Players can dive as deeply as they want into the groundless (or transcendent?) abyss of meaning and self-knowledge; however, regardless of how much they attempt to question themselves, they are inevitably locked in the solitary I-perspective given by how they see their own experience. Essence is privileged, but at the cost of a blind spot.

In the public space of firms and family businesses, this focus on the individual is expanded to include the several levels of organization and the multiple games that occur in the place. Specifically, individual coaching sessions form the backbone of the process – particularly for the leaders, but also for any players who need to address issues untreatable in the public domain, face-to-face conversations provide an ideal, still unparalleled medium to study and internalize the abstract (but all too personal) concepts about self, identity, truth, communication, and power as practices that have significance in one's life. Three settings are added to the individual coaching: silent, ethnographic observation of meetings, and group encounters, in order to record how players behave in uncontrolled conditions; seminars with peers, members of the same divisions, or task groups to collectively study common problems, allow players to jointly reflect about their experiences and errors, and introduce the experience of cooperation in the study of dissonances (which commonly lead to personal polarizations); and meetings between individuals or groups dealing with difficult, wicked, or ill-structured problems that have become personalized and intractable by the routine practices of families or businesses.

Together, these four contexts provide players with an opportunity to analyze the practice through three different perspectives – life as seen from inside, in the coaching sessions; life as seen by an outsider, when they receive the feedback about the spontaneous behavior observed in the meetings; and behavior under real conditions of active learning, as experienced in the individual sessions and collective seminars. One can, then, evaluate the possibilities of error and learning related to the real, ideal, and social selves – the daily enacted, but often only tacitly lived negotiations of identity through which actors fulfill the double need of realizing themselves and growing up to the demands of the social game they play with others under the premises of the normative, prescriptive, or conceptual concepts of the culture in which they are embedded. The trade-off here is between the richness that can be derived from the study of the errors in the practice and the need players usually have to preserve their identity, appearance, and reputation – the basis of a tough exchange game, which often leads actors to preserve deeper issues from the sweeping gale of rationality and from the light of the (always deconstructive) public language game. Contradictions, silences, and defense become obvious, and many times create untouchable areas deeply preserved from the study of error. By working with players in a public setting like the firm or the family – rather than in the private environment of sessions in an office – social presentation, real practice, and the mismatches between essence and appearance are privileged, but many times at the cost of depth.

Considering these trade-offs and the risks implied by any change, this (hopefully creative) clash between theory and practice, or between abstraction and theory-in-use, happens differently in the four settings. In the *individual sessions*, the experience of error, as signalized by conflict, surprise, frustration, or "negative" emotions, is the starting point from which one derives the theoretical concepts and abstract perspectives aimed at illuminating the practice – the result is a loosely organized, but meaningful mosaic of new concepts and paradigms tailored to the needs of the practice. *Seminars* do not address private issues of the actors – which must be protected from the pressures of the group – but allow the study of the collective difficulties and, with the evolution of the group, the treatment of the masks, social selves, and social games already exposed elsewhere in the firm or family. Starting from a more structured didactic approach, but with ample space for the discussion of the practice, they provide a context for the combination of experience with a logically organized framework of the theory; the end result is a jointly negotiated new perspective of the theoretical and practical problems posed by the players, a process in which the change agent is actively present in shaping the creation of novel, hopefully useful, definitions of the situation. The passive *observation of meetings*, followed by individual and/or group feedback, brings the richness of a more detached perspective, the social game being left to take its "natural", contingent, spontaneous course. Finally, *the mediation* of the already-existing conflict situations brings to the fore the full clash of the antagonisms, but within the limitations provided by the artificial (hopefully more rational, focused on second-order dilemmas) setting in which negotiations occur. In these four instances, the (always fragile) premises of the change game of learning are trust, rationality, and good-will. However, even when these are not present – which always happens in any complex system where multiple interests and perspectives are at stake – the public discussion of difficult issues is a powerful tool to effect change, a means to negotiate (or impose?) a common vocabulary, and, often, an instrument of sensemaking that provides good explanations and things to talk about, regardless of the efficacy in prediction or of the fact that many players never actually change, just learn to behave according to the ideals they have to profess in public.

Finally, the whole process of change and culture tweaking depends on the agreement that, in the context of the intervention and of the culture envisioned for the place, learning from the error overcomes (or at least competes with) accountability for the error. This agreement, in turn, depends on the intangible, unenforceable and personal decision to impart a creative, playful, meaningful (yet serious) purpose to the discussion. Thus, whenever deeper values or concepts are called into question, limit situations take the form of paradigmatic encounters in which the previous alliances – with the change agent or among the members of a family or firm – may turn into conflict. If the process succeeds in guaranteeing fair standards for the clash to occur, avoiding the dangers of radical rupture, covered defiance, or shallow consensus, conflict rises to its true potential to engender change. These situations are the emblematic tests of any learning and relationship based on trust and doubt, the defining experiences of the actors' development as conscious agents. From the continued experience of their efficiency in provoking learning comes the concept that change can be grounded on safety, but only if this is used as a basis to engage players in the game of radically exposing of the contradictions, trade-offs, and paradoxes that underlie the (always personal, always emotional) error signals that arise from naive or non-adapted perspectives about the self or reality. Based on the socially constructed, permanently built *tone* given to the game of change, the treatment of the difficult *themes* implied in the organization of culture extracts the maximum benefit from the double fertilization that occurs when the ambiguity of practice brings new nuances to the theory, which, in turn, is used to illuminate the vectors, levers of manipulation, and root causes of the problems observed in practice.

A Brief Critique

Methodologically, all change interventions we have made so far have been based on four pillars: (a) the use of the case study as the starting point for the evaluation of the theory, which involves the application of the theoretical bases we described to the individuals, groups, families, and firms we worked with; (b) participant observation and action research as the fundamental methodological attitudes, which means that observation was never objective; (c) simultaneous evaluation of, and intervention in multiple levels – the individual actors, their dyadic and triangular relationships, the small groups, and the formal or informal networks; and (d) didactic use of affective and cognitive, experiential and theoretical tools to enrich the interpretation and understanding of the symbolic, material and economic conditions that underly all forms of social organization.

Following these principles, the evaluations and interventions we made strived to be objective, by sticking to the facts and including multiple sources of data; but have always been admittedly subjective, the desired understandings stemming from socially constructed, emergent loops of meaning created in action during the interactions of the change agent with the individuals and groups he worked with. Interpretations aimed for a thick, rather than a technocratic or purely rationalistic, formal description of the system [541]. This option for active participation, naturally, influences the content of the observation: the author's biases and values, on the one hand, and the tendency for conformity to authority, on the other, become powerful influences directing the contingent preferences, meanings, and decisions that drive the process of change. By exchanging the ideal of the detached external observer for the immersed, embedded agent who inevitably directs the flow and appearance of the facts he perceives, we trade the idealized (fictitious?) objective perspective for an understanding marked by an open, but reflective and self-doubting subjectivity.

Looking back on the several processes of change in which we participated brings a double-sided picture. On a first sight, we have indeed observed substantial (real? imaginary? transient?) progress in both families and firms – many individuals understood and applied the proposed approach, various groups and divisions adopted the methodology of change, practical problems were solved due to new concepts, and private and public conversations gradually began to revolve more frequently around the new paradigms (elements such as biases, paranoia, trade-offs, ambiguity, interpretive flexibility, asymmetry of information, or power, for example, were common in the narratives and discussions we heard). In this sense, both theory and method attained a specific form of validity: the (biased? socially constructed? false?) concordance of subjects and agent about the goals and perspectives proposed for the culture.

Several limitations, however, hamper these observations from being seen in anyway as a proof of concept. *First,* even if the observed concordance is taken at face value – a strong assumption, given the normative pressures for change, the bias for consensus, and the ambiguity introduced by silence and non-participation – convincing stories pass the test that defines what is a good explanation, but do not guarantee accuracy in prediction or description of reality. Players and change agents alike may, easily, have been deceived by the pleasing redundancy of shared (?) beliefs and silences, using the harmony of the socially constructed common social world to buffer the less comforting experience of facing the dissonances of reality. *Second,* the relatively short duration of the interventions, ranging from a few months to two years, prevents any assumption about long-term changes that could have become part of the culture of the place. Rather, learning was slow; even after many months, contradictions were common; and the new learned forms clearly competed with many other habits in the practice of the actors. In our experience, or at least with the method we propose, any attempt to work with culture can only work if it designed as a project to extend in time and, even so, only imperfectly ingrained in the practice. *Third*, the interventions we made were restricted to the *social* paradoxes of management and organization. The interface between culture, strategy, and the material practices of the place was never completely addressed. This would have involved a sweeping change in the routines that govern the disposition of property, power, status, and rank – the application of a rule of coherence linking the ideals of the culture to all the processes and regulations that characterize the day-to-day routine of the firm or of a family business (incentive systems, mechanisms of control, rules of accountability and decision, paths of succession and career progression, treatment of errors and ambiguities in the practice, etc. – see Chapter 5, Note 5). Since this was not done, players changed their vocabulary but the practices remained strongly conditioned by routines and pressures contradictory to the proposed culture, suggesting that the acceptance may have been ceremonial [35]. The undiscussable values that govern families and their businesses – profit, influence, pride, and self-aggrandizement through myths of identification – were barely scratched. It seems that here, as in the history of mankind, the cultural superstructure can at most give a softer tone to a harsh game that is, in fact, defined by the substructural, materialistic, economic forces that determine for whom and how the means and modes of production are organized.

Methodologically, our change projects – as any attempt to (rationally?) deal with organizational culture – have systematically suffered from several limitations that prevent us from drawing firm conclusions from the findings. Interviews, interventions, and conclusions were recorded a posteriori and by the same person who directed the change process; note-keeping was limited to a minimum, to preserve the positive effect of spontaneity in the social intervention (at detriment of reliability); and moreover, observation was always associated with actions and interactions. As in an action research, the roles of critical observer-researcher and change agent were enacted by the same person, who immersed in the trade-off between participant influence and scientific neutrality became a part of the phenomenon under observation. Probably as in any theory, but certainly more intensely than in a traditional scientific account, any changes we may have observed in the practice can thus never be seen as a link between theory and practice due to the deeper, self-fulfilling nature of the social fact. It is impossible to know whether what we saw was interpreted in the same way by other players or persisted in other settings, as one would expect from the tone that should (supposedly) characterize any genuine culture.

Notwithstanding these limitations, we hope this work, by grounding the discussion on the *a priori* acceptance of the antinomies brought by ontological oscillation, perspectivism, and complexity, may help to reconcile the deconstructive thrust of post-modern relativism with the rational, idealistic (or functionalistic?) push to find an order. Within organizational studies, in specific, we hope to renew the interest in interpretative work and make scholars closer to the practice of the systems they study; future research could better map the main trade-offs, ambiguities, and paradoxes of the firm, as well as the interplay between the social fact, strategy, and managerial dilemmas. Our attempt to explore the interface between the human sciences (sociology, anthropology, psychology, history of ideas) and the practical object of study seems particularly relevant in the field of family businesses. New studies, we expect, should go beyond simplistic paradigms that do not take into account the complex nature of social life and concentrate first on the similarities of family businesses with other forms of organization, and only then focus on the (small) peculiarities that make it a unique object of research. Future work in these areas, we expect, will illuminate the deficiencies and blind spots of the synthesis we presented and bring broader systems of meaning that target the task of putting, in a single text, the opposite vectors of organization and the creative, fragmenting exposure of its contradictions.

A Final Summary

We started this monograph by exposing the contradictions and paradoxes consistently found both within and between the discourses and practices of everyday life: be it in the family or in the firm, actors are often trapped in self-created loops of misunderstanding and miscommunication and tend to disregard the (coherence-based) logics of rationality and appropriateness by constantly shifting from calculating to idealistic perspectives. We showed how the illogical, yet realistic combination of truth, cover-up, and self-deception is in the core of the ambiguity, of the conflict, and of the skepticism that so often erode the belief in the true nature of the family or in the meaning of work when these are dealt with spontaneously. We postulated that an awareness of the contradictions brought by complexity, economy, multitasking, and depth of meaning could minimize the negative impact that silences, taboos, conflicts, and distances commonly have on the unity of the family or the maintenance of strategic or operational efficiency. We then suggested that seeing social actions as games may be a necessary tool to foster the management of meaning involved in any projects of culture and change.

The game perspective. Theoretically, we started by discussing how the formal obeisance to myth and ceremony, which is usually interpreted as the fruit of ideology or false consciousness, may be reframed as inherent to any culture whenever the game perspective is used to unify the dichotomy between the rule-based world of ideas and the loosely organized world of practice. We proceeded to discuss how this game-perspective reconciles the double-sided human experience of seeing life from inside, embedded of agency, and from above, as a structurally organized set of rules of the game – by seeing the purity of the ideal and the contradictions of practice as interrelated dimensions of the same cultural game, the construct may embrace the symbolic and the material elements of social life, the seriousness of truth, the multiplicity of potential interpretations, and the contradictions between paradigmatically distinct perspectives of seeing and valuing reality. We postulated that, as games increase in number and complexity, and as differences of power among players decrease, the combinations of games and the self-fulfilling cycles of reality creation would make it increasingly difficult to make any predictions or find an order for the observed reality.

In the real processes we experienced, change was framed as a game in which the change agent and the players could jointly analyze their theoretical doubts and the practical problems experienced on an everyday basis. The goal of the game was associated with learning. The relentless process of uncovering the paradoxes of the system triggered resistances, which were then framed as necessary steps in the playful attempt to reach a higher, meaningful, but rule-based cultural game, emphasizing the potential social function of conflict [399]. The game framework was clearly helpful in explaining interactions, relationships, conflicts, personal scripts, frames, and other experiences related to the micro-sociological level of individuals and small groups. As complexity increased, however, the predictive value of the paradigm decreased and we could retain only its metaphorical or rhetorical power. This was particularly relevant for the development of the habit of seeing the game from above and learning to think about the structural and structuring elements of each situation. The game perspective was, thus, both a tool to explain reality (in the micro-level of the individuals, interactions, relationships, and small groups) and an instrument to think and create sense-making stories and meaningful narratives about it (at all levels).

Games and the management of meaning. In the attempt to apply the construct of games to organizational culture, we then discussed theoretically how any culture, in order to be meaningful, depends on the interplay of three forces – the structuration of the game, associated with top-down decisions and the definition of a common vocabulary; its enactment in local action spaces, related to the resonance the game acquires for the players; and the unexplainable and unpredictable interplay of the multiple rules, players and games that compete for the primary spots on the social stage. We questioned how one could connect the macro-sociological structuring forces and the micro-sociological personal and interpersonal vectors by engaging the mechanisms with which individuals confer relatively stable meanings to the surrounding world, identifying themselves with the place, the task, the family, the firm, or the culture. Finally, the management of meaning was suggested as a fundamental task of leadership, one that involves both the attention to formal structures and the creation of sustainable illusions that can be superimposed on, and give a transient, but common (symbolic? cultural? aesthetic? affective? ethical?) color to, the instrumental games of everyday life.

In our work, this theory of practice was (partially) put in place through the establishment of formal governance rules to establish the limits, of informal vocabularies of concepts and motives to guide the dialogs in the system, and of loosely organized sets of practices and habits lived in the practice [154]. Formal structuration, in the guise of the written contracts and articles of association, defined what could and could not be done within the rules of the game – they created the boundary-conditions, the limits whose violation could lead to conflict, legal enforcement, or rupture of the relationship. Simultaneously, the development of concepts and practices related to the ambiguities, trade-offs, and errors in the processes of communication and negotiations of truth and value aimed to provide the informal structural framework of a loose meta-game that attempted to reconcile unity and diversity, opening space for both the enactment of differences and for the creation of common meanings.

In the real processes we experienced, the implementation of the projects of culture we proposed was fragmented, fluctuating, and dependent on contingent and imposed, rather than emergent and spontaneous activity. This points to the existence of a deeper, more interesting nested problem involved in any project of culture and organizational design: culture, at least to the extent it can be influenced by the brief work of a few years, seemed to remain a function of power and of the directions given by power, without ever crossing the line after which it becomes intrinsic to the social system. Idealism, thus, was frequently swamped by the pressures of the practice and momentary interests that diverted players from the proposed and professed path of change. There were pockets of resistance that could not be touched because the structural changes required for it to be broken – necessary, but unwanted or impossible lay-offs, coercion, or blockages of undesired communication pathways – would go against the institutionalized paths for the organization and bring an (undesired, unacceptable) ideological flavor of authoritarianism to the proposed project of culture. We observed that change can definitely happen on the individual level, is more erratic in small groups, but was not sustainable and did not become ingrained as a true organizational culture. Overall, the long-term, affective and transcendent (?) objectives of maintaining a family together or keeping the business as a symbol of the name were always in shock with the more mundane factors of everyday life and offered the change agent a different lever of manipulation, but in no means a guarantee, that a true culture could be put in place.[2]

Organizational culture as a problem. This blend of short-term success and failure of persistent implementation, local modulation toward change and lack of diffusion, and acceptance of the immediate work without institutionalization of change strongly suggests that processes of cultural change may indeed be risky and more limited in scope than one may have desired, especially given the short-term goals of the present-oriented, action-generator engine of the firm. This echoes several skeptical remarks about the inherent contradictions that separate realism and idealism: "Is there an alternative? Can managers [or leaders in a family business] sustain an awareness of the contradictions, paradoxes, ambiguities, and ambivalences of life (as intelligence, human beauty, and learning require) while espousing a rhetoric of simplicity, clarity, consistency, and certainty (as managerial norms and practices require)?" [566]. Were the observed changes "really there" or they reflected just the ceremonial enactment of the change agent's ideals and theories? What if the pursuit of disinterestedness, inherent to the proposed cultural illusion, is always a covered-up manifestation of charismatic power, false consciousness, misrecognition, and social conformity to the ideals of change? Where is the fuzzy boundary that separates ideology from idealism, or rhetoric from truth and self-deception? And more importantly, to which extent are one's theories and practices – including the one we presented in this essay – prosaic fictions that may have an interpretative or positivistic tone, but are simply a projected dream of the players, inevitably tainted by the self-referential traps of social construction?

These questions, of course, address the impossibility of solving the problem of validity of this work – or ultimately, of any belief in a common culture or meta-culture based on samples of one or fewer and backed only by self-reinforced iterations or bouts of social consensus [200]. Therefore, we invite leaders, actors and change agents interested in being truthful to the facts to accept they are probably engaged in a playful game of constructing a culture without ever knowing to which extent they are living what they think and say they are living; and simultaneously, to counteract the pull of the illusion with the equally playful game of continuing to work toward the order they envision while always deconstructing the meanings they create. Given all these limitations, then, where would we place this monograph? As an attempt to circumvent these simplifications and address the complexes and ambiguities of organizational change, this is a story about stories, a meta-view that aspires to combine in a single essay the hands-on experience of a practitioner and the doubt-prone curiosity of someone who wants to tackle the theoretical problems brought by practice [22]. It searches for coherence, but is not amenable to any form of empirical testing. It is broad and theoretical, rather than detailed and case-oriented. Furthermore, it suffers from all limitations of perspective of the viewpoint from which the problem was addressed: in writing these pages, not only have we constantly rubbed against our own idiosyncratic limits of observation and synthesis, but also faced the virtual impossibility of translating the free-floating nature of life into the logic-bound rules of the language game. It is therefore as a heuristic perspective, or as a group of general "guides to research" or thought, rather than as a scientific system or a set of prescriptions for action, that we expect this essay to be seen.

Notes

1 Applying Goffman's framework to organizations, one could say that a culture in which error, ambiguity, power, conflict, self-interest, or untruth are all part of the game decreases the chance that these will be seen as irreversible breaking-frame events that disrupt a naturally lived game on which players are engrossed. If one assumes that actors are complex and in flow, and exchange the perspective of truth for the view that identities are illusions that romantically organize an inner complexity marked also by self-interest, pride, power, or status games, the intermittent emergence of these error signals comes to be seen as expected events, and not as violations that disrupt the flow of identification and "cannot be effectively ignored" because the frame of the game does not apply to them ([86]: 347).

2 As Augier and March remark while writing about business schools "education can be organized to provide grace, meaning, delicacy, and elegance to human life, not because those attributes can be shown to yield competitive advantage but because they are basic elements of an educational faith... Questions of faith and beauty require conversations that differ from conversations over utilitarian questions. In the end, they are linked to a sense of identity and aesthetic quality. What is essential to being human? What brings beauty to human life? And how are the essential nature of education and its beauty reflected in an institution and its practices?" ([567]: 408). The same applies to change processes aimed at developing a meaningful organizational culture.

Appendix 2

Didactic Material Used During the Change Process

One of the more difficult problems involved in implementing the process of change we suggest involves the translation of the abstract meta-concepts we described into the everyday words and practices shared by the players. In our interventions, this difficulty was addressed by coupling a hands-on approach to learning – which privileged the study of errors derived from the emotion-driven (but chaotic) flow of the practice – with formal theoretical approaches including brief texts, written feed-back about the meetings, and plenary sessions with formal presentations of the content. The following figures were extvracted from the didactic material used in these instances. They furnish a sample of what was given to participants to aid the process of learning.

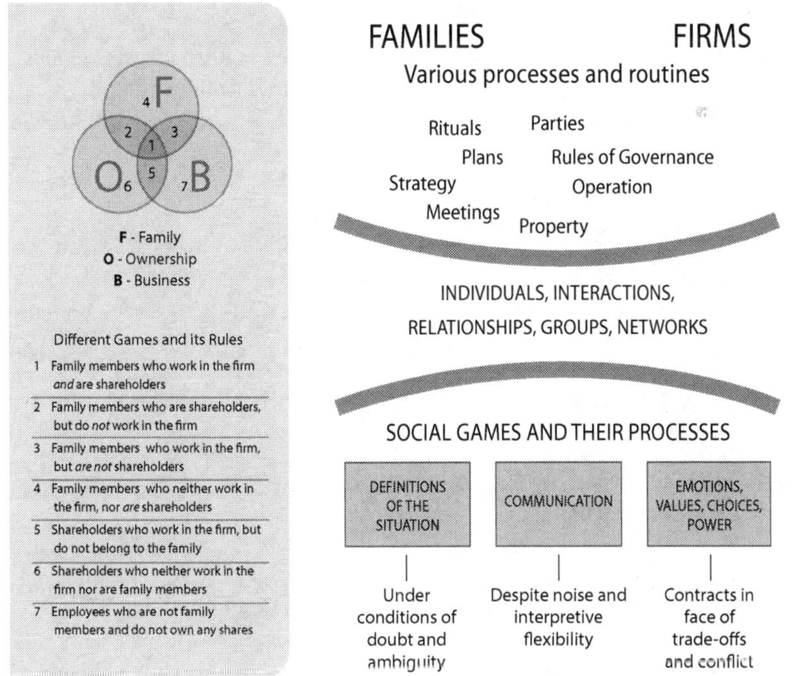

Figure 1 Family Business: Two Frameworks, Two Definitions of the Situation.

Figure 1 shows two frameworks by which family businesses can be seen. In the left, business, ownership, and family are seen as fundamentally different games whose rules must be understood and reconciled by the creation of formal governance systems. On the right we see the interpretive lens we propose: family businesses rely on (tacit and explicit) rule-based interactions, relationships, groups, and networks, which, in turn, depend on processes of communication, truth-creation, and negotiation of values.

During the interventions, each participant was instructed to place himself and the others on the subsectors of the Venn diagram on the left and urged to think about the different rules that characterize the family, the business, and the ownership games. The concept was used as a basis for the creation of formal documents required by the governance system proposed to the firm. Following this exercise, this view was deconstructed by showing how all social systems, including one's personal life, depend on negotiations of truth, doubt, values, and contracts that occur during daily enacted processes of communication. Change and learning were linked to each other by showing how these tend to occur tacitly.

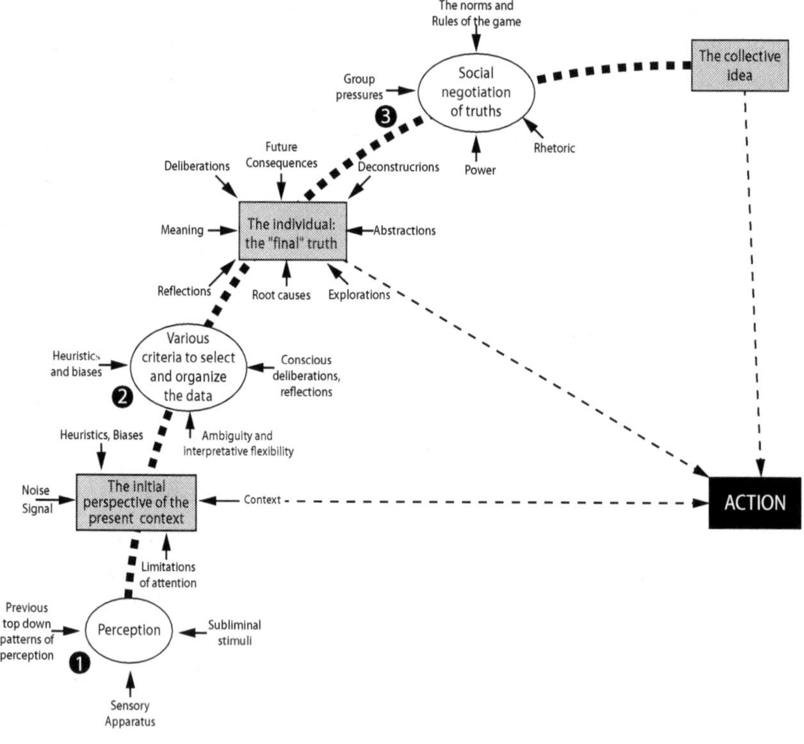

Figure 2 Definitions of the Situations: Steps in the Creation of Truth.

Figure 2 shows how "truths" and definitions of the situation are created during a long process of pruning and organization of stimuli. *First,* subliminal and conscious stimuli, bottom-up and top-down mechanisms of attention, and previous experiences determine what is perceived. Perceptions are organized according to a fast, tacit process that creates the initial perspective of the present, in which percepts are interpreted according to a (hypothetical) context. *Second,* one considers various potential interpretations and reaches the final "truth" or conclusion. *Third*, individual truths are socially negotiated during processes of communication. The apparently neutral, rational negotiations of meaning are, then, linked with the ubiquitous social pressures for conformity, cohesion, rhetoric, power, and obedience to institutionalized directions of interpretation.

In our interventions, the concepts shown in this figure were used both to deconstruct the naive-realistic perspective and to give players a tool to interpret their conflicts under a common premise in which errors could be seen as a consequence of expected violations of the normatively expected rationality, and not necessarily incompetence, disinterest, or dishonesty. This approach, in turn, served as a tool for sensemaking and organization *and* as the basis for the creation of collective debiasing mechanisms.

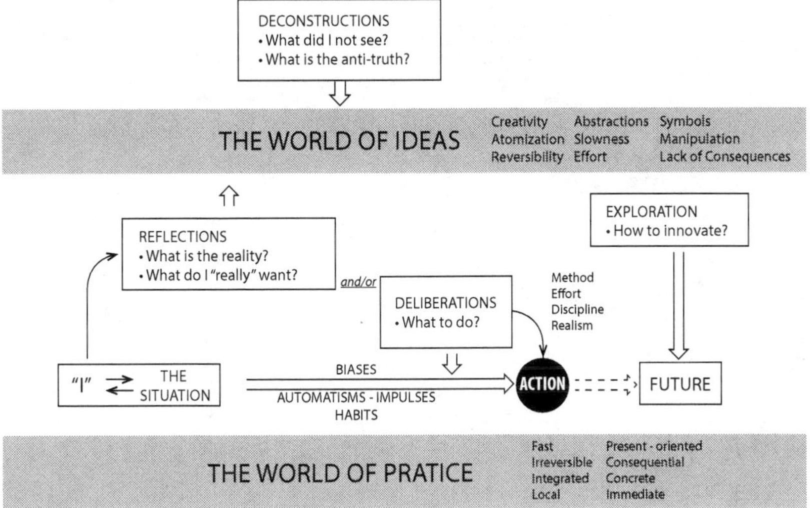

Figure 3 The World of Practice and the World of Ideas.

Figure 3 shows learning from experience as a cycle that starts in the world of practice, passes through the world of ideas, and goes back to practice. Since the concrete, theory-laden facts of the world of practice are created and organized according to biased, context-dependent factors and to rules of taken from parameters present in the world of ideas, individuals and groups alternate between different definitions of the situation that pull them to different sides. Living in the world of practice (or "System 1") is the more natural way of life, whereas the world of ideas (or "System 2") kicks in when there are problems or when reason is formally required to prevail [184]. The four complementary modes in which reason can be used – deliberations, reflections, explorations and deconstructions – have different purposes and generate different definitions of the situation. They are, then, seen as both complementary and competing with each other and with the habitual responses of the practice.

During the seminars and individual sessions, this meta-concept was in the basis of the construction of a vocabulary that embraced both the paradoxes involved in the process of definition of situations and the ideal of a shared, inclusive view of the facts. This framework was used to reframe problems in which players complained about their (or others') lack of objectivity, digressions, alienation, or conflicts between different definitions of the situation. It was also used to illuminate the relevance of tacit expertise and of emergent processes of deliberation, which focus on the practice and not only in theory.

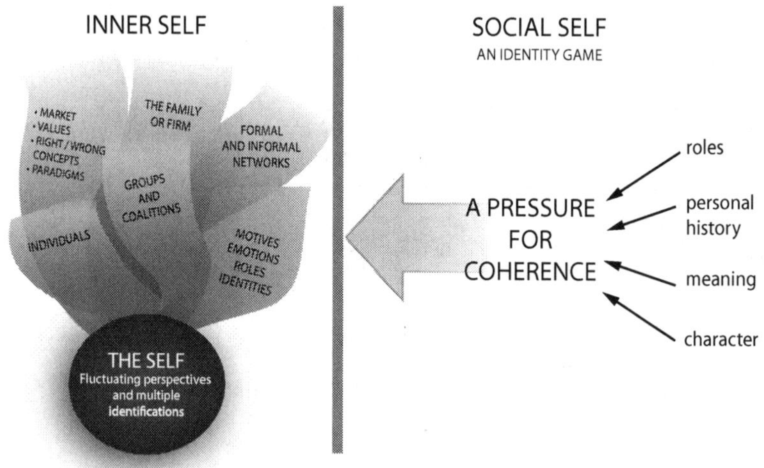

Figure 4 Multiple Levels of Ontological Oscillation and Identification.

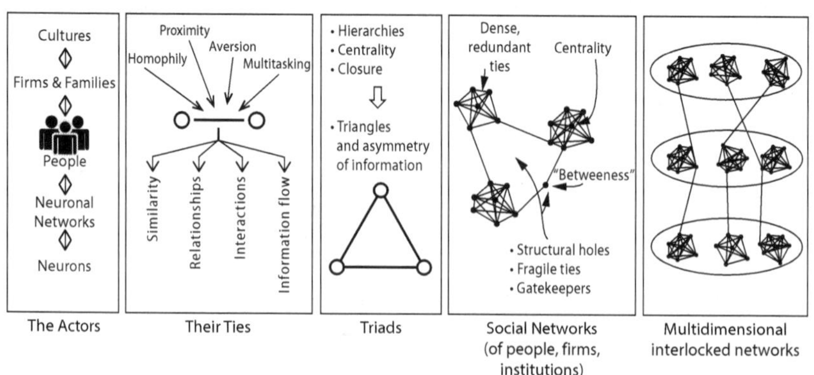

Figure 5 Various Levels of Analysis and Social Organization.

Figures 4 and 5 show the various forms of organization of the social fact, both for the individual and in the system. Figure 4 depicts the difference between the individual inner self – engaged in a permanent ontological oscillation by which players alternate in identifying with and giving being to different entities and processes – and the social self, which responds to constant demands to conform to the roles and expectations of appropriateness implied by the identities they sell. Figure 5 shows various levels of analysis through which families and firms can be seen.

These frameworks were used to deconstruct any illusions of consensus or expectations of strict adherence to specific strategies, goals, to the family, or the firm. It also illuminated how the game perspective, if interpreted in the form of a predictable construction of meaning, fails to address the complexity of social facts. Loose coupling was, then, seen not as deficiency or violation of the ideal of organization, but as a necessary condition that maintains social systems relatively ordered while preserving some degree of freedom for the actors. The task of organization was, then, reframed as resulting from a complementary use of order and slack, freedom, and constraint.

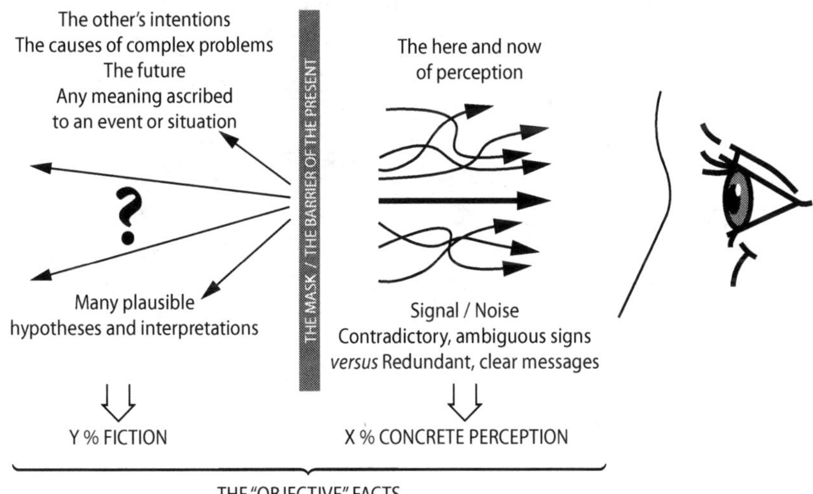

Figure 6 Ambiguity and Interpretive Flexibility.

Figure 6 illuminates some blind spots of naive realism. First, "objective" facts are deconstructed as a mix of perception and interpretation – a cognitive construction by which the crude objects of perception are assumed to have behavior, relations, essence, and attributes that vary depending on how they are interpreted, or contextualized. Second, ambiguity is explained as a fruit of the encounter between the need to create a stable truth and the fact that complex signs allow many different plausible, potentially true interpretations. Observe that silence, noise, and contradictory signs increase the percentage of fiction involved in the creation of "objective" facts.

This framework was used to introduce doubt when players came with certainties regarding the behavior of other people or their views of reality, as well as to reframe polarizations due to dogmatic or rigid beliefs in partial truths. Error, commonly seen as an avoidable mistake linked to lack of attention, laziness, dishonesty, self-interest, or other violations of the identity game, was frequently reframed as a consequence of the fact that players are always making bets about ambiguous facts. The management of doubt was then put side by side with the management of truth.

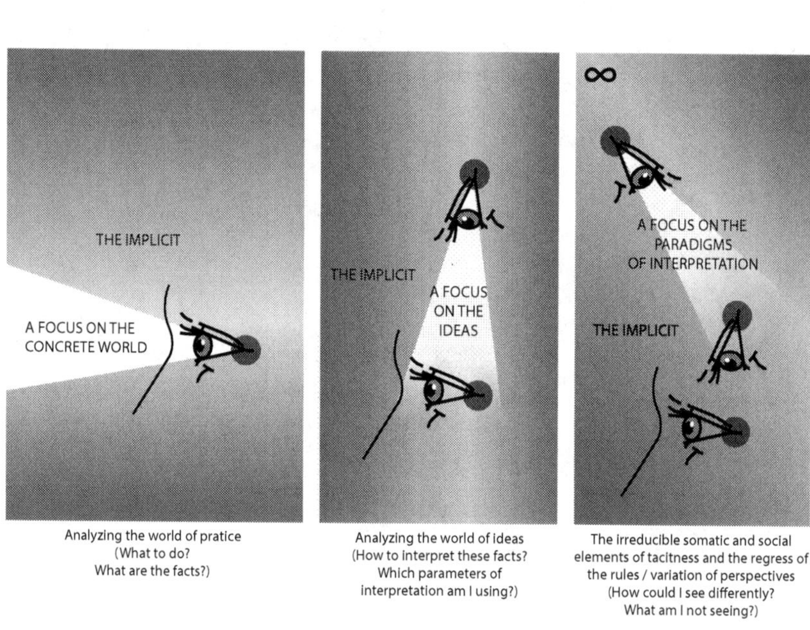

Figure 7 Tacitness and the Regress of the Rules.

Figure 7 shows the interplay between tacitness and awareness. The left panel shows how players focused on the concrete world are (necessarily) unaware of the implicit interpretations used to create the facts. The middle panel shows that, in order to study one's bases of interpretation, ideas, or strategies, one has to momentarily accept the perceived reality as a given and take the focus away from the possibilities of action. Finally, when focused on questioning the paradigms behind the ideas, it is necessary to forget problems related to their validity or practical application. The symbol of the infinite in the right panel symbolizes the fact that one can always deconstruct a system of meaning by imagining another meta-meaning; in doing so, however, one inevitably becomes blind to the parameters used in the deconstruction, which then have to be studied by another meta-meta-game (ad infinitum).

During the interventions, this figure was used to deconstruct the usual managerial views of the relationship between tacit and explicit knowledge. Conflicts between adherents of formalization and processes, on the one hand, and experts, on the other, were seen as part of an ambiguous trade-off choice. The concept of the infinite regress – and of the need to stop the flow of deconstructions in order to establish an (arbitrary, temporary) reality – were used to show the (lack of) logic behind many interminable discussions in which the alternation of nested problems, levels of analysis, and search for a fundament seemed to introduce an irreducible, paradoxical, and hopelessly irrational element in the core of the attempt to organize meaning.

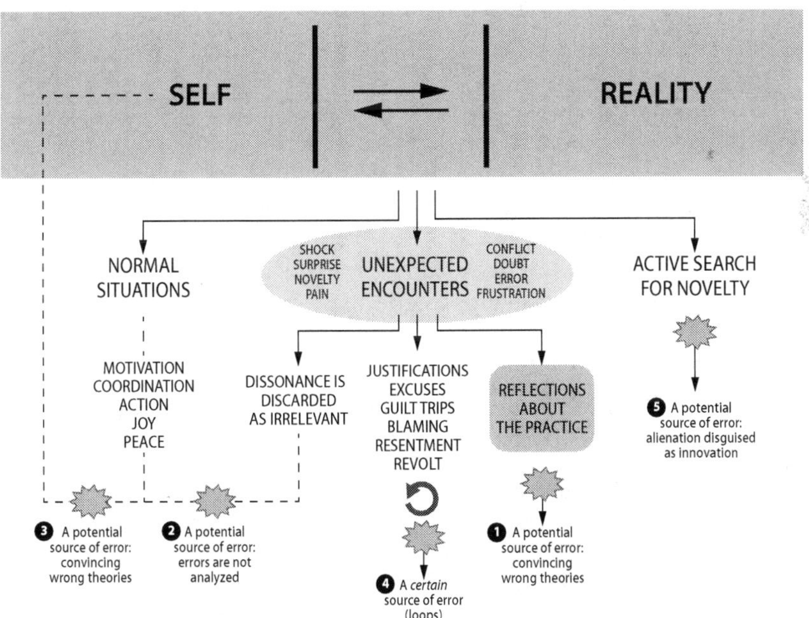

Figure 8 Learning from Experience and Novelty.

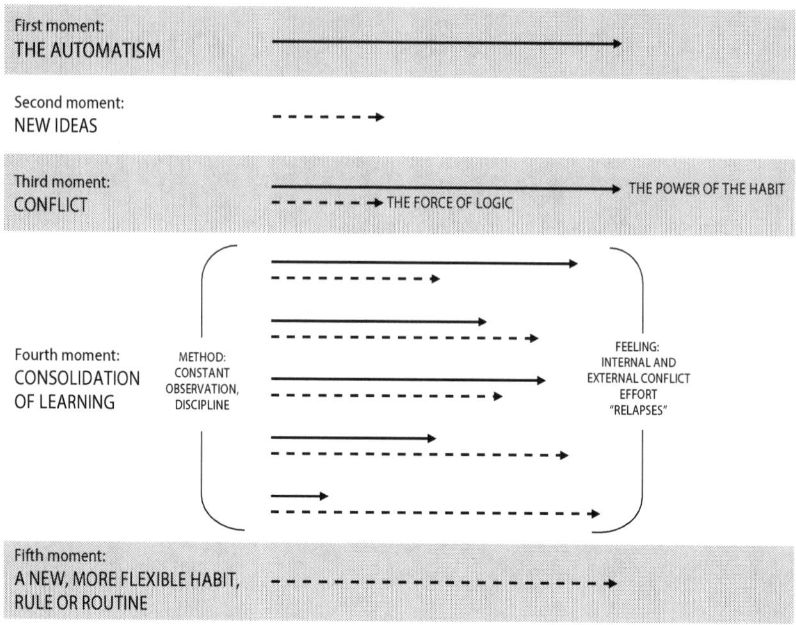

Figure 9 Reasoning and Implementation in the Learning Process.

Figures 8 and 9 show the study of error, the pursuit of novelty, and implementation of learning as interrelated, but competing features of learning. Figure 8 shows the trade-offs involved in learning from experience (the study of error) or innovation (the pursuit of new ideas). Several sources of complications are shown: (1) Reflections may follow wrong chains of inference or be based on false premises, creating wrong truths; (2) Relevant error signals may be discarded as irrelevant, or irrelevant errors may be studied in excess; (3) Success, pleasure, or social consensus may be equated with truth, preventing actors to think about optimal or better solutions or disguising relevant sources of error; (4) When error signals are denied or justified, actors do not think about change; (5) Bad ideas are framed as innovations and true error signals given by the practice are discarded as relevant in order to pursue the novel idea, increasing the possibility of failure. In Figure 9, the automatic responses of the world of practice compete with the rational understanding typical of the world of ideas: even though the initial understanding may occur quickly, its implementation depends on frequent, daily conflicts between habit and the new idea until the new idea may become a habit.

These concepts were central to the interventions we made – from the first day, players were instructed to carefully observe their practice and select situations of conflict, doubt, frustration, or paralysis as materials for individual and group sessions; error was then framed as a good, useful platform for learning rather than as an accountable mistake. Later, these concepts were also used to illuminate the deficiencies of learning from experience, the trade-offs between exploration and exploitation, and the existence of multiple, contradictory definitions of the situation in the same individual and social system. These concepts helped actors to take the maximum benefit from the errors they experienced; to understand how justifications, excuses, guilt, blame, and indignation prevent learning from the error; and to illuminate how the games of truth, accountability, and learning give different meanings to error (respectively, a mistake to be corrected, a failure to be punished, or a sign to be studied).

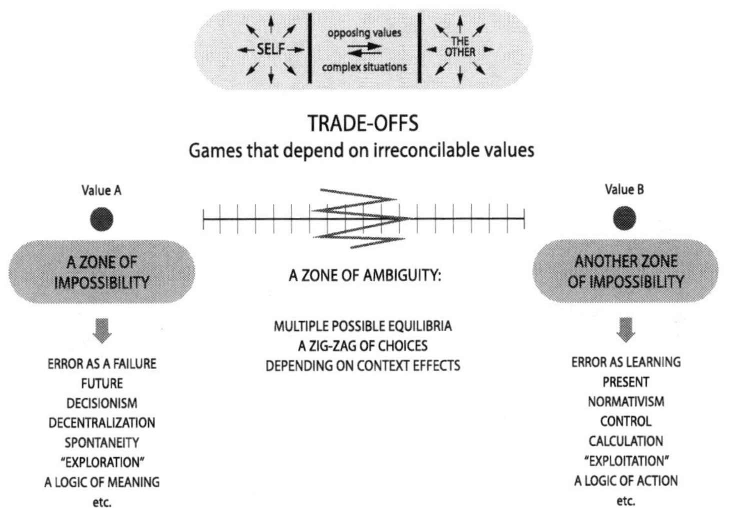

Figure 10 Multitasking and Trade-offs.

Figure 10 presents a stylized version of a multitasking game involving two opposing and mutually exclusive, but equally relevant values mixed in a complex activity. These games may be seen as a continuum in which two zones of impossibility demarcate a larger middle zone of ambiguity. In the zones of impossibility, the denial of the complementary, opposite value leads to complete instability of the game; in the zone of ambiguity, choice involves various equally valid equilibria in which one value is (necessarily) traded-off by the other. Because there is no optimal choice, and the option for one value always brings to the fore the deficiencies derived from not choosing the other, trade-off situations lead to an unstable zig-zag that responds to specific effects of context, and not to preplanned (rational?) strategic decisions.

This framework was used to illuminate many conflict situations in which actors, polarized by the focus on one side of the trade-off situation, disregarded their own blind spot and personalized the discussion. Framing these situations as trade-offs helped the process of organization because players could agree on a common, more abstract definition of the situation; deconstructed the ideals of equilibrium, best choice, and perfect rationality; accepted that choices can be relatively incoherent depending on context situations; and exchanged a first-order dilemma – what to do with a concrete, emotionally laden problem – for a second-order, more abstract dilemma, namely, how to decide, under situations of ambiguity, what to do when facing trade-off limit situations. The joint forces of organization and arbitrary power (the role of the leader to make a final decision) were then reconciled within the framework of a relational contract.

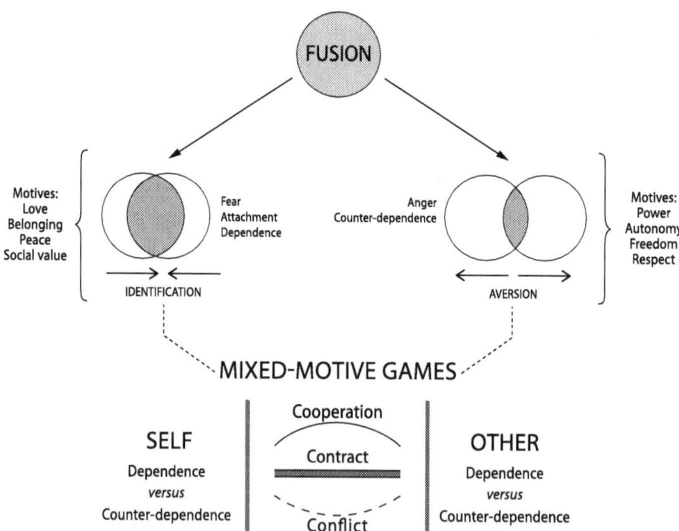

Figure 11 Emotions as Private Signs of Value and Instruments of Communication.

Figure 11 shows how the poles of attraction and repulsion, naturally present as the emotions of fear, attachment, and anger, are in the core of the adult motives of belonging, independence, autonomy, power, dependence, and counter-dependence. These motives, in turn, form the emotional flip sides of all mixed-motive, cooperation-conflict exchanges that involve the combination of a contract and of disputes within this contract. These opposite motives can be reconciled and stabilized only through the use of masks and games, which harmonize the contradictions by framing differences of value as part of the complex identities and interests exchanged in the social game.

In the practical work, these concepts were used to clarify the atavic duality friend-enemy. They illuminated how every complex social game occurs as a mix of dependence and counter-dependence, giving actors a framework to understand how even well-intentioned players often show unexpected facets and motives. They integrated conflict, divergences, and individualism with organization, contract, and cooperation through a meta-view that reframes dissensus as an expected occurrence within cooperative, idealistic games. We could, then, deconstruct naive beliefs of cooperation, enmity, paranoia, disinterested behavior, absolute loyalty, or attachment.

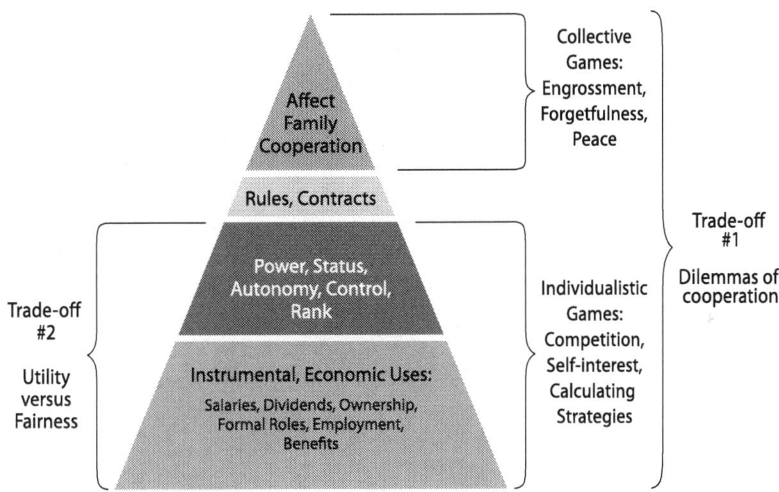

Figure 12 Values, Games, and their Trade-offs.

In **Figure 12**, the "pyramid of games" compresses into one figure several crucial concepts of the proposed vocabulary of motives. Basically, all social games were described as serving utilitarian, economic motives, organized in social games that also involved stratification (power and status relationships) as well as occasional identification or meaning. The *appearance*, *tone* of the game, or rules of illusion to which players promise to return, and *not* any essential feature of cooperativeness or enmity, were then framed as constituting the desirable, aesthetic, ethical and affective values that give distinctiveness to the culture.

Two main trade-offs are due to the superposition of these opposed motives, interests, and sub-games in the context of the same relation. In the dilemmas of cooperation players are required to choose between individualistic and collective games (Trade-off # 1); in the trade-off # 2, exemplified by the ultimatum game, actors are split between utilitarian interests and fairness. As shown in the figure, these trade-offs and contradictions are regulated by more or less fragile, tacit or explicit rules and contracts.

This construct was used as a tool to deconstruct naive conceptions of social games as being either cooperative or conflictive, dismissing the naive, but frequent ideas that engrossment, spontaneity, or meaning are antithetical to calculation. This meta-view created the bases for the reframing of personal conflicts as second-order dilemmas: rather than seeing others as friends or enemies, actors were invited to see every relationship as involving both features. Social exchanges emerged, then, in their full expression of transient, illusory games that emphasize, tame, organize, or cover-up the individualistic drives allowing the alternation of moments of engrossment and conflict.

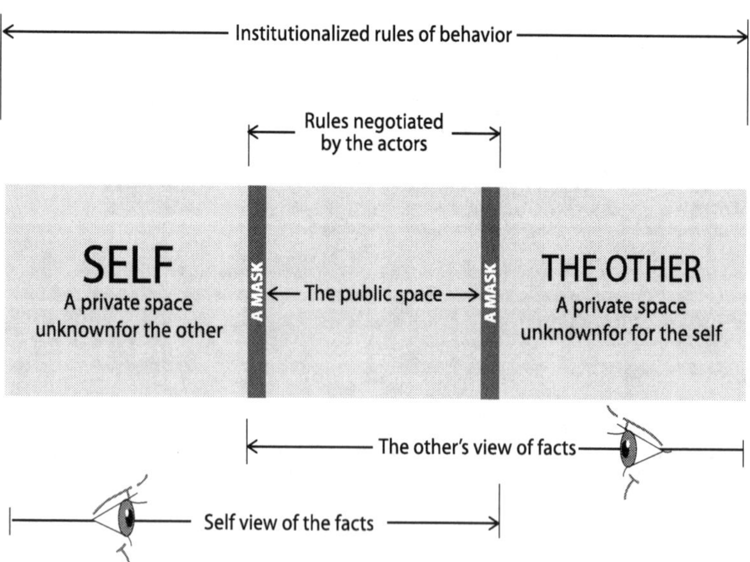

Figure 13 The Micro-Structure of Social Games and its relation to networks and culture.

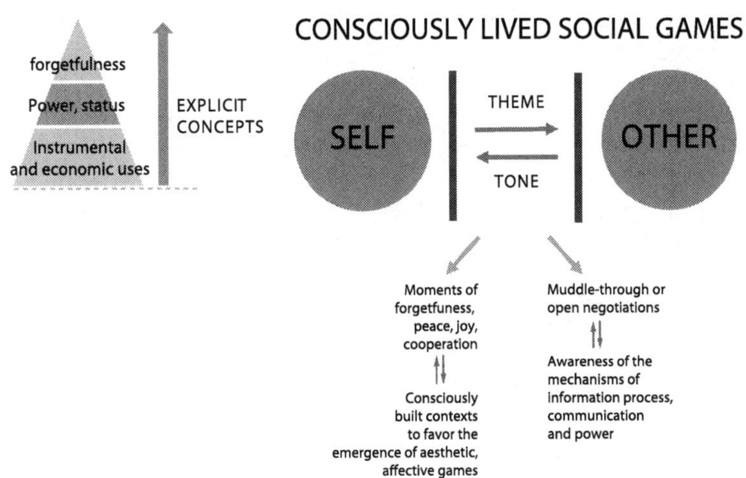

Figure 14 Spontaneity, Engrossment, and Forgetfulness in the Absence of Misrecognition.

Figures 13 and 14 display the basic elements of a social game: (a) the single actor, who has an (only partially conscious) access to his own motives, impulses, thoughts and feelings, (b) the mask, which filters the impulses and creates a social self adapted to the specific rules of each game, (c) the public space, where theme and tone are (tacitly and explicitly) negotiated, (d) the internal world of both actors, which by being unknown to the others introduces leads to asymmetry of information; (e) and the rules of the game that define each interaction, relationship, role, or norm in a social structure and culture. These rules are both negotiated by the actors and given by the institutionalized views of how the social game should occur. Observe how the existence of masks introduces a relevant asymmetry of information: the self' and the other's views of the fact area necessarily different due to the data players have access to. Figure 14 suggests how an explicit vocabulary of motives and practices can serve as a basis for legitimate moments of forgetfulness or engrossment – if actors are aware of the conflicting interests involved in all mixed-motive games, it is possible to create contracts, be more prepared for conflict, and then open up for the spontaneity required by any true engrossment in a game without falling into the traps of ideology. This includes the awareness that identification will be broken at some moment, bringing new conflicts and negotiations.

These concepts helped actors to see social games from above, allowing them to better understand the interactions and relationships and to deconstruct the idea that social life is natural. By doing this, we introduced them to a meta-view that integrates disparate concepts such as calculation, strategic thinking, spontaneity, truth, and mask, fostering an alignment based not on concrete values or attitudes, but on a common, more abstract vocabulary. Spontaneity was, then, reframed as a fragile state that occurs in habitual and meaningful games, a feeling of naturalness that must be associated with calculating, strategic organization of contexts conducive to it; conflict was reframed as a rupture of meaning that can potentially be treated from within the game, leading to renegotiations and new contracts.

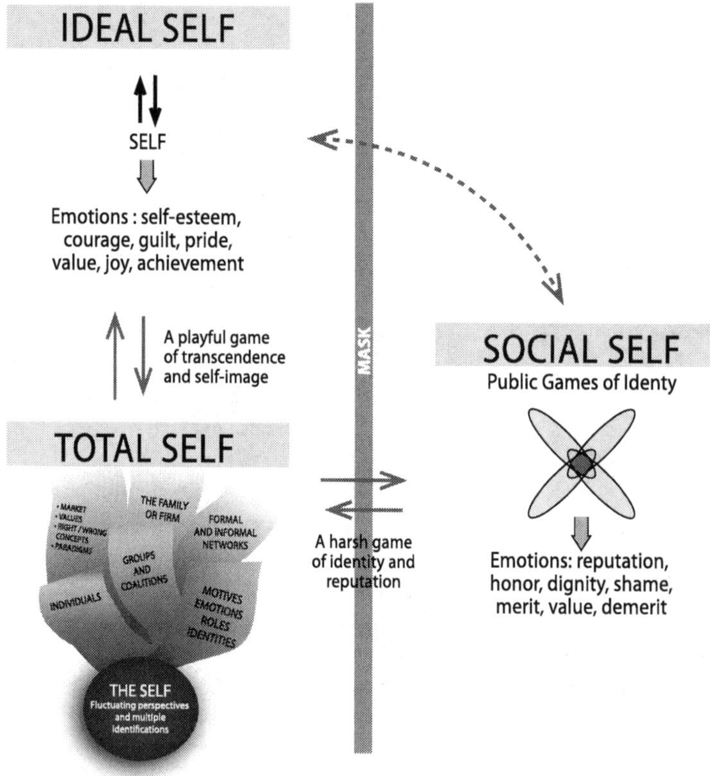

Figure 15 Social Emotions – Self and Other-Based.

Figure 15 shows how social emotions differ depending on how they are directed to an external audience or to one's own self. Emotions related to the external world (or social self) involve a game of identity and reputation. Emotions related to the internal world (or ideal self) are associated with transcendence or inner responsibility. The intimate relationship that exists between social and ideal selves is reflected in how players see their inner game of transcendence. When actors actually *believe* in the institutionalized fictions of identity and free-will, framing the pursuit of the ideal self as a serious or real game, they tend to see guilt, self-esteem, personal merit, or demerit as legitimate (?) feelings or concepts; the internal game is, then, rigid. In contrast, when players dissociate social and ideal selves, the internal (moral) game of transcendence becomes playful, and errors are accepted as a mistake to be corrected but not as justification for self-punishment. The (transcendent) games that emphasize the pursuit of idealism, ethical, aesthetic, or affective ideals are, in this case, playfully detached from the (mundane) preoccupations with reputation, identity, appearance, or social value.

These concepts were used as a tool to deconstruct rigid ideals of identity, which commonly lead to personalization, polarization, and association of error with moral flaws. By deconstructing the concept of free-will and identity, actors were led to reframe these as constructs of a game by which players organize their inner (chaotic) self in other-oriented ordered social self (the public identity) or internally based ideal self (the personal benchmark for action). Error and violations of order could, then, be seen as expected occurrences in a game of coherence and became integrated into the concept of culture as a serious, but also playful, loosely coupled game of unity.

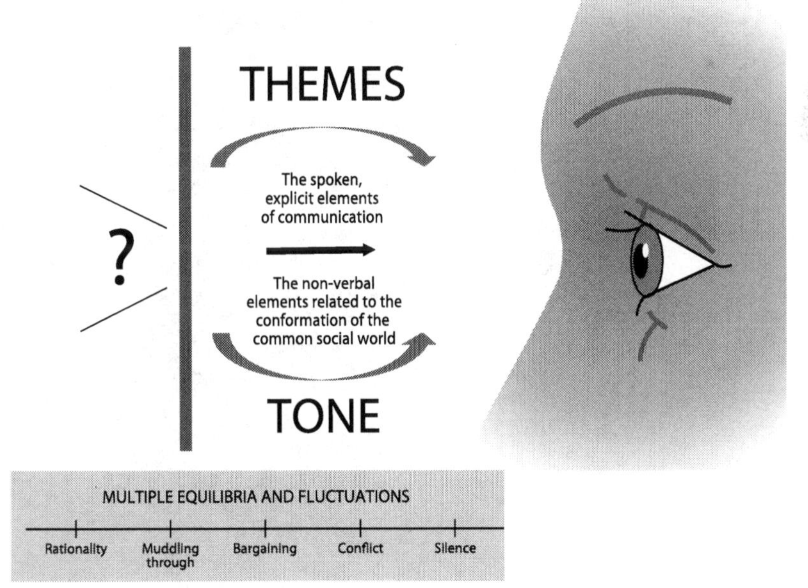

Figure 16 Theme and Tone in Communication.

In **Figure 16**, understanding and knowledge of other people are displayed as interpretive acts that always involve an imperfect synthesis of the explicit theme of communication and a generally implicit, unspoken tone that signals the attitude, posture, and intentions of the other actor. The theme refers to the object of communication or contention. The tone – often the most important element of the communication – signals the proposition the actor is making concerning issues pertaining to the social game, such as hierarchy, distance, intimacy, openness, etc. The real motives, intentions, goals or thoughts of the other actor are unknown. However, as they have to be taken into account to define further action, they serve as the fundament for how conflict and contract are treated within communicative games (rationally, by muddling through scientific, ethical, empirical, or logical discussions, or alternatively through bargaining, silence, or conflict).

This framework was used to make players attentive to how communication is inevitably embedded in definitions about the underlying total social game. This understanding, in turn, served as a tool to refine players' responses to others, avoiding typical traps in which personal polarizations appear as radical responses to principal-agent contexts, doubt, ambiguity, trade-offs, ultimatum-game situations, or dilemmas of cooperation. It also helped them to create better scripts to resolve difficult issues – specifically, the modulation of the tone (toward cooperation) was often used as a tool to counteract the treatment of dissensus (avoiding unnecessary conflict).

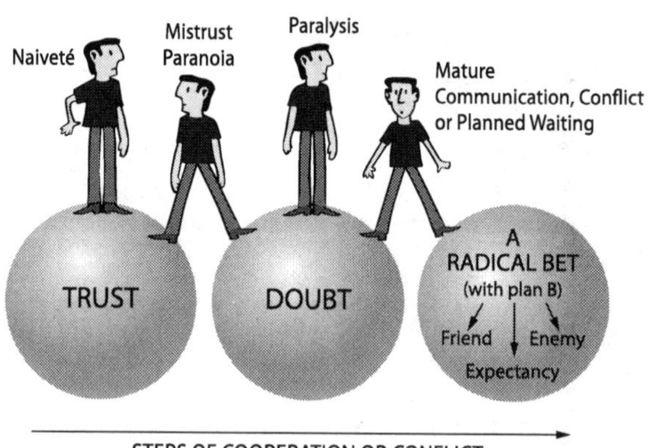

Figure 17 Naive Realism, Paranoia, and Consciousness.

Figure 17 opposes the perspective of naive realism, typical of a metaphysics of truth, with the combination of methodical doubt and radical bet, which characterizes social life as seen through the lens of the game perspective. Three elements bring the necessity of doubt: the existence of the mask, which introduces the asymmetry of information; the fact that players are complex and in flow; and the view of social life as a multiplicity of contradictory games, each of them integrating selfish and disinterested motives and played in several levels of analysis depending on the actors' (unpredictable) ontological oscillation. Doubt, however, leads to paralysis – in order to act, then, players *are required* to make a bet about the basic (momentary) disposition of the others, framing them as friends, enemies, or doubtful entities. This deconstruction dismantles common ideas that trust, faith, and guarantee of truth are necessary for cooperative games; or that conflict and violations of contract refer to permanent dispositions of character, as suggested by doubt and paranoia. It also displays the fact that every social game is based on irrational, uncertain *bets* about the others (the fundamental attitude of rationality, honesty, and will).

In the interventions, this framework was introduced as part of the concepts daily used by players in their conversations and reflections about social exchanges. It was a potent tool to counteract egocentric, paranoid biases. In addition, it substituted a second-order dilemma that happens in the world of the ideas for the concrete dilemmas typical of the world of the practice – specifically, rather than evaluating the others as presented in the moment of the interaction (which leads to naive, absolute, context-dependent trust, or paranoia), players were instructed to consider the context and all past situations and make conscious *bets* about the "basic disposition" of the other (while knowing that these bets are uncertain and may be changed). The framework, then, integrated truth and doubt and gave players a meta-concept that facilitated the organization.

- Truth, honesty, respect
- Doubt and conflict are normal
- All actors open up to change their own viewpoints
- A leap of faith – a bet in the family, in the partners, in the firm
- No unpractical discussions: beware of useless arguments about the past
- Do not question each other's intentions, honesty, or good will

- Proposals grounded in the practice
- Focus on future decisions
- One theme at each time
- All themes exhaustively treated
- Politeness
- No gossiping, finger-pointing
- Avoid empty abstractions
- Adequate tone even during conflict

A basic Trade-off	Normativism: Emerging preferences and pacts Multiple iterative dialogues	*versus*	Desicionism: A unilateral sovereign decision to stop the doubt and make a bet

Figure 18 The Tone: Some Rules about How to Negotiate the Rules.

Figure 18 shows some norms suggested in the families with which we worked. It also shows a draw-back of rationality: as deliberations last longer or become sterile due to irreducible trade-offs or ambiguities, they go against the logic of action and require an act of power to force a definition of the situation. This decisionism must be embedded in the organization of the place and become part of the common vocabulary, lest it may be perceived as an illegitimate exercise of authority (for a similar example in the scientific field, see [568]).

This schema was used to suggest that, in addition to (irrational) bets about the disposition of others, productive communication requires rules of rationality that facilitate the flow of the conversation. These rules about how to negotiate the rules attempt to stabilize the ontological oscillation, skepticism, biases, and disorganization that tend to hamper the flow of communication, trying to guarantee an adequate tone of the social game upon which various themes can be treated. Notice that rationality attempts to adequate the usually chaotic, disorganized flow of communication by suggesting directions derived from the (normative) views of the scientific methodology. Therefore, it introduces some rigidity in the process and always contrasts with emergent, System 1 choices or with rational muddling-through decision-making processes directed to a logic of action.

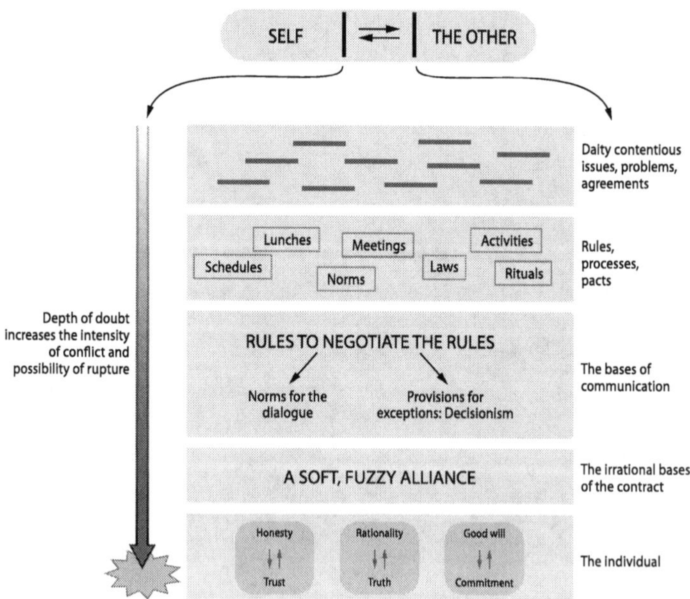

Figure 19 Fiction and Reality in the Social Contract.

Figure 19 shows five layers in which one can decompose the pacts that regulate negotiations in the micro-sociological world of the interactions and relationships. The top two layers involve the explicit problems and the rules used to stabilize the facts of the practice (the *theme* of the communication). These issues are negotiated according to (tacit or explicit) rules about how to negotiate the rules that give the *tone* of the game – general norms for the dialog and provisions for the use of power in case of limit situations. Observe that all tangible problems daily faced by the players are grounded on the intangible suppositions and irrational *bets* about the others' identity and disposition to engage in the game or wage war (see Figure 16). Also observe that genuine cultures and relationships depend on two conditions of belief: actors *have to* believe that both themselves and the others are honest, rational, and committed in order to *feel* that the game is true. Notice, finally, how this model explains well the personal interactions and relationships, but *not* complex social systems such as families, firms, nations, or larger groups. These depend as much on habit, action, automatisms, institutions, social structure, and imposed rules than on mutually agreed pacts.

In the interventions, this schema was used to emphasize how irrationality, interpretation, and decisionism are inevitably involved in the construction of the most clear pacts celebrated by players. We also used the schema to help players prepare scripts for the negotiation, in particular when dangerous problems led to serious conflict, rupture, or organizational silence due to questions about each other's identities.

Bibliography

1 March, J.G., Rationality, foolishness, and adaptive intelligence. *Strategic Management Journal*, 2006. 27 (3): 201–14.

2 Roberts, J., *The modern firm: Organizational design for performance and growth*. 2004, Oxford: Oxford University Press.

3 Martin, J., *Organizational culture: Mapping the terrain*. 2002, Thousand Oaks: Sage.

4 Hannan, M.T. and J. Freeman, The population ecology of organizations. *American Journal of Sociology*, 1977. 82: 929–64.

5 Wack, P., Scenarios: Shooting the rapids. *Harvard Business Review*, 1985. 63 (6): 1–14.

6 Porter, M.E., *Competitive strategy: Techniques for analyzing industries and competitors*. 1998, New York: Free Press.

7 DiMaggio, P.J. and W.W. Powell, The iron cage revisited: Institutional isomorphism and collective rationality in organizational fields. *American Sociological Review*, 1983. 48 (2): 147–60.

8 Burgelman, R.A. and A.S. Grove, Let Chaos Reign, then rein in chaos – repeatedly: Managing strategic dynamics for corporate longevity. *Strategic Management Journal*, 2007. 28 (10): 965–79.

9 Davis, J.A., *Fundamentals of the family business system*. 2007, Boston: Harvard Business School.

10 Tagiuri, R. and J. Davis, Bivalent attributes of the family firm. *Family Business Review*, 1996. 9 (2): 199–208.

11 Bourdieu, P., The economy of symbolic goods, in *Practical reason; on the theory of action*, P. Bourdieu, Editor. 1998, Stanford University Press: Stanford. pp. 92–126.

12 Mintzberg, H. and J.A. Waters, Of strategies, deliberate and emergent. *Strategic Management Journal*, 1985. 6: 257–72.

13 Krackhardt, D., Endogenous preferences: A structural approach, in *Debating rationality: Non-rational aspects of organizational decision making*, J. Halpern and R.N. Stern, Editors. 1998, Cornell University Press: New York. pp. 239–47.

14 Davis, J.A., *Fundamentals of family business system governance* (Note 9–807–019), 2007, Boston: Harvard Business School.

15 Berger, P.L. and T. Luckman, *The social construction of reality; a treatise in the sociology of knowledge*. 1966, New York: Anchor Books.

16 Stinchcombe, A.L., *Information and organizations*. 1990, Berkeley: University of California Press.

17 Friedberg, E., *Local orders: Dynamics of organized action*. 1997, Greenwich: JAI Press.
18 Cohen, M.D., J.G. March, and J.P. Olsen, A garbage can model of organizational choice. *Administrative Science Quarterly*, 1972. 17 (1): 1–25.
19 Beyer, J., Ideology, values, and decision making in organizations, in *Handbook of organizational design volume 2: Remodeling organizations and their environments*, P.C. Nystrom and W.H. Starbuck, Editors. 1981, Oxford University Press: Oxford. pp. 167–202.
20 Augier, M. and J.G. March, Realism and comprehension in economics: A footnote to an exchange between Oliver E. Williamson and Herbert A. Simon. *Journal of Economic Behavior & Organization*, 2008. 66 (1): 95–105.
21 Weick, K.E., *The social psychology of organizing*. 1979, New York: McGraw Hill.
22 March, J.G., Organizational consultants and organizational research, in *The pursuit of organizational intelligence*, J.G. March, Editor. 1999, Blackwell: Malden. pp. 325–37.
23 Stinchcombe, A.L., Social structure and organizations, in *Handbook of organizations*, J.G. March, Editor. 1965, Rand McNally: Chicago. pp. 142–93.
24 March, J.G. and H.A. Simon, *Organizations*. 1993, Cambridge: Blackwell.
25 Cyert, R.M. and J.G. March, *A behavioral theory of the firm* (1963). 1992, Malden: Blackwell.
26 March, J.G., *The ambiguities of experience*. 2010, New York: Cornell University Press.
27 Nietzsche, F., *Writings from the late notebooks (1885–1888)*. 2003, Cambridge: Cambridge University Press.
28 Wittgenstein, L., *Philosophical investigations; the German text, with a revised English translation* (1953). 2001, Malden: Blackwell.
29 Crozier, M., *The bureaucratic phenomenon*. 1964, Chicago: The University of Chicago Press.
30 Bourdieu, P., The forms of capital, in *Handbook of theory and research for the sociology*, J. Richardson, Editor. 1986, Greenwood: New York. pp. 241–58.
31 Huizinga, J., The waning of the middle ages (1919). *Great books of the Western world*, v. 61. 1990, Chicago: Encyclopaedia Britannica. pp. 245–394.
32 Weick, K.E., *Making sense of the organization*. 2001, Malden: Blackwell.
33 Goffman, E., *Interaction ritual; essays on face to face behavior*. 1967, Garden City: Anchor Books.
34 Brunsson, N., *The consequences of decision making*. 2007, Oxford: Oxford University Press.
35 Meyer, J.W. and B. Rowan, Institutionalized organizations: Formal structure as myth and ceremony. *American Journal of Sociology*, 1977. 83 (2): 340–63.
36 Simon, H.A., *Administrative behavior*. 1957, New York and London: The Free Press.
37 Polanyi, M., *The tacit dimension*. 1967, London: Routledge & K. Paul.

38 Argyris, C., *Knowledge for action: A guide to overcoming barriers to organizational change*. 1993, San Francisco: Jossey-Bass.

39 Engeström, Y. and A. Sannino, Studies of expansive learning: Foundations, findings and future challenges. *Educational Research Review*, 2010. 5 (1): 1–24.

40 Burrell, G. and G. Morgan, *Sociological paradigms and organisational analysis*. 1979, Farnham: Ashgate.

41 Yammarino, F.J. and F. Dansereau, Mulilevel issues in organizational culture and climate research, in *The handbook of organizational culture and climate*, N.M. Ashkanasy, C.P.M. Wilderom, and M.F. Peterson, Editors. 2011, Sage: Thousand Oaks.

42 Ramirez, R. and C. Selin, Plausibility and probability in scenario planning. *Foresight*, 2014. 16 (1): 54–74.

43 Merton, R.K., The self-fulfilling prophecy. *Antioch Review*, 1948. 8 (2): 193–210.

44 March, J.G., *The pursuit of organizational intelligence*. 1999, Malden: Blackwell. p. 397.

45 Levinthal, D.A., Adaptation on rugged landscapes. *Management Science*, 1997. 43 (7): 934–50.

46 March, J.G., Learning to be risk averse. *Psychological Review*, 1996. 103: 309–19.

47 March, J.G., *A primer on decision making: How decisions happen*. 1994, New York: Free Press.

48 Ferrater Mora, J., Verdad, in *Diccionario de Filosofia*, J. Ferrater Mora, Editor. 1979, Alianza: Madrid. pp. 3397–408.

49 March, J.G., Exploration and exploitation in organizational learning. *Organization Science*, 1991. 2 (1): 71–87.

50 Martin, J. and C. Siehl, Organizational culture and counterculture: An uneasy symbiosis. *Organizational Dynamics*, 1983. 12 (2): 52–64.

51 Merton, R.K., The Thomas theorem and the Matthew effect. *Social Forces*, 1995. 74 (2): 379–422.

52 Calabrò, G., *Valores. Enciclopédia Einaudi*, v. 37. 1995, Lisboa: Imprensa Nacional - Casa da Moeda. pp. 265–74.

53 Friedberg, E., Organização, in *Tratado de Sociologia* (1992), R. Boudon, Editor. 1996, Zahar: Rio de Janeiro. pp. 375–412.

54 Crozier, M. and E. Friedberg, *The actor and the system: The politics of collective action*. 1980, Chicago: University of Chicago Press.

55 Drees, J.M. and P.P.M.A.R. Heugens, Synthesizing and extending resource dependence theory: A meta-analysis. *Journal of Management*, 2013. 39 (6): 1666–98.

56 Moe, T.M., The politics of structural choice: Toward a theory of public bureaucracy, in *Organization theory: From Chester Barnard to the present and beyond*, O.E. Williamson, Editor. 1995, Oxford University Press: Oxford and New York. pp. 116–53.

57 Mannheim, K., *Ideology and utopia: An introduction to the sociology of knowledge* (1936). 1985, San Diego: Harcourt Brace & Company.

58 Schumpeter, J.A., *Capitalism, socialism and democracy* (1950). 2013, New York: Routledge.

59 Becker, M.C., T. Knudsen, and J.G. March, Schumpeter, Winter, and the sources of novelty. *Industrial and Corporate Change*, 2006. 15 (2): 353–71.

60 Hempel, C.G., *Aspects of scientific explanation and other essays in the philosophy of science*. 1965, New York: The Free Press.

61 Darwall, S., *The British moralists and the internal "ought": 1640–1740*. 1995, Cambridge: Cambridge University Press. p. 352.

62 Foucault, M., *Power/knowledge: Selected interviews and other writings 1972–1977*. 1980, New York: Pantheon.

63 Rousseau, J.-J., *O Contrato social* (1762), n.d., Cultrix: São Paulo.

64 Cilliers, P., Complexity, deconstruction and relativism. *Theory, Culture and Society*, 2005. 22 (5): 255–67.

65 Hobbes, T., Leviathan, or matter, form and power of a commonwealth ecclesiastical and civil (1651). *Great books of the Western world*, v. 23. 1952, Chicago: Encyclopaedia Britannica. pp. 41–283.

66 Edmondson, A. and B. Moingeon, Learning, trust and organizational change: Contrasting models of intervention research in organizational behavior, in *Organizational learning and the learning organization; developments in theory and practice*, M. Easterby-Smith, L. Araujo, and J. Burgoyne, Editors. 1999, Sage: London. pp. 157–75.

67 Geertz, C., Blurred genres: The refiguration of social thought. *The American Scholar*, 1980. 49 (2): 165–79.

68 Vaihinger, H., *The Philosophy of "as if": A system of the theoretical, practical and religious fictions of mankind*. 1935, London: Routledge & Kegan Paul.

69 Coleman, J.S., *Foundations of social theory*. 1990, Cambridge: Belknapp Press.

70 Engeström, Y., Activity theory as a framework for analyzing and redesigning work. *Ergonomics*, 2000. 43 (7): 960–74.

71 Goffman, E., *Encounters: Two studies in the sociology of interaction*. 1961, Indianapolis: Bobbs-Merrill Company. 152 p.

72 Weick, K.E., Organized sensemaking: A commentary on processes of interpretive work. *Human Relations*, 2012. 65 (1): 141–53.

73 Barnard, C.I., *The functions of the executive*. 1956, Cambridge: Harvard University Press.

74 Schein, E.H., Coming to a new awareness of organizational culture. *Sloan Management Review*, 1984. 25 (2): 3–16.

75 Von Neumann, J. and O. Morgenstern, *Theory of games and economic behavior*. 1944, Princeton: Princeton University Press.

76 Homans, G.C., Social behavior as exchange. *American Journal of Sociology*, 1958. 63: 597–606.

77 Williamson, O.E., *The economic institutions of capitalism*. 1985, New York: The Free Press.

78 March, J.G. and P.J. Romelaer, Position and presence in the drift of decisions, in *Ambiguity and choice in organizations*, J.G. March and J.P. Olsen, Editors. 1979, Universitetsforlaget: Bergen. pp. 251–76.

79 Selznick, P., *Leadership in administration: A sociological interpretation* (1957). 1997, Berkeley: University of California Press.

80 Holmstrom, B. and P. Milgrom, Multitask principal-agent analyses: Incentive contracts, asset ownership, and job design. *Journal of Law, Economics, & Organization*, 1991. 7: 24–52.

81 Zajonc, R.B., Feeling and thinking: Preferences need no inferences. *American Psychologist*, 1980. 35: 151–75.

82 Huizinga, J., *Homo Ludens: A study of the play-element in culture.* 1955, London: Routlege & Kegan Paul.

83 Robichaud, D., H. Giroux, and J.R. Taylor, The metaconversation: The recursive property of language as a key to organizing. *Academy of Management Review*, 2004. 29 (4): 617–34.

84 Nietzsche, F., *The gay science* (1887). 2001, Cambridge: Cambridge University Press.

85 Simmel, G., *The sociology of Georg Simmel* (1908). 1964, Glencoe, Illinois: The Free Press.

86 Goffman, E., *Frame analysis; an essay on the organization of experience.* 1974, Cambridge: Harvard University Press.

87 Schmitt, C., *Political theology; four chapters on the concept of sovereignity* (1922). 2005, Chicago and London: Chicago University Press. p. 70.

88 Czarniawska-Joerges, B., *Narrating the organization: Dramas of institutional identity.* 1997, Chicago: University of Chicago Press.

89 Levinthal, D., Explorations in the role of novelty in organizational adaptation: An introductory essay, in *Explorations in organizations*, J.G. March, Editor. 2008, Stanford University Press: Stanford. pp. 97–105.

90 Weber, M., *On charisma and institution building: Selected papers.* 1968, Chicago: University of Chicago Press.

91 Lord, C.G., L. Ross, and M.R. Lepper, Biased assimilation and attitude polarization: The effects of prior theories on subsequently considered evidence. *Journal of Personality and Social Psychology*, 1979. 37 (11): 2098–109.

92 Argyris, C. and D.A. Schon, *Organizational learning: A theory of action perspective (Addison-Wesley series on organizational development).* 1978, New York: Addison-Wesley.

93 Armor, D.A. and S.E. Taylor, When predictions fail: The dilemma of unrealistic optimism, in *Heuristics and biases: The psychology of intuitive judgment*, T. Gilovich, D.W. Griffin, and D. Kahneman, Editors. 2002, Cambridge University Press: Cambridge. pp. 334–47.

94 Barnard, A.J., Family and kinship, in *The new encyclopaedia britannica*, R. McHenry and Y.C. Hori, Editors. 1995, Encyclopaedia Britannica: Chicago. pp. 59–75.

95 Héritier, F., Parentesco, in *Enciclopédia Einaudi*, 1997, Imprensa Nacional da Casa da Moeda: Lisboa. pp. 27–80.

96 Dugatkin, L.A., *Cooperation among animals.* 1997, Oxford & New York: Oxford University Press.

97 Schelling, T.C., The strategy of conflict: Prospect for a reorientation of game theory. *Journal of Conflict Resolution*, 1958. 2 (3): 203–64.

98 Yamagishi, T., Social dilemmas, in *Sociological perspectives on social psychology*, K.S. Cook, G.A. Fine, and J.S. House, Editors. 1995, Allyn and Bacon: Boston. pp. 311–34.

99 Schmitt, C., *The concept of the political* (1932). 2007, Chicago: Chicago University Press. 126.

100 Hamilton, D.L. and S.A. Crump, Entitativity, in *Encyclopedia of social psychology*, R.F. Baumeister and K.D. Vohs, Editors. 2007, Sage: Thousand Oaks. pp. 301–2.

101 Chiva, I., L'ethnologie de la France rurale il y a trente ans. *Ethnologie française*, 2007. 37 (HS): 103–7.

102 Bourdieu, P., The forms of capital, in *Handbook of theory of research for the sociology of education*, J.E. Richardson, Editor. 1986, Greenword Press: Santa Barbara. pp. 46–58.

103 Padgett, J.F. and W.W. Powell, The problem of emergence, in *The emergence of organizations and markets*, J.F. Padgett and W.W. Powell, Editors. 2012, Princeton University Press: Oxford and Princeton. pp. 1–29.

104 Griffin, A.S., S.A. West, and A. Buckling, Cooperation and competition in pathogenic bacteria. *Nature*, 2004. 430 (7003): 1024–27.

105 Bergman, T.J., et al., Hierarchical classification by rank and kinship in baboons. *Science*, 2003. 302 (5648): 1234–6.

106 de Waal, F.B.M. and L.M. Lutrell, The formal hierarchy of rhesus macaques: An investigation of the bared-teeth display. *American Journal of Primatology*, 1995. 9 (2): 73–85.

107 Lusseau, D. and M.E.J. Newman, Identifying the role that animals play in their social networks. *Proceedings of the Royal Society of London - Biological Sciences (Biology Letters)*, 2004. 271(S477–S481).

108 Reynolds, V., Kinship and the family in monkeys, apes and man. *Man*, 1968. 3 (2): 209–33.

109 Carsten, J., The substance of kinship and the heat of the hearth: Feeding, personhood, and relatedness among Malays in Pulau Langkawi. *American Ethnologist*, 1995. 22 (2): 223–41.

110 Gouzoules, S. and H. Gouzoules, Kinship, in *Primate Societies*, B. Smuts, et al., Editors. 1987, University of Chicago Press: Chicago. pp. 299–305.

111 de Waal, F.B.M., *Chimpanzee politics: Power and sex among apes*. 1982, Baltimore: Johns Hopkins University Press. p. 235.

112 McGrew, W.C., L.F. Marchant, and T. Nishida, eds. *Great ape societies*. 1996, Cambridge University Press: Cambridge. p. 328.

113 Moore, J., Savanna chimpanzees, referential models and the last common ancestor, in *Great ape societies*, W.C. McGrew, L.F. Marchant, and T. Nishida, Editors. 1996, Cambridge University Press: Cambridge. pp. 275–92.

114 Héritier, F., Casamento, in *Enciclopédia Einaudi*, 1997, Imprensa Nacional da Casa da Moeda: Lisboa. pp. 140–46.

115 Murdock, G.P., *Social structure*. 1949, New York: The Free Press.

116 Godelier, M., Homem/mulher, in *Enciclopédia Einaudi*, 1997, Imprensa Nacional da Casa da Moeda: Lisboa. pp. 147–64.

117 Evans-Pritchard, E.E., *Kinship and marriage among the Nuer*. 1951, Oxford: Clarendon Press.

118 Childe, V.G., The new stone age, in *Man, culture, and society*, H.L. Shapiro, Editor. 1960, Oxford University Press: New York. pp. 94–110.

119 Anderson, M., Approaches to the history of the western family, 1500–1914. *New studies in economic and social history*, M. Sanderson, Editor. 1980, Cambridge: Cambridge University Press. p. 88.
120 Lévi-Strauss, C., *The elementary structures of kinship* (1949). 1969, Boston: Beacon Press.
121 Segalen, M., *Historical anthropology of the family*. 2002, Cambridge: Cambridge University Press.
122 Hamilton, W.D., The genetical evolution of social behavior. *Journal of Theoretical Biology*, 1964. 7 (1): 1–52.
123 Eliade, M., *The myth of the eternal return; or cosmos and history* (1949). 1991, Princeton: Princeton University Press. p. 196.
124 Scheffler, H.W., Kinship semantics. *Annual Review of Anthropology*, 1972. 1: 309–28.
125 Meyer, A.D., How ideologies supplant formal structures and shape responses to environments. *Journal of Management Studies*, 1982. 19 (1): 45–61.
126 Lévi-Strauss, C., The family, in *Man, culture, and society*, H.L. Shapiro, Editor. 1960, Oxford University Press: New York. pp. 261–85.
127 Freud, S., Totem y Tabu (1913), in *Obras Completas*, 1981, Biblioteca Nueva: Madrid. pp. 1745–850.
128 Héritier, F., Família, in *Enciclopédia Einaudi*, 1997, Imprensa Nacional da Casa da Moeda: Lisboa. pp. 81–94.
129 Héritier, F., Endogamia/exogamia, in *Enciclopédia Einaudi*, 1997, Imprensa Nacional da Casa da Moeda: Lisboa. pp. 125–39.
130 Young, M. and P. Wilmott, *Family and class in a London suburb*. 1968, London: Routledge & Kegan Paul.
131 Marx, K., *A contribution to the critique of politcal economy* (1859). 1970, Moscow: Progress Publishers.
132 Cherlin, A., Changing family and household: Contemporary lessons from historical research. *Annual Review of Sociology*, 1983. 9: 51–66.
133 Gouesse, J.-M., Parents, famille et mariage en Normandie au XVIIe et XVIIIe siècles. *Annales Economies, Sociétés, Civilisations*, 1972. 4–5.
134 Kondo, D.K., *Crafting selves: Power, gender, and discourses of identity in a Japanese workplace*. 1990, Chicago: Chicago University Press.
135 Creed, G.W., "Family values" and domestic economy. *Annual Review of Anthropology*, 2000. 29: 329–55.
136 Ochs, E. and T. Kremer-Sadlik, How postindustrial families talk. *Annual Review of Anthropology*, 2015. 44: 87–103.
137 Flandrin, J.-L., Families in former times: Kinship, househould and sexuality. *Themes in the social sciences*, J. Goody and G. Hawthorn, Editors. 1979, Cambridge University Press: Cambridge. p. 265.
138 Baxter, I.F.G., Family law, in *Encyclopedia britannica*, R. McHenry and Y.C. Hori, Editors. 1995, Encyclopedia Britannica: Chicago. pp. 76–83.
139 Héritier, F., Masculino/feminino, in *Enciclopédia Einaudi*, 1997, Imprensa Nacional da Casa da Moeda: Lisboa. pp. 11–26.
140 Goode, W., *World revolution and family patterns*. 1963, Glencoe: Free Press.
141 Taylor, FW., The principles of scientific management. *Bulletin of the Taylor Society*, 1916. 2 (5): 13–23.

142 Perrow, C., *Complex organizations: A critical essay*. 1993, New York: Random House.
143 Chandler Jr., A.D., *The visible hand: The managerial revolution in American business*. 1977, Cambridge: Belknap.
144 Shenhav, Y., From Chaos to systems: The engineering foundations of organization theory, 1879–1932. *Administrative Science Quarterly*, 1995. 49: 557–85.
145 Koeberle-Schmid, A., D. Kenyon-Rouvinez, and E.J. Poza, *Governance in family enterprises: Maximizing economic and emotional success*. 2014, Hampshire: Palgrave Macmillan. p. 272.
146 Williamson, O.E., Opportunism and its critics. *Managerial and Decision Economics*, 1993. 14: 97–107.
147 Brunsson, N., The organization of hypocrisy; talk, decisions and actions in organizations. 2006, Oslo: Universitetsforlaget AS. p. 242.
148 Weick, K.E., Educational organizations as loosely coupled systems. *Administrative Science Quarterly*, 1976. 21 (1): 1–19.
149 Weber, M., Household, enterprise and oikos, in *Max Weber economy and society; an outline of interpretive sociology*, G. Roth and C. Wittich, Editors. 1978, University of California Press: Berkeley. pp. 370–84.
150 Weber, M., *The theory of social and economic organization*. 1964, New York: Prentice Hall.
151 Meierhenrich, J. and O. Simons, eds. *The Oxford handbook of Carl Schmitt*. 2016, New York: Oxford University Press.
152 Stack, G.J., Political leadership & nihilism: A study of Weber and Nietzsche (review). *Journal of the History of Philosophy*, 1987. 25 (2): 309–12.
153 Rorty, R., From logic to language to play: A plenary Address to the Inter-American Congress. *Proceedings and Addresses of the American Philosophical Association*, 1986. 59 (5): 747–53.
154 Mills, C.W., Situated actions and vocabularies of motives. *American Sociological Review*, 1940. 5 (6): 904–13.
155 Swidler, A., Culture in action: Symbols and strategies. *American Sociological Review*, 1986. 51 (2): 273–86.
156 Tolstoy, L., *Anna Karenina: A novel in eight parts* (1877). 2001, London: Penguin.
157 Mahoney, J. and K. Thelen, eds. *Explaining institutional change: Ambiguity, agency and power*. 2010, Cambridge University Press: Cambridge.
158 Milgrom, P. and J. Roberts, Complementarities and fit strategy, structure, and organizational change in manufacturing. *Journal of Accounting and Economics*, 1995. 19 (2–3): 179–208.
159 Shorter, E., *The making of the modern family*. 1976, New York: Basic Books.
160 Dawson, P., Organisational change stories and management research: Facts or fiction. *Journal of the Australian and New Zealand Academy of Management*, 2003. 9 (3): 37–49.
161 Leitner, K., *A primer on ethnomethodology*. 1980, New York: Oxford University Press.
162 March, J.G., The business firm as a political coalition. *The Journal of Politics*, 1962. 24 (04): 662–78.

163 Geertz, C., Centers, kings and charisma: Reflections on the symbolics of power, in *Local knowledge: Further essays in interpretive anthropology*, C. Geertz, Editor. 1983, Basic Books: New York. pp. 121–46.

164 Podolny, J.M., Networks as the pipes and prisms of the market. *American Journal of Sociology*, 2001. 107 (1): 33–60.

165 Padgett, J.F. and W.W. Powell, *The emergence of organizations and markets*. 2012, Princeton: Princeton University Press.

166 Kadushin, C., *Understanding social networks: Theories, concepts, and findings*. 2012, Oxford: Oxford University Press.

167 Burt, R.S., *Structural holes*. 1992, Cambridge: Harvard University Press.

168 Burt, R.S., *Brokerage and closure: An introduction to social capital*. 2005, Oxford: Oxford University Press.

169 Park, W.-W., A comprehensive empirical investigation of the relationships among variables of the groupthink model. *Journal of Organizational Behavior*, 2000. 21 (8): 873–87.

170 Malcolmson, J.M., Relational incentive contracts, in *The handbook of organizational economics*, R. Gibbons and J. Roberts, Editors. 2013, Princeton University Press: Princeton and Oxford. pp. 1014–65.

171 Wikipedia contributors. "Blind men and an elephant." Wikipedia, The Free Encyclopedia. Wikipedia, The Free Encyclopedia, 6 Mar. 2020. Web. 29 Nov. 2013..

172 Gigerenzer, G. and R. Selten, *Bounded rationality: The adaptive toolbox*. 2001, Cambridge: MIT Press.

173 Simon, H.A., A behavioral model of rational choice. *Quarterly Journal of Economics*, 1955. 69: 99–118.

174 Schumpeter, J.A., Development (1932). *Journal of Economic Literature*, 2005. 43 (1): 108–20.

175 Thompson, J.D., *Organizations in action: Social Science bases of administrative theory* 1967, New York: McGraw Hill.

176 March, J.G. and J.P. Olsen, The uncertainty of the past: Organizational learning under ambiguity. *European Journal of Political Research*, 1975. 3 (2): 147–71.

177 Silverman, D., *The theory of organisations*. 1970, New York: Basic Books.

178 Griffin, D. and A. Tversky, The weighing of evidence and the determinants of confidence. *Cognitive Psychology*, 1992. 24: 411–35.

179 March, J.G. and T. Weil, *On leadership*. 2005, Malden: Blackwell.

180 Nystrom, P.C. and W.H. Starbuck, To avoid organizational crises, unlearn. *Organizational Dynamics*, 1984. 12 (4): 53–65.

181 Levitt, B. and J.G. March, Organizational learning. *Annual Review of Sociology*, 1988. 14: 319–40.

182 Levinthal, D. and J.G. March, The myopia of learning. *Strategic Management Journal*, 1993. 14: 95–113.

183 March, J.G., The technology of foolishness, in *Ambiguity and choice in organizations*, J.G. March and J.P. Olsen, Editors. 1979, Universitetsforlaget: Bergen. pp. 69–81.

184 Kahneman, D., *Thinking, fast and slow*. 2011, New York: Farrar, Strauss and Giroux. p. 499.

185 Sloman, S.A., Two systems of reasoning, in *Heuristics and biases: The psychology of intuitive reasoning*, T. Gilovich, D.W. Griffin, and D. Kahneman, Editors. 2002, Cambridge University Press: Cambridge. pp. 379–96.
186 Demers, C., *Organizational change theories; a synthesis*. 2007, Los Angeles: Sage.
187 Jung, C.G., et al., *O Homem e seus Símbolos*. n.d., Rio de Janeiro: Nova Fronteira.
188 Gabriel, Y., The unmanaged organization: Stories, fantasies and subjectivity. *Organization Studies*, 1995. 16 (3): 477–501.
189 Perrow, C., Why bureaucracy? in Perrow, C. *Complex organizations: A critical essay*. 1986, Random House: New York. pp. 1–49.
190 Martin, J., et al., The uniqueness paradox in organizational stories. *Administrative Science Quarterly*, 1983. 28 (3): 438–53.
191 Patriotta, G., Sonsemaking on the shop floor: Narratives of knowledge in organizations. *Journal of Management Studies*, 2003. 40 (2): 349–75.
192 Weick, K.E., Sensemaking in organizations,1995, Thousand Oaks: Sage.
193 Carroll, G.R. and A. Swaminathan, Why the microbrewery movement? Organizational dynamics of resource partitioning in the U.S. brewing industry. *American Journal of Sociology*, 2000. 106 (3): 715–62.
194 Bruner, J., The narrative construction of reality. *Critical Inquiry*, 1991. 18 (1): 1–21.
195 Felin, T. and N.J. Foss, Social reality, the boundaries of self-fulfilling prophecy, and economics. *Organization Science*, 2009. 20 (3): 654–68.
196 Budge, G.S. and R.W. Janoff, Interpreting the discourses of family business. *Family Business Review*, 1991. 4 (4): 367–81.
197 Rhodes, C. and A.D. Brown, Narrative, organizations and research. *International Journal of Management Reviews*, 2005. 7 (3): 167–88.
198 Descartes, R., *Discourse on the method of rigthly conducting the reason and seeking for truth in the sciences* (1637). v. 28. 1990, Chicago: Encyclopaedia Britannica. pp. 263–91.
199 Corballis, M.C., The uniqueness of human recursive thinking: The ability to think about thinking may be the critical attribute that distinguishes us from all other species. *American Scientist*, 2007. 95 (3): 240–8.
200 March, J.G., L.S. Sproull, and M. Tamuz, Learning from samples of one or fewer. *Organization Science*, 1991. 2: 1–13.
201 Ketokivi, M., S. Mantere, and J. Cornelissen, Reasoning by analogy and the progress of theory. *Academy of Management Review*, 2017. 42 (4): 637–58.
202 Smets, M., et al., *The CEO Report: Embracing the paradoxes of leadership and the power of doubt*. 2015, Oxford and New York: Said Business School/Heidrick & Struggles.
203 Simonson, I., Decision making, in *Encyclopedia of social psychology*, R.F. Baumeister and K.D. Vohs, Editors. 2007, Sage: Thousand Oaks. pp. 224–8.
204 Dehaene, S., et al., Conscious, preconscious, and subliminal processing: A testable taxonomy. *Trends in Cognitive Sciences*, 2006. 10 (5): 204–11.
205 James, W., The principles of psychology (1891). *Great books of the Western world*, v. 53. 1952, Chicago: Encyclopaedia Britannica. p. 897.

206 Russell, B., *The analysis of mind* (1921). 2017, Whitorn: Anodos Books.

207 Koehler, D.J., L. Brenner, and D.W. Griffin, The calibration of expert judgment: Heuristics and biases beyond the laboratory, in *Heuristics and biases: The psychology of intuitive judgment*, T. Gilovich, D.W. Griffin, and D. Kahneman, Editors. 2002, Cambridge University Press: Cambridge. pp. 686–715.

208 Gilbert, D.T., Inferential correction, in *Heuristics and biases: The psychology of intuitive judgment*, T. Gilovich, D.R. Griffin, and D. Kahneman, Editors. 2002, Cambridge University Press: Cambridge. pp. 167–84.

209 Artinger, F., et al., Heuristics as adaptive decision strategies in management. *Journal of Organizational Behavior*, 2014. 36 (1): S33–S52.

210 Gilovich, T., D. Griffin, and D. Kahneman, eds. *Heuristics and biases: The psychology of intuitive judgment*. 2002, Cambridge: Cambridge University Press.

211 Loock, M. and G. Hinnen, Heuristics in organizations: A review and a research agenda. *Journal of Business Research*, 2015. 68 (9): 2027–36.

212 Tversky, A. and D. Kahneman, Judgement under uncertainty: Heuristics and biases. *Science*, 1974. 185 (4157): 1124–31.

213 Gigerenzer, G. and W. Gaissmaier, Heuristic decision making. *Annual Review of Psychology*, 2011. 62: 451–82.

214 Kahneman, D., Maps of bounded rationality: Psychology for behavioral economics. *The American Economic Review*, 2003. 93 (5): 1449–75.

215 Kahneman, D., A perspective on judgment and choice: Mapping bounded rationality. *American Psychologist*, 2003. 58 (9): 697–720.

216 Epley, N. and E.A. Caruso, Egocentric Ethics. *Social Justice Research*, 2004. 17 (4): 171–87.

217 Gigerenzer, G. and H. Brighton, Homo heuristicus: Why biased minds make better inferences. *Topics in Cognitive Science*, 2009. 1 (1): 107–43.

218 Smith, V.L., Constructivist and ecological rationality in economics. *The American Economic Review*, 2003. 93 (3): 465–508.

219 March, J.G. and J.P. Olsen, *Ambiguity and choice in organizations*. 1979, Bergen: Universitetsforlaget. p. 408.

220 McCloskey, M.M. and S. Glucksberg, Natural categories: Well defined or fuzzy sets? *Memory & Cognition*, 1978. 6 (4): 462–72.

221 Murphy, G.L., The downside of categories. *Trends in Cognitive Sciences*, 2003. 7 (12): 513–14.

222 Winkielman, P., et al., Prototypes are attractive because they are easy on the mind. *Psychological Science*, 2006. 17 (9): 799–806.

223 Forgas, J.P. and S.M. Laham, Halo effect, in *Encyclopedia of social psychology*, R.F. Baumeister and K.D. Vohs, Editors. 2007, Sage: Thousand Oaks. pp. 409–10.

224 Doerr, C.E., Dillution effect, in *Encyclopedia of social psychology*, R.F. Baumeister and K.D. Vohs, Editors. 2007, Sage: Thousand Oaks. pp. 248–50.

225 Hanko, K., Focalism, in *Encyclopedia of social psychology*, R.F. Baumeister and K.D. Vohs, Editors. 2007, Sage: Thousand Oaks. pp. 352–53.

226 Russell, J.A. and B. Fehr, Fuzzy concepts in a fuzzy hierarchy: Varieties of anger. *Journal of Personality and Social Psychology*, 1994. 67 (2): 186–205.

227 Kahneman, D. On the psychology of prediction. *Psychological Review*, 1973. 80, 237–51.

228 Redelmeier, D.A., J. Katz, and D. Kahneman, Memories of colonoscopy: A randomized trial. *Pain*, 2003. 104 (1–2): 187–94.

229 Brickman, P., D. Coates, and R. Janoff-Bulman, Lottery winners and accident victims: Is happiness relative? *Journal of Personality and Social Psychology*, 1978. 36: 917–27.

230 Schkade, D.A. and D. Kahneman, Does living in California make people happy? A focusing illusion in judgements of life satisfaction. *Psychological Science*, 1998. 9: 340–6.

231 Florowsky, G., The study of the past. R.H. Nash, Editor. 1969, Dutton: Boston.

232 Fischhoff, B., Hindsight is not equal to foresight: The effect of outcome knowledge on judgment under uncertainty. *Journal of Experimental Psychology: Human Perception and Performance*, 1975. 1 (3): 288–99.

233 Gilovich, T. and V.H. Medvec, The temporal pattern of the experience of regret. *Journal of Personality and Social Psychology*, 1994. 67 (3): 357–65.

234 Medvec, V.H., S.F. Madey, and T. Gilovich, When less is more: Counterfactual thinking and satisfaction among olympic medalists. *Journal of Personality and Social Psychology*, 1995. 69: 603–10.

235 Ohman, A., Fears, phobias and preparedness: Toward an evolved module of fear and fear learning. *Psychological Review*, 2001. 108: 483–522.

236 Buehler, R., D. Griffin, and M. Ross, Inside the planning fallacy: The causes and consequences of optimistic time predictions, in *Heuristics and biaes: The psychology of intuitive judgement*, T. Gilovich, D. Griffin, and D. Kahneman, Editors. 2002, Cambridge University Press: Cambridge. pp. 250–70.

237 Langer, E.J., The illusion of control. *Journal of Personality and Social Psychology*, 1975. 32 (2): 311–28.

238 Mehlman, R.C. and C.R. Snyder, Excuse theory: A test of the self-protective role of attributions. *Journal of Personality and Social Psychology*, 1985. 49 (4): 994–1001.

239 Fitch, G., Effects of self-esteem, perceived performance, and choice on causal attributions. *Journal of Personality and Social Psychology*, 1970. 16 (2): 311–15.

240 Mischel, W., E.B. Ebbesent, and A.M. Zeiss, Determinants of selective memory about the self. *Journal of Consulting and Clinical Psychology*, 1976. 44 (1): 92–103.

241 Greenwald, A.G. and M.R. Banaji, Implicit social cognition: attitudes, self-esteem, and stereotypes. *Psychological Review*, 1995. 102 (1): 4–27.

242 Greenwald, A.G., The totalitarian Ego: fabrication and revision of personal history. *American Psychologist*, 1980. 35: 603–18.

243 Alloy, L.B. and L.Y. Abramson, Judgment of contingency in depressed and nondepressed students: Sadder but wiser? *Journal of Experimental Psychology: General*, 1979. 108 (4): 441–85.

244 Lewinsohn, P.M., et al., Social competence and depression: The role of illusory self-perceptions. *Journal of Abnormal Psychology*, 1980. 89 (2): 203–12.

245 Freud, S. eds. *Mourning and melancholia. Standard edition of the complete psychological works of Sigmund Freud.* Vol. 14. 1917, London: Hogarth Press.
246 Haselton, M.G. and D. Nettle, The paranoid optimist: An integrative evolutionary model of cognitive biases. *Personality and Social Psychology Review*, 2006. 10 (1): 47–66.
247 Isaacowitz, D.M., The gaze of the optimist. *Pers Soc Psychol Bull*, 2005. 31 (3): 407–15.
248 Shleifer, A., Psychologists at the gate: A review of Daniel Kahneman's thinking, fast and slow. *Journal of Economic Literature*, 2012. 50 (4): 1–12.
249 Tversky, A. and D. Kahneman, Belief in the law of small numbers. *Psychological Bulletin*, 1971. 76: 105–10.
250 Epley, N., Base rate fallacy, in *Encyclopedia of social psychology*, R.F. Baumeister and K.D. Vohs, Editors. 2007, Sage: Thousand Oaks. pp. 102–3.
251 Epley, N. and T. Gilovich, Putting adjustment back in the anchoring and adjustment heuristic: Differential processing of self-generated and experimenter-provided anchors. *Psychological Science*, 2001. 12 (5): 391–6.
252 Keysar, B. and D.J. Barr, Self-anchoring in conversation: Why language users do not do what they "should", in *Heuristics and biases: The psychology of intuitive judgment*, T. Gilovich, D.W. Griffin, and D. Kahneman, Editors. 2002, Cambridge University Press: Cambridge. pp. 151–66.
253 Wainer, H. and H.L. Zwerling, Evidence that smaller schools do not improve student achievement. *The Phi Delta Kappan*, 2006. 88 (4): 300–3.
254 Piaget, J., *Psychology of intelligence* (1947). 1960, Tutowa: Littlefield, Adams & Co.
255 Ferrater Mora, J., Deber ser, in *Diccionario de Filosofía*, J. Ferrater Mora, Editor. 1990, Alianza: Madrid. pp. 718–19.
256 Starbuck, W.H., M.L. Barnett, and P. Baumard, Payoffs and pitfalls of strategic learning. *Journal of Economic Behavior & Organization*, 2008. 66 (1): 7–21.
257 Ribeiro, R., Levels of immersion, tacit knowledge and expertise. *Phenomenology and the Cognitive Sciences*, 2013. 12 (2): 367–97.
258 Bayley, P.J., J.C. Frascino, and L.R. Squire, Robust habit learning in the absence of awareness and independent of the medial temporal lobe. *Nature*, 2005. 436 (7050): 550–3.
259 Nonaka, I. and H. Takeuchi, The knowledge-creating company: How Japanese companies create the dynamics of innovation. 1995, Oxford: Oxford University Press.
260 Tsoukas, H., *Complex knowledge: Studies in organizational epistemology*. 2005, Oxford: Oxford University Press.
261 Ribeiro, R., Knowledge transfer. Ph.D. Thesis, in School of Social Sciences. 2007, Cardiff University: Cardiff. p. 257.
262 Ribeiro, R., Tacit knowledge management. *Phenomenology and the Cognitive Sciences*, 2013. 12 (2): 337–66.
263 Goffman, E., The nature of deference and demeanor. *American Anthropologist*, 1956. 58 (3): 473–502.

264 Porter, M.E., The five competitive forces that shape strategy. *Harvard Business Review*, 2008(Jan.): 78–93.

265 Czarniawska-Joerges, B., On imitation and fashion: How new ideas travel around the world, in *A theory of organizing*, B. Czarniawska-Joerges, Editor. 2008, Edward Elgar: Cheltenham. pp. 92–104.

266 Abrahamson, E., Managerial fads and fashions: The diffusion and rejection of innovations. *The Academy of Management Review*, 1991. 16 (3): 586–612.

267 Ribeiro, R. and H. Collins, The bread-making machine: Tacit knowledge and two types of action. *Organization Studies*, 2007. 28 (9): 1417–33.

268 Husserl, E., *L'idée de la phénoménologie; cinq leçons*. 1970, Paris: Presses Universitaires de France. p. 136.

269 Lakoff, G. and M. Johnson, *Metaphors we live by*. 1980, Chicago: University of Chicago Press.

270 Collins, H., Bicycling on the moon: Collective tacit knowledge and somatic/limit tacit knowledge. *Organization Studies*, 2007. 28 (2): 257–62.

271 Wheatley, T. and J. Haidt, Hypnotic disgust makes moral judgments more severe. *Psychological Science*, 2005. 16 (10): 780–4.

272 Kahneman, D. and G. Klein, Conditions for intuitive expertise: A failure to disagree. *American Psychologist*, 2009. 64 (6): 515–26.

273 Festinger, L., Cognitive dissonance. *Scientific American*, 1962. 4: 93–107.

274 Wise, R.A., Dopamine, learning, and motivation. *Nature Reviews Neuroscience*, 2004. 5 (6): 483–94.

275 Engestrom, Y., Activity theory as a framework for analyzing and redesigning work. *Ergonomics*, 2000. 43 (7): 960–74.

276 Weaver, W., Science and complexity. *American Scientist*, 1948. 36 (4): 536–44.

277 Churchman, C.W., Guest editorial: Wicked problems. *Management Science*, 1967. 14 (4): B141–B142.

278 Simon, H.A., The structure of ill structured problems. *Artificial Intelligence*, 1973. 4: 181–201.

279 Perrow, C., A Framework for the comparative analysis of organizations. *American Sociological Review*, 1967. 32 (2): 194–208.

280 Campbell, D.E. and J.S. Kelly, Trade-off theory. *The American Economic Review*, 1994. 84 (2): 422–6.

281 Burt, R.S., Structural holes and good ideas. *American Journal of Sociology*, 2004. 110 (2): 349–99.

282 Jaffe, A.B., Innovation, in *Emergent trends in the social and behavioral sciences*, R. Scott and S.M. Kosslyn, Editors. 2015, Wiley. pp. 1–15.

283 Rittel, H.W.J. and M.M. Webber, dilemmas in a general theory of planning. *Policy Sciences*, 1973. 4: 155–69.

284 Bartz, J.A. and J.E. Lydon, Close relationships and the working self-concept: Implicit and explicit effects of priming attachment on agency and communion. *Pers Soc Psychol Bull*, 2004. 30 (11): 1389–401.

285 Rotteveel, M., et al., Stronger suboptimal than optimal afective priming? *Emotion*, 2001. 1 (4): 348–64.

286 Schacter, D.L., I.G. Dobbins, and D.M. Schnyer, Specificity of priming: A cognitive neuroscience perspective. *Nature Reviews Neuroscience* 2004. 5 (11): 853–62.

287 Raz, A. and J. Buhle, Typologies of attentional networks. *Nature Reviews Neuroscience*, 2006. 7 (5): 367–79.

288 Todd, P.M., G. *Gigerenzer, and ABC research group, ecological rationality: Intelligence in the world*. 2011, New York: Oxford University Press.

289 Brunsson, N., The irrationality of action and action rationality: Decisions, ideologies and organizational actions. *Journal of Management Studies*, 1982. 19 (1): 29–44.

290 Fleck, L., Gênese e desenvolvimento de um fato científico (1980). 2009, Belo Horizonte: Fabrefactum.

291 Hannan, M.T. and J. Freeman, Structural inertia and organizational change. *American Sociological Review*, 1984. 49 (2): 149–64.

292 Geertz, C., *Local knowledge: Further essays in interpretive anthropology*. 1983, New York: Basic Books.

293 Isen, A.M., K.A. Daubman, and G.P. Nowicki, Positive affect facilitates creative problem solving. *Journal of Personality and Social Psychology*, 1987. 52 (6): 1122–31.

294 Engestrom, Y. and A. Sannino, Studies of expansive learning: Foundations, findings and future challenges. *Educational Research Review*, 2010. 5: 1–24.

295 Armstrong, J.S., How to make better forecasts and decisions: Avoid face-to-face meetings. *The International Journal of Applied Forecasting*, Fall 2006. 5: 3–15.

296 Dodgson, M., D.M. Gann, and N. Phillips, Organizational learning and the technology of foolishness: The case of virtual worlds at IBM. *Organization Science*, 2013. 24 (5): 1358–76.

297 Weber, M., The meaning of "ethical neutrality" in sociology and economics, in *Max Weber on the methodology of the social sciences*, E.A. Shils and H.A. Finch, Editors. 1949, Free Press: Glencoe. pp. 1–47.

298 Hume, D., *A treatise of human nature* (1739). 2000, Oxford: Oxford University Press. p. 622.

299 Bentham, J., *The principles of morals and legislation* (1789). 1948, New York: Hafner Press.

300 Simon, H.A., *Administrative behavior; a study of decision-making processes in administrative organization*. 1957, New York: The Free Press.

301 Thaler, R.H. and C.R. Sunstein, *Nudge: improving decisions about health, wealth, and happiness*. 2008, New York: Penguin Books. p. 312.

302 Sunstein, C.R., *Choosing not to choose: Understanding the value of choice*. 2015, Oxford: Oxford University Press. p. 219.

303 Granovetter, M., Economic action and social structure: The problem of embeddedness. *American Journal of Sociology*, 1985. 91: 481–510.

304 Hochschild, A.R., Emotion work, feeling rules, and social structure. *The American Journal of Sociology*, 1979. 85 (3): 551–75.

305 Byrne, R.W. and N. Corp, Neocortex size predicts deception rate in primates. *Proceedings of the Royal Society B: Biological Sciences*, 2004. 271: 1693–99.

306 Ekman, P., Darwin, deception, and facial expression. *Ann NY Acad Sci*, 2003. 1000 (1): 205–21.

307 Darwin, C., The expression of emotions in man and animals (1872), in *From so simple a beginning: Darwin's four great books*, C. Darwin and E.O. Wilson, Editors. 2005, W. W. Norton: New York. pp. 1255–1478.

308 Gordon, S.L., The sociology of sentiments and emotion, in *Social psychology; sociological perspectives*, M. Rosenberg and R.H. Turner, Editors. 1990, Basic Books: New York. pp. 563–92.
309 Ashraf, N. and O. Bandiera, Social incentives in organizations. *Annual Review of Economics*, 2018. 10 (1): 439–63.
310 Cacioppo, J.T. and H.S. Nusbaum, Component processes underlying choice. *PNAS*, 2003. 100 (6): 3016–17.
311 Tellegen, A., D. Watson, and L.A. Clark, On the dimensional and hierarchical structure of affect. *Psychological Science*, 1999. 10 (4): 297–303.
312 Larsen, J.T., P. McGraw, and J.T. Cacioppo, Can people feel happy and sad at the same time? *Journal of Personality and Social Psychology*, 2001. 81 (4): 684–96.
313 Russell, J.A., A circumplex model of affect. *Journal of Personality and Social Psychology*, 1980. 39: 1161–78.
314 Faith, M.L. and J.F. Thayer, A dynamical systems interpretation of a dimensional model of emotion. *Scandinavian Journal of Psychology*, 2001. 42: 121–33.
315 Ekman, P., R.W. Levenson, and W.V. Friesen, Autonomic nervous system activity distinguishes among emotions. *Science*, 1983. 221 (4616): 1208–10.
316 Schneider, B., M.G. Ehrhart, and W.H. Macey, Organizational climate and culture. *Annual Review of Psychology*, 2013. 64: 361–88.
317 Lutz, C., The domain of emotion words in Ifaluk. *American Ethnologist*, 1982. 9: 113–28.
318 Russell, J.A., Culture and the categorization of emotions. *Psychological Bulletin*, 1991. 110 (3): 426–50.
319 Cialdini, R.B., *Influence; Science and practice*. 2009, Boston: Pearsons.
320 Clore, G.L. and Y. Bar-Anan, Affect as information, in *Handbook of social psychology*, R.F. Baumeister and K.D. Vohs, Editors. 2007, Sage: Los Angeles. pp. 12–15.
321 Kelley, A.E., T. Schochet, and C.F. Landry, Risk taking and novelty seeking in adolescence: Introduction to Part I. Ann NY *Acad Sci*, 2004. 1021 (1): 27–32.
322 Kagan, J., J.S. Reznick, and N. Snidman, Biological bases of childhood shyness. *Science*, 1988. 240: 167–71.
323 Schwartz, C.E., et al., Inhibited and uninhibited infants "grown up": Adult Amygdalar response to novelty. *Science*, 2003. 300 (5627): 1952–3.
324 Zajonc, R.B., Mere exposure: A gateway to the subliminal. *Current Directions in Psychological Science*, 2001. 10 (6): 224–8.
325 Nietzsche, F., *The birth of tragedy and other writings* (1872). 1999, Cambridge: Cambridge University Press.
326 Freud, S., *Civilization and its discontents* (1927). 2010, New York: Norton & Norton.
327 Madsen, K.B., *Theories of motivation; a comparative study of modern theories of motivation*. 1964, Cleveland, Ohio: Howard Allen.
328 Fehr, E., Human behaviour: Don't lose your reputation. *Nature*, 2004. 432 (7016): 449–50.

329 Riezler, K., Comment on the social psychology of shame. *The American Journal of Sociology*, 1943. 48 (4): 457–65.

330 March, J.G. and J.P. Olsen, The logic of appropriateness, in *The oxford handbook of public policiy*, R.E. Goodin, M. Moran, and M. Rein, Editors. 2008, Oxford University Press: Oxford. pp. 689–708.

331 Haidt, J., The emotional dog and its rational tail: A social intuitionist approach to moral judgment. *Psychological Review*, 2001. 108 (4): 814–34.

332 Chatterjee, A. and D.C. Hambrick, It's all about me: Narcissistic chief executive officers and their effects on company strategy and performance. *Administrative Science Quarterly*, 2007. 52: 351–86.

333 Rosenthal, S.A. and T.L. Pittinsky, Narcissistic leadership. *The Leadership Quarterly*, 2006. 17: 617–33.

334 Ranganath, K. and B.A. Nosek, Implicit and explicit attitudes, in *Encyclopedia of social psychology*, R.F. Baumeister and K.D. Vohs, Editors. 2007, Sage: Thousand Oaks. pp. 465–6.

335 Parks-Stamm, E.J., A. Achtziger, and P.M. Gollwitzer, Implementation intentions, in *Encyclopedia of social psychology*, R.F. Baumeister and K.D. Vohs, Editors. 2007, Cambridge University Press: Cambridge. pp. 461–3.

336 Schuman, H., Attitudes, beliefs, and behavior, in *Sociological Perspectives on Social Psychology*, K.S. Cook, G.A. Fine, and J.S. House, Editors. 1995, Allyn and Bacon: Boston. pp. 68–79.

337 Baccus, J.R., M.W. Baldwin, and D.J. Packer, Increasing implicit self-esteem through classical conditioning. *Psychological Science*, 2004. 15 (7): 498–502.

338 Strati, A., The aesthetic approach in organization studies, in *The aesthetics of organization*, S. Linstead and H. Hopfl, Editors. 2000, Sage: London. pp. 13–34.

339 Jepperson, R. and J.W. Meyer, Multiple levels of analysis and the limitations of methodological individualism. *Sociological Theory*, 2011. 29 (1): 54–73.

340 Keeney, R.L. and H. Raiffa, *Decisions with multiple objectives: Preferences and value tradeoffs*. 1976, New York: Wiley.

341 Emerson, R.M., Social exchange theory. *Annual Review of Sociology*, 1976. 2 (1): 335–62.

342 Molm, L.D. and K.S. Cook, Social exchange and exchange networks, in *Sociological perspectives on social psychology*, K.S. Cook, G.A. Fine, and J.S. House, Editors. 1995, Allyn and Bacon: Boston. pp. 209–35.

343 Schrodinger, E., *What is life*? 1944, Cambridge: Cambridge University Press.

344 Kerckhoff, A.C., Social stratification and mobility processes: Interaction between individuals and social structures, in *Sociological perspectives on social psychology*, K.S. Cook, G.A. Fine, and J.S. House, Editors. 1995, Allyn and Bacon: Boston. pp. 476–96.

345 Mortimer, J.T. and J. Lorence, Social psychology of work, in *Sociological perspectives on social psychology*, K.S. Cook, G.A. Fine, and J.S. House, Editors. 1995, Allyn and Bacon: Boston. pp. 497–523

346 Argyle, M. and J. Dean, Eye-contact, distance and affiliation. *Sociometry*, 1965. 28 (3): 289–304.

347 Sommer, R., Studies in personal space. *Sociometry*, 1959. 22 (3): 247–60.

348 Leffler, A., D.L. Gillespie, and J.C. Conaty, The effects of status differentiation on nonverbal behavior. *Social Psychology Quarterly*, 1982. 45 (3): 153–61.

349 Godfrey, D.K., E.E. Jones, and C.G. Lord, Self-promotion is not ingratiating. *Journal of Personality and Social Psychology*, 1986. 50 (1): 160–115.

350 Stiles, W.B., D.A. Shapiro, and J.A. Firth-Cozens, Verbal response mode use in contrasting psychotherapies: A within-subjects comparison. *Journal of Consulting and Clinical Psychology*, 1988. 56 (5): 727–33.

351 Stiles, W.B. and S.M. Putnam, Verbal exchanges in medical interviews: Concepts and measurement. *Social Science & Medicine*, 1992. 35 (3): 347–55.

352 Tuzlak, A. and J.C. Moore Jr., Status, demeanor and influence: An empirical reassessment. *Social Psychology Quarterly*, 1984. 47 (2): 178–83.

353 Hsu, G. and M.T. Hannan, Identities, genres, and organizational forms. *Organization Science*, 2005. 16 (5): 474–90.

354 Zuckerman, E.W., The categorical imperative: Securities analysts and the illegitimacy discount. *American Journal of Sociology*, 1999. 5 (1398–1438).

355 Cooper, J., E.E. Jones, and S.M. Tuller, Attribution, dissonance, and the illusion of uniqueness. *Journal of Experimental Social Psychology*, 1972. 8 (1): 45–57.

356 Suls, J., False uniqueness bias, in *Encyclopedia of social psychology*, R.F. Baumeister and K.D. Vohs, Editors. 2007, Sage: Thousand Oaks. pp. 344–5.

357 Weber, M., *Economy and society; an outline of interpretive sociology* (1919)1978, Berkeley: University of California Press.

358 Lindblom, C.E., The Science of "muddling through". *Administration Review*, 1958. 19 (2): 79–88.

359 Singer, T., et al., Empathy for pain involves the affective but not sensory components of pain. *Science*, 2004. 303 (5661): 1157–62.

360 Hardin, G., The tragedy of the commons. *Science*, 1968. 162 (3859): 1243–8.

361 Doebeli, M., C. Hauert, and T. Killingback, The evolutionary origin of cooperators and defectors. *Science*, 2004. 306 (5697): 859–62.

362 Olson, M., *The logic of collective action; public goods and the theory of groups*. 1965, Cambridge: Harvard University Press.

363 dos Santos, M., D.J. Rankin, and C. Wedekind, Human cooperation based on punishment reputation. *Evolution*, 2013. 67 (8): 2446–50.

364 Frank, S.A., Mutual policing and repression of competition in the evolution of cooperative groups. *Nature*, 1995. 377 (6549): 520–2.

365 Marlowe, F.W., et al., The 'spiteful' origins of human cooperation. *Proceedings of the Royal Society B: Biological Sciences*, 2011, (278): 2159–64.

366 Milinski, M., Tit for tat in sticklebacks and the evolution of cooperation. *Nature*, 1987. 325 (6103): 433–5.

367 Ramírez, R., The aesthetics of cooperation. *European Management Review*, 2005. 2 (1): 28–35.

368 Riolo, R.L., M.D. Cohen, and R. Axelrod, Evolution of cooperation without reciprocity. *Nature*, 2001. 414 (6862): 441–3.

369 Rockenbach, B. and M. Milinski, To qualify as a social partner, humans hide severe punishment, although their observed cooperativeness is decisive. *Proceedings of the National Academy of Sciences*, 2011. 108 (45): 18307–12.

370 Jensen, K., et al., What's in it for me? Self-regard precludes altruism and spite in chimpanzees. *Proceedings of the Royal Society of London - B. Biological Sciences*, 2006 (FirstCite Early Online Publishing): 10.1098/rspb.2005.3417.

371 Trivers, R.L., The evolution of reciprocal altruism. *Quarterly Review of Biology*, 1971. 46 (1): 35–57.

372 Axelrod, R. and W.D. Hamilton, The evolution of cooperation. *Science*, 1981. 211 (1390–6).

373 Clutton-Brock, T., Breeding together: Kin selection and mutualism in cooperative vertebrates. *Science*, 2002. 296 (5565): 69–72.

374 Clutton-Brock, T.H., et al., Costs of cooperative behaviour in suricates (Suricata suricatta). *Proceedings of The Royal Society Of London. Series B. Biological Sciences*, 1998. 265 (1392): 185–90.

375 Cockburn, A., Evolution of helping behavior in cooperatively breeding birds. *Annual Review of Ecology and Systematics*, 1998. 29 (1): 141–77.

376 Mesterton-Gibbons, M. and E.S. Adams, Behavioral ecology: The economics of animal cooperation. *Science*, 2002. 298 (5601): 2146–7.

377 Mitani, J.C., D.A. Merriwether, and C. Zhang, Male affiliation, cooperation and kinship in wild chimpanzees. *Animal Behaviour*, 2000. 59 (4): 885–93.

378 Alcock, J., *The triumph of sociobiology*. 2001, Oxford: Oxford University Press. p. 257.

379 Jensen, K., J. Call, and M. Tomasello, Chimpanzees are rational maximizers in an ultimatum game. *Science*, 2007. 318 (5847): 107–9.

380 Fehr, E. and K.M. Schmidt, A theory of fairness, competition, and cooperation. *The Quarterly Journal of Economics*, 1999. 114 (3): 817–68.

381 Nowak, M.A., K.M. Page, and K. Sigmund, Fairness versus reason in the ultimatum game. *Science*, 2000. 289 (5485): 1773–5.

382 Bazerman, M.H., T. Giuliano, and A. Appelman, Escalation of commitment in individual and group decision making. *Organizational Behavior and Human Performance*, 1984. 33 (2): 141–52.

383 Fehr, E. and S. Gachter, Altruistic punishment in humans. *Nature*, 2002. 415 (6868): 137–40.

384 Piazza, J. and J.M. Bering, The effects of perceived anonymity on altruistic punishment. *Evolutionary Psychology*, 2008. 6 (3): 487–501.

385 Thucydides, The history of the Peloponnesian War (430 a.C.). *Great books of the Western world*, R.M. Hutchins, Editors. Vol. v. 6. 1952, Chicago: Encyclopaedia Britannica. pp. 345–616.

386 Brosnan, S.F. and F.B.M. de Waal, Evolution of responses to (un)fairness. *Science*, 2014. 346 (6207): 1251776.

387 Cameron, L., Raising the stakes in the ultimatum game: Experimental evidence from Indonesia. *Economic Inquiry*, 1999. 37 (1): 47–59.
388 Nietzsche, F., *On the genealogy of morality* (1887). 1994, Cambridge: Cambridge University Press.
389 Karagonlar, G. and D.M. Kuhlman, The role of social value orientation in response to an unfair offer in the ultimatum game. *Organizational Behavior and Human Decision Processes*, 2013. 120 (2): 228–39.
390 Nelissen, R.M.A., et al., Fear and guilt in proposers: Using emotions to explain offers in ultimatum bargaining. *European Journal of Social Psychology*, 2011. 41 (1): 78–85.
391 Sanfey, A.G., et al., The neural basis of economic decision-making in the ultimatum game. *Science*, 2003. 300 (5626): 1755–8.
392 Forber, P. and R. Smead, The evolution of fairness through spite. *Proceedings of the Royal Society B: Biological Sciences*, 2014. 281 (1780): 20132439.393. Kahneman, D., J.L. Knetsch, and R. Thaler, Fairness as a constraint on profit seeking: Entitlements in the market. *The American Economic Review*, 1986. 76 (4): 728–41.
394 Singer, T., et al., Empathic neural responses are modulated by the perceived fairness of others. *Nature*, 2006. 439 (7075): 466–9.
395 Conradt, L. and T.J. Roper, Activity synchrony and social cohesion: A fission-fusion model. *Proceedings of the Royal Society of London - B. Biological Sciences*, 2000. 267: 2213–18.
396 Cherkaqui, M., Estratificação, in *Tratado de Sociologia*, R. Boudon, Editor. 1992, Zahar: Rio de Janeiro. pp. 107–65.
397 Berlinerblau, J., Toward a sociology of heresy, orthodoxy, and doxa. *History of Religions*, 2001. 40 (4): 327–51.
398 Simmel, G., *Conflict and the web of group-affiliations*. 1955, New York: Free Press.
399 Coser, L., *The functions of social conflict*. 1956, New York: Free Press.
400 Gibbs, J.P., Norms: the problem of definition and classification. *The American Journal of Sociology*, 1965. 70 (5): 586–94.
401 Bobbio, N., Poder/autoridade, in *Enciclopédia Einaudi*, v. 14 1989, Casa da Moeda: Lisboa. pp. 58–103.
402 Albertone, E.A., Pacto, in *Enciclopédia Einaudi*, 1989, Casa da Moeda: Lisboa. v. pp. 11–43.
403 Asch, S., Opinions and social pressure. *Scientific American*, 1955. 193 (5): 31–5.
404 March, J.G., M. Schulz, and X. Zhou, *The dynamics of rules; change in written organizational codes*. 2000, Stanford: Stanford University Press.
405 March, J.G., *Explorations in organizations*. 2008, Stanford: Stanford University Press. p. 464.
406 Hamilton, V.L. and D. Rauma, Social psychology of deviance and law, in *Sociological perspectives on social psychology*, K.S. Cook, G.A. Fine, and J.S. House, Editors. 1995, Allyn and Bacon: Boston. pp. 524–47.
407 March, J.G., Bounded rationality, ambiguity, and the engineering of choice. *The Bell Journal of Economics*, 1978. 9 (2): 587–608.
408 March, J.G., Wild ideas: The catechism of heresy, in *The pursuit of organizational intelligence*, J.G. March, Editor. 1999, Blackwell: Malden. pp. 225–8.

409 Wells, D., et al., Creative deviance: A study of the relationship between creative behavior and the social construct of deviance. *College Student Journal*, 2006. 40 (1): 74–7.
410 Burgelman, R.A., Intraorganizational ecology of strategy making and organizational adaptation: Theory and field research. *Organization Science*, 1991. 2 (3): 239–62.
411 Macaulay, S., The real and the paper deal: Empirical pictures of Relationships, complexity and the urge for transparent simple rules. *The Modern Law Review*, 2003. 66 (1): 44–79.
412 Mouzas, S. and M. Furmston, From contract to umbrella agreement. *The Cambridge Law Journal*, 2008. 67 (1): 37–50.
413 Strong, T.B., Foreword: The sovereign and the exception; Carl Schmitt, politics, theology, and leadership, in *Political theology; four chapters on the concept of sovereignity* (1922), C. Schmitt, Editor 2005, University of Chicago Press: Chicago. pp. vii–xxxiii.
414 French, J.R.P. and B. Raven, The bases of social power, in *Studies in Social Power*, D. Cartwright, Editor 1959, Institute for Social Research: Ann Arbor. pp. 259–69.
415 Boyd, R., et al., The evolution of altruistic punishment. *PNAS*, 2003. 100 (6): 3531–5.
416 Clutton-Brock, T.H. and G.A. Parker, Punishment in animal societies. *Nature*, 1995. 373 (6511): 209–16.
417 de Quervain, D.J.-F., et al., The neural basis of altruistic punishment. *Science*, 2004. 305 (5688): 1254–8.
418 March, J. and H. Simon, *Organizations* (1958). 2ed. 1993, Cambridge: Blackwell. p. 287.
419 Panchanathan, K. and R. Boyd, Indirect reciprocity can stabilize cooperation without the second-order free rider problem. *Nature*, 2004. 432 (7016): 499–502.
420 Bendix, R., *Max Weber*. 1960, Berkeley and Los Angeles: University of California Press.
421 Eldrige, J.E.T., ed. *Max Weber: The interpretation of social reality*. 1971, Michael Joseph: London.
422 Otto, R., *The Idea of the Holy; an inquiry into the non-rational factor in the idea of the divine and its relation to the rational* (1928). 1958, London: Oxford University Press.
423 Levy-Bruhl, L., *How natives think* (1912). 1926, London.
424 Michels, R., *Political parties; a sociological study of the oligarchical tendencies of modern democracy* (1915). 1962, New York: The Free Press. p. 379.
425 Wilden, A., Informação, in *Enciclopédia Einaudi*, R. Romano, Editor. 2001, Imprensa Nacional - Casa da Moeda: Lisboa. pp. 11–77.
426 Danchin, E., et al., Public information: From nosy neighbors to cultural evolution. *Science*, 2004. 305 (5683): 487–91.
427 Townley, B., Foucault, power/knowledge, and its relevance for human resource management. *Academy of Management Review*, 1993. 18 (3): 518–45.
428 Spinoza, B.d., Ethics (1677). 2nd ed. *Great books of the Western world*, M.J. Adler, Editor. Vol. 28. 1990, Chicago: Encyclopaedia Britannica. pp. 589–697.

429 Schutz, A., *Collected papers*. 1964, The Hague: Nijhoff.

430 Meier, H., *The lesson of Carl Schmitt: Four chapters on the distinction between political theology and political philosophy*. 1998. Chicago: The University of Chicago Press.

431 Lindblom, C.E., Still muddling, not yet through. *Public Administration Review*, 1979. 39 (6): 517–26.

432 Lipset, S.M., Introduction to Michels political parties (1911), in *Political parties*, R. Michels, Editor 1960. pp. 15–39.

433 Pettigrew, A.M., Towards a political theory of organizational intervention. *Human Relations*, 1975. 28 (3): 191–208.

434 Goffman, E., The interaction order: American sociological association, 1982 Presidential Address. *American Sociological Review*, 1983. 48 (1): 1–17.

435 Hinde, R.A., Interactions, relationships and social structure. *Man*, 1976. 11 (1): 1–17.

436 Lewis, S.A., C.J. Langan, and E.P. Hollander, Expectation of future interaction and the choice of less desirable alternatives in conformity. *Sociometry*, 1972. 35 (3): 440–7.

437 Machiavelli, N., The prince (1513). *Great books of the Western world*, R.M. Hutchins, Editor. Vol. 23. 1952, Chicago: Encyclopaedia Britannica. pp. 1–38.

438 Douglas, M., Converging on autonomy: Anthropology and instittutional economics, in *Organization theory: From Chester Barnard to the present and beyond*, O.E. Williamson, Editor. 1995, Oxford University Press: Oxford & New York. pp. 98–115.

439 Mouffe, C., *Agonistics: Thinking the world politically*. 2013, London: Verso.

440 Gil, J., Poder, in *Enciclopédia Einaudi*, v. 14. 1989, Imprensa Nacional Casa da Moeda: Lisboa. pp. 58–103.

441 Plato, Apology (~380 a.C.). *Great books of the Western world*, v. 7. 1952, Chicago: Encyclopaedia Britannica. pp. 200–12.

442 Burawoy, M., *Manufacturing consent: Changes in the labor process under monopoly capitalism*. 1979, Chicago: University of Chicago Press.

443 Thompson, E.P., Time, work-discipline, and industrial capitalism. *Past and Present*, 1967. 38 (2): 56–97.

444 Henrich, J., et al., In search of Homo economicus: behavioral experiments in 15 small-scale societies. *The American Economic Review*, 2001. 91 (2, Papers and Proceedings of the Hundred Thirteenth Annual Meeting of the American Economic Association): 73–8.

445 Blumer, H., The methodological position of symbolic interactionism, in *Symbolic interactionism: Perspective and method*, H. Blumer, Editor. 1969, University of California Press: Oakland. pp. 1–60.

446 Trevino, L.K., R.H. Lengel, and R.L. Daft, Media symbolism, media richness, and media choice in organizations: A symbolic interactionist perspective. *Communication Research*, 1987. 14 (5): 553–74.

447 Grossman, S. and O.D. Hart, An analysis of the principal-agent problem. *Econometrica*, 1983. 51 (1): 7–46.

448 Neale, M.A. and T.Z. Lys, *Getting (more of) what you want: How the secrets of economics & psychology can help you negotiate anything in business & life*. 2015, London: Profile Books.

449 Gibbons, R. and R. Henderson, Relational contracts and organizational capabilities. *Organization Science*, 2011. 23 (5): 1350–64.

450 Vedel, M., A.-M. Holma, and V. Havila, Conceptualizing inter-organizational triads. *Industrial Marketing Management*, 2016. 57: 139–47.

451 McPherson, M., L. Smith-Lovin, and J.M. Cook, Birds of a feather: Homophily in social networks. *Annual Review of Sociology*, 2001. 27: 415–44.

452 Dalton, D.R. and C.M. Dalton, Integration of micro and macro studies in governance research: CEO duality, board composition, and financial performance. *Journal of Management*, 2011. 37 (2): 404–11.

453 Mintzberg, H., The manager's job: Folklore and fact. *Harvard Business Review*, 1975. 53 (4): 49–61.

454 Marmaros, D. and B. Sacerdote, How do friendships form? *Quarterly Journal of Economics*, 2006. 121 (1): 79–119.

455 Reagans, R., Close encounters: Analyzing how social similarity and propinquity contribute to strong network connections. *Organization Science*, 2011. 22 (4): 835–49.

456 Guetzkow, H., Communications in organizations, in *Handbook of organizations*, J. March, Editor. 1965, Rand MacNally: Chicago. pp. 534–73.

457 Banerjee, A., et al., The diffusion of microfinance. *Science*, 2013. 341: 363–73.

458 Aral, S. and M. Van Alstyne, The diversity-bandwidth trade-off. *American Journal of Sociology*, 2011. 117 (1): 90–171.

459 Pettigrew, A.M., Information control as a power resource. *Sociology*, 1972. 6 (2): 187–204.

460 Goldhaber, G.M., *Organizational communication*. 1990, Dubuque: Wm. C. Brown.

461 Lickert, R., *New patterns of management*. 1961, New York: McGraw-Hill.

462 Simon, H., D.W. Smithburg, and V.A. Thompson, *Public administration*. 1950, New York: Knopf.

463 Putnam, L.L., N. Phillips, and P. Chapman, Metaphors of communication and organization, in *Handbook of organization studies*, S.R. Clegg, C. Hardy, and W.R. Nord, Editors. 1996, Sage: London. pp. 375–408.

464 Ruddle, K., In pursuit of agility: Reflections on one practitioner's journey undertaking, researching, and teaching the leadership of change, in *Mapping the management journey; practice, theory, and context*, S. Dopson, M. Earl, and P. Snow, Editors. 2008, Oxford University Press: Oxford. pp. 320–40.

465 Daft, R.L. and R.H. Lengel, Organizational information requirements, media richness and structural design. *Management Science*, 1986. 32 (5): 554–71.

466 Cyert, R.M. and J.G. March, An epilogue, in *Explorations in organizations*, J.G. March, Editor. 2008, Stanford University Press: Stanford. pp. 52/78.

467 Eisenberg, E.M., *Strategic ambiguities: Essays on communication, organization, and identity*. 2007, London & New Delhi: Sage.

468 Whalen, P.J., et al., Human amygdala responsivity to masked fearful eye whites. *Science*, 2004. 306 (5704): 2061-.

469 Winston, J.S., et al., Automatic and intentional brain responses during evaluation of trustworthiness of faces. *Nature Neuroscience*, 2002. 5 (3): 277–83.
470 Weisfeld, G.E. and J.M. Beresford, Erectness of posture as an indicator of dominance or success in humans. *Motivation & Emotion*, 1982. 6: 113–31.
471 Grandjean, D., et al., The voices of wrath: Brain responses to angry prosody in meaningless speech. *Nature Neuroscience*, 2005. 8 (2): 145–6.
472 Adolphs, R., Social cognition and the human brain. *Trends in Cognitive Sciences*, 1999. 3 (12): 469–79.
473 Gallese, V., C. Keysers, and G. Rizzolatti, A unifying view of the basis of social cognition. *Trends in Cognitive Sciences*, 2004. 8 (9): 396–403.
474 O'Keefe, B.J., The logic of message design: Individual differences in reasoning about communication. *Communication Monographs*, 1988. 55 (1): 80–103.
475 Weber, M.S. and H. Kim, Virtuality, technology use, and engagement within organizations. *Journal of Applied Communication Research*, 2015. 43 (4): 385–407.
476 Balle, F., Comunicação, in *Tratado de sociologia*, R. Boudon, Editor 1996, Zahar: Rio de Janeiro. pp. 561–93.
477 McPhee, R.D. and P. Zaug, Organizational theory, organizational communication, organizational knowledge, and problematic integration. *Journal of Communication*, 2006. 51 (3): 574–91.
478 Kaplan, S., Strategy and powerpoint: An inquiry into the epistemic culture and machinery of strategy making. *Organization Science*, 2010. 22 (2): 320–46.
479 Ter Hoeven, C.L., W. van Zoonen, and K.L. Fonner, The practical paradox of technology: The influence of communication technology use on employee burnout and engagement. *Communication Monographs*, 2016. 83 (2): 239–63.
480 March, J.G., Ibsen, ideals, and the subornation of lies. *Organization Studies*, 2007. 28 (8): 1277–85.
481 Levitt, B. and J.G. March, Chester I. Barnard and the intelligence of learning, in *Organization theory: From Chester Barnard to the present and beyond*, O.E. Williamson, Editor. 1995, Oxford University Press: New York and Oxford. pp. 11–37.
482 Ashforth, B.E., S.H. Harrison, and K.G. Corley, Identification in organizations: An examination of four fundamental questions. *Journal of Management*, 2008. 34 (3): 325–74.
483 Kunda, G., *Engineering culture: Control and commitment in a high-tech corporation*. 2006, Philadelphia: Temple University Press.
484 Slovic, P., et al., The affect heuristic, in *Heuristics and biases: The psychology of intuitive judgment*, T. Gilovich, D. Griffin, and D. Kahneman, Editors. 2002, Cambridge University Press: New York. pp. 397–420.
485 Bargh, J.A. and T.L. Chartrand, The unbearable automaticity of being. *American Psychologist*, 1999. 54 (7): 462–79.
486 Ross, L. and A. Ward, Naive realism: Implications for social conflict and misunderstanding, in *Values and knowledge*, T. Brown, E.S. Reed, and E. Turiel, Editors. 1996, Lawrence Erlbaum: Hillsdale. pp. 103–35.

487 Kruger, J. and D. Dunning, Unskilled and unaware of it: How difficulties in recognizing one's incompetence lead to inflated self-assessments. *Journal of Personality and Social Psychology*, 1999. 77: 1121–34.

488 Ross, M. and F. Sicoly, Egocentric biases in availability and attribution. *Journal of Personality and Social Psychology*, 1979. 37 (3): 322–36.

489 Ross, L., D. Greene, and P. House, The false consensus effect: An egocentric bias in social perception and attribution processes. *Journal of Experimental Social Psychology*, 1977. 13: 279–301.

490 Pronin, E., C. Puccio, and L. Ross, Understanding misunderstanding: Social psychological perspectives, in *Heuristics and biases: The psychology of intuitive judgment*, T. Gilovich, D.W. Griffin, and D. Kahneman, Editors. 2002, Cambridge University Press: Cambridge. pp. 636–65.

491 Gilovich, T., V.H. Medvec, and K. Savitsky, The spotlight effect in social judgment: An egocentric bias in estimates of the salience of one's own actions and appearance. *Journal of Personality and Social Psychology*, 2000. 78 (2): 211–22.

492 Vorauer, J.D. and M. Ross, Self-awareness and feeling transparent: Failing to suppress one's self. *Journal of Experimental Social Psychology*, 1999. 35 (5): 415–40.

493 Gilbert, D.T. and P.S. Malone, The correspondence bias. *Psychological Bulletin*, 1995. 117: 21–38.

494 Buehler, R., Planning fallacy, in *Encyclopedia of social psychology*, R.F. Baumeister and K.D. Vohs, Editors. 2007, Sage: Thousand Oaks. pp. 671–3.

495 Ichheiser, G., Misunderstandings in human relations: A study in false social perception. *American Journal of Sociology*, 1949. 55, Part 2, viii: 1–70.

496 Davidson, W.P., The third-person effect in communication. *The Public Opinion Quarterly*, 1983. 47 (1): 1–15.

497 Gawronski, B., Fundamental attribution error, in *Encyclopedia of social psychology*, R.F. Baumeister and K.D. Vohs, Editors. 2007, Sage: Los Angeles. pp. 367–9.

498 Miller, D.T. and R.K. Ratner, The disparity between the actual and assumed power of self-interest. *Journal of Personality and Social Psychology*, 1998. 74 (1): 53–62.

499 Quattrone, G.A. and E.E. Jones, The perception of variability within in-groups and out-groups: Implications for the law of small numbers. *Journal of Personality and Social Psychology*, 1980. 38 (1): 141–52.

500 Pronin, E., et al., You don't know me, but I know you: The illusion of asymmetric insight. *Journal of Personality and Social Psychology*, 2001. 81: 639–56.

501 Thompson, V.A., *Modern organization: A general theory*. 1961, New York: Knopf.

502 Wason, P.C., On the failure to eliminate hypotheses in a conceptual task. *Quarterly Journal of Experimental Psychology*, 1960. 12 (3): 129–40.

503 Koriat, A., S. Lichtenstein, and B. Fischhoff, Reasons for confidence. *Journal of Experimental Psychology: Human Learning and Memory*, 1980. 6 (2): 107–18.

504 Chapman, G.B. and E.J. Johnson, Incorporating the irrelevant: Anchors in judgment of belief and value, in *Heuristics and biases: The psychology of intuitive judgment*, T. Gilovich, D.W. Griffin, and D. Kahneman, Editors. 2002, Cambridge University Press: Cambridge. pp. 120–38.

505 Merton, R.K., The self-fulfilling prophecy, in *Social theory and social structure*, R.K. Merton, Editor. 1968, Free Press: New York. pp. 475–90.

506 Czarniawska-Joerges, B., *Exploring complex organizations: A cultural perspective*. 1992, Newbury Park: Sage.

507 Janis, I.L., *Victims of groupthink*. 1982, Boston: Houghton-Mifflin.

508 Gross, E., Symbiosis and consensus as integrative factors in small groups. *American Sociological Review*, 1956. 21 (2): 174–79.

509 Skov, R.B. and S.J. Sherman, Information-gathering processes: Diagnosticity, hypothesis-confirmatory strategies, and perceived hypothesis confirmation. *Journal of Experimental Social Psychology*, 1986. 22 (2): 93–121.

510 Nelson, N.F., Identification as the basis for a theory of motivation. *American Sociological Review*, 1951. 16 (1): 14–21.

511 Rossi, P.H. and R.A. Berk, Varieties of normative consensus. *American Sociological Review*, 1985. 50 (3): 333–47.

512 Davis, J.A., Governance of the business family (Note 9–807–020), 2007, Boston: Harvard Business School.

513 March, J.G., *Explorations in organizations*. 2008, Stanford: Stanford University Press.

514 Freud, S., Psycologia de las masas y analisis del yo (1921), in *Obras Completas*, 1981, Biblioteca Nueva: Madrid. pp. 2563–610.

515 Green, M.J. and M.L. Phillips, Social threat perception and the evolution of paranoia. *Neuroscience & Biobehavioral Reviews*, 2004. 28 (3): 333–42.

516 Hofstadter, R., *The paranoid style in American politics*. 1964, Boston: Harvard University Press.

517 Kramer, R.M., The sinister attribution error: Paranoid cognition and collective distrust in organizations. *Motivation and Emotion*, 1994. 18 (2): 199–230.

518 O'Reilly III, C.A., et al., Narcissistic CEOs and executive compensation. *The Leadership Quarterly*, 2014. 25: 218–31.

519 Resick, C.J., et al., The bright-side and the dark-side of CEO personality: Examining core self-evaluations, narcissism, transformational leadership, and strategic influence. *Journal of Applied Psychology*, 2009. 94 (6): 1365–81.

520 Shapiro, D., *Neurotic styles*. 1965, New York: Basic Books.

521 Ey, H., P. Bernard, and C. Brisset, *Tratado de psiquiatría*. 1978, Barcelona: Toray-Masson.

522 Sapolsky, R.M., *Behave; the biology of humans at our best and worst*. 2017, New York: Penguin Press.

523 Schelling, T.C., Bargaining, communication, and limited war. *Journal of Conflict Resolution*, 1957. 1 (1): 19–36.

524 Schelling, T.C., *La estrategia del conflicto* (1960). 1964, Madrid: Tecnos.

525 Schelling, T.C., *Strategies of commitment and other essays*. 2006, Cambridge: Harvard University Press.

526 Kuhn, T.S., *The structure of scientific revolutions*. 1962, Chicago: University of Chicago Press.

527 Braybrooke, D. and C.E. Lindblom, *A strategy of decision; policy evaluation as a social process* (1962). 1970, New York: The Free Press. p. 267.

528 Thorngate, W., "In General" vs. "It Depends": Some comments of the Gergen-Schlenker debate. *Personality and Social Psychology Bulletin*, 1976. 2 (4): 404–10.

529 Ross, L. and R.E. Nisbett, *The person and the situation: Perspectives of social psychology*. 1991, New York: McGraw-Hill.

530 Thaler, R.H., *Misbehaving; the making of behavioral economics*. 2015, New York & London: Norton.

531 Norberg-Schulz, C., *Genius loci: Towards a phenomenology of architecture*. 1980, New York: Rizzoli.

532 Norberg-Schulz, C., The phenomenon of place. *Architectural Association Quarterly*, 1976. 8 (4): 3–10.

533 Saloner, G., A. Shepard, and J. Podolny, *Strategic management*. 2001, New York: Wiley.

534 Weick, K.E., Puzzles in organizational learning: An exercise in disciplined imagination. *British Journal of Management*, 2002. 13: S7–S15.

535 Argyris, C., *Reasons and rationalizations; the limits of organizational knowledge*. 2004, New York: Oxford University Press. p. 242.

536 Chesterton, G.K., *Heretics*. 1907, New York: J. Lane Company.

537 Schein, E.H., *Organizations: Rational, natural and open systems*. 1992, Englewood Cliffs: Prentice Hall.

538 Martin, J., *Cultures in organizations: Three perspectives*. 1992, New York and Oxford: Oxford University Press.

539 Huizinga, J., *Men and ideas: History, the middle ages, the renaissance*. 1960, London: Eyre & Spottiswoode. pp. 245–394.

540 Huizinga, J., *Erasmus and the age of reformation* (1924). 2014, Princeton: Princeton University Press.

541 Geertz, C., *The interpretation of cultures*. 1973, New York: Basic Books.

542 Burnham, J., The Machiavellians: Defenders of freedom – a defense of political truth against wishful thinking. 1943, Washington, DC: Gateway.

543 Greene, J. and J. Haidt, How (and where) does moral judgment work? *Trends in Cognitive Sciences*, 2002. 6 (12): 517–23.

544 Greene, J.D., et al., An fMRI investigation of emotional engagement in moral judgment. *Science*, 2001. 293 (5537): 2105–8.

545 Roberts, J. and G. Saloner, Strategy and organization, in *The handbook of organizational economics*, R. Gibbons and J. Roberts, Editors. 2013, Princeton University Press: Princeton. pp. 799–849.

546 Geertz, C., Found in translation: On the social history of the moral imagination, in. *Local knowledge: Further essays in interpretive anthropology*, C. Geertz.. 2000, New York: Basic Books. pp. 36–54

547 Gibbons, R. and R. Henderson, What do managers do? Exploring persistent performance differences among seemingly similar enterprises, in *The handbook of organizational economics*, R. Gibbons and J. Roberts, Editors. 2013, Princeton University Press: Princeton. pp. 680–731.

548 Carter, P. and N. Jackson, An-aesthetics, in *The aesthetics of organization*, S. Linstead and H. Hopfl, Editors. 2000, Sage: London. pp. 180–96.
549 Starbuck, W.H., Organizations as action generators. *American Sociological Review*, 1983. 48 (1): 91–102.
550 Morrison, K., *Marx, Durkheim, Weber: Formations of modern social thought*. 1995, London: Sage.
551 Milinski, M., D. Semmann, and H.-J. Krambeck, Reputation helps solve the 'tragedy of the commons'. *Nature*, 2002. 415 (6870): 424–6.
552 Meyer, A., P.J. Frost, and K.E. Weick, The organization science jazz festival: Improvisation as a metaphor for organizing - overture. *Organization Science*, 1998. 9 (5): 540–2.
553 Schelling, T.C., Game theory: A practitioner's approach. *Economics and Philosophy*, 2010. 26 (1): 27–46.
554 Joas, H. and W. Knöbl, *War in social thought; Hobbes to the present*. 2013, Princeton & Oxford: Cambridge University Press. p. 325.
555 Green, R., *The ethical manager: A new method for business ethics*. 1994. Macmillan: New York.
556 Smircich, L. and G. Morgan, The management of meaning. *The Journal of Applied Behavioral Science*, 1982. 18 (3): 257–73.
557 Cristi, R., *Decisionism. The encyclopedia of political thought*, 2014: 831–3.
558 Liu, W., Knowledge exploitation, knowledge exploration, and competency trap. *Knowledge and Process Management*, 2006. 13 (3): 144–61.
559 Zellweger, T., *Managing the family business: Theory and practice*. 2017, Cheltenham: Edward Elgar.
560 Swartz, D., *Culture and power; the sociology of Pierre Bourdieu*. 1997, Chicago: University of Chicago Press.
561 Henrich, J., Social Science, enhanced: Cooperation, punishment, and the evolution of human institutions. *Science*, 2006. 312 (5770): 60–1.
562 Lotem, A., M.A. Fishman, and L. Stone, Evolution of cooperation between individuals. *Nature*, 1999. 400 (6741): 226–7.
563 Blau, P.M., *The dynamics of bureaucracy: A study of interpersonal relationships in two government agencies*. 1955, Chicago: University of Chicago Press.
564 Waelti, P., A. Dickinson, and W. Schultz, Dopamine responses comply with basic assumptions of formal learning theory. *Nature*, 2001. 412 (6842): 43–8.
565 Ribeiro, R., Remarks on explicit knowledge and expertise acquisition. *Phenomenology and the Cognitive Sciences*, 2013. 12 (2): 431–5.
566 March, J.G., Poetry and the rhetoric of management: Easter 1916. *Journal of Management Inquiry*, 2006. 15: 70–2.
567 Augier, M. and J.G. March, The pursuit of relevance in management education. *California Management Review*, 2007. 49 (3): 129–46.
568 Aronson, J.K., et al., Key concepts for making informed choices. *Nature*, 2019. 572 (7769): 303–6.

Index

Note: Page numbers followed by "n" denote endnotes.